D1200628

Review

£25.95.

COMMUNICATIONS
IN TRANSITION

301.16072 MAN

COMMUNICATIONS

IN TRANSITION

WITHDRAWN

NOV 17

SAINT LOUIS UNIVERSITY

Issues and Debates
in Current Research

Edited by

Mary S. Mander

P
91.3
.C64
1983

PRAEGER

PRAEGER SPECIAL STUDIES • PRAEGER SCIENTIFIC

Library of Congress Cataloging in Publication Data

Mander, Mary S.
  Communications in transition.

  Bibliography: p.
  Includes index.
  1. Communication—Research—Addresses, essays,
lectures. I. Title.
P91.3.M36   1983   001.51   83-13985
ISBN 0-03-062938-1

Published in 1983 by Praeger Publishers
CBS Educational and Professional Publishing
a Division of CBS Inc.
521 Fifth Avenue, New York, NY 10175 U.S.A.
© 1983 by Mary S. Mander

All rights reserved

3456789   052   987654321

Printed in the United States of America
on acid-free paper

PREFACE

The origin of this book lies in several conversations with my colleagues at the Pennsylvania State University. As the reader will see, the title has been variously interpreted by the authors contributing to the volume. Originally, though, I settled on <u>Communications in Transition</u> because I conceived it to be a companion to Eugene White's book, <u>Rhetoric in Transition</u>. From this inchoate embryo the book evolved. At times it took unexpected paths and amazing directions, such that the final product surprises even me. Nevertheless, the original intention behind the book remained with it throughout its journey.

The purpose of this volume is not to settle issues and debates in communications once and for all. Rather, its intention is to generate a scholarly dialogue about questions central to postmodern times, questions concerning the nature and process of communication.

I am indebted to many people for their support in this endeavor: to Carolyn Marvin, Dick Barton, and Bill Rawlins whose advice was reliable and thus valuable; to Robert S. Brubaker whose collegial and financial support was much appreciated; and to Joyce Diehl and Diane Roan who prepared the final manuscript for publication.

Mary S. Mander

EDITOR'S INTRODUCTION

The research studies collected here are somewhat arbitrarily divided into two parts: "New Directions in Communications Research," and "Emerging Issues and Debates in the Social Sciences Tradition." I use the word "arbitrarily" because in some sense those contributions labeled "New Directions" predate those presumed to be "older." Also, it is entirely unclear whether the chapter by Hawes belongs in Part II or the piece by Grossberg belongs in Part I. However arbitrarily placed, all chapters in this volume had in common an intellectual pursuit: the attempt to discover order in collective life — whether the collectivity is society at large or subgroups in society, for example, scholars, policemen, or children.

"Something is happening to the way we think about the way we think," argued Clifford Geertz (1980). His observations about genre shifting and genre mixing in social science today are borne out by the studies in this book. In this connection a cautionary note, one borrowed again from Geertz, must be introduced. This volume does not assume a two-cultures viewpoint, that is, that communications scholars belong to a brotherhood in which scientists and humanists borrow from the accumulated wisdom of polarized camps. Rather, at the heart of this volume is the recognition that the lines formerly grouping scholars of communications into intellectual camps have "blurred." This regrouping of intellectual communities holds out the promise that futile arguments over method may now be replaced by more fertile investigations into the social paradigms to which we adhere.

Thus it is that each section of the book is best read as an echo chamber of the other. Recurrent topics and themes are treated in both parts: problems of context, of history, of form, of power; questions of meaning, of structure, of understanding, of mediation. For this reason, the overall character of the book is that of a dialogue. It is an extended conversation raising questions to which no answer — definitive or otherwise — is sought. It is a conversation based on the principal importance of asking the right questions. Such is the spirit of Thomas Pynchon who wrote: "If they can get you asking the wrong questions, they don't have to worry about the answers."

Finally, we ought to note that the book itself is a cultural artifact, a piece of evidence from which we can extract the images used by scholars to interpret or ascribe meaning in communication. As such it is a testimony to the power and fragility of human beings in their quest to understand social life. It is this phenomenon of human existence to which Walter refers in Malraux's <u>Anti-Memoirs</u>: "The greatest mystery is not that we have been flung at random between the profusion of matter and of the stars, but that within this prison we can draw ourselves images powerful enough to deny our nothingness."

Mary S. Mander

CONTENTS

PART I

NEW DIRECTIONS IN COMMUNICATIONS RESEARCH

1
INTRODUCTION
James W. Carey

I find it difficult to fairly characterize and introduce the chapters that follow. They are by design and nature diverse. They derive from what Whitehead called inconsistent backgrounds. The problems they address are various; their disciplinary origins divergent; their hopes and expectations incongruent; their theoretical positions and methodological injunctions contradictory; and even their styles of exposition at variance.

What binds them together is the fullest meaning of the title Communications in Transition. They are written against the background of a sea change, observed or desired. None of them are apocalyptic but all recognize the necessity of reformulating our received notions about communications in the light of rapidly changing circumstances. However one wishes to characterize the present changes in communication — a revolution, a restructuring, a reconfiguration — everyone seems pretty much in agreement that something rather fundamental is underway. The most obvious and dramatic change is in the technology of communications and the possibility it opens up for reconsidering the entire evolution of the structures and artifacts of human communication. But the change in technology is but part of a general social process in which an entire industry will be reorganized, forms of human association rearranged, and the styles and juxtapositions of cultural products reworked. The only thing that will not change, on the evidence of these studies, is the pattern of ownership and control, however much that is to be desired. These changes in the concrete world of human practice and activity lead, in turn, to an insistence on theoretical revision. At various points the studies call for destroying the distinction between theory and history whereby theoretical work will become historical and historical work theoretical. In another place they call for dislodging communications history from its professional sponsors in the crafts, releasing the captive so to speak, and wedding it to new sponsors in the history profession itself. Another study argues for a more grounded theory of communications by tying it to the problems of power and desire that occupy European postmodernist thought. Another finds promise in a reinvigorated critical scholarship working at the point where a Marxist political economy meets Marxist ideological analysis. Finally, and perhaps most interestingly, there is a call for a reconstruction of our ideas about rhetoric around the problems of international discourse, the public realm, and the nature of public life.

The theme of communications in transition echoes in the objective analysis of the scene of contemporary communications, in the subjective reflection on that scene through the call for intellectual revision, and, lastly, in the very "structure of feeling" that animates the studies: the sense running through them that the earth is moving under our feet, that our moorings — intellectual, social, even emotional — are being swept away.

I share much of this sense of transition and many of the hopes and directions advocated by these chapters. I have reservations too and they are perhaps best summed up in Goethe's maxim, which I slightly twist: Be careful what you hope for when you are young for you will get it, when you are old. The questions and reservations that make me something of a skeptic at this particular feast revolve around the ghosts that are still in the machine.

There is an assumption in the chapters, an assumption both dangerous and easily made, that the struggle with positivism — in our case behaviorism and functionalism — is over. On the contrary. Despite the heady days of the late 1960s and 70s, positivist assumptions continue to guide the practice, theory, and technology of communications. As an old maxim has it, what is ushered out by the front door merely comes back through the window. Oddly enough, positivism — that desire for metaphysical comfort, grounded knowledge, what John Dewey called the neurotic quest for certainty — often comes back through the least likely of portals, those labeled history or postmodernism. But it is the nature of the thought, not the labels we put upon it, that will determine its consequences for us.

There is also a desire that traces the studies that can only be called the desire for theoreticism. There is a lament within them concerning the inadequacy of various theories of one kind or another. Yet the temptation in the face of these inadequacies is always to look for another theory: a new theory of history, of freedom, or of communications itself. The radical response is avoided: communications, technology, and freedom are not the sorts of things one has theories about. The demand we should make is not that people have theories but that they have something interesting to say about the subject, that they make a contribution to a meaningful conversation. Perhaps all the talk about theory, method, and other such things prevents us from raising, or permits us to avoid raising, deeper and disquieting questions about the purposes of our scholarship.

A final trace on the studies is the commitment to professionalism. Many modern conflicts turn upon the question of which professional group has responsibility for the authoritative analysis of which social question. So in these chapters the debate often turns on which intellectual movement, theoretical group, or national tradition will provide the authoritative analysis. A problem is dislodged from one professional group only to be lodged with another. I'm not unsympathetic to this problem; in fact, I've contributed to it. However, the professionalization of intellectual life, of social problems, results in the constriction of the conversation of our culture to those who are legitimated by one device or another. It reduces social action to conflicts among middle-class intellectuals.

Finally, the chapters speak to our continuing inability to find a way to satisfactorily analyze technology in general, communications technology in particular. Insofar as communications is in transition, the transition is, at the moment, primarily technological, not for reason of any determinism, but simply because technology remains the active, imaginative sector of our common life. Other sectors change as a derivative of technological innovation that is driven by the search for profit, power, and efficiency. Our analytic and political control over technology is weak because we have no point outside the technological complex from which to unhinge it and we are more than a little, albeit silently, in love with power. Virtually all intellectual positions, even those labeled critical, are mere reflexes and reflections of the phenomenon under analysis. Any attempt to stand outside the complex and to judge it invites the dismissal of nostalgia or utopianism, more often the former these days. It is apparently no longer within our province to use either the past or the future as a standard of judgment or aspiration. The result is a wholesale evacuation of the public sphere in the name of hardheadedness. To write without regard for the past or hope for the future is surely the hallmark of modernism, the strongest impulse among us. To assume, however, that the transition to the future requires the wholesale diremption of the painfully won collective knowledge of the species is certainly nihilism of a high order.

Chapter 2 of this volume ends with a quote from Alexis de Tocqueville, a melancholy quote, to the effect that the search for democracy and equality is a long voyage in which one wearies of ever seeing the destination for the mirage. De

Tocqueville asks, in effect, if humans are destined to roam for-ever upon the sea of hope. The only honest and hopeful answer is yes, if we are not to live what Nietzsche called mankind's longest lie (though my quotation is from Richard Rorty [1982, p. 208]): "that outside of the haphazard and perilous experiments we perform there lies something (God, Science, Knowledge, Rationality or Truth [should we add History?]) which will, if only we perform the correct rituals, step in to save us." In the transition of communications we might try to go forward to basics, to recognize there is no final destination for our studies, no fixed and immutable truth to be unearthed in our research, no end, blessedly, to the argument. Life is not like history or theory or technology. It is, alas, more like a conversation. As Kenneth Burke has reminded us, it is a conversation underway when we enter. We try to catch the drift of it; we exit before it's over. About the best we can do is accept the advice of Michael Oakeshott (1962, p. 131) and follow the "intimations of our tradition" using customs and traditions that are "the footprints of thinkers and statesmen who knew which way to turn their feet without knowing anything about a final destination."

The hope I have for these studies and the reason I commend them to the invisible reader is not that they will provide theo-ries, resolve conflicts, chart new directions, or point to final destinations. That is simply the wrong way to think about schol-arship. Rather, they will enlarge the conversation about commu-nications, a conversation that, almost against our will, has become central to the direction of modern life.

2
COMMUNICATIONS THEORY AND HISTORY
Mary S. Mander

In preparing this chapter on history and communications theory I frequently found myself given over to the pessimism of Samuel Beckett, who wrote: "I have nothing to say and I can only say to what extent I have nothing to say." Rather than surrender, in the fashion of romance, and make bafflement and concern over contemporary communications research the subject of this exploratory study (compare Kernan 1982, p. 33), let me begin by making a few observations about the problems of such research and then suggest an alternative route.

PROBLEMS IN CURRENT RESEARCH

Since the 1960s at least two new approaches and research methodologies, critical and cultural, have emerged in the United States to challenge the hegemony exercised in the field by social scientific research. Nevertheless, communications research still generally is defined in empirical terms, the logic of which is induction. The majority of those who engage in this pursuit view communication as that branch of science dealing with human interaction. This approach to the study of mass communication developed out of the work of early pioneers in mass communication research at Yale and Columbia; but put in a larger context it is a descendant of the revolution in science in the

A version of this chapter was presented at the biannual meeting of the International Association of Mass Communications Research, Paris, 1982. I wish to thank William Rawlins and Nick Jankowski for their helpful comments.

seventeenth and eighteenth centuries. While stressing direct observation, men of Descartes's and subsequent generations tended to disregard history as a legitimate scholarly pursuit. Heightened consciousness of the logic of intellectual activity led to the Cartesian criterion for legitimate scholarly endeavors: questions of Cartesian criterion for legitimate scholarly endeavors: questions of definition, rules of inference, and rules of logical transformation. Consequently, Descartes and his contemporaries denied to history any claim to be a serious study. History to them was a mere confusion of memories, travelers' tales, fables, moral reflections, and gossip (Berlin 1981). It constituted the blunderings of irrational experience.

In many regards, contemporary scholars of communication view history as merely tangential to communications theory. In effect they believe that history is beneath the study of serious men and women seeking to understand the nature and process of communication. Even a scholar of the stature of Paul Ricoeur, in writing of objectivity in history, implies that something is awry when he says:

> This desire for objectivity is not limited to a critique of documents, as a narrow positivism would have it. On the contrary, it even encourages great synthesis. Its near rationalism is of the same nature as that of modern physics, and in this respect there is no reason for history to have an inferiority complex (Ricoeur 1965, p. 25; emphasis added).

Moreover, the success of the natural sciences in establishing general principles or laws of nature led eventually to an optimism that similar success might be had in the field of human behavior. Unfortunately, the stability of events in the world of nature is not replicated in the social world. In fact, if natural events were as capricious as human events, then natural science would be replaced by natural history (Gergen 1973, pp. 309-10). Yet we are so used to defining communications in terms of the empirical paradigm that we no longer are able to recognize the commitments of holding such assumptions.

Much of the communications research done in the United States today represents "only" an accumulation and classification of data, rather than theories that pinpoint the nature and process of communication. I put the word "only" in quotation marks to suggest that quantitative methods do contribute ultimately to our understanding of the subject. However, much of what is written in this vein is repetitive and too narrowly focused; many of us seem content to be dunces studying corners. To avoid reducing complicated literature to the level of a stereotype, it should be pointed out that leaders in the field recognize these problems (for example, Katz, Blumler, and Gurevitch 1974; Kline 1972; McQuail 1969; Gerbner and Gross 1976). Nevertheless overconfidence in certain methodologies to deliver the goods has resulted in an unquestioning attitude toward the assumptions that lie hidden beneath the paradigm. It is my contention that the protopositivist paradigm has surrendered its exclusive authority to explain communications by virtue of its constant rearrangement of the parts that make up the paradigm and by its inability to offer little more than conflicting speculations about communications phenomena — for example, the effect of television violence on the behavior of children.

At the same time, however, problems have developed with the two emergent approaches: critical studies and cultural studies. As to the former, what might have offered a breath of fresh air instead has rigidified, in some cases, into a bitter line of hostility and an ideology of fixed antagonism (compare Kernan 1982, pp. 31-32). A posture that ironically smacks of elitism summarily dismisses research lying outside Marxist concerns as "naive" or "irrelevant." On the other hand, some of the work of the cultural school has substituted a kind of messianic homiletics for painstaking scholarship and rigorous thought. A posture of inflexible certitude in the "rightness" of certain explanations of phenomena has replaced an open-minded and dispassionate interrogation of the evidence. Nothing much can be done about this situation until we understand the roots of this elitism, evangelism, and arrogance. It may very well be that the emotional tone of these postures reflects their perceived marginality in the field (compare Tudor 1976).

Finally, the majority of the concepts used in contemporary literature seem remote and detached from real experience. We collect data, and we use them to generate explanatory models that we hope eventually will lead to fundamental laws or theories of communication. Yet, as Gregory Bateson has pointed out, "about fifty years of work in which thousands of clever men have had their share, have in fact produced a rich crop of heuristic concepts, but, alas, scarcely one single principle worthy of a place in the list of fundamentals" (Bateson 1972, p. xix). In its present state communications research has generated a number of quasi-theoretical speculations, but we have not advanced fundamental knowledge by even a centimeter.

At this point a caveat must be introduced. Qualitative and quantitative methods are best regarded as two ends to a continuum. The example frequently used to demonstrate the relationship of the two is water. Change in water as it begins to drop in temperature can be measured quantitatively by degrees. Yet when water freezes, a qualitative change has taken place. It is not my intention here to reduce intellectual matters in communications to a choice of "to count or not to count"

(Christians and Carey 1981). As Christians and Carey (1981) have pointed out, "counting, even the more elaborated forms of counting, are among the most extraordinary and indispensable tools invented by humans. No one can get by very long without such tools, and simple arguments about quantifying versus nonquantifying distort and even obscure the real intellectual problems." Invariably when one proceeds to point out the limitations of a particular method or a body of literature, guerrilla warfare breaks out and one is accused of sniping at the so-called enemy. The purpose of this critique is not to polarize parties into positions they would not wish to hold for very long (compare Tudor 1976). Rather my argument is an attempt to shed light on the failure of communications researchers to advance fundamental knowledge — to generate a cohesive theory of communications.

To be sure, scholars in other fields of research — psychology, anthropology, and sociology, especially symbolic interactionism — have made observations similar to those offered here (Strauss 1971; Tudor 1976; Geertz 1973, pp. 87ff; Barton 1979; Gergen 1973). Anselm Strauss (1971), in examining the critical and theoretical works in social science, observed that the limitations of the literature were rooted in its underemphasis of historical content and its overemphasis on quantitative analysis (compare Handlin and Handlin 1964). Qualitative studies best generate theories; quantitative methods best test those theories (Tudor 1976).

Nevertheless models and metaphors establish categories of what is possible and what is impossible. We describe the growth and decline of cultures, the rise and fall of nations. The metaphor of growth is one of the oldest and most tenacious in the history of the West. To glance at the universe and see it in terms of a machine, as Newton did, or an organism, as social Darwinists do, is all right; to mistake the attributes of analogy for attributes of reality can have serious repercussions (Nisbet 1970, p. 7; Geertz 1980). By using empirical models in communications research, we have paid the price of excluding what is most real and most central to human experience: historicity. Ironically, this making of communication independent of history, this conception of communication in abstraction, comes at a moment in time when electronic media, by all appearances, have increased human interaction.

My principal contention is that communications research is primarily an historical pursuit and that without the historical dimension current research cannot transcend historical circumstances. The result will be that in the year 2082 historians will look into our literature with the idea of understanding life in this century. Yet communications scholars will find little of value in what we have said. In other words, unless the historical dimension is taken into account, our research reports run the risk of becoming charming period pieces.

The thrust of this argument is that history provides context, a phenomenon closely related to meaning (Bateson 1972; Hirsch 1976). That is, without the historical dimension, which provides the context of a communicative act, the meaning of a communicative act cannot be fully or truly understood. Moreover, an analysis of the logic underlying both history and science will show how and why communications research must include the historical dimension. The ensuing argument owes much to the writings of Isaiah Berlin and Gregory Bateson.

THE LOGIC OF SCIENCE AND HISTORY

First of all, there are three crucial differences between a scientific, quantitative approach to communications research and an historical, qualitative approach. The first has to do with the differences between the logic of science and the logic of history. In the sciences, we can safely put our confidence in general laws and theories rather than in specific phenomena. For example, if on a cloudy day someone said the sun did not rise, we know that despite its apparent absence from the skies, it is there. The laws of science assure us this is so. In history this is not the case. If an historian were to cast doubt on or explain away an eyewitness account solely because he put his faith in some abstract theory, we would fault him for altering the facts to fit the theory. Selective reading of the evidence to fit ideology is an act of fraud in history. Herein lies a major difference between the methods of history and the quantitative methods used in the sciences and the majority of communication research in the United States. Communications research in the scientific tradition acts as an X-ray machine, wiping out everything except what subjects have in common. Qualitative studies, on the other hand, seek to capture the unique pattern, the peculiar characteristics of their subject (Berlin 1981, pp. 113ff).

Moreover, there is between the two schools a striking difference between the canons of explanation and logical justification. In the scientific tradition, links between propositions are logically apparent. In research relying on statistical measures, even if such symbols of inference as "because" and "therefore" were omitted, the logical construction of the research is evident in the order of its component propositions. Not so in history, although the canons of rigor equally apply. If signposts like "therefore," "whereupon," or the irresistible "thus" were omitted, the logical force of an account would largely disintegrate (Berlin 1981, pp. 116-17).

A third difference between the two approaches, and the most important for this argument, has to do with the ancient dichotomy between substance and form. General laws in the sciences like the laws of conservation or gravity concern **substance** or matter. However, communication, whether defined as a mental happening or as objective social facts and artifacts, concerns **form** or order (Bateson 1972, p. xxv). The inability of the quantitative methodologies to deliver durable theories of communication may be connected to this dichotomy. Scientific measures build bridges to substance. Qualitative methodologies, especially history, build bridges to form rather than substance. History, rhetoric, literature, philosophy — all deal with humanly created symbol systems; all are concerned with reality construction. Since communication concerns **form**, history has the potential to enrich communications theory dramatically. The remainder of this chapter is devoted to an analysis of history and communications. An examination of certain traits common to literate and oral cultures will be used to shed light on contemporary culture. In this analysis I will restrict myself to very few characteristics. I cannot, for example, treat the importance of cunning in oral societies, or the effect a medium of communication has on social structure. Nevertheless, the ensuing examination of the past is intended to provide a **context** for understanding communication in what many call an "electronic culture."

COMMUNICATIONS AND HISTORY

At the heart of communication, however defined, is the fact that it is mediated. Because all communication is mediated, the nature of communication is necessarily connected to historically dependent dispositions (compare Gergen 1973, pp. 318-19). Communication is the historical creation of a culture rather than a natural expression identical for all human beings, independent of time or geography. As theorists we should begin to take this into account, to treat no form of communication as normative, and to allow communication in its various appearances to act, if I may borrow a phrase from Malraux (1978), as "voices of silence." Just as in sociology, psychology, and related studies cross-cultural methods are used to generate durable theories, enduring theories can be achieved in communications through the methods of history. Only then will our literature transcend time and speak effectively to later generations.

To illustrate what I mean, let me return to Malraux, who reminds us that the Middle Ages had no concept of art. For that matter, neither the Greeks nor the Egyptians had a word for it (Malraux 1978, p. 53). What we call art, Malraux argues, was originally parts of other institutions. Icons were an aid to prayer in churches; portraits were visible reminders of the genealogy of noble houses. After the Renaissance, the museum, which reified the concept of art by removing cultural objects from their context, led artists to create to prescription the kinds of works that fit the museum's definition of art: the masterpiece.

What began with the actual museum was extended by the camera into a musée imaginaire. The camera made reproductions available to all. More importantly, though, by blowing up fine details, such as a small portion of an illustrated letter in the Book of Kells, the art album emphasized style. Photography allowed each style to stand on its own. Equal scale also meant loss of proportion, or the creation of "fictitious" art (p. 24). Concomitantly, a priori aesthetic theories were discarded, as people began to realize that the gothic statue was not a botched attempt by a sculptor who started out to make a classical statue and failed (p. 20). In the musée imaginaire, no style is normative; all styles are voices of silence: The sheer juxtaposition of these voices testifies to man's ability to shape reality, to impose a peculiarly human accent upon it (Kernan 1982, p. 20).

What Malraux did in 1953 to cast light on the nature of art and aesthetic experience, many scholars in communications and related fields are attempting to do with regard to literacy in particular. The Russian psychologist Lev S. Vygotsky (1978), influenced by the Marxist notion that man has no fixed human nature but transforms his nature through the use of tools, expanded the concept of mediated human nature to the use of symbol systems. His essays on the effects of a written language system on intellectual processes influenced a recent study in the United States on the psychology of literacy (Scribner and Cole 1981). Goody and Watt (1968) have elucidated the ways in which literacy led to new ways of classifying knowledge (compare Graff 1981). Similarly, in anthropology, significant findings concerning the evolution of the mind have led to reformulations about the nature of human nature (Geertz 1973). Elizabeth Eisenstein (1979) and M. T. Clanchy (1979) both have contributed works that analyze the effects of the spread of literacy on the content and organization of knowledge (compare Lowe 1982; McLuhan 1962; Innis 1951, 1972). Finally, classicist Eric Havelock (1967, 1978, 1982) spent the last 50 years examining the far-reaching effects of the Greek alphabet on human thought.

Unfortunately, readers who are unacquainted with the broad spectrum of these and other works latch onto McLuhan, Innis, or Ong and, based on these admittedly flawed pieces, dismiss this approach as "technological determinism" (for example, Williams 1980, pp. 50-63; Bell 1979). An immature reading of Havelock's Preface to Plato has led others to the error of oversimplification of literate vis-à-vis preliterate thought. As Havelock (1982, p. 9) points out, "the complete genius of the literature and philosophy under inspection is understandable as neither oralist nor a flaccid compromise between the oral and the literate but as the product of a dynamic tension between them."

The corpus of Havelock's work attempts to unearth the meaning and significance a set of poems had for Greeks living in the ninth century. Like him, cultural historians of communication seek to reconstruct past worlds through scrupulous collection and examination of the evidence and critical piecing together of clues. This tradition, which goes back to Vico and Herder, relies on Vico's fantasia, a form of knowledge best translated as "reconstructive imagination" (Berlin 1976). History's object is not merely to collect and describe data. (Too often, in fact, historians become involved in debates over minor facts [A. Strauss 1971], but this is a limitation of imagination, not a limitation of imagination, not a limitation of the subject matter.) Rather the sheer juxtaposition of forms of knowledge, meaning, and communications of past worlds with our own provides a context for understanding the nature and process of communications. Past worlds act as "voices of silence."

ORAL AND LITERATE CULTURES

In a society that communicates via the spoken word, such as Greek society before the reappearance of writing in the seventh century B.C. or Hebrew culture before the time of Christ, communication is closely connected to social control. Social control is exerted at both the individual and collective levels; it is not so much an exploitative control, exercised by the elite over their inferiors. Rather it is best thought of as a means of imposing order over chaos, or investing outside-the-skin reality with meaning and significance. Control is achieved in several ways, but here I will mention only two: the phenomenon of naming and the use of genealogies.

First of all, control is achieved in oral cultures by naming objects and persons. In Genesis, for example, Adam named the animals, an act that signified his superiority over the beast and his power over the animal kingdom. Likewise, in Greek religion, when a god was conceived, it was invested with a name, a name usually derived from the sphere of activity over which the deity had jurisdiction. As long as the name was understood, the god's powers were limited: "Through his name the god is permanently held to that narrow field for which he was originally created" (Cassirer 1953, p. 20). Knowledge of the name imposes a kind of control over the named person or object.

Likewise, in strictly oral cultures the genealogy, or the naming of one's ancestors, functioned as a mnemonic of social relationships (Goody and Watt 1968). A genealogy cannot be regarded as an accurate list of one's ancestors, in the sense that constant generation of offspring results in a constant lengthening of the genealogy. Consequently, new births must be accompanied by genealogical shrinkage, or telescoping — a trait, like ellipsis, very characteristic or oral cultures. The social function of remembering (or forgetting) one's ancestors is to legitimize present social institutions, the existing social and ideological picture. The past is used as a means for acting in the present (Goody and Watt 1968, pp. 32, 37, and 45).

As paradoxical as it may seem, oral societies hold that whatever can be known can be influenced — gods, devils, moons, or stars. The realm of the supernatural can be brought under the sway of its influence. All that is known is alterable, through manual skills supplemented with magic. In so-called advanced, literate societies, all that is natural is knowable. The supernatural — that is, God in his heaven — is thought to be beyond the human provenance. While the secrets of the universe can be discovered and understood, chance and the secrets of God lie outside human reach (Feibleman 1968, pp. 69-70). Ultimately, then, the coming of the alphabet loosened the stranglehold humankind had upon the gods.

With the advent of the Greek alphabet a slow process of separation took place in Western culture. There was an episte- mological separating out or division made between body and soul, past and present, religion and politics, myth and science, fact and fiction, particular and universal, public and private, and the divine and the natural. The Greeks likewise divided knowledge into separate cognitive disciplines: for example, philosophy, natural science, language, and literature (Goody and Watt 1968, p. 54). The invention of the printing press reinforced these divisions. Printing made knowledge accessible to all; at the same time literacy also made knowledge easy to avoid (Phillpotts 1931, p. 162-63). In a literate culture, nonlogical modes of thinking flourished alongside the logicoempirical.

The history of communications indicates that as literacy spread, meaning in communications became increasingly indepen- dent of the time and place of communication, the behavioral context. The purest example of this phenomenon can be found in the works of the British essayists (for example, John Locke's An Essay Concerning Human Understanding). In this kind of writing meaning is explicit; meaning is made explicit by minimizing the number of possible interpretations of the text (Olson 1977, p. 262). The image of Newton, the mathematical genius of his time, bent over the scriptures and calculating from them the date the universe was created, provides an ironic commentary on this phenomenon taken to an extreme.

After the printing press was invented, communication came to mean publication (Corcoran 1979). Writing became a powerful in- tellectual tool. "No longer did general premises rest on com- mon-sense intuition" (Olson 1977, p. 269). Instead, meaning depended on the logical implications of statements and resulted in the construction of counterintuitive models of reality. Luther denied that meaning of the scriptures rested on an interpretive context, the oral tradition of the Roman Church (Olson 1977, pp. 263-72). Copernicus, without the aid of a telescope, generated a theory of the universe that defied common sense (Eisenstein 1979). In other words, literacy and the printing press did to communication what the museum did to cultural artifacts: Both made communication independent of behavioral context.

Finally, in literate cultures communication is closely connected to the human experience that things are not always what they seem, to the discrepancy between appearance and reality. This distinction provides the novelist, the philosopher, and the historian with their raison d'être. "Save the appearances, Plato said, and turn them into realities" (Gass 1971, p. 7). After the alphabet, death became the only plain, unambiguous statement left to us (G. Steiner 1975, p. 36).

Since the invention of broadcasting, scholars have attempted to come to grips with the new technology and its social impact. While thousands of books and articles have been written to explain electronic culture, we are probably no closer to truly understanding it today than we were 30 years ago when Berelson, Hovland, Lazarsfeld, and Merton did their work (compare Barton 1979). Since then hundreds of men and women have followed their leadership. (As Geertz [1973, p. 88] reminds us, in art this "solemn reduplication" is called academicism.)

If we apply the caution of Havelock to contemporary culture, we must conclude that in a society like ours, in which communication is both written and spoken, meaning and communication will result from a dynamic tension between the literate and the oral. Rather than see in the future the demise of the book, the decline of literacy, the disappearance of a particular form of logic, or the rise of the global village, it is more sensible to look for a convergence of characteristics peculiar to each culture: stories as a means of social control and the enduring discrepancy between appearance and reality.

CONTEMPORARY CULTURE

Some scholars believe that television is our chief instrument of enculturaltion and social control (for example, Gerbner and Gross 1976; Newcomb 1978). However, these studies, while they acknowledge the mythic basis of media use, emphasize the role of the media as a means for controlling the "masses" and keeping them in service to the status quo. For the most part they have concerned themselves with violence — to the neglect of most other types of television programs, not to mention radio and music.

Studies of this sort assume that the meanings people derive from media can be made perfectly explicit by ensconcing them in an experimental design. Yet explicitness is a goal appropriate only for a particular kind of communication. In oral communication, meaning cannot be divorced from the behavioral context. Empirical studies of media use impose one set of rules on human experiences that operate according to a different set of rules. As Schutz (1944, p. 500) pointed out, in a different context, "the knowledge of the man who acts and thinks within the world of his daily life is not homogenous; it is (1) incoherent, (2) only partially clear, and (3) not at all free from contradictions."

The argument here is not that statistical measures tell us nothing about media use. Rather statistical analysis, a product of literate culture, is limited in its ability to determine the meanings people derive from television programming because it ignores the behavior context. Behavioral context cannot be divorced from the communicative act in oral culture.

Television programs do influence members of the audience in complex and various ways. For example, research in the popular culture tradition delineates the needs and desires formula art addresses. Cawelti (1976) has indicated that certain moral fantasies are connected to story types. In action adventure stories the hero overcomes all obstacles and dangers; victory over death is the moral fantasy at the center of this kind of show. The moral fantasy at the heart of romance is love triumphant and enduring; in mystery stories it is the assertion of a rational order over chaos, secrecy, and irrationality. Finally, in monster shows terror is domesticated by objectifying it in the form of a clearly defined monster, which, once seen, dissipates that fear. The moral fantasy operating here is our dream that the unknowable can be known and related to in a meaningful way.

Comedy programming rests on a similar appeal, in the sense that the humor usually is connected to a situation thought to be dangerous but which turns out to be harmless. Humor and terror, laughter and fright, are closely related experiences.

In the sense that television programming functions to reassure members of the audience that behind the apparent chaos of the world there is order, it exercises some form of social control. We constantly reassure ourselves that despite the tragedies of life, despite the complex ambiguities with which we must deal, the world operates according to a benevolent moral principle. At the individual level, television programming provides a kind of mnemonic of social relationships, recipes for proper conduct. These recipes are both schemes of action as well as schemes of interpretation (compare Schutz 1944). They are schemes of action because television, whether one is speaking of news, public affairs, or serials, is essentially drama (Esslin 1982), and drama is a mode of thinking. We often construct scenarios of future activities in our heads. They are schemes of interpretation in the sense that storytelling is and always has been a means by which men and women invest meaning and significance into their daily lives (see Gerbner and Gross 1976).

Likewise, stories function to resolve the ambiguities of human experience, the discrepancy between reality and appearance. Television programming provides a scheme of interpretation. Studies of television and its impact need to examine this process rigorously. Because such examination concerns everyday life, it is a particularly fortuitous opportunity to construct a viable theory of communication. With that in mind, I would argue that any contemporary theory of communication is adequate to the extent that it allows the kinds of questions to be raised that everyday life puts to ordinary people. These are the questions that alternately haunt us and flee from us. A theory of communication is significant to the degree that it addresses such questions — "for the everyday questions of ordinary life are always addressed to those ultimate appearances which we remember must be saved" (Gass 1971, p. 9). Thus television, while it is extremely limited in its ability to deal with abstract ideas, because it is drama, is an unlimited resource for exploring concrete situations and ordinary living.

Finally, history indicates that with the advent of a new medium of communications there is a concurrent shift in the institution that "decides" which interpretation, which set of symbol systems, is the "true" one. Thus television programming is connected to social control at the collective level to the extent that a coherent world view is derived from it. The dominant institution of an electronic culture can be identified as that institution which profits from that particular world view. However, and this is extremely important, to dominate one must exist outside the world view propagated, one must perceive another's truth as illusion, one must not "buy into" the world view of those who are dominated (Greenblatt 1980). Marxist scholars tend to identify the corporation as the dominant institution of electronic culture, but I am inclined to suspect that the corporation was the dominant institution of the previous century. The corporation does not exist outside the world view it propagates. The institution of dominance in an electronic culture is not the church, it is not the government, nor is it the corporation. There seems to be a blurring of these institutions today. Rather, the institution of dominance is the media.[1]

CONCLUSION

I have argued that history is essential to the construction of communications theory. In examining past cultures and identifying certain traits, I have attempted to provide a context for understanding contemporary culture.

However (and here's the rub), every piece of history is an exercise in world-making itself, a fiction of sorts. "Every 'resurrection' sorts out what it recalls" (Malraux 1978, p. 67; compare Finley 1965, pp. 295ff). In seeking to make the world over into the shape we desire, history openly enacts those human gestures that are at the base of all human institutions. While this may be seen as its greatest strength by some, it is also viewed as history's greatest weakness. Researchers are leery of history's remaking of the world. Clio does not evince their confidence or command their respect. While we make up our worlds, it seems to be entirely unsatisfactory to know that we do so (Kernan 1982). Instead, communications scholars turn to more "reliable" fields. Statistical methodologies, in the view of many, lend precision to their work. Yet precision at the price of context has yielded small returns.

Let me conclude with a poignant passage from the Recollections of Alexis de Tocqueville, whose Democracy in America received renewed interest in the United States in the 1950s, an era dominated by phrases like "the lonely crowd," "the quest for community," "the eclipse of community," "the organization man," and the master word, "alienation" (Nisbet 1977, p. 68). The passage is apropos, given that what I have argued here has been argued by others more learned and eloquent than I (Berelson 1959; Gans 1972; Carey 1975b; compare Golding and Murdock 1978) and yet decades later the state of research has little changed. In speaking of humankind's search for democracy and equality, he wrote:

> I do not know when this long voyage will be ended; I am weary of seeing the shore in each successive mirage, and I often ask myself whether the terra firma we are seeking does really exist, and whether we are not doomed to rove upon the seas forever (Nisbet 1977, p. 75).

To avoid the weariness and pessimism evident in this passage, communications research must push on, via history, to construct theories of communication that are durable. Regrettably, however, the organized amnesia characteristic of schools of communication in the United States, unless tended to, will ensure the failure of our studies to transcend history and speak effectively to future generations.

NOTE

1. I have some misgivings about this last statement. One could argue, for example, that the university exists outside the world view propagated by the media.

3
SPACE, TIME, AND CAPTIVE COMMUNICATIONS HISTORY
Carolyn Marvin

In the now conventional discussion of the disappointing quality of communications history within the field (Carey 1974; Stevens and Garcia 1979; McKerns 1977), the most obvious thing perhaps has not quite been said: For most of its existence the study of communications history in the United States has been a captive of its patron, the professional media training program. While research on problems that are central to communications history has flourished outside the field in recent years (Clanchy 1979; Darnton 1979; Eisenstein 1979; Havelock 1982; Stock 1983), investigation within it has remained detached from the shaping minds and influences of historiography in the last half-century. Communications scholars have contributed little to the work and thinking of mainstream historians, nor have they been influenced in any very perceptible way by the rather spectacular and fruitful developments that have vivified recent historical discourse (Stone 1980; Higham and Conklin 1979; Le Roy Ladurie 1979; Braudel 1969; Rabb and Rotberg 1982). The fact that there has been little discussion of this point is a troubling sign, I think, of the degree to which the relationship between communications history and its patron is still a stifling one, though lately it is a symbiosis showing distinct signs of strain.

This situation is not unique in historical studies associated with professional training. In 1959 Bernard Bailyn, the distinguished historian of the American Revolution, warned historians of American education, a group constituted within similar professional curricular boundaries, of the hazards of isolation from the active center of historical research, writing, and teaching (Bailyn 1960). He faulted especially the restrictive definition of education as a subject for research to formal instruction alone, as though an understanding of other educational forms and practices were not essential to an intellectually serious history of education, and as though the history of formal instruction could properly be understood apart from them. Bailyn advised educational historians not to confuse the justification of current professional norms and notions with the pursuit of historical understanding. All past instruction had not prophetically aimed, as conventional historiography had it, at the profession of teaching and the institution of schooling as educational practitioners had come to believe in it in the twentieth century. The impulse among educational historians to discover in history the "intimate relationship between their hitherto despised profession and the destiny of man" was motivated by understandable but not scholarly concerns (Bailyn 1960, p. 8).

The parallels with communications history are painful and exact. Communications history within the field has been, on the whole, an isolated endeavor. Its clients certainly have not been historians of all persuasions, or even an educated public, but mainly journalism teachers and their students. The subject matter of communications history also has been organized around a professional notion of what counts. Its research focus generally has been limited to the history of professional mass media. Even within that narrow compass, this meant for years an exclusive concern with the history of printed media. The history of spoken discourse, of telephony, telegraphy, museums, libraries, parades, festivals, correspondence, of literacy, of graffiti, of fashion and etiquette, of sound and visual recording, dance, maps, gossip and taboo, of the sonic landscape, of prayer, of the organization of knowledge, of dictionaries, spelling, and a thousand other components of communications have not merely been ignored or slighted within the field. They have barely been recognized.

Finally, the questions addressed by captive communications history have emerged primarily from modern professional constructions of the proper role of the elite urban press projected on past time.[1] From the fixed-point frame of reference in which captive communications historians have worked, the modern urban press is an end-point of evolution, if not exactly a professional perfection of autonomous news media institutions and products, increasingly professional news staffs, and whiggishly maturing audiences. The rosy reconstruction of journalism history as a morality play in which bad journalists and big government struggle against good journalists and emerging professional standards portrays the past as a quainter, somewhat less accomplished version of our own present, as "the present writ small," to borrow Bailyn's description of educational historiography (1960, p. 9).

There are certainly journalism historians who do not accept this traditional framework for press history, and who believe that the concerns of communications history should be broader. Such discussions alarm some guardians of the applied professional curriculum. They fear that an expansion of communications history or any other nonapplied area of the curriculum will reduce the time students have for cultivating professional skills. Others are concerned that such changes could endanger the academic legitimacy of the applied curriculum, the traditional raison d'être for most communications programs, and the final protector of the journalism historians themselves, who have no protectors elsewhere. This practical tension between the applied and academic curriculum within communications programs has furnished the terms of what debate there has been among the captive historians and their patrons.

THE UNEXAMINED LIFE OF THE AMERICAN NEWSPAPER

In my view this issue, though serious, is not the most crucial one for communications history. I believe the structural distortions of a profession-driven concept of communications history are much deeper. To take one pertinent example, I believe that even the meaning of the historical term "newspaper" has a falsely secure ontological and analytical status; that we know much too little about the adequacy of the evolutionary model of the past taken for granted in journalism history; that the shape of newspaper history never has been examined independently of powerful professional notions of what ought to be and to have been; that what is regarded as the "solid basis of fact" (Carey 1974, quoting Theodore Peterson, p. 3) needing only amendment by inspirited investigators may be neither solid nor fact.[2]

Consider how the authors of The Press and America, a standard reference work, and the bedrock text for most college courses in journalism history, set the conceptual boundaries of their entire historical narrative with a definition of their subject that has remained unchanged through four editions (Emery and Emery 1954, 1962, 1972, and 1978). (For statistics on journalism history text use, see Endres 1978, p. 2.) Inexplicably adapted from a 1928 German text (Groth 1928, pp. 21ff) and offered without theoretical justification or elaboration, this definition sees the "true" newspaper as a commodity published by mechanical means at least weekly, available to all at a single price, concerned with news of interest to a "general public," pitched to an "ordinary" literary skill, timely within the possibilities of available technology, and economically stable "as contrasted to the fly-by-night publications of more primitive times" (Emery and Emery 1978, pp. 4-5; see Dickinson 1929, pp. 9-11 for a contemporary review of Groth).

This list will be perfectly intelligible to journalists, since it reflects a commonsense professional mythology about what newspapers ought to be. Its categories are meant to be roomy enough to surround a large amount of history, including periods when the newspaper was not yet "complete." They suggest that the historical event, newspaper, is a special conceptual, commercial, and moral achievement with fixed characteristics marked by their absence or presence and level of mature development. In this setting the task of newspaper history can only be to explain how past historical actors learned by a series of successively fewer errors and bad guesses to solve the (correctly conceived and real) problems of our present. To make past actors responsible for historical goals that describe modern aspirations is a peculiar and unsupportable charge on the interpretation of the past.

There are other difficulties. To what audience does the term "general public" refer for historical periods in which literacy (what skills at what level of difficulty?) was not yet an "ordinary" achievement in the United States? Does the specification of a criterion of literacy suggest that real newspapers can be apprehended only privately? If so, why? Why is an economically "stable" newspaper more truly a newspaper than one that is not? (What does this criterion suggest about the current classification of The Times of London?) Why wasn't the "party press," the unabashedly partisan early republican press format, that of a "true" newspaper and ours the primitive, or by turn, decadent version?

Such unexamined notions go to the heart of traditional newspaper history. Consider, for example, efforts to establish an origin point for the newspaper in the "newes letter," traditionally regarded as one of the earliest newspaper formats in spite of the model its name suggests (as though it were a misguided effort that could have striven to be the New York Times if its producers had understood things properly).3 The newes letter was comprised of items from private letters, from other newes letters, and from "correspondents" who might be traveling friends of the newes letter proprietor. It was distributed, at first irregularly, to the same taverns and coffeehouses that served as distribution points for letters from abroad and as places to converse about them. Newes letters frequently invited return correspondence and occasionally provided blank pages for readers to add their own news for forwarding to friends. The newes letter was less often the focus of its early proprietors' livelihoods than a sideline or extension of more significant communications roles that did provide such focus. Newes letter proprietors might be local postmasters within whose responsibilities all letters, including newes letters, fell, or job printers working also as booksellers, innkeepers, and

general store keepers, occupations that constituted the central
nervous system of local communication.

The newes letter was not an immature or fumbling prototype
of objective journalism striving for the anonymous perspective
familiar to modern audiences, but an elaboration of customary
habits of letter writing and public discourse in communities of
mutually acquainted persons. The newes letter practiced the
conventions of the personal letter, the private professional
mercantile newsletter, and the tavern conversation, all personal
communication forms with established public dimensions. While all
these forms contributed to the social invention of the modern
newspaper, none was a quaint or deficient version of it.

We know relatively little about the homogeneity or distribution of early news forms from one town or community to the
next, or about differences in their appearance and function in
localities with different histories and cultural mixes, different
geographic, economic, and social circumstances. We know less
about the social economy of personal letters, conversations in
coffeehouses and taverns, the postal service, the pulpit, or
networks of personal friendship and gossip. Taken together, the
practices of these oral and written forms in public and private
settings constituted ecologies of discourse that should be a
principal object of the study of the history of communications.

INSTITUTIONAL AND ARTIFACTUAL MODELS

Our ignorance reflects the prevailing model of the historical
newspaper, a taxonomic illusion that treats evidence and event as
coterminous. The newspaper has been confidently charted
through history as a communications event fully contained in a
product, a concrete object with natural outlines set neatly in
relief against the past and following self-generated internal
rules of development. Instead of placing the newspaper within
larger systems of social signification and practice, systems partly
reflected in the newspaper but also surrounding and containing
it, historians have located the newspaper either in the relatively
impoverished context of editorial practices organized around and
through the professional newsroom or against the thinnest of
background narratives of American political history.

The narrow logic of this institutional model was inherited
both from the newspaper profession and from the self-consciously
scientific "new" historians of the late nineteenth and early
twentieth centuries. In emulation of the much admired examples
of nineteenth-century biology and philology, the new historians
constructed ambitious institutional histories conceptualized in
abstraction from social life at large, and purportedly demonstrating the forward evolutionary movement of human affairs.

The chronologies, periodizations, and organizing concepts they devised framed their subjects for years to come (Handlin 1979, pp. 43-110; Hofstadter 1968, pp. xi-xvii, 3-43).

Journalism historiography faithfully adhered to the reigning historical model of institutions cast in splendid and improving isolation. The stand-alone evolutionary model pried the newspaper of journalism history loose from the rest of the social life and helped preserve it from challenges to its interpretive validity. That model has not worked very much better for the modern newspaper, for it is not only the origin of the "true" newspaper that is in doubt. For example, the captive historians have failed to explore, because their artifactual categories could not suggest them, the historical connections between certain important features of the newspaper-as-wire-service-outlet and network broadcasting.

With the emergence of a national wire service monopoly and a monopoly national telegraph network, local newspapers were often transformed into, or created precisely for the purpose of becoming, outlets on a national electrical communications grid for identical and exclusive "programming" transmitted from a central point. Concentration of news sources and conventions of editorial selection and presentation now strongly associated with broadcasting were familiar to audiences long before the invention of wireless technology and provided economic and cultural templates for its development. Perhaps because communications historians have not asked, conventional historical wisdom continues to see a nineteenth-century newspaper where it has not existed for 100 years. The habit of packaging communications practices and phenomena in the deceptively solid forms and products of technology conceals strategic cultural details and functions that are not isomorphic with any single technological application.

This is not a question of providing a richer or more adequate context, conceived as a kind of pastel wash around the imagined edges of events, but the question of an historically legitimate model of communications. Michael Schudson (1978) has recently challenged the captive mold by casting the penny press of the 1830s in the role of inventor of "objectivity" instead of merely a stage in its evolution, a characterization that augments the traditional reputation of the penny press as inventor of the local feature story. Schudson does not, however, explore why objectivity and local news were new to urban journalism. Were earlier entrepreneurs less imaginative (a notion that sometimes passes for explanation in captive history), or had the rhythm and pattern of life in earlier communities provided other, better networks for collecting, sorting, and distributing familiar and surprising knowledge? Did modern news devices mend deficiencies in older, quainter forms that might have disappeared earlier but for more talented entrepreneurs in the heroic mold, or were structures of social communication reorganized around new relationships in community life and new models for understanding and expressing them?

The "problem of journalism history" (Carey 1974) may be something like the discovery in anthropological and development circles that labels like "peasant" and "tribe" had been too generally applied to widely diverse groups and dissimilar practices.[4] Once investigators began to consider these labels in light of evidence that could be fully appreciated only after they had begun to loosen their intellectual grip, a host of notions that seemed incontrovertibly true and plausible also began to unravel in their wake. The variety of cultural phenomena masked by those labels belied much of the ideological overlay that had connected and supported them. The question for communications history is whether the term "newspaper," and others like "print culture" and "literacy," are applied too generally to dissimilar phenomena, or to misdivide other phenomena that are better grouped together along new classificatory axes.

It must be said that journalism historians have come by the contemplation of their own navels honestly. They, too, are victims of history. In a public description of his plans for one of the first full-scale journalism schools at Columbia University in 1904, Joseph Pulitzer vowed that through all phases of the ambitious historical training he envisioned for journalists "would run the idea of progress, especially the progress of justice, of civilization, of humanity, of public opinion, and of the democratic idea and ideal" (Pulitzer 1904). Pulitzer's perspective was the Progressive one of his period, shaped in the Midwest, shared not only by politicians and reformers but reflected also in the work of academic historians like Turner, Becker, Robinson, Beard, and Parrington.

These scholars and their disciples provided models and organizing questions to which journalism historians of the 1920s and 1930s, a breed that flourished especially in the land-grant schools of the Midwest, turned for their vision of American history. The coincidence of terms in the title of one of the first serious products of the new historical consciousness in journalism, Willard G. Bleyer's Main Currents in the History of American Journalism (1927), and Vernon Parrington's influential Progressive History, Main Currents in American Thought (1927), suggests the attentiveness of early journalism historians to the intellectual ferment of their time. But the Progressive view that took root in the first professional schools of journalism in accord both with the foremost model of American history at the time of their birth and the expectations of a profession in pursuit of intellectual legitimacy never really moved again.

Why? The answer to this question is speculative, but probably not mysterious. It can be sought in the intellectual isolation of journalism historians in their graduate training, in their departments, and in the universities where they work. In most graduate communications programs, core courses provide training in theory and basic research technique, and specialized seminars allow students to pursue special topics or to explore relationships between marginal and mainstream areas. In most graduate programs, communications history is still a special area with a small range of courses. Aspiring communications historians are slighted not only in basic history but often do not get adequate training in their chosen specialty. An awareness of debates and discoveries in history at large, or of the narrower range of work bearing directly on communications history, is built out of the structure of most graduate training in communications history.

The meagerness of this intellectual diet is sometimes justified by pointing to the limited teaching opportunities for historians in professionally based communications programs. It is strengthened by the conviction of other communications faculty that communications history of the usual kind is adequate for students, that it requires and deserves no more than commonsense training. Nor have journalism historians found sympathetic support from colleagues elsewhere in the university, who are often suspicious of the legitimacy of all professional faculty. Journalism historians frequently enjoy little of the camaraderie and support from other academicians, particularly in history, which provides the informal intellectual give and take that disciplines, encourages, and legitimates much academic work.

The mutually constructed nonintercourse between many communications programs and outside academic departments finds communications historians twice exiled. While scholars with history Ph.D.s are regarded as too academically specialized and insufficiently socialized to professional curricular goals to be hired in most communications programs, an advanced communications degree with a history specialization is also inadequate qualification for an appointment in history. Historians with primary training in communications are not prominent in professional scholarly associations of historians, and prominent historians are not active in associations for communications scholars. While these may be problems for communications historians to work out gradually in the course of disciplinary and curriculum evolution, they help explain, I think, why communications historians in the field have blazed few new trails through their own subject.

Permission to take the substantial intellectual risks that are necessary to build a field of knowledge requires an intellectual support system, either in curriculum structure and teaching opportunities in the field, or in a network of sympathetic scholars beyond it. It must include even the freedom to repudiate one's own intellectual heritage. Lacking the confidence of a discipline that takes its own risks, poorly placed to displease its patron, captive communications history has never dared enter the main arena of academic history to insist on the power of its subject to mark a path to the center of historical thought. Claiming only a small and derivative historical territory for its own, journalism historians never imagined a history of communication that might be more than a decorative bauble on the Progressive framework, or might expand and deepen Progressive hypotheses and rebuild them with the special materials available to journalism and communications historians. The failure of captive communications history must be measured by this inability to offer a genuinely fuller understanding of the past, but must also be seen in terms of the limiting conditions faced by many of its scholars.

PRESSURES FOR CHANGE

Ironically, the materials of communications history are just those that might have involved its researchers in the issues that have so engaged mainstream historians during the dramatic twentieth-century shift to social history. Until recently this shift of emphasis has taken place without reference to the work of communications historians, who nevertheless have a critical investment in the relationship of popular to elite history, the history of literacy, the history of large demographic shifts, the history of technology, women's history seen as the expanding area of public discourse permitted them, and the broadly conceived history of the imaginative and practical routine of daily life. This does not mean that mainstream history can or should dictate the program of so-called special areas like communications history.[5] It has always been necessary for historians working at the margins to prove the validity of their claims to center stage.

Although the inadequacies of Progressive journalism history are widely conceded, this dissatisfaction results only partly from internal scholarly discussion. Pressure for change is also a response to changes in the academic fortunes of journalism education and the rising worldly success of what has confusingly been labeled empirical communications studies.[6] During the fiscally prosperous 1960s and 1970s, teachers of professional journalism and social scientists of communication waged a kind of cold war over their shared curriculum. The ascendant star of social scientific approaches to a variety of topics and problems, including the press itself, gave social scientists growing leverage over communications budgets, curricula, and terminology. "Journalism" programs increasingly became "communications" programs.[7] Especially in an age fascinated by television, journalism historians seemed to have little to offer.

To the extent that their legitimacy depended on the tolerance of their professional colleagues, the shift of academic prestige away from vocational journalism training toward experimental and survey research sometimes deprived journalism historians, possessors of modest status outside the field, of status inside many communications programs as well. While the Association for Education in Journalism (organized as a wholly academic group in 1949 in a departure from the more customary partnership of professional journalists and journalism educators) has included organizations of journalism historians since 1951, the International Communications Association, organized in 1950 to further social scientific research in communications, still has no communications history group of any kind.[8]

The appearance of Journalism History in 1974 was a visible sign of the increasing exclusion of journalism historians from traditional forums of communications research. From its first issue Journalism History made itself a center for debate about what a reinvigorated journalism history might be, launching that discussion with an article by James W. Carey, a respected and influential spokesperson for what is usually called the American cultural school of communications studies, which Carey recommended as a research perspective to students of communications history.[9] The cultural school has claimed for its intellectual turf the study of thoughts, feelings, and sensibilities in specific social milieux. It seeks to go beyond descriptive "facts" and institutional analyses of communicative expression to a determination of deeper social meanings, an empirically and theoretically elusive goal in much of the school's work. Although its followers have been articulate about the difficulty of investigating such meaning with the usual assumptions and techniques of communications research, they have not developed rigorous alternative strategies and methodologies that are suited to such problems (Christians and Carey 1981).[10] Whether meanings that satisfy cultural investigators have some claim to validity or are simply possible glosses of significance subject only to the aesthetic preferences of interested observers is not an issue the cultural school has successfully resolved.

The declared allegiances of the cultural school are to Durkheim, Park, Dewey, Thomas, Mead, Wirth, Cooley, and others generally regarded as founding members or early formative influences on the Chicago school of sociology. The cultural school's own subject list for sociological inquiry rests heavily on the historical presumption that an existing organic social unity, variously defined, was destroyed in the movement from community to society. The major temporal markers of that transformation also have varied with the problem under consideration, but most advocates of cultural studies would probably agree that whatever starting point for social disintegration is chosen, things have only gotten worse, and that the technologization of communication is largely responsible for rendering human experience demeaningly vicarious and artificial.

This is a sweeping historical hypothesis, in support of which there has emerged no cultural school of communications history research, properly and self-consciously speaking, no distinctive corpus of cultural research models, data, or strategies. The cultural school's definition of social life as communication has produced a few scholars to carry the debate, in Fernand Braudel's words, "right into the heart of history" (1969, p. 73).[11] Because the cultural school has generated no substantial historical body of knowledge of its own, its champions have had to look elsewhere for evidence to support a typically nostalgic construction of history, sometimes without adequate guidelines for judging the quality of historical work cited in behalf of that perspective.

The American cultural school's resistance to the intellectual evangelism of contemporary social science has also not been entirely consistent. While members of the school have questioned the capacity of reductionist models to handle and explain complex social meaning, they have also appealed to models of inquiry in anthropology, ethnography, and sociolinguistics — that is, to social sciences whose practitioners have labored to develop highly rigorous models and methodologies that are capable of approaching some aspects of human meaning and experience in an explanatorily rich and empirically reliable way (for example, Hymes 1967).

GRAND THEORY IN MEDIA HISTORY

There is an historian whose work exemplifies for some enthusiasts of cultural studies a theory of history that treats communications as the nerve center of social possibility and change. Harold Adams Innis conceived Western history as a succession of competitive struggles of centuries' duration among communications technologies serving competing elites and cultural values. His thesis has seldom been examined in light of its historical adequacy. Innis's most extended presentation of his communications theory of history, Empire and Communications (1950), is a somewhat breathless account of what almost seems to be a list of every important fact in communications history from 4000 B.C. to 1950. In fact, this historical narrative is perilously sketchy. A second book, The Bias of Communication (Innis 1951), offers only a slightly expanded analysis. Innis does not present his chronology of historical events as unique or possessed of multiple levels of explanation and structure, but as the epiphenomenal expression of great technological transformations in media that constitute the bone structure of historical epochs.

Innis set himself the problem of accounting for the rise and fall of "empire" in the history of such transformations. He hypothesized that empires rise out of partnerships between durable media and portable media, and that the outcome of adversarial encounters between civilizations depends on the comparative efficiency with which media controlled by contending powers facilitate the administration and control of territory on the one hand and the succession and continuity of authority on the other. Innis did not elaborate this hypothesis in sufficient historical detail to explain the mechanics of its claim, much less to make them convincing. He never proved whether the real history behind history is the history of media, as he asserts, or whether media only carry the struggles of history on their backs, and explanations of fundamental change lie elsewhere.

For Innis, assertions of media presence count as declarations of historical efficacy in the absence of detailed evidence for concrete media effect in particular historical circumstances. When Innis does note specific historical claims, the result is sometimes jarring. His account of the French Revolution in this sentence, "The policy of France, which favoured exports of paper and suppression of publication and which increased printing in Holland and England, created a disequilibrium, which ended in the Revolution" (1950, p. 159), is not credible and not atypical. Minus an argument from detailed evidence, Innis stretches the fabric of history across a spare two-dimensional frame of "time" and "space" coordinates said to be manifest in communication — the process, according to Dewey, in which society exists. The hopeful and immodest ambition of this attempt to sort vast and complex collections of human experience into typologies devoid of any obstinate paradoxes of particularity owes something to a reductive structuralism that has characterized not a little recent social science theory.

Innis's fundamental historical dynamic does not begin at this abstract level. It begins in the plausible argument that political and cultural control over space requires the capacity to move information easily from the center of power to its periphery and back, from which it follows that the portability of the medium is a critical factor. In a parallel way, he argues, successful control over the imaginative time of tradition requires media like stone that endure. Less plausible is the next level of the argument, in which the physical characteristics of media generate typical habits of thought and disposition for entire cultures. If media last, according to this claim, then the cultures to which they belong respect tradition and permanence. If media move information rapidly across space, then the cultures to which they belong value life that is fast paced and present-oriented.

Innis uses the term "bias" to specify media orientation. Time-biased media render the passage of time unimportant in the transmission of messages. However far back in time a message is launched, it remains unimpeded and undistorted. People separated by generations can have the same message in their hands. Time-biased messages fade over space. Spoken language, clay, parchment, and stone are time-binding media, according to Innis (1950, pp. 7-8, and passim; 1951, pp. 3-4, 33-34, and passim). They are typically durable and difficult to transport. They are said to foster hierarchy, decentralization, provinciality, religious tradition, and permanence. Space-biased media render the expanse of space unimportant in the transmission of messages. From no matter how geographically distant a point a message is launched, it remains unimpeded and undistorted. Space-biased media are light and fragile and permit those separated by vast reaches to have the same message in their hands. Space-biased media are ephemeral, and the messages they carry fade over time. Paper, celluloid, and electronic signals are space-binding media. They are said to give rise to centralization, bureaucracy, secularism, imperialism, and force.

The elliptical narrative in which this scheme is presented leaps from technological "fact" to social "effect." Though Innis's theory of media determinism radically challenges conventional historical explanations of political change, it seems to have no consequences at all for conventional periodizations, nor for conventional labeling and sequences in political history. The "facts" on which it is built are culled from a variety of secondary sources without discussion of the interpretive contingencies on which such facts depend. Innis treats categories like technological innovation, bureaucracy, decentralization, religion, and secularism as if they described razor-sharp, clean-boundaried, precise, and unproblematic phenomena, just as he finds it expedient to characterize Greek or British or French culture along one or two dimensions. Students of culture may be justifiably suspicious of this reductive tendency in the historical description of complex civilizations.

Innis also takes the operation of time and space biases as ideally effective. He assumes an always successful connection between centers of power and peripheries of spatial and temporal geography, an identity between the possibility of control and its reliable exercise that was rarely borne out in the premodern historical record with which he is particularly concerned, and probably operates more erratically in the present than is generally assumed. The representation of shifts in media efficiency as transformations of enabling conditions requires a supporting history of transportation effectiveness, an element largely missing in the Innisian account.

Absent a history of transportation, media and the values they embody compete for dominance by a process Innis also never analyzes or elaborates empirically. Just as some media are always present and by implication effective for Innis, so some media are always dominant in a way that has determinative cultural consequences. Theoretically, dominance is the result both of leaps in efficiency, or effective competition among media, and monopolies of knowledge, or failed competition. Monopolies of knowledge have the same evils as economic monopolies in stifling adaptiveness and diversity. They occur when obstacles of cost or skill give effective control of particular media to exclusive groups. Monopolies of knowledge introduce social instability and "invite" challenge from competing media and bodies of knowledge. Social stability, of which empire is the most dramatic historical example, occurs when a single authority controls both space-binding and time-binding media.

In Innis's narrative, "dominant" sometimes means politically dominant in the sense of being administered or controlled by reigning political authority. At other times it means socially dominant (in the sense of being the channel through which most people communicate most of the time), or economically dominant (though Innis, whose work was mostly in economic history, never offers figures comparing media for this purpose), or morally dominant (in the sense of dictating prevailing values). At different points it has all these meanings, but they are assumed rather than demonstrated, and this makes them tautological as well.

Innis writes as if "space-binding" and "time-binding" were mutually exclusive, independent, and constant physical properties of media operating on culture. In the details of his historical account, however, the effective properties of old and new media constantly shift in relation to one another, as if there were after all an ecology of mutually adjusted communications functions. Innis specifies no general principle for circumstances in which the physical characteristics of media fully shape the social expression organized by their means, or, alternatively, in which they do not. In the resulting confusion, cultural characteristics exactly opposite from those predicted by a "technological" definition of media are occasionally attributed to media in particular historical situations.

Innis portrays the ancient Babylonian empire, for example, as an uneasy alliance between a temple-based priesthood in the south organized around sacred writing on clay tablets, and a centralized, militarily ambitious northern monarchy organized around stone media and architecture (1950, pp. 26-54). The heaviest and most enduring of all ancient media is thus held responsible for classic space-binding cultural traits of military expansion and secular political interest, where, according to the theory of media bias, there should be an overlapping and unconquerable constellation of time-binding influences on social organization.

Either spatial and temporal biases are potentially equally present in all media and are variously elicited in circumstances that can be specified, or they reside separately and unvaryingly in media with distinctive physical characteristics. They cannot logically do both. Having argued that the success of Hitler's aural and therefore temporal radio appeal was a theoretically consistent reaction to the distortion of Western civilization by the spatiality of the printed word, for example, Innis cannot then claim that radio overcame the impulse of printing toward decentralized nationalism, and successfully commanded vast new territories, without contradicting himself (1951, pp. 80–81). A world constructed in the spatial, centralized image of print cannot also be a decentralized community battling the paradoxically expansionist tendencies of an ephemeral aural medium like radio.

Besides making such a posteriori adjustments without explanation, Innis frequently introduces external factors to explain media effects without acknowledging the extratheoretical character of this extramedia explanation. He makes much, for example, of the strength of the Greek oral tradition, which he credits with resisting the absorptive threat of a written alphabet and with being the "reason" the Greeks were able to break the advancing wave of Persian empire (1951, pp. 53, 58–59, 66, 75, 84). Since all ancient cultures had an oral tradition of some kind, what made that tradition strong in one culture instead of another was not the oral tradition itself and must be explained in other terms. If external influences determine the effectiveness of media and even, as in the case of Babylonia, shape that effect in violation of some inherent "bias," then it is not media that make a historical difference, but other political, economic, and religious factors that operate through them.

These are not the only logical puzzles in Innis's theory. Except to construct the history of media competition in a deterministic and narratively dramatic way, it is not clear why any medium should be capable of only a single bias at a time, or how it is that "space" and "time" are mutually exclusive categories of analysis. Media do not exist as communications phenomena or events except in socially invented practices for transmission, storage, and retrieval. Innis seems to have regarded storage and retrieval not as variable social practices but as consistent extensions of assumed transmission properties of media, and to have classified all media accordingly.

The actual history of memory innovations drastically diminishes the suggestiveness of Innis's scheme for sorting media by the presumed consequences of bias. While Innis has argued, apparent contradictions aside, that print is as pure a case of spatial bias as history offers, Elizabeth Eisenstein (1979) has argued that the most important consequence of the printing press was to make writing permanent. While manuscripts were fragile and unevenly dispersed across geographical space, and survived best when they were inspected least, typographical fixity saw the printed word through all disasters that had previously diverted human energy from cultural preservation. Eisenstein, as is now well known, argues that several cultural renaissances that preceded the quattrocento Renaissance failed to take hold for lack of effective preservative techniques. After Eisenstein, it is difficult to argue convincingly that print is ephemeral. In Innis's terminology, print binds space and time with equal success.

If the capacity to move information over long distances and to store a lot of it are significant measures of media effectiveness, the two watershed developments in communications history after language and writing are printing, which greatly increased the capacity for transmitting and storing written messages, and computing, which is telegraphy with a memory, radio with a memory, and television with a memory. What printing did for writing, computing does for all electronic media.

These definitions of effectiveness are seriously inadequate, however, most of all because they leave the crucial problem of meaning unaddressed. The very anthropologists, ethnographers, and sociolinguists to whose example the enthusiasts of cultural studies have so strongly appealed argue that the pattern and richness of meaning can be established finally only in its particularities (Hymes 1967). Few cultural enthusiasts would be likely to insist that culture is so inconsequential a system of human meaning that messages moved over time and space will arrive undistorted in circumstances of utterly different cultural dimension and significance. That very notion, however, is the thrust of a theory of technological determinism. Innis failed to realize that meaning is not in the technological object, but only in the particular practices to which society puts it. Every technological object is already the expression of meanings and choices in a larger social order. Innis's error was the same as that of the journalism historians who assumed that media are objects with natural outlines, rather than a range of possibilities responding to changes in cultural time and space.

CONCLUSION

It is not surprising that communications history, increasingly studied by scholars outside the tradition of journalism history, shows signs of becoming an adopted child of social history. This shift is a significant and positive departure from its traditional and not notably successful emulation of Progressive institutional history in departments of journalism and communications, and from its acquiescence in that setting to the practical priorities and intellectual categories of professional journalists. Communications history cannot win its fight for intellectual dignity as a captive of professional ideology. Wherever communications history is subordinated to an applied curriculum, it will be distrusted both by professionals who see it as having an irremediable outsiders' perspective on what insiders know and by mainstream historians who see it as the impossible object of irreconcilable intellectual commitments. Whether it can do better under the auspices of social history than it has done as a grudgingly tolerated helpmeet of political history is a more uncertain question. Even the most critical and painstaking attempt to reconstruct the evidence of the past can only use categories that make sense in whatever the present may be. In that sense, all history is Whig history and is in need of constant rediscovery and reinterpretation.

The work of Harold Innis has sometimes been offered to communications historians as an alternative to the generally conceded inadequacies of conventional journalism history. This chapter argues that Innis's schematic media determinism is theoretically and empirically inadequate to the serious account of communications history its students seek. The formulation and investigation of fruitful historical problems in communications or any other area does require, though it cannot be dictated by, disciplined engagement in the central debates within mainstream history, something that also cannot be achieved so long as communications history remains within the warm circle of professional media concerns.

NOTES

1. For evidence of an assumed equivalence between the so-called elite press and newspapers deemed worthy of historical inquiry, see Merrill 1969, Chapters 1-4; and Nevins 1959.

2. Frank Luther Mott once explained that he always worked "with someone looking over my shoulder, as it were — with the sense of writing in a kind of collaboration with someone else, as my wife, a colleague, a close friend . . . . When I write on a journalistic topic, that collaborator is most often another ink-stained wretch" (see Casey 1965, p. 81).

3. Typical examples of reading the present back into the past, and judging the past by modern professional standards, are found in Gordon 1977, pp. 8-13, and Mott 1962, p. 15. A fairer picture of American journalism, comparative rather than evolutionary in presentation, is Marzio 1973 and Lee 1937.

4. I am indebted to Pamela Sankar for discussion on this point.

5. The perils of mainstream appropriation of emerging historical areas are clearly illustrated in the text of an address by Allan Nevins, then president of the American Historical Association, to the Committee on History at the 1959 Association for Education in Journalism Convention in Eugene, Oregon (1959). Nevins surveyed journalism historiography and concluded that: it had been insufficiently critical in identifying good and bad journalism (by standards unspecified, but evidently assumed); that journalism historians had done a poor job of discovering novel evidence to assist in the construction of a fuller political history, as though the only "real" history were political history; and that historians should confine their energies to newspapers worthy of having their history preserved, a criterion that, from Nevins's perspective, excluded most American dailies.

6. For example, Daniel J. Czitrom (1982) titles a chapter on the recent movement of social scientific perspectives into the field of communications, "The Rise of Empirical Media Study: Communications Research as a Behavioral Science, 1930–1960," (pp. 122–46). This is a misnomer. Journalism and communications history were always intended to be empirical, that is, to make and test propositional statements on the basis of evidence. Czitrom and others perhaps improperly confuse the term "statistical" with "empirical."

7. As early as 1944, however, Ralph D. Casey (1944, p. 56), then director of the University of Minnesota School of Journalism, was advising his colleagues at the National Council on Professional Education for Journalism that "the forward-looking teachers acknowledge that today's school of journalism is properly a school of communications." As an exercise in social prognostication, this article is chiefly interesting for its inability to identify what would be the chief new demands on journalism schools in the postwar era.

8. The evolution of these groups is recounted in Summary of Roundtables 1951; Official Minutes 1952; Conversation with Emery 1980.

9. Following Carey's (1974) article in its inaugural issue, Journalism History devoted the entirety of another issue to further discussion and replies to Carey. "A Symposium: History in the Journalism Curriculum" was the topic of Vol. 3 (1981). Though Journalism History has also devoted issues to Native American Indian journalism (1979) and to women's history and journalism (1975), these efforts do not so much challenge basic constructions and assumptions of traditional journalism history as attempt to disguise a seriously flawed theoretical structure by giving it a fashionable vocabulary.

10. Christians and Carey advance four standards for qualitative research, including naturalistic observation, contextualization, maximized comparisons, and sensitized concepts. Nowhere, however, do they wrestle with the translation of these rhetorical notions into concrete research procedures. Much, for example, is made of taking "social wholes" into account in interpretation (p. 355), but no effort is made to specify what a social whole is, so that an aspiring researcher can decide if he or she has gotten hold of one. Similarly, the discussion of maximized comparisons never considers whether or under what circumstances particular comparisons are inappropriate and invalid. In its claim to present strategies and standards for "qualitative" research, this article, the only one I am aware of that represents the culturalist contribution to such discussion in communications, is not merely disappointing but theoretically and methodologically inadequate.

11. Classic culturalist preambles include Carey 1975 and Park 1923.

4
CULTURAL STUDIES REVISITED AND REVISED
Lawrence Grossberg

"Communications in transition": the ascription is a seductive one and perhaps, for that very reason, it is worth interrogating. Its appeal may be in part the result of its apparent innocence, which leaves unspecified not only the direction but also the substance of change. At the same time, it constructs the illusion of autonomy and occludes the sociological, political, and discursive determinations implicated in the process. Whether that autonomy is located in the "natural logic of the subject matter," or in the dialogue among individual scholars, both the specificity and the determinateness of theoretical interventions are glossed over. My own preferred characterization is that communications is the site of a discursive struggle.

My aim in this chapter is twofold:

● To bring to the center a rather expansive discourse that has been largely marginalized and ghettoized. Cultural theory, which is a particularly lively field of theorizing in Britain and Europe, exists for the most part in the gaps and cracks in the American disciplinary apparatus. (The fact that it does exist is evidence that "hegemony is leaky.") Moreover, I want to outline the trajectory of theorizing in contemporary cultural studies.

● To locate the conjuncture of two questions. The first is an epistemological one: How does one understand communication? The second is a political one: How does one acknowledge and intervene in the relations of power involved in contemporary communicative practices? By following the trajectory of cultural theory into what has been called "postmodernism," I will suggest that the struggle in communications theory is not, as is often claimed, between theories of effects or influence and theories of signification or interpretation, but between theories of signification and theories of power (which reconceptualize the notion of effects).

The specificity of cultural theory can be seen in part in the context from which it emerged and into which it reinserted itself: namely, an interrogation of the nature and value of the intersecting social, economic, and political changes constituting "modernization." The uniqueness of its intervention was to locate these processes within culture, taken broadly as the structures and production of meaning. Thus, cultural theory set for itself a double problematic: on the one hand, the primacy of a theory of signification and interpretation; on the other hand, the foundations of a theory of community and politics. As a result, it implicated its own discourse, as cultural, within its sphere of concern. This particular conjunction has not only provided the site for a broad series of theoretical and political arguments, it has also circumscribed a discursive space through the structure of its analytic practice (as the construction of homologies) and the identification of the culture/politics couplet with that of relativism/legitimacy. For just as the issue of interpretation problematizes any epistemological or cultural claim of truth, the confrontation with modernization threatens to undermine the political possibility of community and democracy (Rorty 1982).

The relationship between cultural theory and communication theory is a complex one. Historically, the former was one of the founding discourses from which communication, both as a unified object of study and a discipline, was constituted. Moreover, as communication theory has increasingly turned to questions of meaning, this new theoretical hegemony has attempted to incorporate some of the terms of cultural theory. While communication theory radically segregates questions of signification and politics (even the so-called critical communications theorists rarely threaten this boundary), cultural theory is located at the point of the intersection of these two problematics.

I shall begin by briefly comparing the "founding discourses" of John Dewey and Raymond Williams. While their positions are initially quite similar, the two traditions to which they give rise differ significantly because of Williams's eventual incorporation of the problem of politics into the moment of signification or culture. Thus, rather than understanding power as an external intervention into the processes of culture, the British school of "cultural studies" argues that power is a struggle within and over meaning. As a result, cultural studies have drawn upon contemporary theoretical developments in Marxist theories of ideology and semiotic theories of signification. After outlining these recent developments, I shall briefly discuss some of the work of the Centre for Contemporary Cultural Studies. Raising a number of objections to this work on both theoretical and political grounds, I will suggest the possibility of a cultural theory that reverses the primacy of signification over questions of power. Rather than seeking the truth of politics, I will attempt to locate a politics of truth. Rather than seeking an interrogation of culture and communication through the problematic of signification, I will propose that signification itself be taken as merely one moment within the organization of power and desire.

DEWEY AND WILLIAMS

Given the temporal, geographical, and philosophical distance between John Dewey and Raymond Williams, it is somewhat surprising that they each articulated very similar theories of culture and communication. Of all the contributors to the Chicago School of Social Thought, Dewey (1954) spoke most directly to problems of communication and culture. The particular way in which Dewey described these was, of course, partly determined by his philosophical commitment to pragmatism, which, as a naturalist theory of meaning, argued that meaning was worked out in action or, more accurately, in transaction with the other. In fact, all of life was characterized transactionally: in relation to the world at the biological level, to people at the social level, or to language at the level of the generalized other. For Dewey, the model of all such transactions, at whatever level of human complexity, was ultimately communication.

The pragmatists' commitment to transaction or process was further defined by their acceptance of the evolutionary model (not surprising, given when they wrote). They assumed a hierarchical series of evolutionary levels characterized by homologous processes: Organism is to the world as self is to the social self as individual is to the social as forms of communication are to forms of social life. That is, the structure of the various levels was taken to be the same, a basic process common to all the levels. This assumption was common to the pragmatists, and thus what it meant to be human demanded an answer in terms of some particular form of a more general process. Basically, the pragmatists offered three views of this process. At one extreme, Peirce (with his logical semiotics and, later, Morris with his behavioral semiotics) located human meaning as the product of a semiotic system (signs/structures) as a way into the problem of interpretation. At the other extreme, James grounded his work on a theory of the stream of experience. G. H. Mead seems to have positioned himself somewhere between James and Morris, looking to the analysis of what came to be called "symbolic interactions." There is a clear trajectory in his work from the behaviorism of **Mind, Self and Society** (edited by Morris coinci-

dentally) to the phenomenology of The Philosophy of the Present.
Only Dewey, located somewhere in the middle as well, began
explicitly with notions of communication and sought to elucidate
the relations between forms of communication and forms of social
life (the notion of forms presumably existing somewhere between
structures and processes).

Furthermore, for Dewey, this process of communication was
teleologically defined, inevitably leading toward consensus,
shared meaning, and community. Thus, the process of communication is the same as the process of community and, even more
fundamentally, of social life. The two moments — communication
and community — each reinforce each other and locate themselves in a continuing circle, since communication presupposes
the community that it creates and recreates.

Consequently, if the processes of communication and community were not working, this could not be due to something inherent in the process itself but rather must be due to the
interference of some external force(s). For Dewey, the twin
faces of the failure of modernization — the destruction of community (culture) and the eclipse of the public (politics) — were
both manifestations of the same breakdown of the natural human
processes of communication due to the intervention of outside
forces blocking the flow of necessary communication. The problem was not inherent in the process itself. While the new media
of communication were apparently to blame for the economic,
social, and political dispersion of American culture, the solution
was to be found in those same media. The real enemy was simply
the misuse of the possibilities of the communication media, and
the solution was to restore the process, a question of providing
the knowledge that was needed for people to interpret successfully and act upon reality in shared, rational ways once again.

Thus, the result of Dewey's attempt to think through the
relation of culture, communication, and social life was a particular vision of the mediating function of meaning, through which
the cultural and political realms were describable as homologous
or corresponding processes. Furthermore, the idealist view of
process (albeit a naturalism) assumed a teleology that grounded
and directed political optimism and, apparently, intervention. The
failure of the process could be understood only as the result of
some foreign and external agent or structure blocking the flow
of communication; the solution lay in setting the original processes back in circulation.

This position is similar to the early position of Raymond
Williams, but there are important differences that have defined
the divergent traditions that have arisen out of each. I will
return to this shortly. In an obvious way, the most significant
difference between Williams and Dewey is the starting point.
Williams (1966) raises the question of judging "modernity" by

constituting a tradition of British critical thought — the "Culture and Society tradition" — in which both conservative and populist authors approach the task of judging the new social organizations and relationships through the explicit mediation of the category of "culture." Like Dewey, Williams was a part of a specific generation of writers, working class children who entered into the intellectual elitism of the British university system. They existed in a "border country," living with two conflicting and competing identities and thus they located at the center of their interrogation of modernity questions about the nature of cultural identification and understanding. Williams, in particular, began by identifying the specific ambiguity of the concept of "culture": It refers to a particular social sensibility, a special kind of activity (for example, the arts) and the notion of a whole way of life. As is his wont, he then argued that the changing meaning of the term was related to other historical changes and that underlying these diverse significations — historically and therefore semantically — is the notion of a special (agricultural) process: the tending for natural growth. Williams thus interpreted the idea of culture as a continuous process by which shared meaning is established by common effort. Culture becomes the "community of process" and the process of community is that of communication. Social reality as a shared meaning production is accounted for as a dialogue, not merely between individuals nor between rigidly isolated individuals and reified society but between systems of meaning constantly interacting. Reality is the product of a dialectic of creativity and tradition within the space of the production of shared meaning.

When we turn to the political implications that Williams draws from this view, we find that he continues the impulse of the various writers in the culture and society tradition to locate in the concept of culture itself a standard or measure of social life. For Williams, the ideal of the "community of process" is the measure. He rejects both the conservative defense of art or of some (mythical) organic community and the populist defense of working class culture for its own sake. Rather, what Williams extols if the "long revolution" embodied in the course of modernization, what we might today call the beginnings of a populist social democracy. The problem then becomes one of participation in and access to the media by which the process of community is realized. Thus, Williams attempts to identify both the positive and the negative contributions of modernization to the realization of the ideal of culture.

However, Williams (1965) takes another direction that results from the complexity of the concept of culture and that takes him into radically different questions and directions. Understood as either a sensibility or a way of life, "culture" refers to the social construction of reality through the processes of meaning-production. This is also clearly the function in part of those privileged expressive activities that we also label as cultural (for example, art). Yet this does not account for the latter's special position, their privileging, or their special role in social and cultural life. Generally speaking, Williams proposes to find a way to speak about the relationship between this one unique mode of human activity and the rest of our social lives, understood in terms of our lived experience. Williams then sets out to understand the relationship between art and the totality of lived experience of a particular social moment.

What Williams proposes, as does Richard Hoggart (1958) at the same moment, is that the foundations of cultural studies lie in the intersection of literary and sociological theory. Both suggest that the specifically literary analysis of culture offers a unique insight into the understanding of culture as the whole way of life of a particular social formation. In a sense, the project of cultural studies, as it arises in England, is to understand what it felt like to be alive at a particular time and place through the interpretation of cultural (that is, artistic and communicative) texts (Hoggart 1970). How this is to be accomplished is, then, the unique problem posed by British cultural theory. Williams's solution is somewhere in the gaps of the pragmatists: in the notion of the "structure of feeling." It is this notion that opened up an analytics of interpretation in Williams's work that remained unexplored in the corpus of the Chicago School. It is meant to provide a principle of structure to that which is to be interpreted and which is, apparently, structureless (that is, feelings). Like Dewey, Williams assumes a principle of homologous structures but his is even more encompassing. The "structure of feeling" describes both the "objective" whole way of life and the coherent totality of lived experience. That is, it provides a description of the way in which all of the "pieces" of social existence fit together into an apparently rational whole, both from the objective and the subjective sides. It is precisely this assumption of a homology between these two perspectives that has made Williams's criticism so powerful.

Thus, in order to examine the social significance of any one element in social life it is not sufficient simply to relate it to one of the remaining pieces (for example, literature to the economic). Rather, the interpretation of any moment of social life requires that it be related to the totality of the structure of feeling. Williams's interpretive analytic directs one to look at the relations among all of the elements in a whole way of life. Of course, there is still a problem when one turns to the question of the interpretation of artistic texts, for their relation to the general structures of feeling remains unexplicated. Here, Williams uses the assumption of homologies to replace less sophisticated casual models of the relationship. Williams argues that artistic texts embody, perhaps more clearly than any other form of social practice, the structures of feeling of the social moment of their origin and reception. This is not, however, simply a reflection of an already constituted external structure; rather, artistic texts both refract and constitute the structure of feeling of their social contexts. It is for this reason, according to Williams, that art is so highly valued. It is not only the most articulate entrance into and presentation of the structure of feeling, it is also the most potentially honest and reflexive production of that structure of feeling.

The notion of the structure of feeling, however, problematizes the political implications of the community of process. A consideration of the latter alone led Williams to agree with Dewey that the failure of this process must be due to external agencies interfering with the natural movement of history; similarly, the political task was one of removing blocks to access and restoring natural flows. But this model is undercut to some extent by the competing moment of the structure of feeling, for this seems to suggest that the contradictions and inequalities of a particular social moment are an integral and constitutive moment of culture. It is, however, only as Williams (1974) begins to examine the concrete structures of communication — the actual material processes by which the community of process is both carried out and undermined — that the implicit break with the politics of the Chicago School becomes explicit. Increasingly, Williams began to argue that if the forms of communication and their mirror image in the structures of relationship both produce and reproduce social reality, then these must be seen as concrete human activities. As a result, one must identify the intentions and interests that structure communication itself behind the apparently innocently given communication environment. Such intentions are neither personal nor psychological, however, rather they are constituted within social structures and represent economic and political positions within the social formation. Further, Williams argued that such intentions could be read off, interpreted within, the communicative texts and practices themselves.

Thus, the community of process constantly is contradicted and distended by "the community of culture." The latter points to the necessary materiality of the processes by which social reality is produced, a materiality that incorporates into the process itself questions of power and inequality. These are not two separate processes but two moments — telos and ursprung — of the same process, the social production of meaning. Thus Williams concludes that the question of politics must be raised within the issue of signification, rather than as the result of external interference. Politics is a moment of the cultural process itself; politics is itself an interpretive issue.

The interpretation of culture and communication, then, rests upon the assumption of homologies explicated in the notion of the structure of feeling. Now, in addition, one must find a way of describing these processes not only in terms of the social production of meaning (or of reality as meaningful) but also in terms of the social displacement of reality in processes of meaning-production. Once we recognize that all of culture refracts reality as well as reproducing it as meaningful, then we are committed as well to examining the interests implicated in particular refractions. If both the production of meaningful reality and the displacement of reality within that production are integral moments of the process of culture, then culture studies must interrogate the ways in which communication not only produces but also distorts or deviates from the homologous structuring of culture and social experience.

Thus, despite the fact that both Dewey and Williams began by exploring the same intellectual and historical terrain, each opened up a different discursive space. This has had significant implications for the development of cultural studies in the two countries. Both apparently confronted two distinct problematics. The first (signification) questions the nature and production of meaning. It points to, in Ricoeur's (1970) terms, a hermeneutics of faith. The second issue (power) questions the possibility of distortion or misrepresentation, pointing to a hermeneutics of suspicion. As long as the two problematics remain separated, however, there is the third question of the relationship between the two theories offered in response. William's most significant contribution was to recognize eventually that the theories of communication and miscommunication had to be articulated together, that the question of how texts mean is intersected by the question of how texts relate to and distort reality. This insight suggested that cultural studies fruitfully might locate itself at the site of the intersection of semiotics and the theory of ideology.

On the other hand, the U.S. tradition of "culturalism" that developed out of the work of the Chicago School (Carey 1975, 1977), has taken a very different path. This was the result, in part, of the particular marginalization of this tradition, not only in social theory but in the study of communications as well. Because of its narrower focus on the processes of mass media, American cultural theory has devoted an inordinate amount of its energy to defending itself against the claims of the more "scientific" effects tradition. Furthermore, Dewey's naturalistic idealism provided little direction for concrete theoretical and interpretive practice.

Rather vague and often contradictory notions of the symbolic construction of reality have led to the celebration of epistemological and cultural relativism, and at the same time have undermined the possibility of coherent political critique. While this tradition often provides some of the most sensitive readings of American culture, it does so in an apparently atheoretical way, without any interpretive analytic. In a rather unique paradox, it assumes the mediating function of signification without offering any theory of how this is accomplished or of how it can be dismantled and described. Nor is there any theory of why the production of meaning is itself effectively produced as a representation of the real. Because the role of concrete social and material relations in this process remains unconceptualized, there is no way of addressing the relationship between processes of meaning-production and "intentional displacement." Because the two problematics remain essentially unconnected, there is no apparent place for a theory of the political management of the production of meaning. Despite its impeccable humanistic credentials, the American culturalist tradition seems a less fruitful alternative than the British school of cultural studies, which attempts to link signification and social processes, communication and miscommunication, together.

CULTURAL AND STRUCTURAL MARXISM

The traditional reading of Marx suggests that the social formation could be represented as a dialectic between the base and the superstructure. The former is characterized by the particular mode of production, defined by the dialectic between the forces and relations of production. In capitalism at least, this is determining, and its internal contradictions provide the potential source of revolution. The latter consists of the various political and cultural institutions of the social formation. While the base is often reduced to only the mode of economic production and the superstructure is seen as a mere reflection of the determining base, there are those who would argue that this is an oversimplification of Marx's theory. Nevertheless, in this traditional view, ideology is defined functionally as a representation of the interests of the dominant or ruling class, as the body of "ruling ideas," or as the ideal expression of the dominant material relations. It is, in other words, a hierarchically imposed false consciousness whose function is to hide, via a distortion of reality, the contradictions and interests constituting the social formation in general and the class relations in particular.

Such views have been made a little more sophisticated by recognizing the dialectical nature of the relationship between the base and the superstructure. Furthermore, the simple class analysis on which it initially was based has given way to a more open view in which ideology need not reflect the interests and position of a single dominant class. Instead, ideology can be understood as the site of a struggle and, in particular, of the conflict inherent in the class struggle. However, the real lacuna in this view of ideology is any analysis of how ideology works, of the mediation of reality that it produces, and of the medium through which it is empowered (that is, language).

There have been two major responses to this lack of an adequate theory of either ideology or, more generally, the superstructure. Hall (1980) has described them as "cultural" and "structural" Marxism. In contrast to the traditional conceptions of Marxism, both of these approaches are theoretical and are primarily concerned with the superstructure and its role in constituting power and domination through the operation of ideology. Both are opposed to the economic reductionism of earlier Marxisms, although they retain the basic assumption that the economic is determining in the last instance. Rather than seeing the superstructure or culture as a mere reflex or reflection of economic determinations, however, they argue that culture and ideology have their own real determining role in the social formation. Furthermore, they suggest that the relationship between economic and political processes, on the one hand, and superstructural processes, on the other, always is mediated by other refracting levels of determination. Finally, both are opposed to the totalitarianism of the Stalinist reading of Marx, and both seek to reclaim the political fecundity of Marxist practice.

The argument between them is over the status of experience as a possible beginning point or standard. This issue is not, however, reducible to a simple argument over the primacy of the individual versus the social, since even culturalists like Williams would argue that experience is always social. While it does have implications for issues of subjectivity and the possibility of oppositional practice, the real issue is, I believe, whether one starts with a theory of reality (experience) and distortion or a theory of signification and the production of experience.

The culturalists' revision of Marxism (Williams 1973) emphasizes the "humanistic" rather than the "economistic" side of Marx's writings, especially the earlier Hegelian works. They point to Marx's concern with describing social reality in terms of lived experience. They focus their analysis on the social subject as an active agent who makes history through "praxis," the essential form of creative human activity. Furthermore, they argue that any particular practice must be located within the totality of social life, both as an actuality and as a totalization to be achieved. They maintain a teleological image of history explicated through the eventual resolution of the class struggle. Thus, they continue to describe social experience in terms of class experience, although classes no longer are necessarily seen as homogeneous totalities but rather as an alliance of particular "class fractions," which are determined ideologically and politically, as well as economically. The result is, of course, that particular class alliances may themselves embody contradictions among the various fractions. While class position determines the consciousness with which individuals confront, for example, ideological forms, the model that the culturalists propose for this process is significantly revised in a number of ways. Attempting to escape the limits of the base–superstructure model, they suggest that both of these terms must be seen as processes and as complex sets of often contradictory practices. For example, Williams (1973) prefers to say that "social being determines consciousness"; that is, that the structures of human material practices determine the structures and contours of human consciousness.

Further, the relation of "determination" is seen as a dialectical process of shaping and influencing, rather than the simple production of mirror images. It is the exertion of force that tends to push the other in a certain direction. The processes of determination rarely operate directly; they are mediated through a variety of moments that necessarily distend the possibility of any casual relationship. One of the consequences of this view is that the category of the economic is largely absent from culturalist analyses, except in terms of class experience.

Finally, the concept of ideology either is replaced by or supplemented with Gramsci's (1971) concept of hegemony. Whereas ideology suggests the distortion of reality through a stable system of representation, a content that can be compared to experience, hegemony points to a constant process by which the dominant class alliance wins the consent of the dominated classes by creating representations of reality that are taken as reality itself. Hegemony is a continuous struggle to dominate through consent rather than coercion, through representation rather than falsification, through legitimation rather than manipulation. In the struggle for hegemony, representations of reality are offered in the place of the real and come to be taken as reality, and thus they provide the natural and reasonable limits of "common sense." On the surface this view of the production of meaning as the social construction of reality bears a striking similarity to the theories of American culturalists; but its location within the context of a theory of the class struggle opens up an entire analytic of the concrete processes by which: particular interests are tied to particular representations, and the struggle to produce and maintain consent is carried on concretely. However, because the cultural Marxist's final appeal is to the category of experience, there still remains a moment of distortion within the theory of hegemony, and a moment of correspondence between ideology and reality. Thus the culturalist's project is to compare the ideological representations, now located within the ongoing struggle for hegemony, with the lived experience of particular classes. Cultural Marxism seeks homologies between class positions and systems of representation.

On the other side of the current debate in British cultural studies is structural Marxism, based largely upon the work of Althusser (1970, 1971). Althusser explicitly rejected Marx's early writings as idealist and ideological. He proposes both a new model of the social formation as well as a new theory of ideology, resulting in a radical undermining of the base-superstructure model that he still sees operating in the culturalists' search for homologies. Given the complexity and difficulty of his views, I can provide only a brief outline.

First, according to structural Marxism, the social formation is to be described as a "structure in dominance." It is composed of four levels or ensembles of social practices: the political, the economic, the ideological, and the theoretical. This last level — Althusser's failed attempt to describe the scientific status of Marxist critique and thus to avoid the conclusion that Marxism is itself an ideological practice — need not concern us here. Any social analytic must begin, then, with the complexity of the unity of a structure. This requires that we recognize both the specificity of the levels and their relations, that we identify the contradictions within each level as well as those between them.

The relations among the levels are described in the concepts of "structural causality" and "overdetermination." Althusser distinguishes three kinds of causality. Mechanical causality is the identifiable operation of one isolatable entity on another (the billiard ball model). Expressive causality is the expression of an internal or central principle (such as the spirit of an age or the structure of feeling) in all of the surface phenomena. Structural causality is a cause that exists only in its effects or, more accurately, in the structuration of its effects. Structural causality rejects any appeal to an external agency or to an internal principle. There is no essential structure (even any particular contradiction) that can characterize and explain the social formation. Structural causality operates by overdetermination; that is, every moment in the social formation determines and is determined by every other moment. One cannot, therefore, isolate individual causal relations as if they could exist outside of the structured context. And yet, one cannot reduce any level entirely to the determinations of the other levels, since each level of practice is characterized as well by a semiautonomy. This is not an appeal, however, to some notion of absolute freedom; it rather points to the fact that each level is determined partially by its own history and its own internal logic. As a result, there is and must be a necessary noncorrespondence between the levels in the social formation.

While the culturalists define the social in terms of class experience and structure, Althusser returns to the more traditional Marxist view of the social as defined primarily by the mode of production. Each of the levels, however (political, economic, ideological), as a form of practice, is productive. Thus, one must specify the hierarchical relations among the three levels. This is what Althusser calls the "structure in dominance." At any historical moment, one of the three levels is dominant (that is, most directly and powerfully determining) within the social formation. Which of the three serves this function is itself determined by the economic level in the last instance. But as Althusser quickly adds, the last instance never comes, and it can never come if we are to avoid falling back into economic reductionism. Thus, the structural Marxist view of the social totality within which ideology and culture are effective is significantly different from that of the cultural Marxists: Overdetermination replaces homology.

Althusser's theory of ideology (1971) is also significantly different; it denies that there are homologies between representations and experience. For structural Marxism, ideology is in fact the process by which experience itself is produced. It is the unconscious system of representation of the imaginary relationship between people and their real conditions of existence. It is the production of the meaning, not of reality, but of the way in which we live our relationship to reality, that is, of our experience. In what Althusser describes as a "double specular relation," ideology is a mirror structure within which the individual and reality are produced in a relationship to each other, as subject and experience, respectively. That is, ideology works by positioning the individual in a particular relation to the system of representation. Ideology "hails" or "interpellates" the individual as a subject. It makes the subject apparently responsible for those meanings and, hence, for his or her own experience. The result is that the system of representation appears to be innocently given in the immediacy of our own experience. Whereas, in fact, it is that experience itself that has been produced. Ideology is not a mediation between subjectivity and reality. The subject, which is the transcendental assumption of all humanists, is "deconstructed" and shown to be a necessary product of ideological practice, that which ideology constructs as its own support or bearer. One of the more controversial results of this particular functional theory of ideology is that ideology is a necessary moment of any social formation. There must always be ideology, embodied within the material practices of signification. This would seem at least to problematize the assumption of any utopian reading of history insofar as such readings must appeal to an image of human nature (subjectivity) as universal and essential.

There is an apparent similarity between the structural theory of ideology and the concept of hegemony. Both identify the operation of ideology with the processes of signification and naturalization so that meaning is offered in the place of reality/experience. The power of the structuralist view, however, lies in its explicit articulation of a theory of signification that brings together the moments of representation and misrepresentation. In order to see this more clearly, one must examine the semiotic foundations of Althusser's work and, in particular, his debt to structuralism and poststructuralism.

STRUCTURALISM AND POSTSTRUCTURALISM

The theory of structuralism is built upon distinctions: langue/parole, synchrony/diachrony, paradigm/syntagm, and signified/signifier. Structuralism brackets questions of language use (parole) and history (diachrony) in order to study the underlying system or codes that make possible the concrete usage. It analyzes the system in terms of relations of substitution (paradigms) and contiguity (syntagms). Most significantly, the basic unit of signifying systems — the sign — is described as a unity of signifier and signified. While it is tempting to describe these as a material vehicle and a concept or meaning, respectively, this is not quite accurate for the concept of the sign (and all of structuralism) is based upon the assumption of constitutive difference. Saussure (1959), often regarded as the founder of structuralism, argued that the sign is always arbitrary, that is, that the relationship between the signifier and the signified is neither necessary nor externally defined. The sign does not refer to some external referent nor to some subjective intention; both reality and subjectivity are excluded from structural analyses. Instead, the sign is defined by a series or system of differences. Both the signifier and the signified exist only as spaces within such systems of differences; thus meaning (or more accurately, since we are in the realm of langue, value) is immanent within the system. Any particular signifier is not a concrete matter but a position that is differentiated and therefore given value within the system itself. Similarly, the signified is not a concept in the mind but a place carved out from an amorphous conceptual space. Either one can be filled by a multiplicity of variants or concrete embodiments, but this would take us into the realm of parole. Finally, structuralism argues that there is a necessary correspondence between the system of signifiers and that of the signifieds. It is as if these two distinct domains existed on opposite sides of a common plane; the way in which one inscribes differences on the plane of the signifier determines the inscription of differences on the plane of the signified.

Thus, according to structuralism, language structures conceptual space and the only place for the subject is as a prisoner in the house of language (Jameson 1972).

While Althusser's theory draws heavily upon structuralism, he also draws upon the structural psychoanalysis of Lacan (1977). Together, they represent the transition from structuralism to poststructuralism in their attempt to account for the production of meaning (the signified) and subjectivity in signifying practices. Lacan argued for both the primacy of the signifier and the implication of the subject in language, both of which serve as the foundations for contemporary poststructuralist work. Briefly, Lacan located the origin of desire as a lack that results in the infant's need to become the object of desire of the mother — the phallus. This lack is filled only (and only apparently so) in the Oedipal stage, which involves the child's accession into the domain of language, or what Lacan calls "the Symbolic." By representing oneself in language — the "I" of enunciation — the moment of Oedipal resolution produces a splitting of the individual: the one who speaks and is represented in language and that which can neither speak nor be spoken, the unconscious. Thus, according to Lacan, language is responsible not only for the production of the subject but also for the production of the unconscious (and, hence, the possibility of repression and all that entails psychoanalytically).

This connection of signification and subjectivity opens up a radically new space of critical discourse. No longer content merely to bracket questions of subject and reality — a strategy that inevitably leaves them in their taken-for-granted place — the focus of poststructuralism has turned from signifying structures to processes and practices of structuration. It is, then, a philosophy of the signifier. It takes for granted that signifying practices involve the production of signifiers in relations. Interestingly, this is quite similar to Peirce's pragmatic semiotics in which signification is to be analyzed as the continuous production of material signs. The poststructuralists argue that there is no need to assume the existence of signifieds or meanings within some sort of conceptual space. Rather, language (no longer distinguishing between langue and parole) is a constant sliding of one signifier into another, the production of a chain of signifiers. Meaning is the (imaginary) product of this movement, the result of the need or desire to stop the infinite generation of signifiers and to rest somewhere with an apparently natural meaning. It is, metaphorically, a game of musical chairs in which meaning is simply the product of our bringing the music to a halt. At that point, particular signifiers appear to be in special places (the chairs) or to have special effects that we take as meanings. Thus, there is no "conceptual space of the mind" in which meanings preexist and are organized by the signifying system. Signification is not a mediating function at all.

If there is no conceptual or phenomenological space of meanings, then there is similarly no moment of subjective existence that escapes the determination of signifying practices. The subject — as one who uses language for his or her own projects or as one who creatively binds the signifier and signified together into the sign — is an imaginary product of the very practices the concept seeks to control. This "I" is, simply put, another socially produced reality (Lukacs 1971).

It is important at this point to be clear about the precise claims that are being made. Poststructuralists do not deny that we experience ourselves as subjects, nor that we experience the world as meaningful, nor that these experiences are effective and have real material consequences in the world. Rather, they are suggesting that experience itself must be problematized and destabilized. The categories of experience cannot provide the beginnings of a theory of signification nor the standard for a theory of representation and misrepresentation, for it is these very categories that are the product of signifying practices. Appeals to experience, as if it existed outside of the production of meaning, and appeals to subjectivity, as if it were not positioned by and within signifying practices as the source and locus of meaning, are at the very root of our inability to theorize the processes of meaning-production and their relation to power (Coward 1977).

The practice of poststructural criticism takes a number of closely related forms. Basically, it attempts to "deconstruct" any apparently transparent, given, essential, totalizing, or transcontextual moment; such moments may be categories of experience, philosophically privileged concepts, or particular texts. Deconstruction destablizes the claim of any term to contain its own meaning within itself by dispersing its apparently given unity and meaning into the processes of its production. The result is that meaning always becomes "undecidable."

Such deconstructive practices have taken two basic forms (Coward and Ellis 1977). The first form of deconstruction involves a kind of philosophical critique by which any attempt to identify a stable meaning in a particular concept is undermined. This does not entail the denial of meaning or of the effectivity of the experience. Rather it is a constant deferral of one's ability to locate such a meaning. Even the structuralist's claim that meaning is constituted in relations (often binary) of difference is undermined by destabilizing the very category of difference; the ability to locate a stable moment of difference within which one can describe the particular constitution of meaning is again deferred. It is this notion of a difference that is constantly deferred, thus always pushing meaning away from us, that Derrida (1976) calls "differance." Difference and hence meaning constantly are produced and deferred, always pushing themselves further into the infinite possibilities of such production, leaving only traces of their operation for us to find. "Differance" is the ongoing inscription or articulation of differences and, hence, it is that ongoing movement of the production of meaning that cannot be said to exist outside its concrete products.

The second form of deconstructive practice also disperses meaning into the processes of its production. However, such processes are located in concrete reading practices. The result is that the explosion of meaning is not given in a deferral but rather in the infinite possibilities of the continued generation of meaning in readings. Focusing generally on texts, such "dissemination" (Derrida 1981) explodes the very category of "the text" in general and any particular text into the context of reading. If meaning is a product of the various codes that traverse the text, then the text always exists and is carried beyond itself into a domain of intertextuality. The meaning of a text is undecidable outside of particular readings; hence the text cannot be said to have a meaning or even a closed set of possible meanings. But this does not mean that one can claim that texts have no meaning, for this would merely be to substitute a void, an absence, for the assumption of a presence. Deconstruction, then, dissolves the boundaries of the text by continuing the connotative reverberations and webs of its discourses. Meaning is not the product of some reified text, nor of some privileged "perspective" belonging to the reader. Rather, meaning is a function of the context produced by particular reading practices and the possibility of new readings opens the text to an infinite possibility of meaning.

There are a number of problems, however, with such deconstructive practices. First, they continue to privilege experience by defining their project as accounting for the production of the categories of experience. Thus they fail to radically problematize the semantic boundaries of such experiences and thus question only their claim to primacy and stability. The alternative would be to take experience itself as one material fact among others. Second, they actually do not give an account of the production of the subject in concrete terms and appeal instead to universally necessary processes. Neither Althusser's theory of ideology nor Derrida's theory of "differance" gives an adequate account of how these processes work to produce the subject. In fact, everything ultimately is reduced to a trace of these processes. This suggests that they may in fact be functioning as new transcendentals, that is, universal processes that determine but are not determined by historical contexts.

However, it is not only the existence of the subject that needs to be explained; it is also the possibility of the breakdown or failure of the production of the ideological or discursive subject. For it appears that both Derrida and Althusser reconstitute a unified subject. It is, on the one hand, the necessary and almost mechanical result of the operation of signifying practices. On the other hand, it is the assumption of their own critical practices: in Althusser's claim for the scientific (that is, nonideological) status of Marxist analysis, and in Derrida's apparently innocent, undetermined, and playful reading subject.

This raises a significant theoretical and political problem. If the subject (as it is experienced within the terms of Western culture) is the product of signifying practices (either ideological or discursive), then how is it possible to move beyond the mechanical reproduction of this subject? How is deconstructive practice possible? And how is revolutionary action (even in terms of the production of revolutionary discourse) possible? If one cannot explain the necessity of the production of the subject, how is one to explain the possibility of the revolutionary subject? For example, in Derridean terms, why do the reading practices in which we are implicated function in the way they do? Derrida's attempt to incorporate some moment of historical and political determination — in his appeal to logocentrism — would throw us back into an expressive theory of causality.

The poststructuralist response to these problems largely has come from the work of the group associated with the journal Tel Quel, in two related interventions. The first proposes a critical vector that moves in the opposite direction from the playful and infinite possibilities of dissemination. It interrogates the moment at which the productivity of the sliding of the signifiers is halted; it looks at the ways in which meaning is determined by reading practices and the contextual constraints within which readings are accomplished. Thus, reading in itself seems to be the determined product of textual, intertextual, and cultural codes. For example, Barthes's (1974) reading of a realist short story offers something other than an explosion of the meaning of the text. On the one hand, he argues that the realist text is read precisely as a realist text, that the chain of signifiers is structured, directed, and ultimately stopped in determined ways. This determination is the operation of codes that can be located only in the intertext of our socially determined reading practices. This determination of meaning cannot be accounted for in terms of some stable structuring of the text, nor in terms of the subjective appropriation of the text. Yet, on the other hand, Barthes argues that this particular text also deconstructs the very possibility of its own meaningfulness as realism by constantly playing off, against its own codings of language and sexuality, the image of that which resists all attempts at coding — the image of castration. The result is that Barthes exhibits both the intertextual determination of meaning and the instability if not impossibility of any such meaning. Similarly, in A

Lover's Discourse (Barthes 1978), he demonstrates how a particular intertextual set of discursive practices carries the speaker along, constructing not only a highly emotionally charged language but the speaker as the subjective source of such emotions: To be a lover is to exist within a web of clichés.

The second intervention into a politics of and for poststructuralism derives from Kristeva's (1975; Grossberg 1983a) attempt to appropriate and rework both Althusser and Lacan. Both of these end up suggesting that the individual is inserted into an already defined space of subjectivity that leaves little room for either political or discursive oppositional practice. Kristeva seeks to theoretically locate the possibility of multiple and even contradictory subject-positionings. While Barthes apparently is satisfied to ascribe this to the effects of competing reading practices, Kristeva argues that it is the result of the conflict between language and desire that takes place within the production of meaning or significance. There are two moments to this process, two lines of force and determination: the symbolic and the semiotic. The former points to the Lacanian, Althusserian, and Derridean view of signifying practices and their necessary production of a particular subject-position. The second moment, the semiotic, which is also signifying, implicates the unconscious in its opposition to the constraints of social codings. The semiotic is the eruption of libidinal drives into and through the structures of the symbolic. It is also an interruption, an articulation of that which cannot be articulated symbolically. According to Kristeva, the subject is constantly produced in the struggle between these two moments within significance. Although symbolic practices seek a stable subject position, semiotic practices constantly disrupt and destabilize the possibility of any such mechanical reproduction. If the subject is never produced once and for all and if there is, at the very heart of the production of meaning and subjectivity, a moment of opposition, then the possibility of a revolutionary subject — one that would disrupt the stability of the ideological and discursive subject — always exists. Obviously, this view is not incompatible with that of Barthes. The strongest poststructuralist position will be one that combines a theory of the relationship of desire and discourse with the recognition that the subject is determined by the multiplicity of signifying practices available to him or her. The result is that subjectivity is not produced as a stable unity but rather is always being produced in fragmented and contradictory ways. The subject (even of experience) is not a single position but always a determined structuration of multiple positionings.

THE RETURN OF CULTURAL STUDIES

While U.S. cultural and communication theorists have, for the most part, ignored these theoretical arguments, they have had a decisive impact on the development of cultural studies in England, through the work of the Centre for Contemporary Cultural Studies (Hall 1980). While the Centre's initial problematic involved the attempt to examine the relationship between social practices and the ways they are represented in discourse (and ideology), its theoretical growth has led it to question this dichotomy. Rather than separating questions of representation and determination, the Centre has attempted to think these two moments together at the intersection of structuralism and Marxism while focusing on questions of the relative autonomy and the specificity of cultural practices.

At the same time, while the concerns of the Centre have always been much broader than those of traditional communication studies, their work increasingly has attempted to bring these two discourses together. For example, Hall (1982) has rewritten the history of communication theory through the history of the Centre. He argues that the problem of communication theory is that of consensus, and he identifies three historical moments in the theoretical elaboration of the discipline. In the first stage, consensus was understood in terms of shared norms. Anyone not participating in the structure of shared norms was characterized as deviant and their experience as anomic. The second stage was constructed upon the recognition that the world is meaningful and that most people act according to operative definitions of the situation. The deviant was placed into a subculture that offers its own construction of meaningful reality. The third stage, defining the current position of the Centre, argues that the world "has to be made to mean." Not only is meaning produced, but the claim to representation is also produced. The definition of the situation is neither given nor innocent but is rather the product of an ongoing "struggle over meaning" (Volosinov 1973). Consequently, subcultures must be located within the social and cultural struggle to produce consensus.

This has led the members of the Centre first to critique and then to extend Althusser's theory of ideology and to locate it within the concept of hegemony (Hall 1977). First, they reject the pessimistic conclusion that ideology always functions to reproduce the conditions of the existing social formation. Consequently, they tend to underemphasize the notion that ideology works by producing subject-positions (Coward 1977) and substitute a process of the negotiation of and struggle over identities. Second, since meaning itself is never given in language but always a product of social practices of signification, and since the production of consent takes place within a struggle over meaning, the Centre (Hall et al. 1980) has attempted to use contemporary semiotic theories to explore the "articulation of ideology in and through discourse." This entails rejecting Althusser's apparent identification of ideology and language. This has significant implications and had led to an extension of Althusser's argument that ideology always must be located within the ensemble of practices of the social formation. For if the ideological import of any particular text cannot be read off directly from the text itself, then one must explore the social practices that enter into the determination of the ideological effect. Using the work of Laclau (1977), the Centre has argued against the culturalist reading of hegemony in terms of class experience and suggested instead that there is no necessary "class-belongingness" of specific ideological practices. There is no simple correspondence between class position and ideological practice, despite the fact that there may be "traditional" couplings or "traces" that do, in special cases, allow for such a reading. Finally, drawing upon Bourdieu's theory (1980) of the social distribution of cultural capital, the Centre has attempted to find ways to describe the different cultural resources available to the various class fractions and subcultures involved in particular struggles over meaning. Consequently, the Centre has developed an analytic for interpreting ideological texts based upon the differentiation of the contexts of production and reception, or, in their own terms, of encoding and decoding (<u>Working Papers in Cultural Studies</u> 1971-77).

The Centre's attempt to bridge the gap between structural and cultural Marxism, however, has placed it in a number of contradictions that it has been unable to resolve in its actual interpretive practice. This can be most clearly seen if we consider two of the most often cited examples of the Centre's work: Morley's two studies of the "Nationwide" television program, and Hebdige's (1979) interpretation of subcultural style. Morley's study, partly coauthored by Brunsdon, is the clearest illustration of both the strengths and weaknesses of the Centre's theory of encoding and decoding. In the first part (Brunsdon and Morley 1978), the authors undertake a semiotic reading of the text to reveal the "preferred reading" encoded into the text. This refers to the attempt, in the production of the text, to structure it in ways that will determine that the audience will interpret it within the ideological terms of the economic and political hegemony of the media. In the second part (Morley 1980), the author attempts to describe how differential readings of the program are not only possible but also are actualized by particular groups of audience members, identified primarily by their class position. Hall (1973) has described these alternative readings as either negotiated or oppositional; the latter is defined by its direct struggle with the hegemenous coding, the former by the mediation of other codes and social positions. Morley attempts to reconstruct the audience's interpretation of the text through a questionnaire that identifies the "cultural capital" of the audience within already developed theories of class resources (using sociological and sociolinguistic categories). Morley (1981) himself has acknowledged the many problems with and weaknesses of his work, both semiological and sociological. In the first place, there are problems concerning how one reads a text semiotically to identify the preferred ideological meaning, especially without appeals to issues of subject-positioning. In the second place, the reconstruction of the decoding of the text is based upon the identification of cultural resources with class experience and the description of class position in terms of traditional sociological variables. Finally, the study leaves open at the end the question of the relationship between the two moments of encoding and decoding. There is no concrete analysis of the struggle between representation and determination embodied within this particular context of social relations and practices. This has led some of the Centre's contributors (Corrigan and Willis 1980) to question the analysis of reading practices in terms of experience and to seek a semiotic description of cultural resources. They argue that one cannot assume a correspondence between practice and identity (that is, between role performance and role internalization). Using semiotic theory, they suggest that the multiple and contradictory positionalities of the social subject determine differential relations (openness and accessibility) to different discourses. The problem for cultural analysis is to find ways of describing the relations between discourses and the noncoded, extradiscursive resources of the working class. Such knowledge, albeit not articulated, is embodied within "cultural forms" that are amenable to semiotic reading.

The notion that the cultural resources can be deciphered as signifying practices underlies Hebdige's study of subcultural style. It is worth considering his position in some detail since it is perhaps the most complete example of the Centre's work. Hebdige (1979) offers the concept of "style" as the mediating term through which the interpretation of any concrete subcultural form must pass. In essence, his argument is that a subcultural style is a representation of and an imaginary solution to the particular experienced contradictions within class culture. Let us begin by asking first, how subcultural styles work to signify and, second, what it is that they represent. One must ask what distinguishes a subcultural style from the systems of representation of the dominant culture. Hebdige's response is that styles are obviously fabricated and display their own codes. Consequently, they deny and disrupt the "deceptive innocence of appearances" on which the hegemony is built and maintained. The naturalness of the meaning of reality, of the world of experience, of the circuit connecting object and sign is problematized and ultimately rejected. The social processes of production and reproduction, depending as they do on the processes by which objects are given meaning and transformed into signs, are contradicted in the very practice of style. Here we can begin to examine the function and operation of style: as communication, bricolage, homology, and signifying practice. Style primarily communicates "a significant difference" and thus a group identity. It marks its members as different from the rest of the world as it simultaneously defines and represents a "forbidden identity." The remaining three terms of the series explain how this function is carried out. Style is a form of "bricolage" that uses the commodities of a conspicuous consumption culture in a particular way, as a form of what Baudrillard (1978) calls a "semiotic guerilla warfare" against the innocence of the surfaces of hegemonic reality: "These humble objects can be magically appropriated; stolen by subordinate groups and made to carry 'secret' meanings: meanings which express, in code, a form of resistance to the order which guarantees their continued subordination" (Hebdige 1979, p. 18). Style fits these objects together in a particular "symbolic fit" or homology that forms a unity, not only with other stylistic objects but also with the group's relations and situations. Subcultural style exhibits a consistency and coherence that can only signal that "the objects chosen were, either intrinsically or in their adapted forms, homologous with the focal concerns, activities, group structure, and collective self-image of the subculture" (p. 114). There must then be an underlying level of style at which it is able to generate this appropriation of objects into an homology: style exists finally as signifying practice. Different styles embody different modes by which objects are transformed into signs. Such signifying practices not only produce the circuit between object and sign in various ways but also that between sign and subject. They position individuals and group in language and, thus, represent identities in the last instance.

However, we can take this last point further and ask what it is that is represented in style or, from the other direction, how style is determined. Hebdige's most general response is that subcultural styles represent "group experience," but the group is, at least initially, apparently broader than the subculture: Style is "a coded response to the changes affecting the entire community" (p. 80), which in turn is defined largely in terms of class experience. However, drawing upon Althusser, Hebdige argues that style represents the way in which class is lived (p. 74). A subculture is "a form of resistance in which experienced contradictions and objections to [the] ruling ideology are obliquely represented in style" (p. 133). Avoiding the obvious appeal to the material conditions of class existence, Hebdige argues that style gives expression to the particular contradictions within the way in which a group lives its relationship to the economic reality (class structure).

Yet Hebdige refuses any such simple correspondence; instead he argues that the experience responded to in style is overdetermined. It responds to a number of other moments within the historical social formation, including hegemonic attempts to represent and appropriate its own existence. Further, the particular experiences coded and responded to within subcultural styles in England are predicated upon the assumed identification of the position of blacks and working class white youth. Their styles can be interpreted as a "series of mediated responses to the presence in Britain of a sizeable black community" (p. 73). Finally, there is a particular "generational consciousness" that responds to the more general "breakdown of consensus" in postwar Britain. Youth cultures, while confronting and experiencing the class contradictions of their working class roots, attempt to define a position for themselves that can "negotiate a meaningful intermediate space somewhere between the parent culture and the dominant ideology: a space where an alternative identity could be discovered and expressed. To this extent, they were engaged in that distinctive quest for a measure of autonomy which characterizes all youth sub- (and counter) cultures" (p. 88).

The final stage in the argument is to address the issue of the relation between style as signifying practice and as a representation of lived contradictions. Hebdige's answer lies in the "obliqueness" with which these contradictions are represented: Style can be read as "maps of meaning which obscurely re-present the very contradictions they are designed to resolve or conceal" (p. 18). That is, style represents experienced contradictions in an eternal circle so that the representations themselves appear as an (imaginary) solution. The signification of style is a magical one by which the identity it produces provides the appearance of an experiential resolution of the contradictions. Because this resolution is only magical, that is, because it works by appropriating commodities into a "spectacular" style, it is always open to reappropriation. It can always be reincorporated into the hegemony, either through the mass production and recommodification of its signs or through an ideological renomination of the subculture. Because of its oblique and magical effectivity, it is impossible to maintain this as an absolute distinction. Subcultures remain based in leisure activities and, consequently, the gap between an appropriated and a reappropriated commodity cannot provide the basis of a reading of style. However, because every subculture moves through a "cycle of resistance and defusion," the interpretation of style must focus on the "outrageous" spectacle, that moment in which style transforms objects into subcultural signs, rather than on the signs as "objects-in-themselves." Hebdige's argument then would suggest an interpretive practice built upon the structuration of identities in response to experience rather than the search for homologies between texts and experience.

Nevertheless, his actual reading belies his own argument and points to the contradictions within the Centre's theoretical practice. First, the fact remains that Hebdige assumes a series of homologies and structures his analysis accordingly. There is a correspondence between any particular moment of a subcultural style and the general characterization of that style, and between the style and the lived experience of the subculture. This double homology, re-presented in the undecidable relation between style as communication and as signifying practice, throws us back into the search for phenomenological correspondences. Second, not only are the descriptions of the two regimes — experience and style — radically separated, but each is also problematic. The experience of the group is described in essentially interactionist terms and, apparently, taken as an innocently given starting point. What appears to be its overdetermination is merely a description of a part of its conjunctural specificity (class, age, race). Its ideological production, which would implicate style itself in the process, is ignored in favor of the class determination of experience. In fact, Hebdige's description of the experience behind and represented within it; style is represented as part of the subcultural experience so that its description is in phenomenological rather than material terms. The result is that Hebdige fails to specify the particular nature of the struggle over meaning within subcultural style. He is satisfied with glossing over this theoretical problem in the notion of an "imaginary" solution, but this serves only to reiterate its place within an ideological struggle.

There have been at least two responses within the Centre to the inadequacies of Hebdige's reading despite its richness. McRobbie (1980) has pointed to the "structured absence" of any consideration of the place of women within subcultures. Indeed, she seems to argue that questions of sexual power cannot be dealt with adequately within the Centre's current theoretical position because it lacks a theory of pleasure. The result is that there is no theory of leisure and, hence, there is a serious flaw in their reading of subcultures. We can identify, however, at a deeper level the Centre's inability to deal with the challenge posed by feminism and sexual politics. For the question is, fundamentally, whether cultural power can be conceptualized on the model of hierarchical domination and the ideological production of experience (Foucault 1978; Adams 1978). Can the relations of power organized around the distinction between male and female be theorized within a framework of signification and experience? If the oppression of women is not merely a question of symbolic meaning, then the call for a theory of desire and power challenges the phenomenological roots of any theory of the social production of the real as meaningful. What if behavior is not just a function of the interpretation of the situation and if the effect of social practices is more, or actually less, than the meaning of the practice?

The second response to the gaps in Hebdige's analysis emphasizes overdetermination and the materiality of social practices. Thus, in his recent work, Hebdige (1981a, 1981b) increasingly attempts not only to treat the object as an image but the image as an object to be located in an overdetermined historical moment:

> It is perhaps only in this way by outlining the connections and breaks between groups of separate but interlocking statements that we can begin to imagine the particular dimensions of a language which is now largely lost to us and to appreciate not only the historical conditions under which that language was originally constructed but also the social conflicts and shifts in power which were registered inside it and which ultimately led to its dispersal and decline (1981a, p. 40).

Similarly, Chambers has argued that specific cultural texts must be seen as constituting "an active, contradictory, cultural practice whose choices, relations and possibilities are being continually forged and transformed by the social relations that traverse it" (Chambers 1981, p. 39). Thus, the cultural power of such texts — their implication in a struggle over meaning — demands an analysis of "the interlocking effects of cultural powers, and institutional apparatus . . . and the social relations that invest them" (p. 37). What is significant in these arguments is, ultimately, the absence of any appeal to experience as the other side of the cultural production of meaning. Implicit in their position is a critique of the Centre's fundamental assumptions. In particular, instead of reconciling notions of hegemony and the structural theory of ideology, the Centre falls back into a model of expressive causality and reconstitutes the division between base and superstructure. There remains, at the core of its position, the contradiction between experience as the product of an ideological struggle and as the articulation, however displaced, of class position. This contradiction is reproduced in the ambiguity of their critical practice: Seeking to describe overdetermined cultural practices, they conclude by uncovering homologies. In Hebdige's recent work on the image and Chamber's analyses of popular music, we find the theory of overdetermination clearly displacing the search for homologies. Both argue for an examination of the specific articulation of social practices onto other practices. Yet both continue to decipher the meanings of a symbolic form. It is this (the primacy of signification) that, I would like to suggest, is at the root of the inability of cultural studies to construct a practice adequate to the theory of overdetermination. This is, in turn, the result of beginning with the question of the relationship between culture and society, for this inevitably privileges and differentiates cultural practices as essentially significatory. In the concluding section of this chapter, I would like to propose an alternative approach to the issues of communication and culture based on the project of postmodernism. Rather than thinking of our task as the interpretation of meaning, or even as the deconstruction of meaning, I want to suggest that meaning itself must be located as an effect within a broader theory of power and desire.

CULTURE, POWER, AND DESIRE

The irony of cultural theories built upon the reduction of the real to the meaningful is that they are unable to argue for either the truth of their own interpretations or for the validity of their political interventions. Structuralists struggle to find an adequate description of "theoretical" or critical practice that would enable them to ground their politics in a comparison of experience and reality. Culturalists are forced to appeal to transcendental utopian principles while at the same time acknowledging that these are themselves the product of ideological practices. Questions of power and determination are, for both, conceptualized as either coercion (violence, oppression) or consent (reproduction, the struggle over meaning).

The attempt to understand both culture and politics within a theory of signification is a result of the modernist assumption — at the center of philosophical thought since Kant — that the world is only available to us as already and always meaningful. But the fact that there are no uninterpreted phenomena is not sufficient to argue that, therefore, the real exists only as the meaningful. Even the Marxist supplement that the world must be made to mean is taken as the limited claim that there is a politics implicit within any particular signifying practice. However, it can also be read to suggest that the world — the real — is always other than the meaningful and that signification is one strategy for the production of the real in terms of particular relations of power. Thus, there is a politics of the problematic of interpretation or signification itself (Baudrillard 1980). To speak as if one were not always and already implicated in a universe of significations may appear to be nothing but self-delusion. The task, however, is to find a way of talking about the real without falling into either positivism or relativism, without either sounding naive or becoming trapped within the discourse one uses. Obviously, I can only begin to suggest the possibility of the project in this limited space.

Such an argument against meaning is at the root of the post-modernist project: the search for an immanent critical practice that would not appeal to any transcendental terms (as ground, origin, or essence). This, of course, demands that they seek new writing practices as well. Consequently, it denies any apparent unity or totality and emphasizes discontinuity, difference, fragmentation, and rupture. Rejecting teleology, it makes history the very context and substance of our existence. Disrupting metaphors of depth (and hence the problematic of meaning), it imprisons itself within the materiality of surfaces. Excluding any claim of transparency, innocence, or freedom, it contextualizes all of reality in terms of processes of chance, change, and determination. This all may be summarized by saying that the postmodernist begins by rejecting the appeal to the givenness of experience and, consequently, argues that subjectivity, meaning, and truth are produced effects that may, in turn, have their own effects.

There are, of course, a variety of postmodern practices. Poststructuralism, for example, attempts to fragment the categories of experience and multiply the possibilities of meaning. However, it consequently relocates itself within a philosophy of signification refusing any connection to the real (Grossberg 1983a). It is content to define its task in terms of the problematizing and production of the categories of (signifying) experience. An alternative postmodern practice (Deleuze and Guattari 1981) subtracts such transcendental moments and adds more connections and effects and functions. One asks not what the event means, but what it does and what are the conditions of its existence as a material fact. Events may have effects that contradict or even occlude each other. Such effects need not take place through the mediation of meaning, consciousness, or ideology. In fact, the production of particular meanings (or struggles) can be treated as one such material effect. This is not the same as the behaviorist's attempt to substitute effects for meaning, nor the rhetorician's reduction of effects to particular domains of individual response. Thus, cultural practices must be located not only in a context within which social facts determine interpretations and vice versa, but in other regimes in which texts have asignifying effects and are determined through asignifying practices. The result is that, rather than locating power in the context of signification, signification is to be located in the context of relations of power.

While a theory of signification totalizes itself and represses the real, this postmodernism describes a reality that is always pluralizing itself. The real is like crabgrass (not just metaphorically, either), constantly extending itself by producing effects at some place other than itself; its existence is only in the tangled web of often inseparable lines ("rhizomatic flows"). Reality is its own production — "a monism of plurality" — as lines of "effectivities" (Foucault 1981), "desiring productions" (Deleuze and Guattari 1977), or "intensities" (Lyotard 1977a, 1977b). If the existence of an event is only the plurality of its effects, located in its others (that is, its contextuality), analysis is no longer interpretive. The analysis of an event, instead, maps the connections or relations between that point and all of the other points that effect or are effected by it. Defining the nature of the event beforehand (for example, as the unity of a signifying practice) results in simply retracing the boundaries of the particular "regime." For in fact, reality is "territorialized." Lines of effect (desire) are not only continuously erupting to and from multiple points; desire apparently flows in ways that continuously transgress and (re-) constitute particular structures and organizations. We might describe the real, then, as a "machinic apparatus" producing and extending itself but also inscribing boundaries upon its surfaces that direct the flows of desire and the possibilities of the real. Power, always local and plural, is the struggle over the configuration of effects included within and producing the contours of the real. Power territorializes, deterritorializes, and reterritorializes the vectors of effectivity; it defines "the real" as the places at which effects can be produced and circumscribes the possibilities of connections.

The analysis of a cultural practice, then, examines its functioning within a material context of desire and power. Drawing a map of its network of effects (that is, its place in a particular machinic apparatus that is never totalized), one interrogates the conditions of its existence: the emergence of its particular effectivity. Its specificity is shattered into the plurality of regimes of effects traversing it and its place within an organization of power. While some of its effects may be mediated through the production of meaning, it does not follow that the description of these effects requires an interpretive detour. Moreover, while there may be effects that are precisely describable as the production of meaning and thus raise the problematic of signification within analysis, we should not assume a unity of signifying practices and effects, nor a homogeneity of interpretive procedures. In fact, both the multiplicity of signifying practices and the inscription of regimes of signification can be examined through the ways in which they modify the structurations of desire. So that, for example, the existence of the individual is always fractured and contradictory, determined not only as multiple subjectivities within the regimes of signification, but also as multiple objectivities of desire and power within asignifying regimes (Foucault 1978).

The cultural analyst is confronted with the task of constructing a machine with apparently only one instruction: Include this particular piece understood as a conjuncture of specific effects. The analyst then produces an analytic machine that maps the real by drawing lines connecting the specific practice to and locating it within multiple regimes. One will necessarily transgress some of the boundaries already inscribed upon the real, and at the same time will inscribe or reinscribe others. The analytic machine not only maps but also reaches into and intervenes in reality. Its truth is not representational but political. Because it itself is connected to some of reality, the analytic machine is always a deterritorializing and reterritorializing of desire. Consequently, the truth of any statement is its existence within a particular regime of effects. Not only must these truth-effects be seen as a form of power, but the fact that any particular statement has a place within this regime is itself an effect of power. The regime of truth is a particular production of boundaries that privileges particular discursive practices. Within its borders, statements are empowered and protected in specific ways; they are both allowed to intervene and protected from intervention.

The production of analytic machines may be likened to a topography of cultural practices. One reconstructs the complexity of a multidimensional surface only by mapping the various planes that traverse the surface. Insofar as each singular place inescapably is implicated with the others, it carries traces of the multiplanar existence of any of its points. Topography, beginning as cartography, draws the lines within a regime; but by invoking those traces, it seeks to dissolve the boundaries of the regimes and map the multiple and contradictory connections among the points across regimes. For example, Hebdige (1982) has begun to examine the place of "youth" in society:

> The vectors of power I want to trace cut across a number of heterogeneous sites: discursive categories, institutions and the spaces between institutions. Those sites are "youth," "sexuality," "fashion," "subculture," "display" and its corollary "surveillance." . . . many of these sites are themselves quite clearly "superficial." . . . A conventional presentation of history in which selected themes are carefully pursued along a single line leading from a finished past to a yet-to-be completed present will have to be abandoned. Instead I want to posit each site as a terminus in a circuit within which a different kind of

knowledge, a different kind of truth can be generated; a knowledge and a truth which can't be encapsulated within the confines of a discrete historical "period," one which sets out, instead, with the best of intentions: to pull the Father's beard.

Similarly, I have proposed an analysis of rock and roll (Grossberg 1983b) that maps its contradictory functions at particular conjunctural moments in order to describe the specificity of its relationship to youth cultures. Thus, one begins by fracturing the cultural form and locating its effects within a determinate multiplicity of social regimes, both signifying and asignifying. By beginning with the fact of its popularity, the particular machinic functioning of rock and roll can be described: it is an affective organization of and resistance to the contradictory demands of desire and power made upon and constituting postwar youth culture. Importantly, only a part of this existence can be explained by appealing to rock and roll's intermittent site within signifying regimes. Rather, it is only by locating the multiple sites of its effectivity that one is able to invoke its particular affective politics.

If the result of such analysis is to inevitably implicate cultural practices within relations of power, it also restructures the possibility, indeed the necessity, of political intervention. For on the one hand, it suggests that every description not only defines a site of intervention but is itself already an intervention. Moreover, it directs that such interventions cannot be grounded upon either utopian teleologies or opposition to general structures of domination and repression. Nor can particular interventions be justified from a place outside the analysis of the particular context of power. If power is always local, then struggle too must be defined locally: One resists particular structurations of reality within relations of power. But if resistance always seeks to deterritorialize, its success always threatens to reterritorialize. Hence, one must continuously seek to intervene in ways that undermine the propensity of any "truth" to reinscribe relations of domination, oppression, and so on. It seems reasonable to suggest that any particular intervention be located within an alliance of ongoing resistance in what might be described as a network of "social anarchy" (Grossberg 1983a).

I have described only the outlines of a postmodern theory of cultural studies, which reinscribes the problematic of signification and communication within the context of an analytic of the real. As a theoretical project it is paradoxical, since it would replace theorizing with concrete analysis. As a political project its conclusion records an undecidability that can be escaped only in the concreteness of political struggle. That is, it demands that political action and goals be defined within the particular context of struggle rather than by an appeal to theoretical or utopian principles. As a theory of communication, it opens new possibilities for the discipline by interrogating the place of communication within the production of the real, a place that we recently have begun to take for granted.

5
THE ROLE OF POLITICAL ECONOMY IN THE INFORMATION AGE
Janet Wasko

Around town, around the world. Around home, around the office. The telecommunications revolution is happening, now. You've yet to see all its benefits. But more and more things that used to take days to accomplish can now happen in seconds. . . . Telecommunications has been called "the industry that defines the 80's" (Contel advertisement, Wall Street Journal, February 28, 1983).

In the information industry . . . we are in the midst of a technological revolution which promises true abundance. The evolution of new forms of delivery systems and new program suppliers presents the American public with a momentous opportunity — an opportunity to have unfettered access to a broad diversity of video programming (U.S. House 1981, p. 244).

Recent developments in communications and information technologies have stimulated widespread discussion of a fundamental change — a shift from industrial society to an information society based on information as a basic resource: The Information Age.

While new technologies are making possible increased and faster production of information, other media technologies are providing wider distribution of information and entertainment. As a result, established media are undergoing a process of displacement or redefinition of their economic, political, and cultural roles. Importantly, these processes are occurring within a continually shifting political and economic climate; struggles are erupting over control and power in local, national, and international arenas (Mosco and Wasko 1983b).

While the introduction of new information processing systems and techniques already is contributing to a major transformation of the workplace (see Mosco and Wasko 1983a), these technologies are also following us home. Computers and information delivery systems combined with more familiar home communications systems promise no less than a revolution in the ways that people receive and use information. An example is provided by Vincent Mosco's description of videotex in his book, Pushbutton Fantasies:

> Over 98% of all U.S. households have telephones and television sets. It would not be a very complex procedure to turn these common devices into a videotex system. But videotex is much more than television or even interactive cable television. Videotex can provide enormous amounts of information as well as its other interactive services in both the home and office. So videotex promises to be a mass-based phenomenon with the combined attention-grabbing power and pervasiveness of the television and the telephone (Mosco 1982, p. 9).

Videotex and other such systems will most assuredly pose competitive challenges to established communication and media systems, such as the postal system, newspapers, books, and magazines. Yet home videotex and other new distribution systems, such as direct broadcast satellites, are still only "fantasies." Other new communications technologies are already realities that threaten traditional media sources. The growth of cable, subscription TV, multipoint distribution systems, satellite superstations, and home video systems (tape and disc), offer new distribution outlets to challenge older ones, such as over-the-air ("free") television and motion picture theaters. With these new distribution possibilities, program suppliers are scrambling for new alliances, with companies both within and outside the communications and entertainment industries. Indeed, throughout these industries, there are continuously shifting alliances and struggles for new markets, as established companies and a few new ones converge their interests with other large corporations and financial institutions (see Hamelink 1983; Wasko 1982; Schiller 1981).

These emerging technologies have prompted important debates in both policymaking and communications research circles. Interestingly, these discussions involve some of the classic concerns of political economy: the structure of media and information industries and questions of ownership and control of communications resources.

While this might be seen as an encouraging trend, there must be at least some concern with the questions as they are framed within these various debates. A brief look at the issue of media concentration and ownership in a few recent studies may provide examples of some of these problems, as well as point to the role that critical communications research might play in reframing these important questions.

POLICYMAKING FOR THE INFORMATION AGE

New technological possibilities in the communications/information field, together with the political/economic climate of the 1980s, have prompted a major reexamination of the regulatory framework for broadcasting and telecommunications. The process of deregulation of communications has accelerated during the Reagan administration, as various government bodies and agencies challenge the existing rules and regulations, in quest of increased diversity and more efficient competition.

The traditional focal point for setting communications regulatory policy has been the Federal Communications Commission (FCC), where special studies have been prepared to support the deregulatory process and to confront the changes anticipated from new communications technologies. Several of these studies examine specifically the question of media ownership.

In October 1980 the Network Inquiry Special Staff offered its final report on the FCC's regulatory approach to commercial television networks. In New Television Networks: Entry, Jurisdiction, Ownership and Regulation, staff members examining ownership regulations suggested that, in light of new technologies, "a systematic and coherent set of ownership policies" be adopted. They further advised that the tools used in antitrust policy and economic analysis be employed by the FCC in these questions (FCC 1980, pp. 13-14).

A special study of the FCC's policy on cable ownership was presented in November 1981. The study's conclusions provide an example of the issues raised:

We find that the underlying goals of the Commission's ownership policies — the promotion of competition in the economic marketplace and in the marketplace of ideas — are met when a wide range of media, both video and non-video is available. Our analysis suggests that the market for video programming and many of the other services that cable can provide is workably competitive and in most cases not susceptible to monopolization. . . . [W]e believe that in general a policy of extending free entry into cable to all interested first is most likely to contribute to a rapidly growing, technologically dynamic industry that meets consumers' needs (Gordon, Levy, and Preece 1981, pp. 4-5).

Further consideration of FCC ownership policies was included in a staff report issued in December 1982 in connection with the FCC's proposed elimination of the broadcasting network-cable system cross-ownership prohibition. In considering Measurement of Concentration in Home Video Markets, the Office on Plans and Policy suggested that national ownership rules are inappropriate for video delivery markets, while many of the policies concerning ownership and concentration in local markets be reexamined carefully. The report argued that the FCC should encourage competition and diversity, rather than mandate these results (Levy and Setzer 1982, pp. 100-07).

Although the FCC has been especially active in considering these issues, media ownership questions also have been debated in Congress as part of efforts to rewrite the Communications Act of 1934. These questions are confronted directly in Telecommunications in Transition: The Status of Competition in the Telecommunications Industry, a report on hearings held by Representative Wirth's Committee on Telecommunications in 1981. The report acknowledges the importance of media ownership questions as follows:

> An ownership analysis of the mass media is a much more important undertaking than in most industries. Heavy concentration in the spark plug manufacturing industry, for example, is significant to consumers of spark plugs. The ownership characteristics of the mass media, however, concern far more than the price and efficiency of a consumer product. It is the control of the creation and dissemination of information — the information, in the form of both ideas and images, that serve to shape our social, cultural and political thinking. An understanding of who and how many possess that power becomes an integral component in assessing the competitive responsiveness of the information marketplace (U.S. House 1981, p. 277).

In addition to these studies, hearings have been held on Media Concentration by the House Committee on Small Business in 1980 (U.S. House 1980), as well as being considered by the Federal Trade Commission in its Symposium on Media Concentration (FTC 1979). Of course, various antitrust suits by the Department of Justice regularly confront ownership questions in the media and information industries.

From these few examples, it appears that policies concerned with ownership are studied and made in a fragmented, unsystematic fashion, similar to most policies involving communications and information. As one who is familiar with the policy process, Wilson Dizard notes in his book, The Coming Information Age:

. . . policy questions dealing with the new information environment are moving into the public agenda in a variety of ways and at different political levels. The effort is fragmented, discursive, and complex reflecting the division of power in a sensitive area of national policy. Meanwhile, the communications and information structure is expanding rapidly, largely as a result of incremental decisions and actions based primarily on their immediate utility to commercial interests (Dizard 1982, p. 133).

It is certainly not the first time that policy vacuums have provided possibilities for the interests of communications industries to prevail (see Schiller 1969; Mosco 1979). Yet in the previously mentioned government studies, when conclusions or recommendations are made, they most often are generally supportive of these commercial interests, whether by the assumptions that are made or the specific questions as they are posed.

Most recently, the common, and often admitted, assumption is the need for deregulation. Evidence is gathered to support the process. Competition is stated as the desired goal in most cases; questions are framed in terms of the marketplace and consumers. Economic analysis is offered to assess levels of competition in the economic marketplace and in the marketplace of ideas.

An example of this orientation is provided by the following statement by the Wirth Committee report:

The overarching societal interest in today's communications industry is to establish markets that can accommodate the vast changes in technology that have occurred over the last several decades so that their enormous productivity-enhancing powers may be fully realized. The evidence submitted to the Subcommittee supports the proposition that a competitive market provides greater assurance that this societal interest will be more fully met than under any other market structure. This conclusion, combined with the irrefutable evidence of technological dynamism now pervasive in this sector of our economy, leads us to believe that the only proper direction of legislation is the vigorous encouragement of competition (U.S. House 1981, p. 32).

Interestingly, the notion of public interest often is virtually absent the debate. Apparently, the public's interest must compete in the information and entertainment marketplace, where public means consumers. The image repeatedly conjured up is one of the sovereign consumer casting dollar votes in the unfettered marketplace of ideas.

The obvious, but unstated, bias, then, is for private ownership and a commercial price system for the production and distribution of information and entertainment. Little, if any, attention is given to other forms of ownership or means of support, such as public or municipal systems. As Thomas Guback has observed in his study of ownership and concentration in the theatrical film industry,

> the bulk of debate is not about alternatives to capitalist ownership, nor even about how to change monopoly tendencies within capitalism, but about how to manage them while preserving the system as a whole. As this appears to be the acceptable arena for debate, discussions about media ownership necessarily will remain on the technical level, which is where the owners would undoubtedly like to keep them (Compaine et al. 1982, p. 277).

Furthermore, the debate takes place with little, if any, public participation in the policymaking process. Although still adhering to the notion of public as consumers, Dizard makes this observation also:

> Communications and information policy, by its very nature, requires broad public input. . . . A weakness of our current approach to the new information environment is that decisions are being made, and options closed, every day that should be open to public scrutiny. At a time when to take action to strengthen communications and information patterns in this country through the end of the century, an important element in the decision process is often missing — the views of individual consumers (Dizard 1982, p. 134).

The deregulation process, with this marketplace criteria for the distribution of ideas and entertainment, is proceeding at an increasingly rapid pace in these various arenas of "public" policymaking. It may be appropriate at this point, then, to examine how communications research contributes to this process.

PERPETUATING THE MYTHS: MAINSTREAM COMMUNICATIONS
RESEARCH ON OWNERSHIP QUESTIONS

In light of these activities within policymaking circles, it may not be surprising that there has been increased attention recently to industry structure and media ownership questions by communications researchers. Important contributions have been made by the two editions of Who Owns the Media?, edited by

Benjamin Compaine (1982), in addition to a number of other studies (see Howard 1982; Meyer et al. 1980; Seiden 1974; Frech and Nielsen, n.d.).

Yet despite some of the evidence gathered, conclusions very often are made by these researchers that reflect a policy orientation. In other words, similar questions are asked, with familiar assumptions made. Indeed, some researchers seem compelled to go out of their way to defend the status quo, regardless of evidence presented.

Compaine, for example, attempts to avoid the issue of quality or diversity of information, yet still manages to conclude that

> within the broad boundaries established on the one hand by the First Amendment and on the other hand by economic structure that has evolved to implement it, the evidence of ownership patterns would appear to support the argument that the underlying structure of the system is able to encourage a robust exchange and competitive flow of ideas, entertainment, information and commerce throughout the media (Compaine et al. 1982, p. 465).

Another observation is based on the addition of a few new firms to the list of leading communications corporations. It is concluded, therefore, that new technology creates "its own democratic process in the world of media ownership and gateways of information" (Compaine et al. 1982, p. 464).

Again, ownership questions are considered within a narrow framework, usually employing quantitative assessments of individual industries, with limited measures of competition. Market concentration is again the primary focus, while questions of ownership concentration and corporate control are often neglected. Indeed, when they are considered, conclusions again are made on the basis of limited information; thus, very often, familiar myths concerning corporate control/ownership are perpetuated.

For instance, by looking only at the number of stockholders and their shareholdings, Compaine concludes that there is widespread control over media/information companies (Compaine et al. 1982, pp. 455-65). While this indeed may seem to be the case, if one looks only at these limited measures of ownership, a more careful analysis of direct and indirect means of control and influence, both inside and outside these corporations, seems to be required before such conclusions can be made.

Most importantly, though, these studies of market and ownership concentration need to be considered within a much larger framework. Again, as Guback has pointed out,

> although market shares may shift periodically, and a merger now and then may create even larger enterprises,

the industry remains fixed within the capitalist sector of the economy, which means it is owned and managed by a single class. This establishes the medium's functions. Ultimately, that is the principal measure of concentration. Identification of the specific who (or what) within that class only serves to pinpoint more precisely where the profit motive is interpreted. It does not change the nature of that motive (Compaine et al. 1982, p. 250).

In other words, locating the center of power or control must be accompanied with research on structural questions that examine the limits and constraints placed on communications and information systems by the processes of commercialization and privatization, as well as the process of deregulation (see Murdock 1982).

As an example, the question of diversity is a major concern of policymakers and researchers, yet is most often considered only in quantitative terms. As Graham Murdock has argued,

the first aim of any television policy should be to maximise the diversity of provision by ensuring that the available programming expresses or provides a platform for as full a range of views, opinions and forms of expression as is practicable. But diversity is not multiplicity. It is possible greatly to increase the number of channels and the number of goods in circulation without significantly extending diversity. More does not necessarily mean different. It also can mean more of the same or the same thing distributed in a variety of ways (Murdock 1981, p. 12; emphasis in the original).

Concern over the number of conduits available must be accompanied with consideration of the quality and range of content offered by these channels, when owners and managers share the same goals or motivations.

Certainly a wide range of research questions needs to be studied in connection with ownership issues, including more careful analysis of structural constraints and limitations. Most importantly, media and information industries must be seen in light of general economic trends, within the context of actual power relations of society as a whole. Thus, research in this area has only just begun.

REFRAMING THE QUESTIONS IN CRITICAL COMMUNICATIONS
RESEARCH: DISCOVERING AN INTEGRATED CRITICAL THEORY

One might expect that critical communications research would be sympathetic to these questions and their reformulation. However, this is not necessarily the case, despite the recent claims that most critical work primarily is interested in ownership and control issues (Rogers 1982).

It is important to point out again that the critique of communications and information systems involves different research approaches and interests. Communications research itself cannot continue to be characterized, as some insist, by the false dichotomy of critical versus empirical. Nor can critical research be described in the simplistic and misleading terms offered by mainstream researchers. There is a rich diversity of critical research that examines a wide range of questions and issues, and employs a variety of research techniques. In addition, there is much debate within critical research defining the area and developing critical theory (see Slack and Allor 1982; Halloran, n.d.).

Indeed, one of the liveliest debates continues to focus on the relative importance of questions of ideology and political economy. Most recently, Stuart Hall (1982) has proclaimed "the end of political economy" for Marxist theory as a whole.

On the other hand, it has been argued that much critical work overemphasizes ideological or superstructural questions, in neglect of infrastructural context. Certainly, this overemphasis has been claimed for Marxist theory, generally, as well as for critical communications theory (see P. Anderson 1976; Smythe 1977).

Considering the changes occurring as a result of new technologies, as well as the emphasis on assessing communications/information developments in terms of the marketplace, there seems to be an ever more pressing need for ongoing, historically founded, critical analysis of industrial structure and policies for communications and information questions. Of course, this critique must be done within the social context or the actual social setting, thus in conjunction with ideological questions.

As Nicholas Garnham (1972, p. 145) has argued: "In order to understand the structure of our culture, its production, consumption and reproduction and the roles of mass media in that process, we increasingly need to confront some of the central questions of political economy in general. . . ." Rather than an end to research in the political economy of communications, then, its role becomes even more crucial in understanding these shifting patterns of control and power in the new age of information; in suggesting the actual future of the information society; in examining whether or not there is indeed a fundamental change in the nature of capitalist society when information is a basic resource; and, importantly, in pointing to the contradictions and alternatives necessary to promote true diversity and public participation in communications and information processes.

While there can be no end to ideology, or to political economy, critical communications research must work toward an integrated theory, as well as point to forms of resistance and struggle within the constantly evolving information age (see Murdock 1978; Halley 1981; Mosco and Wasko 1983a). Most assuredly, this is a tall task, yet one that becomes more urgent as the "information revolution" unfolds around us.

6
MESSAGE ANALYSIS IN INTERNATIONAL MASS COMMUNICATION RESEARCH: A RHETORICAL EXAMPLE
Richard L. Barton

In the realm of international media systems there is the general assumption that messages have meanings that impact on the cultures that use them. The Canadian government's policy that attempts to restrict the amount of U.S. media content in broadcast programming is one manifestation of this assumption. The Canadians view their content rule as "an instrument . . . to implement cultural objectives" (Report of 1982, p. 288). Similarly, the New World Information Order debate reveals, among Third World countries, the belief that international mass communication content generates meanings that intrude upon, challenge, and replace essential cultural symbology. "Electronic colonialism" is the accusatory pejorative that has emerged to describe, among other things, presumed message effects (McPhail 1981, pp. 18–21). Despite these assumptions of message influence, the research in international mass communication is not organized for the systematic study of media content. Instead, the studies proceed primarily through the wide lens of the "political economy" of mass communications. This perspective, typically based in classical Marxism, focuses on the importance of economic processes and productive structures. Major issues include control exercised through media ownership and the ideological implications of control for culture industries such as broadcasting (compare Boyd-Barrett 1982). Meanwhile, Hur's (1982) recent review of the American literature in international mass communi-

This is a revised version of a paper presented to the biannual meeting of the International Association of Mass Communications Research, Paris, 1982.

cation research neither reveals nor recommends message analysis beyond content analysis methodology.

The study of international media processes lags behind the general trend in mass communication study of systematically investigating the formal qualities of media discourse (see, for example, Curran, Gurevitch, and Woollacott 1982, p. 22). However, the significance of content and the need for careful explication of media texts in international communication research have been suggested in earlier research. Boyd-Barrett (1977) includes "specific media contents" among the four major components of the international communication process, but he assigns this component a strictly economic function in terms of its ability to achieve "market penetration." On the other hand, Griffith's (1973) call for the detailed explication of international communication texts predicts the textual analyses that now flourish in many other areas of mass communication study: "Although the deciphering of esoteric communications requires the most rigid standards and the careful explication de texte . . . the skill remains, like the reconstruction of the text of a fragment of Sappho, an art" (p. 519). Because international mass communication involves the interaction of message systems, some knowledge of message structures promises clearer understanding of the implications of electronic communication between cultures.

It is my purpose here to undertake a rhetorical analysis of an American noncommercial television documentary. Through the analysis I want to reveal the discursive potential of the documentary as an international media message and thereby evaluate the usefulness of message analysis for international communication study.

DOCUMENTARY AS INTERNATIONAL DISCOURSE

The international exchange of television documentary is a common occurrence, especially among Western nations. This communication form provides a convenient focus for the analysis of message structure in international discourse. Documentary has been described historically as a discursive form (Stott 1973). For Nichols (1981) the relationship between discourse and ideology is important: A central question is how to understand this form of discourse (documentary) in relation to ideological effect. . . (p. 243). Chaney, meanwhile, acknowledges the discursive nature of documentary, but his Marxist vision, typical especially of the British political economy research, overlooks the ideological significance of the organization of the text. What was once a medium of public discourse, we are told, now simply provides a record of collective experience that is mainly relevant to the producing institution's organizational purposes and routines

(Chaney 1981, p. 134).   While it is evident that the discursive potential of documentary is constrained by social, political, and economic factors that influence form, it is simplistic to assume that because documentary is so constrained, it irrevocably has lost its potential to induce social discourse.   Surely the Canadians, as determined as they are to reduce U.S. media influence, would not easily be convinced by such content-free explanations.   Explanations based in Marxist political economy tend to restrict the notion of ideology to mediated "false consciousness" created by politically oppressive economic forces.   The study of international media discourse needs to account for a broad range of forms, including controversial documentaries that require precise analysis.   Therefore, such studies would be better situated in Althusser's notion of ideology.   For Althusser, ideology expresses the themes and representations through which men relate to the real world (compare Curran, Gurevitch, and Woollacott 1982, p. 24).   This definition encourages the analysis of discourse in media texts.

THE BASIS OF RHETORICAL ANALYSIS

What seems to be missing from contemporary discussions about the discursive role of documentary is a clear understanding of the interaction of critical method and the form of the messages under analysis.   Two points are of concern:

- The critical method chosen must be capable of revealing the constituents of social discourse.   This is an issue of methodological suitability; of using critical tools that are appropriate for the task at hand.
- The form of the message itself requires analysis in the process of criticism, including the conventions, appeals, and accommodations that are offered to audiences.   The message must be analyzed in a way that accounts for "essential formative principles that are intrinsic to the content and grow organically within it to offer meaning beyond rote convention, even beyond producers' intent" (Barton and Gregg 1982).[1]

The idea that rhetoric functions to induce actions in human agents who attend to messages is basic to rhetorical studies (Burke 1969a, p. 81).   While the rhetorical force of a television documentary routinely is implied in documentary analysis (compare Chaney 1981; Nichols 1981), the meanings of "rhetorical function" and "rhetorical features" of documentary have been less clearly specified.   Rhetorical theory suggests that all rhetoric is situational; it comes into being as a response to a situation.   A situation invites or needs a discourse that is participatory and capable of altering reality (Bitzer 1968). The present analysis is rhetorical because it concerns itself with documentary as a persuasive form for international publics. Documentary has rhetorical potential because strategies of rhetorical invention are used to organize audio–video materials to achieve symbolic inducement.

Social reflexivity, a sociological term associated with rhetoric, describes the dialectic between the individual and society as an ongoing process. This dialectic allows the individual audience member to consider alternatives to present social conditions and to understand how to engage in a political response to those conditions (Dalgren 1981). One concern in this rhetorical analysis is how the form of the rhetorical elements in audio–video combinations might contribute to social reflexivity in a situation that is internationally rhetorical.

THE DOCUMENTARY

"Paul Jacobs and the Nuclear Gang" was produced in 1979 by Jack Willis in collaboration with Saul Landau. This 60-minute color documentary was the first offering in the American Public Broadcasting Service (PBS) series entitled "Non-Fiction Television," under the auspices of the Independent Documentary Fund at WNET, Channel 13 in New York. The film was made with a total budget of $65,000. The film organizes, extends, and concludes 20 years of research and filming by journalist–film-maker–activist Paul Jacobs on the subject of nuclear testing in the Utah–Nevada area. This documentary deals with the systematic attempt by the U.S. government, primarily through the Atomic Energy Commission, to suppress information about the threat to the health of the people and animals posed by low-level radiation. We are told that the suppression was designed to protect the national security missions of the nuclear weapons and nuclear energy program.

A preliminary analysis of the film reveals the following characteristics that seem to combine to make this an appropriate documentary for this rhetorical analysis.

• The film deals with the suppression of public discourse as its major topic. The U.S. government is accused of preventing public discourse because it would have the potential to lead to further political action that would interfere with weapons and energy development using nuclear materials.
• This documentary was produced as the premiere piece in what was widely cited as the model of independent documentary production in the United States, the PBS "Non-Fiction Television" series. The series was intended to be politically provocative, nonconventional, and controversial. Its role in

public discourse is perceived as the series' most important function. This particular documentary is typical of the radically democratic documentary in that it attempts to dignify the usual (the typical American citizen) while leveling the extraordinary (the nuclear energy systems and the bureaucracy that embraces them) (Stott 1973, p. 49).

- In the tradition of social documentary this program seeks to correct a wrong by making appeals to the emotions and the intellect.
- In order to understand the reflexive potential of documentary form we need to survey the social context in which it functions as communication. The sociopolitical climate influences the ability of rhetorical strategies to generate audience response. A documentary about the Black Plague is likely to have less reflexive potential than historical appeal when presented to an American audience of the 1980s.

While this documentary was produced in 1979, it continues to have currency in the world's sociopolitical affairs. One issue around which much of the documentary is built, human and animal cancers resulting from nuclear bomb tests in Utah-Nevada, is an important political-legal issue in the U.S. federal courts. In August 1982 a federal judge, vacating his own 1956 decision in the Utah-Nevada case, declared that the government had withheld information, pressured witnesses, and had been intentionally deceptive ("Federal Integrity," August 8, 1982). As of November 1982, over 1,000 Utah citizens were seeking compensation for what they believed were nuclear-related medical problems ("U.S. Rests Its Defense," November 17, 1982). The worldwide citizen's movement of 1982-83 to place a freeze on nuclear weapons provides an international audience for whom the rhetorical appeals of this documentary might be effective. This documentary exists within an active international rhetorical situation that is capable of generating and responding to social discourse about nuclear contamination.[2]

THE RHETORICAL ANALYSIS

Briefly summarized, the piece hinges on a rhetorical strategy that invokes the audience to respond through two processes: first, identification with cancer victims whose illnesses are attributed to nuclear weapons testing and nuclear energy programs, and ultimately, direct participation in the political issue of nuclear contamination. The invocations are developed through two dominant formal elements: mythological framing and unmasking of the method of documentary construction. These main elements are supported by the presentation of five additional structural features: acts of sacrifice, implied consensus, dispersed narration, dramatic irony, and historical proofs.

Many victims eventually and dramatically are revealed to have died from nuclear-induced cancers. As they personally unravel their troubled histories involving nuclear contamination, the victims assume the collective role of a prophetic vanguard for the rest of us. Early in the piece, the producers confront us with the idea that we already are involved personally: We share the victims' dilemma. The association of international publics with these victims is made by one nuclear scientist who reveals that "one pound of plutonium has the potential to induce cancer in every person on earth" and that "each nuclear reactor makes 500 pounds of it each year." The international audience is appealed to again as a physician concludes: "Everyone in the world now has plutonium in his tissues."

THE MYTHOLOGICAL FRAMING OF THE DOCUMENTARY

The overall binding structure of the piece is a mythic one; a narrative is developed in which characters exhibit superhuman behavior (Frye 1957, p. 366). The mythic structure serves the purpose of relating the characters to each other while inviting us to share their dilemma; it produces a romanticized context for the emergence of the main heroic figure, Paul Jacobs.[3] Mythic structure, with its traditional appeal for audience response, is an appropriate foundation for documentary discourse.

The announcements of the deaths of these victim/narrators, whose personal histories we have witnessed, are dramatized by the technique of superimposing over their video images, while they talk, their names and dates of death (see Table 1). These characters are presented in a way that assigns them to a chorus-like function reminiscent of the Greek theatre. They serve to remind us that we are part of a shared destiny. They interact with each other and with the camera, revealing the appeal of the common man whose trust has been betrayed. They are the social consciousness of the piece; they play a normative role. The victims appear, retreat, then reappear even after their deaths are announced as their presence is extended in Paul Jacobs's language, which reiterates many of their pleas. When the carefully crafted invitation for us to identify with the victims through their intensely personal dialogue is abruptly withdrawn in the death announcements, a poignant sense of loss is invoked.

The sacrificial treatment of the victims in the documentary agitates a response to the proposed cause: government suppression of information about the hazards of nuclear energy. The rhetorical structure, then, is developed so that coherent units, such as the personal histories of the characters, are extended and interrelated to other units in the documentary. Themes common to the individually structured units are moved toward an apparent consensus among the antinuclear voices of the piece. Meanwhile, the antinuclear arguments are made more attractive through the technique of dispersing the function of narration among a range of citizen-characters. The construction presents a universal appeal that moves beyond one specific group of victims and, more significantly, beyond one nation of victims.

However, the strategy of developing close identification with characters, then sacrificing them for emotional rhetorical appeal, is most dramatically engineered to create the climax of the documentary. It is revealed that Paul Jacobs himself has cancer. The revelation develops Jacobs into a hero figure within the mythic context already introduced. The camera, in close-up, shows him with trousers down, injecting morphine into his thigh, we learn, to kill the pain of his rapidly spreading cancer (see Table 2). He and his doctor believe the cancer was caused by his picking up a microscopic piece of plutonium at a so-called hot-spot while he was covering the story at an atomic bomb test site. His comments during this sequence combine with this visual material to create appalling dramatic irony. "All cancer patients who use morphine," he says, "learn very quickly that it's either that or a lotta pain." Here, then, is Paul Jacobs in the midst of his roles as narrator, interviewer, filmmaker, and political activist, succumbing to the malady that he has been revealing to us through the suffering of others. The revelation of his own cancer proposes a reflexive function for the documentary. His cancer, besides enhancing his credibility as a source of information about this issue, extends and intensifies the rhetorical effect introduced earlier — of moving us from outside the story to being involved in it. Jacobs has moved from apparent observer to the center of experience. His dedicated action has become the ultimate response. The inference offered by the progression of events is that we, as audience, are next, and by implication the suggestion is that the alternative to our suffering the same fate is to take political action; to work against the suppression of information by the pronuclear establishment. Jacobs discusses his transition from observer to victim (see Table 3): "I was filming Elmer Jackson, the way you people are filming me. I was talking to Elmer Jackson while he was up on his horse. And he had to get down off the horse a couple of times because he couldn't take the pain. I have the pain now, I know what the pain is like, now I know how Elmer felt."

The function of this rhetorical structure is to set up a kind of self-consciousness that requires the viewer to define his relationship to the characters and to the issues. The comparison is an uncomfortable one. It requires decisions about investing

TABLE 1
Nuclear Victims

	Nonsynchronous Audio		Synchronous Audio	Video
	Spoken Commentary	Music		
1			(Max)	Medium close-up
2			I've thought a lot	of Max, smiling
3			of times why the	as he talks.
4			hell did it have to	Superimposed title:
5			happen to me. Why	"S. Max Brinker-
6			couldn't it happen	hoff died February
7			to Joe Blow. But I	27, 1978."
8			guess he wants to	
9			get by as bad as	
10			I do, you know.	
11			(woman next to	
12			Max, whose hus-	
13			band died from	
14			cancer)	Cut to two shot of
15			Sometimes I'd like	Max with woman.
16			to take a poke at	
17			somebody, I don't	
18			know who.	
19			(Dr. James Livermore,	
20			Department of Energy)	Cut to medium shot
21			To my mind the	of
22			standards are	Livermore.
23			adequate and serve	
24			public health and	
			safety.	
			(Helen)	
25			These men had	Cut to extreme
26			these ideas that it	close-up of
27			wasn't hurting any-	woman. Super-
28			body. And they don't	imposed title:
29			want anybody to	"Helen Reichman
30			declare them differ-	died February 14,
31			ently, I think.	1978."

	Nonsynchronous Audio		Synchronous Audio	Video
	Spoken Commentary	Music		
32			That's the whole	
33			thing. They didn't	
34			want to be made	
35			fools of.	
			(Paul)	
36			They said there's	Cut to medium
37			no correlation	shot of bed-
38			between radiation	ridden cancer
39			and disease.	patient. Super-
40				imposed title:
41				"Sgt. Paul
42				Cooper died
43				February 8, 1978."
44			That you got	Zoom into
45				extreme closeup.
46			and that's	Dissolve
47			ridiculous.	to closeup of Jacobs.

TABLE 2

Paul Jacobs as Victim and Unmasking Documentary Method

	Nonsynchronous Audio		Synchronous Audio	Video
	Spoken Commentary	Music		
	(Jacobs)			
1	What's your reaction			Extreme close-up
2	to what's been			of bedridden
3	happening?			cancer patient.
4			(Patient)	
5			Well, I think it's	
6			a very poor situa-	
7			tion. I think the	
8			Pentagon has been	
9			doing a lot of	
10			covering up over	
11	Coverin' up of		the years.	
12	of what?			
13			Stuff like this,	
14			that's been happenin'!	Tilt-pan to patient's
15			See, they don't want	hand as he talks.
16			to admit that it's	Close-up of
17			happened to us.	hand.
18	That man's			
19			(Jacobs continues)	
20			Got no more reason	Cut to Jacobs
21			to be here ...	with hospital
22				mask on,
23			Reason he's here	walking out of
24			cause	patient's hospital
25				room.
26			he trusted, trusted	
27			people in whom he	
28			had (door slams)	
29			no basis for	Closes door,
30			giving that kind	removes his mask.
31			of trust.	

Nonsynchronous Audio		Synchronous Audio	Video
Spoken Commentary	Music		

#			Synchronous Audio	Video
32			And all cancer	Cut to extreme
33			patients who use	close-up of Jacobs
34			morphine learn	rubbing his upper
35			very quickly	left thigh with a
			that it's either	cotton swab, trousers
36			that or a lotta	down to his knees,
37			pain.	pinches skin between
38				fingers, inserts
39				hypodermic needle
40				into thigh. Plunger
41				of needle is slowly
42				pushed.
43			And that choice	Tilt-up to Jacobs's
44			is a fairly easy	face.
45			one. The	Pull back to
46			danger is to get	medium close-up as
47			(pause) there is	he puts his hypo-
48			a possibility of	dermic apparatus
49			getting addicted	away.
50			to the morphine.	
51			One has to be	
52			careful for that.	
53				

91

emotions past the point of the usual empathy for the documentary as temporary text. Many of the characters to whom we have been carefully introduced, whose language and pain have become familiar, have been sacrificed. The forced comparison of our relationship to their pain and to the issue itself suggests we are passive. We are, therefore, invited through the interactional elements of rhetorical form to a more active level of participation. We are confronted now with two exigencies (Bitzer 1968) requiring a rhetorical response: nuclear proliferation, and the suppression of social discourse. The choices of response are clear: Continue to observe the pain of others, share the experience of pain with them, or take political action that will work to alleviate the pain and social injustice that it represents.

UNMASKING THE DOCUMENTARY METHOD

The rhetoric of this documentary turns in on itself. It is meta-communicative; the film's rhetoric unmasks its own method by dropping the claims to the conventions of objectivity and the structural features that are characteristic of journalistic documentary.

This formal element is obvious in a scene in which Jacobs subjectively evaluates the information that has been given to him as an interviewer. A dying, bedridden cancer patient, whose cancer is said to be from his exposure as a soldier in an atomic bomb test, says he believes the Pentagon is "covering up." Jacobs is shown walking out of the man's hospital room, removing his protective face mask, and saying: "That man's got no more reason to be here. . . . Reason he's here 'cause he trusted people in whom he had no basis for giving that kind of trust" (see Table 2). These elements of "subjective rhetoric" do not exist in isolation but interact (Roeh 1982, p. 86). This example of "subjective rhetoric" is built upon in the scene in which Jacobs reveals his own cancer.[4]

Together the scenes generate a persuasive force through dramatic irony. We are invited to share the "secret" of the manipulation of the argument against nuclear proliferation and the overall effect is to personalize the invitation beyond that likely in a more conventional treatment. The effect is ironic because here, as in drama, we are asked to understand, simultaneously, two perspectives: that of the speaker and that of the documentarian as he unmasks his method (Hirsch 1968, pp. 55–56). From their offset perspective, each voice compounds the effect by revealing insights about the other. The tone generated by the dramatic irony is one of informality; it is invitational; it suggests that the producers have nothing to hide. This approach serves to enhance the credibility of the antinuclear position.

The sounds and images revealed in the unmasking do not exhibit the "packaged" characteristics of conventional American network documentary. Instead, they seem to extend an invitation to the audience to peek behind the scenes; to observe in the manner of cinema verité. The rhetorical control inherent in conventional documentary packaging using "detached objectivity," in effect, is traded away in order to enhance Jacobs's credibility as narrator/hero.

TREATMENT OF THE PRONUCLEAR POSITION

On the other hand, the producers selected and organized materials to represent the pronuclear argument so that the rhetorical invitation extended is quite different from that of the antinuclear argument. Two major patterns for the pronuclear position emerge. First, official government film, shot at the time of the atomic bomb tests in the 1950s, is excerpted so that the official, inflexible, and authoritarian style of the military is the prevailing message. A typical sequence uses footage from the U.S. government series entitled "The Big Picture" (see Table 4). We see the heart of an atomic bomb blast, then the shock-wave, and troops assembled at the test site to witness the direct effects of the blast. The narrator, speaking over strident military march music, explains:

Men who have experienced their first atomic explosion, moving out of their trenches toward the blast area with the mushroom cloud still hanging in the air, have acquired an invaluable first-hand knowledge of the effect of nuclear devices.

The second pattern, interactive with the first, juxtaposes the extremely personal and dramatic comments of the victims with the government film footage. The collison works to argue that the military position is impersonal, hypocritical, and inhumane. It also implicates military policies with the plight of the victims. Again, dramatic irony is the element at work. Here it creates the rhetorical effect of alienating the audience from the pronuclear position. The film footage above cuts directly to a close-up of a cancer patient whose jaw has been destroyed beyond recognition by cancer (see Table 4). Through severely distorted speech he reveals how his cancer is believed to be associated with his assignment as a paratrooper, to carry out a drop mission into a bomb test site minutes after the blast. The pattern of mixing dated, authoritarian, and obviously propagandistic government film against the personal interviews of the victims works to rigidify the pronuclear position — in effect, to

TABLE 3
Paul Jacobs's Identification with Elmer Jackson

	Nonsynchronous Audio		Synchronous Audio	Video
	Spoken Commentary	Music		
1			(Jacobs)	Medium close-up
2			And then it spread	of Jacobs
3			from my lungs through-	seated.
4			out my whole body	
5			into my bones, and	
6			my spine. And in my	
7			ribs. And my hip	
8			where it is most	
9			painful now. And I	
10			don't know where	
11			next and I don't	
12			know for how long.	Extreme close-up
13			One thing I didn't	of Jacobs
14			understand before:	riding in car.
15			I was filming Elmer	
16			Jackson the way	
17			you people are	
18			filming me. I was	
19			talking to Elmer	
20			Jackson while he	
21			was up on his	
22			horse. And he had	
23			to get down off	
24			the horse a couple	
25			of times, because	
26			he couldn't take the	Cut to medium
27			pain.	shot of Jackson
28				on horse.

94

	Nonsynchronous Audio		Synchronous Audio	Video
	Spoken Commentary	Music		
29		Outdoor sounds	(Jackson)	
30			And so I went into	
31			my home and my	
32			wife met me at	
33			the door. And she	
34			says, heavens, what's	
35			the matter with	
36			your face and your	
37			eyes? And I said	
38			well, I was just	
39			in that atomic	
40			fallout that was	
41			caused from the	
42			blast this morning	
43			in Nevada, and	
44			she said your eyes	
45			look terrible	
46			and your face is	
			all blistered.	
47		Auto sounds	(Jacobs)	
48			I didn't know what	
49			he meant by the	
50			kind of pain that	
51			comes from radiation	
52			and the nausea that	
53			comes from chemo-	
			therapy. That was	
54			just words to me.	
55			Didn't really have	
56			any significance.	Cut to close-up of Jacobs in ear.

TABLE 3 (continued)
Paul Jacobs's Identification with Elmer Jackson

	Nonsynchronous Audio		Synchronous Audio	Video
	Spoken Commentary	Music		
57		Outdoor sounds	(Jackson)	Cut to close-up
58			I had a large	of Jackson feeling
59			growth on my	left side of neck
60			neck — seemingly	as he talks.
61			came overnight,	
62			and was about	
			the size of an egg.	
			(Jacobs)	
63		Auto sounds	I have the pain	Cut to close-up
64			now. I know what	of Jacobs.
65	(Jacobs)		that pain is like.	
66	Now I know how			Shot out of window
67	Elmer felt.			of houses as car rolls by.

96

TABLE 4
The Use of Historical Proofs

	Nonsynchronous Audio		Synchronous Audio	Video
	Spoken Commentary	Music		
1	(Male narrator)			Medium close-up of
2	Heavy silence hangs	Orchestral music		helmeted soldier.
3	over ground zero,	building to a		
4	the target area,	crescendo under		Cut to wide shot of
5	and the trenches in	commentary until		bomb test site.
6	which the soldiers wait.	bomb blast.		Cut to sand-bagged
7	The countdown			trenches.
8	announces the detonation.			Cut to extreme
9				close-up of soldier
10				counting down
11			Bomb blast sound	through a walkie-
12				talkie.
13				Cut to two soldiers
14				with heads down as
15				blast occurs.
16			Sounds of fire	Cut to close-up of
17			storm, wind, blast	soldier with flash
18			continuing	of blast reflecting
19			through these	off him.
20			scenes.	Medium shot of
21				tank.
22				Long shot of site,
23				disintegrating
24				buildings.
25	(Male narrator)	Triumphant		Long shot of mush-
26	Men who have experienced	March music		room cloud rising
27	their first atomic			with soldiers
28	explosion, moving out			moving under the
29	of their trenches			cloud.
30	toward the blast area			

TABLE 4 (continued)
The Use of Historical Proofs

	Nonsynchronous Audio		Synchronous Audio	Video
	Spoken Commentary	Music		
31	with the mushroom			Cut to a medium
32	cloud still hanging			shot of soldiers
33	in the air, have			moving toward
34	acquired an invaluable			camera in the desert.
35	first-hand knowledge			
36	of nuclear devices.	(Music Out)		Cut to close-up of
37	(Major Patrick)			man (identified by
38	I flew cloud sampling			superimposed title),
39	missions.			Major Richard H. Patrick.
				His right jaw is
				severely deformed,
				etched away. Cut to
40	And later on		Sound of plane	aerial view down-
41	participated in flying		flying	ward through
42	a drop-test mission.			cloud cover.
43	I retired from			
44	the Air Force in			Cut to shot of
45	1963 and approxi-			bomber. Cut to
46	mately eight			extreme long shot of
47	months later I had		Sound of explosion	H-bomb exploding.
48	what I thought			Cut to medium
49	was a toothache.		Sound of	shot of air-borne
50	However, it was		bomber.	B-29 bomber
51	diagnosed as			viewed from side.
52	cancer.		(Sound Out)	

freeze it in history, to encrust its rhetoric within flawed arguments. The arguments have been proved through time to be scientifically naive and bureaucratically deceptive. Historical hindsight is made to work against the pronuclear position. The documentary is not about the business of journalistic balance; nor is it committed to the conventions associated with that approach. It is openly rhetorical in construction, seeking to persuade through a combination of emotional and logical appeals. In this sequence a direct confrontation between the spokesman for the two positions is avoided. Instead real victims in the midst of their suffering are set against the impersonal formalized bureaucratic face of the nuclear establishment. Historical proofs are at work.[5] As a result, the antinuclear ideology seems less confrontational. What we see are the inhuman effects of a bureaucracy operating in secrecy.

The only accommodation made to the pronuclear position, to balance what might be seen as unfair treatment through the manipulation of dated military rhetoric from the film archives, is the inclusion of recent interviews with nuclear industry spokesmen who argue that they were operating as best they could with the knowledge available to them at the time. But the final force of this argument is lost in the repeated pattern of revelations of how the government systematically worked to prevent public disclosure of the potential hazards of nuclear development. The idea that public discussion of the threat of nuclear contamination was thwarted intentionally emerges as the final impression.

The documentary, on the surface, seems to be in two parts. The second half of the documentary was made after Jacobs's death and without his guiding hand. The focus is changed by investigating problems at nuclear submarine plants in Portsmouth, New Hampshire and at Rocky Flats, Colorado, where triggers for nuclear devices are made. But the producers use Jacobs's remarks, obviously filmed when he was quite ill, to unify the piece by further developing the mythic structure. His language seems to have taken on an heroic quality. It is relatively primitive in its symbolic structure, international in its appeal for morality. It is less concerned here with specific examples of the nuclear contamination problem.[6] A Faustian allusion sets the tone for the overriding argument about the right to public discourse. Jacobs says:

Nuclear physicists are saying in order to have energy you must make a bargain with the devil. They think it's worth it. And, . . . they've forgotten the social purpose of science. And no one raised the question . . . who says we have to have nuclear energy? No one raised the question of whether the public might be willing to cut back on energy in other forms and do without that Faustian bargain . . . not run the kind of risk that we're running now.

His style, here broad-stroked and moralistic, helps bind together the otherwise dissimilar halves of the documentary by pointing to the moral issues to which they relate and reiterating the central point of the documentary: that positive social objectives are achieved through social discourse. Someone must, he implores, "raise the question." The mythic structure, in the final analysis, has combined its elements for this focused appeal through Jacobs as hero. Social action is the rhetorical act of "raising the question" in the face of the pronuclear opposition.[7]

CONCLUSIONS

The analysis suggests that in order for documentary to have the potential for international social discourse it must itself have a structure that presents audio-image elements in a dynamic and interactive way involving basic symbolic forms that have universal appeal. Documentary reflexivity, it appears, springs from a content structure that is itself reflexive.

This documentary derives its potential for discussion among international publics primarily from a structural counterpoint between the conventions of the documentary genre as a whole and rhetorical elements that violate the assumptions inherent in those conventions. Of the two major ideological positions treated in this documentary, the antinuclear is placed within a dynamic, complex mythic structure that involves intimate language of personal histories, dramatic irony achieved through unconventional audio-video revelations, and a subjective rhetoric that lays bare the methods and attitudes of the producers with the effect of enhancing their credibility. The pronuclear position, while dynamically countered with the opposing ideology, is characterized in this treatment as historically static, authoritarian, and defensive.

The documentary's structure changes from an emphasis on the externally applied artificial shaping devices (camera angle, detached narrator, stock video transitions) of television's conventional form to a form that develops more organically through the interaction of the content elements themselves (Barton and Gregg 1982). Jacobs's narrator-role evolving into the victim-role is the predominant example of organic formal development. The formal development works to make the documentary more suitable for international discourse. While the technical conventions of American television might be recognized and "read" internationally, the features of the mythic structure that emerge from the organic form of this discourse move the audience appeals beyond the level of superficial structures of television production to the more basic, universal set of mythic symbols that are shared interculturally.

This analysis does not suggest that the discursive potential inherent in the structure of "Paul Jacobs" will necessarily be transformed into reflexive action on each presentation. Such conclusions require analyses of many communication variables and the combination of social science methods with detailed analyses of content. However, the discursive potential revealed in this example does suggest that international mass communication research needs to look more closely at manipulation of form as argument. Here is a documentary structure that is sensitive to, and involved with, the process of soliciting social discourse about a significant international political issue. Discovering these structures and making judgments about their meanings in the context of the documentary requires critical methods that are more concerned with intrinsic features of form than with the application of extrinsic political and economic principles that overlook the special features of the work in question. The analysis suggests that documentary television is an inherently rhetorical form, and that of American forms, independent TV documentary has greater potential for international social reflexivity than U.S. network documentary because it intentionally moves beyond organizational and formal constraints that might inhibit rhetorical invitations to political discourse.

Clearly, the relationship between message forms and organizational constraints is an important one in this case. The study reveals the need to combine methods of message analysis with methods concerned with control inherent in media organization structures. A collaborative approach seems to promise more precision than now exists in our study of the effects of cultural imprints on interpersonal messages that are communicated electronically. However, the research traditions in international mass communication and the methods they represent seem to be isolated both ideologically and geographically. Sustained international effort will be required to negotiate the collaboration.

NOTES

1. Barton and Gregg (1982) argue that the distinction between organic and conventional form must be accounted for if the critic is to understand rhetorical appeals in nonfiction television.

2. One British reviewer who saw this documentary on BBC 2 comparatively analyzes it with two contemporary British TV social documentaries (Wilce 1979). Meanwhile, an American reviewer

labels this documentary "an important contribution to public knowledge about the threat of nuclear radiation" (Sklar 1979).

3. The structure of this documentary specifically recalls Frye's notion of romance in which there is a dialectical conflict between a hero and his enemy (Frye 1957, p. 187).

4. Itzhak Roeh (1982) offers a brief discussion of the device of "laying bare the facts" through a subjective presence.

5. The example of the selective use of historical materials follows the rhetorical strategy of using history to induce social action. Frye describes the process as one that "catches the rhythm of history, that seizes on a crucial event or phase of action, interprets it, articulates the emotions concerned with it, or in some means employs a verbal structure to insulate and conduct the current of history" (Frye 1957, p. 327).

6. Robert K. Merton argues that of seven forms of social knowledge, mythic knowledge is the least artificial and most permanent, while technological knowledge is the most artificial and least permanent (Merton 1968, p. 525).

7. The mythic structure is consistent with Frye's notion of the "myth of concern which 'exists to hold society together.'" Frye believes that myth reveals that "what is true is what society does and believes in response to authority" (Frye 1971, pp. 34ff).

7

KNOWLEDGE, FORM, AND ACTION: THREE FACES OF THE NEW RHETORIC

Gerard A. Hauser

The term "rhetoric" may seem out of place in a book like this. The contemporary communications scholar is aware that the term has a technical meaning beyond that of popular parlance: inflated or meaningless talk, as in "mere rhetoric." Even allowing its technical distinction, rhetoric as an area of research commonly is associated with an attitude toward communication that appears outworn in light of contemporary concerns.

It does not study human communication in a manner that lends itself easily to quantification. Rhetoric's focus is on the quality of the message, making its research largely interpretive. It does not frequently address the private realm, in which so much of what Western mass culture values as "authentic" communication occurs and from which so many of our conceptual assumptions about what it means to communicate "authentically" emerge. Moreover, in terms of communication in the public realm, mass communication appears much more consequential as a mode of communication than does rhetoric.

This litany could be expanded, but the point would remain unchanged. Most of these attitudinal concerns stem from a fundamental association of rhetoric with public speaking. While historically accurate, this association misses underlying concerns that always have informed the understanding rhetoricians had of their subject: concerns of method in public reasoning that could warrant confidence, of the suasory dynamics of language that could permit humans to construct social reality, of civic virtue in practical conduct that could promote community. Knowing, being, and doing: These were the concerns of antiquity; they remain the concerns of today.

The contemporary study of rhetoric has expanded beyond its original formulations about speech as it is used in formal address to include investigations into the ways in which symbols induce cooperation, whether in the sharing of attitudes or in the sharing of deeds. While during earlier periods of the modern era there was a separation of rhetoric from communication along humanistic/scientific lines, the increasing awareness that communication is form and that form requires interpretive study (Rabinow and Sullivan 1979) bridges a gulf that once appeared to separate these inquiries. Centering on form also provides opportunities for those interested in rhetorical dimensions of human symbolic activity to share in common scholarly pursuits with those involved in the exploration of other dimensions of human communication.

In this chapter, I will discuss three developments that have been of signal significance in shaping contemporary rhetorical studies:

● the positivist/antipositivist debate and the subsequent recognition that rhetoric is at the heart of their dialectic tension;
● the development of a perspective toward symbolic forms that articulates their inherent suasory characteristics; and
● the emergence of "discourse" as a fundamental category in charting the formation of social will.

I will consider each of these developments in turn. I wish to show how, from these three starting points, three rich areas of inquiry have emerged and how the research activities in these areas are transforming rhetorical studies from thematizing the surface concerns with effective use of language to those of the underlying concerns with knowing, being, and doing.

RHETORIC AND EPISTEMOLOGY

The first characteristic of contemporary rhetorical theory is its focus on rhetoric's epistemic function. To grasp the range and depth of this concern, it is enlightening to recall that in antiquity dialectic or logic was in alliance with rhetoric; together they formed a complete art of communication. Moreover, their union provided rhetoric its philosophical status as a method central to the acquisition and advance of knowledge. Descartes severed that union with his call for a new type of logic suited to scientific investigation. The impact of the Discourse on Method was to strip rhetoric of the testing apparatus that logic had always provided, resulting in rhetoric's degeneration into concerns of style and delivery removed from interpretation of content (Howell 1958). The diminished estate of rhetoric continued into the twentieth century, with the accomplishments of science enforcing the epistemological supremacy of an investigative logic. Modern rhetoric appeared to lack any relationship with the philosophical aspects of communication, precisely the union that historically had been the defining feature that provided rhetoric its illuminating power on the character of thought and action.

During the past 20 years rhetoricians have attempted to reseal this modern version of the wisdom/eloquence split (see Hauser 1979; Johnstone 1981). The revival of epistemologically oriented research in rhetoric is best viewed in the context of ongoing critique of the prevailing positivist epistemology concerning how knowledge is established and acquired. I shall attempt to indicate how rhetoricians have joined this critique and have added to its arguments for the centrality of suasory processes to human knowing.

Perhaps the clearest synthesis of the positivist epistemology is expressed in Carl Hempel's (1942) essay entitled "The Function of General Laws in History." In it he argued that history, contrary to prevailing opinion, should be and, indeed, was concerned with the theoretical function of general laws in its scientific research. While the subject matter of history seems ill-suited to the theory Hempel was propounding, his essay has come to be regarded as "the fullest and most lucid formulation of the positivist theory of explanation . . ." (von Wright 1971, p. 10). His position, now known as the Covering Law Model, held that a scientific explanation consisted of:

(1) a set of statements asserting the occurrence of certain events C_1 . . . C_n at certain times and places,
(2) a set of universal hypotheses, such that
 (a) the statements of both groups are reasonably well confirmed by empirical evidence,
 (b) from the two groups of statements the sentence asserting the occurrence of event E can be logically deduced (p. 36).

As a model of rational thought, Hempel's deductive-nomological theory of explanation is actually an extension of the Cartesian epistemology currently dominant in Western thought. In two important respects the Covering Law Model makes rationalist assumptions. First, codicil 2 endorses the view that explanation must rest on universally true propositions. In Cartesian terms, such propositions are said to be self-evident, being indubitably certain to anyone who understands the terms of the premises employed. These first premises are a priori, not themselves the products of prior demonstrations and the foundations upon which all subsequent demonstrations are built. Indeed, all demonstrative reasoning, when pushed back to its bases, finds certitude only insofar as infinite regress is halted by the ultimate foundation of a premise that is self-evident and, therefore, true. Second, codicile 2b holds logical deduction to be the standard for rational thought. This means that as long as such reasoning is consistent within the rules of the logical system employed, deduced conclusions are guaranteed to be certain. The formal requirements of logic provide the criteria of rationality, thereby limiting knowledge only to those matters that are demonstrably true or false. Clearly a false claim fails both as an explanation and as a report of knowledge. By implication, however, this codicil also excludes any claim that, in principle, is not amenable to demonstration. The whole realm of the nondemonstrable — matters neither true nor false, right nor wrong — are separated from matters of truth. The contingent realm rests on opinions, which are subjective and arbitrary in character, incapable of providing explanation or understanding, and therefore beyond the pale of knowledge.

One hesitates to deny the power of the Covering Law Model, especially in light of accomplishments in the physical sciences where it has long been the paradigm for explanation; but the attempts by its proponents to claim that deductive-nomological reasoning is the universal norm for explanation and the sole criterion of rationality have come under serious attack.

On the face of it, the Covering Law Model cannot explain the occurrence of scientific revolutions wherein the prevailing paradigm of explanation (codicil 2) and prediction (codicil 2b) are violated. Such events seem to escape the explanatory model and yet count as scientifically discovered and confirmed reports of reality (Kuhn 1970). From another perspective the model ignores the apparent evolutionary nature of scientific knowledge. It does not take into account the influence of context on the discovery of new theories, or methodologies, or even questions that emerge from a dialectical exchange of ideas among members of a professional community. Such factors are not detected by logical canons nor by the hypothetico-deductive model of reasoning. Nonetheless they are significant in the judgment of what is or is not considered to be known scientifically or even knowable at any given time (Toulmin 1972). Moreover, the positivist model of rationality encounters serious problems in terms of its ultimate assumption of self-evident starting points. By the model's explicit formulation, whatever is unable to withstand the rigors of logical demonstration is ruled out as providing a rational basis for the explanation and understanding of events. The positivist model classifies nondemonstrable claims as either self-evident or arbitrary. Yet when the model itself is scrutinized for basic assumptions, its starting points appear to be no less arbitrary than those of "irrationalists" and, therefore, must be equally irrational (Bartley 1962). While it is true that the proponents of the model claim that scientific reasoning rests on self-evident premises, the point is extremely difficult to carry since it is doubtful that any practicing scientist would endorse that position willingly.

At the core of these and other objections to deductive-nomological accounts of scientific reasoning is a disavowal of an absolutist epistemology that is both reductionistic and monistic in what it will admit as a knowledge claim. They express the view that human understanding is not confined to logic, especially since logical certainty is an artifact of consistent reasoning within an axiomatic system and need bear no correspondence to material or existential reality. They reject the positivist dichotomy wherein what is not demonstrably certain is regarded as arbitrary. Instead they search for and postulate alternative standards of human rationality and human knowledge (McMullin 1974).

Clearly the issues involved in this controversy are of signal importance to an understanding of rhetoric. Under the shadow of a positivistic model, rhetorical activity is banned from making any contribution to human understanding. Its premises are drawn from opinions; its conclusions are probabilities. At best it can transmit knowledge established scientifically or through other means leading to demonstrable certainties; but it is clearly mistaken to regard rhetorical transactions as epistemic, since rhetorically founded conclusions are merely the agreements of interlocutors on premises arbitrarily chosen and unsystematically extended. Further, any commitments elicited or intensified through rhetoric, per se, are patently irrational since they are without any demonstrable foundation.

Conversely, in the light of antipositivist analysis, systems and means of communication play an important part if not the central role in the development and testing of human understanding (Bartley 1962; Kuhn 1970; Lakatos 1968; Polanyi 1958; Rescher 1977; Toulmin 1958, 1972; Weimer 1979). At the same time, however, the status of and confidence in understanding so rooted remain as significant obstacles to holding rhetorical behavior as rational and not arbitrary. If the universal validity of self-evidence and demonstration are denied, rhetoric then must overthrow the implication that all thought must degenerate into skepticism wherein everything is subjected to unremitting doubt, or irenicism wherein everything is held to be equally true.

These problems, central to the research of philosophers of science, also have provided a context for scholars of rhetoric interested in the relationships of discourse to thought and action. Since just before the Wingspread and Pheasant Run Conferences (Bitzer and Black 1971), rhetorical theorists, commentators, and critics have focused their attention on the epistemic status of rhetoric (Scott 1967). My intention is not to review the literature on this subject (Leff 1978) but instead to consider the dimensions of this ongoing discussion as it relates to the development of research in rhetoric. To this end I shall sketch with broad strokes emerging issues on the nature, type, and domain of rhetorical knowing.

The Nature of Rhetorical Knowledge

The relationship of rhetoric to knowledge has been discussed since Plato first questioned its apparent method (or lack thereof) and epistemic product (opinion). Setting aside the views of the antirhetoricians, there have been three basic positions in the ongoing dialogue. Some, like Aristotle, have maintained that rhetoric is an art of selection. In the given case one proceeds systematically by rhetorical methods to discover what of suasory consequence may be said. It excludes rhetoric from discussion of technical matters, leaving these to science. These questions about determinate entities, namely, ones about their causes, are pursued to their culmination in apodictic proof. Rhetoric's preserve is conceptualized as including questions about indeterminate matters; its movement is from what a public holds generally to be the case to what follows as a basis for judgment and action in the given case. Rhetoric is epistemic in the sense that it leads to the discovery of what is there to be known as a likelihood on such matters.

A second position, advocated by such figures as Cicero, Quintilian, and Vico, has maintained that rhetoric is an art of construction. In novel situations one proceeds systematically by use of rhetoric to create realities heretofore nonexistent. Rhetoric is conceived as an art of invention and proof; its methods are analysis by means of the topics and demonstration by means of performance. One considers indeterminate matters and, through the manifestations of appeals and the judgment of empowered listeners, one makes or creates a determinate outcome. Rhetoric is epistemic in the sense that it constructs a determinate resolution to novel and indeterminate situations. This resolution stands as the rhetor-listener's understanding about a shared dimension of existence and experience.

Finally, there have been advocates, like Richard Whately, who have maintained that rhetoric is an art of adaptation. Knowledge of what is the case is conceptualized as within the preserve of the disciplines proper. Rhetoric alone does not enable one to select which issues and arguments have suasory potential nor to construct a new reality and human understanding of same. Rhetoric as method manages the resources of argument and language to adapt a previously established understanding to the needs, interests, readinesses to respond, and so forth, of listeners. On this conceptual model, if rhetoric is epistemic, it is so only in a most general way; it is surely lacking in the assertive strength of the two preceding models. Its task is to communicate knowledge effectively rather than to provide the avenue to knowledge.

Contemporary discussions on the whole have not emphasized the third position. They have focused primarily on rhetoric as an art of selection or construction. Insofar as one can infer scholarly consensus from 15 years of focused research, it is that we have developed a reasonable case for rhetoric as a way of knowing. What remain at issue are the type of knowledge rhetoric generates and the domain of that knowledge.

The Type of Rhetorical Knowledge

The type of knowledge one claims under the banner of "rhetoric as epistemic" obviously is dependent upon one's prior views about the nature of knowledge. Hence, rhetorically based knowledge is roughly aligned with a conceptual model of what shall count as knowledge in the first place. Here two positions appear to be dominant. The first maintains that rhetorical knowledge is contingent knowledge (Scott 1967, 1976). It is never a certainty because the matters it treats, as Aristotle taught us, do not permit of certainties. Moreover, since it is of the given case, rhetorical knowledge, limited in scope to the here and now, provides at best analogues for the future but surely never anything approaching laws. The second position maintains that all knowledge built upon argumentation is rhetorical knowledge (Brockriede 1975). Since arguments are inherently rhetorical, no area, including the sacred preserves of science, escapes the rhetorical net (Weimer 1977). Hence rhetorical knowledge is not merely knowledge of matters calling for human decisions. Rhetorical knowledge includes everything established through words. With the exception of certain concerns of a purely formal character or matters of ineffability, it is impossible to imagine what is not established as knowledge through presentation and defense, through warranted argument. Thus it would seem either that all knowledge is contingent or that, insofar as they are established via "good reasons," the contingent and noncontingent alike are epistemically established through rhetoric (Hauser and Cushman 1973).

Both of these positions have encountered difficulties. The argument based on contingencies may be attacked on two fronts. First, it assumes there is another form of knowledge, noncontingent or certain in character. From it, rhetorical knowledge may be set apart. If there is another, certain, form of knowing, then rhetorical knowing must be its inferior. The objection is, then, that this model inadvertently subscribes to a rationalist epistemology and thereby undermines its own case (Weimer 1977). Second, by arguing for rhetoric as epistemic in the realm of the contingent, it places emphasis on the subjects that rhetoric treats, on its matter. Opponents may again indicate the inferior epistemic status this position accords rhetoric since, in principle, there are other, noncontingent, bodies of matter that have a firmer claim to being knowledge. Beyond this, however, the contingency position ignores that rhetoric takes on full meaning only in action, where matter and manner fuse (Zyskind 1968, 1970). In fact one may argue that in action matter is a function of manner (Sennett 1978). Rhetorical action is gauged by two criteria: First by the rhetor's selection of issues to be decided; then, after having put the question in a specific way, by the rhetor's determination of what will be the advantageous position to argue.

To avoid these objections the advocates of "good reasons" or "warranted assertions" center on the idea that there simply is no valid argumentation beyond the pale of warranted content claims. The shift from "contingent versus certain matter" to "warranted assertions" avoids the justificationist assumptions of rationalism because all knowledge except that in formal disciplines or matters of ineffability, is established through argumentation to an audience. Significantly, the audience determines whether or not an assertion is "warranted."

However, several objections may be lodged against the "warranted assertions" position. First, it may be saying no more than that all knowledge is relative to the audience. What guarantees that the audience is qualified to assay the metal of the rhetor's claims (Brinton 1982; Croasman and Cherwitz 1982)? Second, if repaired by the imposition of some communal norm, the argument is met by the objection that it creates an elite audience and runs the risk of employing a priori standards of the community — be they scholars, lawyers, or some other relevantly defined special groups (Kuhn 1970). This is a lapse into justificationism (Bartley 1962; Weimer 1977). Third, the justificationism associated with an elite audience may be repaired by a move, along Perelman's (1969) lines, to a universal audience. But the concept of "universal audience" remains to be clearly and finally absolved of the suspicion that the criteria for judgment, and therefore of what will pass muster as knowledge, are left to the good offices of a rhetor's fallible insights and intuitions into what is rational (Johnstone 1978).

Interestingly, each of these objections suggests that a conception of audience is a crucial problem to be resolved in determining the type of knowledge to which rhetoric may lay claim. Scholars increasingly have recognized that if rhetorical epistemology is to avoid the blemish of inferior citizenship, knowledge must be rooted in action (Arendt 1958). Rhetorical action, in turn, requires a theory of audience as certifying agent in discursive transactions, a theory capable of accounting to the rationality of rhetorical acts. Though this theory of audience remains to be developed, recent research on "the public" provides positive signs that such work is already underway (Bitzer 1978; Farrell and Goodnight 1981; Hauser and Blair 1982).

The Domain of Rhetorical Knowledge

Implicit in the concern over the type of knowledge generated by rhetoric are questions about the domain of such knowledge. One might suspect that the differences between the contingent and the warranted knowledge camps would have allied positions on the domain of rhetorical epistemology. At first glance this appears to be so, though at the crux of this matter is a potential for unity, as I shall attempt to indicate.

On the issue of rhetorical epistemology's domain, scholars have advanced two basic positions. The first makes the assumption that only that which is communicated with efficacy has moment epistemologically (Brummett 1976; Carleton 1978). This position holds that knowledge is generated whenever one proceeds systematically to invent ideas, interpret data in their light, express interpretations with thematic unity, and relate these presentations holistically to a framework for understanding experience and existence (Carleton 1978). Such a perspective identifies rhetoric as a method whereby humans come to know rather than as the subject matter communicated; it includes all knowing within its range (McKeon 1971).

The second camp claims that rhetoric's domain is social knowledge, as distinguished from formal and technical knowledge (Farrell 1976). Social knowledge is formed through symbolic relationships on problematic matters that call for public behavior (Bitzer 1978). It is addressed to ontological over ontic matters, to praxis over theory. While social knowledge centers on the contingent and the probable, it is equally sensitive to the audience's role in establishing rhetoric's knowledge claims.

Obviously the foregoing is oversimplified, as a condensation of complex issues necessarily must be. Each of the larger positions I have been sketching has within it several more finely drawn variants and subschools, frequently at odds with one another. Nonetheless, from a distance the differences between the overarching positions seem more apparent than from conceptual incompatibilities. The former addresses the realm of human thought where rhetoric is grounded in method. In this sense its issues are about invention and judgment of the possible and transformation of the possible into the real. It highlights the architectonic potential of communication as the organon of things, thoughts, and actions. The latter addresses the world of affairs where rhetoric is grounded in practice. In this sense its issues are not ones of scientific determination but of public judgment. It highlights the productive aspect of rhetoric that forges consensus and promotes action.

Other approaches to rhetoric have attempted to develop unitary groundings that seal the divisions rampant among scholars working on the epistemology question. Essentially they seem to regard the issues of epistemology as unresolvable and have taken different courses of argument. They do not emphasize the architectonic domain of method nor the productive domain of social knowledge, but rather the groundings of rhetoric in symbolic form or the fusion of theory with praxis in rhetorical action.

RHETORIC AND SYMBOLIC FORM

Those theorists grounding rhetoric in symbolic form developed their perspective concomitantly with those concerned with the rational basis of communication in reaction to the doctrine of logical positivism. Earlier I had discussed the positivists' perspective toward rationality. Embedded in their "rationalism" was an attitude toward language equally inimical to rhetoric.

Initially the positivists and those influenced by them seemed to raise conclusive objections against the possibility of using anything but neutral language meaningfully in rational discourse. Since rhetoric was traditionally concerned with the use of valuative language, this critique appeared to reduce rhetoric to intellectually meaningless verbal display. According to the positivists, all meaningful or "significant" propositions were either "formal" or "factual." Formal propositions, such as those found in logic and pure mathematics, they regarded as tautologies and, therefore, as verifiable through analyses of their constituent parts. Factual propositions, on the other hand, could be verified by such empirical means as raw observation or controlled experimentation. Values, emotions, and other such subjective aspects of human response evoked by messages and influential on listener judgments were to be banned as mere self-reports.

It is doubtful that during the 1930s and 1940s many students of communication were reading firsthand the words of Ayer (1935), Carnap (1935), Russell (1927, 1935), or Ogden and Richards (1930). The views of these writers form through two principal, influential channels: the works of John Dewey (1910, 1922, 1938, 1939, 1948) and the theories of the General Semanticists (Korzybski 1933; Chase 1938; Hayakawa 1941).

Examination of the journals and textbooks on rhetoric and communication makes abundantly clear the profound influence that the thinking of Dewey and the General Semanticists exercised on students of communication during this period. A "cult of facticity" arose, devoted to the notion that pragmatic communication should consist, to the fullest possible extent, of empirically verifiable assertions. Good communication, it was widely thought, should be conscientiously purged of expressive language, leaving listeners to judge the worth and pertinence of ideas on the basis of factual data alone.

As the logical positivist position came under scrutiny, a line of analysis developed that undermined the attempt to restrict rational communication to value neutral language. Shortly after World War II new assessments of the relations among science, communication, and the necessarily evaluative and evocative character of language began to throw into doubt a number of the philosophical and rhetorical foundations upon which the "cult of facticity" had until then rested securely. This reassessment has been discussed by many writers, including such well-known persons as Whitehead (1938), Braithwaite (1953), Rudner (1953), Polanyi (1958), and Kuhn (1970). They and a host of other critics have argued that values are inescapably part of scientific accounts. Most prominently, such critics have stressed that science is a social enterprise, and a valuative enterprise. Obviously each of these conditions involves science in a consideration of values as well as of facts. Importantly they constitute a direct refutation of attempts to escape the evocative character of rhetorical expression through some form of value-free neutral communication. These critiques together argue that such modes of expression are conceptual ideals at best, if not gross distortions of the nature of communication.

While philosophers and methodologists of science were assigning new importance to the _act_ of communicating as part of engaging in science, rhetoricians and critics were advancing a new conception of language as a _medium_ of communication. Such writers as Richard Weaver (1953, 1964), Kenneth Burke (1950, 1954), Paul Newell Campbell (1973, 1975), Wayne Booth (1974), and Richard Gregg (1978, 1981) among others held that not only is it pragmatically impossible to denude language of values, but it is ontologically and epistemologically impossible as well. Indeed, their claims urge the conceptualization of symbolic forms as more than the medium of communicaton but in and of their very nature providing the foundations for ontology and epistemology.

For rhetoricians working in this perspective, language is more than a sign system and more than a mediational medium. Instead these rhetoricians argue that there is no meaning for humans but symbolic meaning (Campbell 1973). Along lines similar to those set forth by Cassirer (1955), these scholars maintain that human perception is grounded in primal forms, such as space, time, cause and effect, thingness, and attribution. The first formations of symbols, they argued, were not to mediate cognitions but for purposes of comprehension by the symbol user. Consequently and significantly it is asserted that the invention and subsequent use of symbols are, from their very origins, the means whereby humans come to know their realities: creating reality's contours; selecting salient elements of the environment for attention, transmission, and preservation; providing shape and movement for meaning. Since Cassirer, Gregg (1981) has drawn on the research findings of cognitive psychologists to advance the claim that symbolic forming is primordial in that it is physiologically grounded. He argues that our sensory organs themselves are so structured as to "resonate" with the structures of nature and, thereby, organize their received data in patterns that create cognitive experiences. The significance of these initial patternings is that, from the first, perceptions are formed in ways mirrored by human symbols, rendering reality as we know it a human construction entirely symbolic in character.

Prior research by those investigating symbolic form had been subject to refutation on the grounds that such research was comprised of subjective interpretations that arbitrarily ascribed meanings to symbolic activities. However, the articulation of the primitive groundings for symbolic forms suggests that these objections may be invalid. Current work shows that patterning is essential to meaning, that patterns shape perceptions and encourage valuations, that patterns are inherently rhetorical in that they have suasory potential, and that recurrent patterns can assume cultural significance. While interpretations of human patternings always are subject to question, nonetheless the inherent relationship between patterning and human cognition makes it possible to provide principled accounts for how symbolic forms (whether verbal or nonverbal) acquire meaning and underwrite all knowledge. The research ahead, then, is likely to be most profitable insofar as it is able to uncover those basic principles guiding the ways in which symbolic forming shapes human communication activity.

RHETORIC AND ACTION

A second strand that has developed in counterpoint to the epistemological question has centered on the problem of the split between theory and practice, a problem long under scrutiny by social sciences in general. By centering rhetorical studies on meaning and action, researchers in the field have attempted to reconceptualize the theory/praxis split in terms of the fusion rhetoric provides. While concerted research in this area is relatively new among twentieth-century rhetorical theorists, the rhetorical tradition has a rich legacy of thought addressed to the problem, as the work of McKeon has demonstrated (see Hauser and Cushman 1973). Moreover, this contemporary concern partakes of the much older social science research tradition of verstehen (Weber 1968).

The use of rhetoric as a basic concept from which to launch social critique is best made clear through contrast of this new stance with traditional theory. Traditional theory is grounded in the writings of antiquity, especially those of Greece. It adopted an Aristotelian concern with discovering available means of persuasion for the given case. Such theory proceeded on the assumption of common ground between speaker and audience, which would provide optimum commitment to consensus forged through public deliberation. Rhetoric was conceptualized as a method for crafting public speeches to persuade audiences about the best means for achieving culturally shared ends. As such, most twentieth-century thinking reflects an instrumental understanding of rhetoric — the effective use of language (Duhamel 1949).

The differences between the Greek experience and those of contemporary Western industrial societies is too well documented to require discussion here. Suffice it to say that as part of the critique of contemporary society, scholars of diverse persuasion have recovered the ancient Greek insight that speech is basic to the human condition (Arendt 1958, 1977; Gadamer 1975; Habermas 1979). Speech is joined to action in the public realm as necessary for politics. Thus, with the death of viable public rhetoric (people no longer give speeches, rhetoric is no longer practiced artfully, mass media has usurped the role of the rhetor), contemporary societies begin to experience political crises.

Theoretically, the action perspective stands between two foci already outlined. It views the extension of rhetoric to include all symbolic acts as undermining rhetoric's status as an art. If everything human is rhetorical and rhetoric becomes the fundament of everything else, then there is no basis for setting artful talk apart from mere talk. For reasons that will become apparent momentarily, the action perspective views the loss of this distinction as consequential. The other extreme is to deal with rhetoric in terms of an ideal that creates a hypostatized view of speech with no bearing on the real world. The action perspective, instead, considers public rhetoric to be in a moribund state and devotes itself to the study of public discourse as it fails today. The consequence of mass industrialized society is not just that we have lost the art of rhetoric. This position maintains that when you lose the art of rhetoric, you lose the possibilities for cultural cohesion and coherence.

It would be a mistake to interpret as nostalgic these observations on the relationship of an artful public rhetoric to culture. A rhetorician's obvious appreciation of well-crafted public statements is not the animus here, nor is there any attempt to lament. The observation is intended to be descriptive within a framework that conceives of rhetoric as a public act dealing with the practical exigencies of life and capable of artful performance. This framework opens an entire area of research into the normative deviations of actual communication practices. This newly emerging aspect of rhetorical studies thus provides critique of how public communication leads a mass to provide the endorsements necessary for institutional authorities and special interests to maintain power and impose their will.

Cast in a different fashion, speech joined with action in the public realm is seen here as a fusion of theory with praxis resulting in the creation of interests. Interests are not theoretically determined and superimposed upon concrete situations; they evolve through the experiences of a lifetime of speaking and acting before strangers. This perspective rejects the objectivist stance, which places the knower outside the realm of descriptive facts and regards facts to be meaningful in and of themselves. Instead, facts have no meaning, holds this view, except as they are experienced and the reality of those meanings can be affirmed only when they are witnessed as real in the public realm. Hence, through the public performance of words and deeds, theory and praxis are fused in human interests. The most basic of these interests is open communication, since all substantive interests are dependent upon communication in the public realm. As words and deeds are publicly enacted without restraints, citizens experience freedom to discover their interests. As restraints are imposed, interests become distorted.

The benchmarks of distortion have yet to be clearly formulated. Among the positions advanced are McGee's theory of ideographs (1980) and of "the people" (1975); Cooper's adaptations of Foucaultian enunciative modalities (1981, 1982); Farrell and Goodnight's adaptation of Habermas to delineate rhetorical crises features (1981); and Hauser and Blair's theory of a rhetorically based public (1982). Taken collectively, however, some common assumptions appear to be emerging. Among these are:

● Mass societies tend to treat audiences as passive; they are asked to purchase and applaud. Publics, on the other hand, have the potential to be active; they are asked their opinions.
● The power of speech and action to effect change is in direct proportion to the diversity and activity of the public.
● Consciousness of potential for collective action with strangers (an active public) is contingent upon space for appearance before strangers (a public realm).

- Access to political problems requires commonsense language.
- Reality can be known only in the public realm.

As these propositions suggest, by focusing on the publicness of rhetoric, this ancient art has been transformed into a normative condition fundamental to public life, to freedom, and to the apprehension of reality.

Emphasis upon the publicness of rhetorical communication thus becomes a theoretically pivotal point. For example, in terms of the last assumption — reality can be known only in the public realm — the relationship between public appearance and reality is used to analyze several dimensions of communication. First, it creates a dialectical tension with privacy and leads the research-er to thematize communication patterns that encourage false consciousness or are manifestly deceptive or duplicitous. Such distortions are likely to occur when insights and intuitions husbanded and sheltered in some private domain are proclaimed as realities or when some philosophy of totality is imposed on experience. Second, this relationship suggests the importance of witnesses: Human realities require competent observers and judges of words uttered and deeds performed in a common realm to certify their worth. This perspective thus leads the analyst to investigate the diversity of those who receive messages as well as the range of messages available to them as witnesses. It also seeks signs of overt responses as indications of reality as it is understood in the public realm. Still further, the public ap-pearance/reality connection suggests the significance of a public realm: Humans require a common space where they can meet to-gether if they are to discover their common world. The re-searcher is thus guided to concerns of access to information, access to media, opportunities for open exchanges of ideas and emotions, restraining forces of institutional or special interest distortions, and like concerns that will define the level and quality of communication in the public sphere.

These extensions of the public appearance/reality assumption have analogous extensions in the other assumptions. They serve to illustrate the potential contributions that may emerge from theoretical and critical work that focuses upon the cluster of concerns gathered about the publicness of rhetorical communi-cation. Such study is about the union of theory and praxis in the words and deeds creating a presentational reality (Hauser and Blair 1982). In important ways, criticism of the rhetoric that passes through the public sphere is an exploration of the human condition.

This vein of contemporary rhetorical studies has begun to join the ranks of interpretive social science as a critical study directed at the explication and assessment of social will formation (Gronbeck 1981). Its researches draw heavily on the hermeneutic tradition of phenomenology (Arnold 1968; Grassi 1976); on the neo-Marxist critical theory of the Frankfurt school, especially as articulated by Habermas (Farrell and Goodnight 1981; McGee 1975); and on the poststructuralist analysis of deconstructivists, especially Foucault's (1972) archaeological method (Cooper 1981, 1982). Each of these approaches considers social will to be constructed by disclosure, which is public, intersubjective, and open to interpretation.

Thus, whereas the traditional understanding of rhetoric encouraged the critic to assess effects in terms of rhetor intents, this conceptualization takes the discourse to possess a life of its own, quite apart from rhetor intentions (McGee 1980), as a presentation that inhabits the common discursive space of the public realm (Hauser and Blair 1982). If there is a fusion of theory and praxis, it occurs in the experiencing of public rhetoric understood in this way.

CONCLUSION

For the first half of the twentieth century, the study of rhetoric was largely historical. Theoretical research focused on the interpretation of significant texts, such as Aristotle's Rhetoric, Cicero's De Oratore, Thomas Wilson's Arte of Rhetorike, or Hugh Blair's Lectures on Rhetoric and Belles Lettres. Critical studies, under the influence of Thonssen and Baird (1948), studied historically significant speeches, like Edmund Burke's "Address to the Electors at Bristol," or significant debates, like Webster and Hayne on "Foote's Resolution," or the rhetorical habits of great orators, like Charles James Fox.

Since the middle of the 1960s the study of rhetoric has been dramatically altered. The assimilation of Kenneth Burke's writings into the mainstream of research and graduate education and the appearance of the journal Philosophy and Rhetoric catapulted rhetorical studies into deeper and broader conceptual vistas. The research of the 1980s shows these twin seeds of intellectual foment now coming to fruition.

Rhetoric is not a cumulative subject, in the sense that it develops new forms of appeals or new devices of language based upon prior research into the uses of symbols. It is not a study that invents or accumulates material truths so much as it provides a stance for uncovering and understanding the content created by human symbolic inducements. The scholarly work in the field is, therefore, appropriately critical in its posture toward communication transactions and philosophical in its commentaries on the significance of rhetoric for human and humane existence.

The three perspectives reviewed in this chapter provide a representative illustration of the contemporary rhetorical posture. Each provides a stance toward human symbolic behavior that affords a view of the way in which knowledge is formed and held, how meanings are formed, how social will is established and modified, how actions are induced, and how the human condition is experienced and understood. As a field, contemporary rhetoric is concerned with the practical necessities of framing public messages, with the interpretive necessities of evaluating the symbolic management of meaning and action, with the philosophical necessities of grounding human conduct and the humanly alterable aspects of the world in the suasory potential of symbolic forming. As such, rhetorical studies are meaningful, and even essential, to the valuative study of the human race.

PART II

EMERGING ISSUES AND DEBATES IN THE SOCIAL SCIENCES TRADITION

8
INTRODUCTION
B. Aubrey Fisher

Throughout history the study of communication, it seems, always has been "in transition." Change and debate have dominated every decade of the twentieth century. The early decades witnessed a debate over disciplinary boundaries of communication and led to the information of professional associations of journalism and speech educators who broke away from teachers of English. The 1930s inaugurated a methodological debate between advocates of critical methods and quantitative researchers. In the 1940s the debate between practitioners and educators developed, to be followed by the 1950s emphasis on the persuasive impact of communication, particularly the subliminal or hidden persuaders of the mass media. During the 1960s the emphasis on source control gave way to the receiver-centered view of communication that focused on the semantic capacity of the perceiving individual. The New Orleans Conference advocated a greater emphasis over message variables during the decade of the 1970s. Residues of these debates remain in the 1980s, but new debates have emerged to maintain the "in transitional" nature of communication study. Nothing seems so constant as the process of change.

Even a cursory review of the chapters that follow will reveal minimal agreement among the authors as to what communication is, let alone how one goes about understanding it. Taken as a whole, these chapters provide the issues for the debates characterizing the decade of communication research in the 1980s. Further, these chapters reflect issues that dominate scholarly argument in the whole of communication study and, to some extent, the whole of the social sciences. This volume will settle none of these issues, of course — that is not its intention — but it does reflect the current state of transition that will be followed, no doubt, by yet another transition during the next decade.

THE ONTOLOGICAL ISSUE

Fundamental to a significant portion of the emerging debates in the social scientific inquiry into communication is the ontological controversy over the phenomenal nature of communication. Of course, one cannot divorce the ontological identity of communication from epistemological considerations of how we come to know about the phenomenon. Hanson (1958) long ago illustrated the impossibility of separating observation from interpretation. That is, one does not just _see_ communication; one sees it _as_ something or other. But most of the epistemological and methodological controversies in communication proceed from different outlooks on the ontological nature of communicative phenomena.

A superb illustration of this ontological difference is apparent when comparing the chapters contributed by Hawes and Poole. To Hawes communication is improvisational linguistic activity interpretable as "text." He specifically denies the separation of language from objective referents, thereby requiring some semantic interpretation internalized within the language user. Rather, Hawes finds the subject/object tension within the text of the language-in-use, that is, "a variable production in the turning of speech/language." The structural aspects of communication, then, are within the text of language in use. Communicational structure is thus, by definition, infrastructure and discoverable within the stream of human discourse.

Poole sees communication as activities that constrain and reflect the internalized choices/judgments made by the user. The structure of communication, then, is a suprastructure to be found in the relationship of language in use with the semantic creations of psychological selves. Given Poole's notion of structure, one can easily understand Poole's interpretation that the "Interact System Model (ISM)" of Fisher and Hawes (1971) is "deterministic" in that some situational factors must have accounted for the structure found in the interaction. Of course, the ISM is also interpretable as an infrastructure of the activities associated only with other activities without any deterministic assumption of some implied suprastructural constraint. As one of the authors of the ISM, I must admit to having been more than a little surprised to see it represented as a deterministic model.

Similar to the ontological difference exhibited in Hawes's and Poole's chapters are the different views of mass media found in the Lindlof-Traudt and Christenson chapters. Lindlof and Traudt, specifically in their referencing of the ethnological research of Lull, see television viewing as a series of situated events interpretable in terms of their infrastructural properties such as indexicality or regularities of occurrence. Christenson, however, sees television (and other mass media) in its association with the viewer's semantic interpretation. Thus, the mass media become environmental resources for learning by the perceiving users.

THE EPISTEMOLOGICAL ISSUE

The ontological differences of these authors lead to an epistemological controversy as to the explanatory model used to understand or acquire knowledge about communicative phenomena. At the risk of oversimplifying an extremely complex issue, one might phrase the central epistemological issue as what the various authors implicitly assume to be the nature of explanation. The following chapters are almost evenly divided between advocates of explanation as interpretation and explanation as prediction. Hawes visualizes communication inquiry as the interpretation of the dialectical tensions within the improvised text of language-in-use. O'Donnell-Trujillo and Pacanowsky view organizational communication as an art form subject to "art-like" interpretation, even in the form of writing fiction. Putnam and Cheney advocate a pluralistic approach to communication but appear to place more emphasis on the interpretive paradigms of historical-hermeneutic and critically oriented inquiries. Lindlof and Traudt advocate their approach to "media-in-use" by families whose viewing habits are interpretable within the range of their ongoing activities.

The remaining authors appear to assume a predictive model of explanation. To Rawlins communication is an attempt to influence others to accept one's presentation of self. The actual communicative act, then, may be an accurate or inaccurate semantic revelation of the "real" or private self of the communicator. To Gouran and Hirokawa group communication is a study of the influences on the members' decisionmaking judgment. To Poole communication is a constraining antecedent influence on the choices made by individuals. Christenson sees the inquiry into media effects as a problem of training receivers (while they are children) to view television and then ascertain their social learning residual to media consumption.

The difference in how these authors view the nature of explanation leads them to two fundamentally different explanatory models. The predictive assumption of explanation leads to the traditional prospective explanatory model. Within such a model the presence of certain specifiable antecedent conditions implies the existence of some specified consequent condition in the traditional "if-then" logic of prospective explanation. If the antecedent condition is known to exist, then one can infer (that is, predict) the existence of the consequent condition. The interpretive implication of explanation, on the other hand, leads to a retrospective model of explanation. Retrospection is an exercise in sense making, that is, making sense out of or interpreting the connections among sequences of events after they have occurred. Whereas prediction suggests past constraints upon present events, sense making suggests that present interpretation finds order in events of the past. The predictive model is based on constraints; the retrospective model is based on reflexivity.

EMERGING DEBATES OF THE 1980s

In some respects the current debates among communication scholars in the social scientific tradition are unique. During previous decades the controversies have focused on subcultural differences in the scientific community (for example, "scientists" versus "humanists") or on intraparadigmatic issues (for example, source-centered versus receiver-centered versus message-centered emphases). The contemporary debates seem more closely aligned to conflict between advocates of differing paradigms. (The term "paradigm" appears here in a very loose usage of the term. Most scholars will agree that, according to Kuhn's [1970] standards, communication is a "preparadigmatic" discipline. But most will also argue that the status of being preparadigmatic is neither deprecatory nor significant). For the first time the traditional social scientific stance of psychomechanism is subject to direct challenge.

The Nature of Self

The traditional social scientific view of the human being is that of a _rational_ self. The view, borrowed largely from psychological researchers, considers attempts to account for human action as the outcome of or logical response to some cognition or perception or belief or value or norm or multivariate combination of internalized motivating influences. The goal of scientific explanation is, thus, to identify those crucial perceptions or cognitions that serve as the enabling variables for (if not determinants of) human action and thereby "account for" that action. Such inquiry must necessarily rely on some observational technique for gathering data concerning psychological disclosure, some manner of inferring what is going on "inside the heads" of communicators.

An alternative to the traditional notion is to view the human as a _cultural_ self situated in social action. Such a view considers the self to be a social being in process, constituted from and by the ongoing experiences of social interaction, that is, communication. In this sense the process of communication accounts for itself reflexively in the history (past/present/future) of that interaction. Viewing the human being as a cultural self does not deny the characteristic of rationality as much as it questions the source of human rationality as some a priori psychological or internalized phenomenon. The rational aspect of self then emanates from the human who reflexively accounts for present action in past interaction and vice versa.

Rawlins is the sole author, of those chapters that follow in this section, to address explicitly the nature of self as central to understanding communication. To Rawlins the communicator's self is highly rational in that the communicator carefully considers "the exigencies of the moment and the needs of the other person . . . in light of an individual's purpose before communication is attempted." Rawlins thus provides the most traditional treatment of the thinking/feeling psychological self who uses behavior, as consciously as possible, to conceal or disclose that self to the other. Behavior thereby becomes defined as an extension of this psychological self into the social arena, but the explanation of communication resides within the communicator's intrapersonal self.

Hawes has established himself as a principal advocate of the alternative view of self (see, for example, Hawes 1977). His communicator acts improvisationally during communication with another and reflexively makes sense of the discourse. Lindlof and Traudt's television-viewing families create rules for their interaction during their interaction, and mediated communication is part of the event-phenomena that constitute their interactions. Along with Putnam and Cheney's historical-hermeneutic and critically oriented inquiry into organizations, O'Donnell-Trujillo and Pacanowsky's art-like view of organizational realities represents the remainder of the authors whose chapters espouse the alternative view of the cultural self. They stand in juxtaposition with the more traditional social scientific view of self represented in the other chapters.

The Nature of Explanation

Generations of students of courses in social scientific theory have been taught the sacred triumvirate, borrowed from the natural sciences, of such theory: explanation, prediction, and control. The key to "scientific" explanation has been assumed to be the ability to make accurate predictions of unknown events after controlling for extraneous or extratheoretic influences on the outcomes. Divorced from the context of explanation has been description (often called "mere description") in that it was assumed not to provide any predictive capacity to anticipate future events. Whereas description has always been considered useful to scientific explanation, it has generally been considered only as a prelude to "real" scientific research that tested predictions in the form of hypotheses. I once served as the referee of a manuscript submitted for journal publication in which the author(s) recognized inherent flaws in the inquiry but argued that normal standards for inquiry did not apply because the observation was "only descriptive."

The growing popularity of naturalistic methods in communication research has given credibility to the attitude that description, leading to knowledge claims, is itself a reasonable and reputable approach to scientific explanation. Phillipsen (1977) advocated such a descriptive purpose in nonlinear research designs, as opposed to the linearity of predictive explanation, as "an indispensable resource in the work of developing an empirically grounded understanding of communication" (p. 50). However, the research methods (for example, ethnology, hermeneutics, phenomenology, discourse analysis) commonly located under the rubrics of "naturalistic inquiry" or "interpretive approaches" are not the only applications of explanation as description. The massive literature on group development (see, for example, Poole 1981) is typically descriptive rather than predictive in its explanatory framework. Much of the literature on relationship development (see, for example, Fisher and Drecksel 1983) is also descriptive.

If the goal of inquiry in any social scientific field is increased understanding and a greater variety of claims to knowledge of the phenomena, then one should find reasonable the claim that description is as likely to meet the goal as is prediction. Of course, the nature of the understanding will differ on the basis of which explanatory model the investigator selects. In terms of practical advice, the predictive model is more precise as to which behaviors ought to be enacted in order to secure the desired goal, whereas the descriptive model is more apt to advocate ongoing adaptive behaviors to communicative situations as their configurations change. Either model is, of course, highly desirable on its own merits. The only unusual characteristic of the two models is that the traditionally unquestioned goal of science as prediction has now been challenged as the sole goal of scientific explanation.

The Nature of Data

Every beginning student of communication learns quickly of Charles Morris's (1946) tripartite division of semiotics into syntactics, semantics, and pragmatics. These categories also serve as a convenient mode of distinguishing another controversial issue in the social scientific study of communication: "What counts as data in communication inquiry?" The study of any phenomenon, including communication, comprises a series of observational transformations and leads to generalizable knowledge claims of succeeding levels of abstraction. The initial transformation in the enterprise of gaining understanding/knowledge is at the level of direct observation — transforming the phenomenal event of communication into data. Data, then, may include structures (syntactics), meanings (semantics), behaviors (pragmatics), or some combination of the three.

Perhaps the simplest manner of identifying data and researchers' differences in what constitutes data is to focus, for the moment, on structures. Explanation requires more than transforming concrete phenomena into data; it also entails finding connections among data, that is, accounting for one datum with another datum. In this way an observer explains communication by structuring the data in some way. Depending upon assumptions of how data are to be structured, the researcher looks for (and invariably finds) specified portions of the communicative phenomena and transforms them into the data of communication.

A recent issue of Human Communication Research (HCR) contains several research reports that illustrate different answers to the question of what counts as data in communication inquiry. Cody et al. (1983) and J. Bavelas (1983) begin with the assumption that perceived aspects of the situation influence communicative behavior and thus transform phenomena into data representing personal perceptions of the situation and intentions to behave. The emphasis is on the semantic aspects of communication such that the process of inquiry reported in either article did not need to include an actual communicative event. Subjects were given questionnaires, asked to imagine themselves in some specified hypothetical situation, and asked to indicate their specific dispositions to behave. Perceptual reactions and behavioral dispositions, both semantic aspects of communication, count as data in these studies. Actual communicative behaviors are unnecessary to the research purpose except as they would serve to confirm or disconfirm the dispositions.

Haslett (1983), reporting research in the same issue of HCR, recorded verbal interactions of preschool-age children and sought to discover how expressed language functions with the expressed language of others across sex and age differences. Haslett structures her data by focusing on the pragmatic aspects of communication and views behaviors as strategies adapted to other behaviors in the sequence of interaction. Data for Haslett are exhibited behaviors functionally structured with other behaviors. For Haslett, unlike the authors of the other two studies, data must include an actual occurrence of communication in order to provide the pragmatic behaviors to be transformed into data.

Naturally the issue of what counts as data is resolvable directly from the ontological/epistemological issues associated with the natures of self and explanation. Rawlins transforms communication, in purely semantic terms, into revelations (with a variable degree of truth) of the communicator's intrapersonal self. Behavior is not significant as behavior (that is, pragmatics) but is valuable only as an insight into the semantic interpretation of the communicator's psychological self. Of course, that semantic interpretation is always under the control of the communicator. Hawes, for example, transforms communication into a script and seeks the pragmatic infrastructures of sequential linguistic behaviors. Gouran and Hirokawa, along with Poole, transform communication into the structures that link behaviors with antecedent dispositional or judgmental choices to behave. At the level of mass communication, Lindlof and Traudt transform television viewing in terms of the family's ongoing regularity and recurrence of other routine behaviors, whereas Christenson seeks the outcomes of learning (semantics) that accrue from having viewed television. Data may be perceptual or behavioral and may involve structural links between perceptions and behaviors or between behaviors and other behaviors.

CONCLUSION

Cronkhite and Liska (1977), introducing a symposium on theoretical controversy in communication, indicated the "history of communication research, like the history of most sciences, is a history of the invention and destruction of myths" (p. 3). When one accepts all scientific knowledge claims as "mythical," then the continual controversies that characterize the history of communication research seem inevitable and quite healthy. The myths that seem to pervade the following chapters depict a clash between semantic myths and pragmatic myths of communication — psychologism versus phenomenalism. In Weick's (1979) terms, one fundamental controversy with far-ranging implications regarding the nature of explanation and of self and of data is that between "enthinkment" and "enactment." Is the process of communication improvisational or structurational, rules-based or effects based? The most obviously correct yet unsatisfying answer to such questions is an emphatic "yes." Advocates of one myth challenge the advocates of another myth; and members on all sides of the controversy advocate one form of mysticism over another.

One thing does become clear in the following chapters and in recent journals and convention programs. The community of communication scholars is developing a rich vocabulary of "god terms" and "devil terms." Nearly all the advocates will denigrate positivism or logical empiricism or determinism or covering laws. The object of rejection is identifiable with a variety of devil terms. Nearly all will praise the virtues of development or evolution or some time-based model of communication inquiry. Some scholars find fault with "science" as a presuppositional constraint on understanding and with "psychologism" as a black-box locus of internalized meanings. To others, these terms (at least conceptually) are more "god-like." Interaction (or, at least, activities) is highly favored. The controversies in communication, then include a certain basis of commonality even though misunderstanding and misconstructions of the other's position dominate these intellectual debates.

One wonders about the future of communication research when the alleged experts in the field cannot agree on even the most fundamental epistemological and ontological issues. Perhaps, as Christenson notes, communication is a "magpie science" feasting on the discarded remains of other sciences. Perhaps society would not be a whit poorer if we threw out all the communication research literature to date. Perhaps controversy over fundamental issues is symptomatic of a healthy and maturing discipline. Perhaps debate and controversy are to be expected in any social science as part of the normal process of inquiry.

Crable (1982) would probably agree with the latter assessment when he writes: "Knowledge-as-status is conferred — and altered — through socially and academically argumentative processes" (p. 262). "A science becomes decadent," according to Cronkhite and Liska (1977), "when it takes its own explanations too seriously and turns in pathological fascination to examine and worship its own intellectual droppings" (p. 3). In the midst of wondering about the resolution of the current debates in communication research, we can all rest assured that, at the very least, communication is apparently not a decadent science.

9
INFORMATION/COMMUNICATION: ADDRESSING THE POWER OF AN UNBALANCED INFRASTRUTURE

Leonard C. Hawes

Conventional wisdom has it that information is the currency of postmodern global economics (Boraiko 1982; Ernst 1982). Certainly information theory and technology, as discursive practices, are inscribed quite densely into the natural and social sciences (for example, Wooldridge 1963; Moles 1966; MacKay 1969; J. Miller 1976). Post-World War II communication research is such a transmuted discourse; its roots are the rhetorics of classical Greece and Rome. Rhetoric was about the affairs of daily living; the study of rhetoric and its methods developed from concerns about the rational conduct of domestic, commercial, and legal matters. Free men, responsible citizens of city-states, aspired to be effective rhetoricians. Aristotle's Rhetoric can be read as a rhetorical psychology; human beings, whose practical actions are motivated by and explained in psychological terms, are influenced by rhetorical techniques. To be an ethical citizen as rhetorician, one had to understand the motivations of one's audiences (Zeller 1955, pp. 95-206).

Rhetorical studies, from the classical to the more contemporary, have positioned the human being, as both subject and object, at their centers. Rhetorical speech is assumed to be purposive and rational; these two properties are brought to language in speech by psychologically motivated interlocutors (that is, speaker/listener). Consequently, prior to the elaboration

John D. Peters and Michelle Egan provided invaluable discussion and criticism prior to as well as during the writing of portions of this manuscript.

of information theory and technology, our understandings of the relationships between speech and language on the one hand and human as subject and object on the other were largely psychological understandings.

The discourse of information theory, primarily Hartley's (1928), Shannon's (1948), and Cherry's (1957), became credited. Communication studies differed from rhetorical studies along several seams information theory provided, the most salient of which is methodological. Rhetorical methods remained critical and historical, whereas communication methods became quantitativee and probabilistic. Nevertheless, the primitive communication model, although elaborated in the discourse of information theory, differed little in structure from rhetorical models; a speaker addresses an audience with an intended purpose and with varying degrees of success. Language became conflated with code; rhetor and audience became sender and receiver; speech became message; interpretation became encoding and decoding; meaning became information; misunderstanding became distortion and noise; effectiveness concerns became efficiency concerns; literacy became numeracy (Singh 1966).

In what follows I argue for a rebalancing of the information/communication dialectic; the first step is to excommunicate both terms from the subsequent discussion. Both pair-terms have occupied central positions in most prior discourses; both are assumed in rather than the focus of study. I intend to thematize both terms — communication and information — by not assuming them but by interrogating them from different perspectives.

The subjective/objective nature of psychological identity as opposed to semiotic identity is discussed in order to see the speech/language dialectic as a universe of signifiers. The multiple levels of signifying chains move and elaborate themselves metonymically and metaphorically. Metonymic movement is the local articulation of difference from identity. Metaphoric movement is the distant articulation of identity from difference. Such movement produces the turning structures of conversing, the animating of which is an interplay of improvising and modulating, both of which are possible through the media of faith and history. Playing as opposed to working is discussed in terms of the turning structures of conversing. With these preliminary steps taken, I then discuss the ideological implications of improvising as the appropriation of power; the power to insinuate. Such power is experienced narratively such that interpersonal action, produced as text articulated in context, is the material infrastructure of cultural value and power arrangements (that is, ideologies).

SUBJECT/OBJECT

Perhaps the most obvious production of contemporary rhetorical and communication theory and practice, and thereby the most stubborn in yielding to critical appreciation, is the psychological subject. Such a subject has motivations, values, attitudes, beliefs, thoughts, and feelings, all organized into cognitive structures, located within the body and formulated as the generative mechanisms of discourse's production. Such a conception of subject produces finely detailed psychological characterizations of the subject/object; it produces much more granular understandings of speech/language. As Grossberg (1979) notes, however, man exists partially in nature and partially in consciousness. John Peters (1982b, p. 5) elaborates:

By objective I mean those phenomena which exist independently of consciousness; an objective phenomenon (a frog, a tree, a stone, an atom) exists in and of itself. By subjective, on the other hand, I mean those phenomena which require a mediating consciousness to come to life; as Jacques Lacan puts it, "every phenomenon of meaning implies a subject": hence phenomena of meaning are subjective.

Contempory semiotics problematizes the subject and produces several alternatives to the psychological subject (Barthes 1967). Husserl (1970) wanted to found arithmetic and logic on a theory of the subject as sign rather than on a theory of subject as psychology. For Husserl, logic became a system of formal relationships between signs. The experience of subjectivity as consciousness became the transparency of unitary expressive signs; that is, signs with sense but no reference. Indicative signs, on the other hand, both express and refer. The sign, for Husserl, then, is the ideal unity of speech and meaning.

As contemporary exemplars of such a model of the subject, consider the centrality of competence in Chomsky's (1965) linguistics, in Hymes's (1974) sociolinguistics, in Habermas's (1979) critical theory, in Cicourel's (1974) ethnomethodology, and in Grice's (1975) natural language analytics. Each presupposes that experience is given directly and immediately to subject. Chomsky presupposes a priori categories of experience; Hymes conceives of communicative competence more in terms of non-grammatical performance features; Habermas posits a universal pragmatics; Cicourel formulates "interpretive procedures" for the competent subject, as does Grice in his work on conversational implicatures. Each of these models also locates the subject at their respective centers.

Ricoeur's (1976) tack is somewhat different; meaningful action is conceived as a text, but the subject is a situated sign that is a sententially structured proposition. Subject is understandable and meaningful to others as proposition or sentence rather than as sign. Furthermore, the meaning of such situated propositions is intersubjective; for Ricoeur, the argument favoring a shift from sign to proposition is that signs refer only to other signs of the semiotic system whereas with propositions, language "is directed beyond itself" (Ricoeur 1976, p. 20). For Ricoeur, as for Jakobson (1962), communication can be modeled without formal or informal reliance on linguistics.

Lacan (1977) and Derrida (1973), rather than treat subject as ideal or situated sign or as sententially structured proposition, formulate subject as text. Analytic interest is in the message; furthermore, the message is presumed to evidence its own foundations without reference to sender and receiver. Messages, as texts, disclose an infinite variety of signifying chains with no material positioning of subject. Such textualization of subject and subjectivity deconstructs sender, receiver, and message. A code, as language, is a description of material relationships articulated and positioned within signifying chains that become, themselves, interlocuted as discourses. Subject comes to be positioned variously throughout interconnected semiotic systems. Thus, according to Coward and Ellis (1977), modeling the subject as text lays the groundwork for a material theory of subject evidenced in materially given signifying practices.

Subject/object is decentered as the sign constantly at the center of speech/language. For cybernetic epistemology (Bateson 1972, pp. 448-66), as the foundation for information theory and technology, language is a resource for producing and controlling messages and their effects (Ashby 1956; Crosson and Sayre 1967). For semiotic epistemology, language is a universe of signifiers moving metonymically and metaphorically, contexturing as discourses; that is, as chains of signifying practices (Barthes 1967). Subject/object is no longer the constant generative mechanism in the worlds of meaning; rather, subject/object becomes a variable in the turning of speech/language. The next section elaborates that understanding.

SPEECH/LANGUAGE

Speech/language is a universe of signifiers turning metonymically and metaphorically, contexturing as discourse. Universe, here, intends space and time. Importantly, however, the spatiotemporal dimensions are given neither a priori nor are they fixed; such a universe articulates itself as its limits of possibility. It marks space in time, thereby producing historical understandings.

Signs are articulations; they are identities marked by differences. For Saussure (1974), a sign is Janus-faced; it is the union of signifier and signified. Barthes (1967, p. 39) says:

> Since Saussure, the theory of the linguistic sign has been enriched by the <u>double articulation</u> principle, the importance of which has been shown by Martinet, to the extent that he made it the criterion which defines language. For among linguistic signs, we must distinguish between the <u>significant units,</u> each one of which is endowed with one meaning (the "words," or to be exact, the "monemes") and which form the first articulation, and the <u>distinctive units,</u> which are part of the form but do not have a direct meaning (the "sounds," or rather the "phonemes"), and which constitute the second articulation.

<u>Signification,</u> however, is not simply a uniting of unilateral entities; that is, a uniting of signifier and signified, inasmuch as signifier and signified are at once term and relation. For Lacan (1968), the signifier is global and made up of a multileveled chain. Each level of this chain is metonymic. Taken on its multiple levels, however, the chain is metaphoric. Signifier and signified "have only a floating relationship and coincide only at certain anchorage points" (Barthes 1967, p. 49). A universe of such multileveled chains of signs is, thereby, a signifying universe. Signifying is an intransitive action whereas, say, representing is a transitive action. Signs articulate themselves intransitively in the dialectical turning of metonymy and metaphor.

METONYMY/METAPHOR

The most primordial movement of a universe of signs is the dialectical turning of metonymy and metaphor. <u>Metonymic movement</u> articulates difference in identity; it produces two-from-one. Simple cell division is a fitting analogue for such movement. Signs signify metonymically. Those signs contiguous to one another signify one another; they are about one another. Signs, whose signifying associations are contiguous and continuous, stand in spatial but atemporal relation to one another. Metonymic movement, then, is a timeless drifting of contiguously local configurings of signs. Localized significations and primitive spatial (that is, mnemonic) memory is possible inasmuch as metonymy is locally articulated. Of necessity, then, metonymizing elaborates a text from within itself.

<u>Metaphoric movement</u> consists of a juxtaposing of signs from different universes. Peters (1982a) elaborates several en-

tailments. Metaphor moves in a logic of discontinuity. Whereas metonymy moves sequentially, metaphor moves in surges and discontiguous leaps. Jakobson (1971) specifies this logic of movement from the principle of similarity underlying metaphor. Jameson (1980, pp. 80-81) argues that the power of a metaphor is strengthened proportionally as the contexts being inmixed differ from one another.

Given that likeness depends on difference, metaphor's ground is metonymy (Peters 1982a, p. 6). The movement of metaphor evolves from contexts of developing metonymies. The structure of such movement ensures the instability of metaphor; it is built on the negation of similarity and is marked in time. As a temporal production, the metaphor dissolves in metonymic drifting. Metaphorical movement suppresses differences only to have metonymic movement dissolve the similarities; the differences evidence themselves again in different forms. "Because of metaphor's unique ability to produce an identity — a new, momentarily self-sufficient world of meaning — by controlling the flow of negation into the liberal, it becomes a dialectical structure par excellence (Peters 1982a, p. 9). The apparent similarity in difference is appropriated as the differences are suppressed until that suppression is negated in the metonymic movement of temporality/atemporality.

CONVERSING/TURNING

Conversing is spoken discourse produced in and by the turning of metonymic and metaphoric signifying practices. From an information theory/practice vantage point, a speaker takes a turn at producing conversation. From a semiotic vantage point, turning is the dialectical movement of texts. As indexical movement, metonymy is not subject-referential by nature; as reflexive movement, metaphor is subject-referential by nature. The turning of metonymy and metaphor is a semiotic change of consciousness. Conversing is punctuated not only by speakership but also by discursive structure.

As conversing approximates metonymic movement it is decreasingly capable of reflexivity and subject-referentiality. Subject can be only another signifier moving in continuously articulated contexts of signifiers. Signifying movement perpetuates itself in the production of its own possibility. In metonymic movement, possibility is reduced to spatiality and such movement is developmental rather than evolutionary. Metonymy lacks the capability of decentering space to produce the possibility of time; consequently, relevance is parochial and memory/history is spatial.

As conversing approximates metaphoric movement it is increasingly capable of reflexivity and subject-referentiality. Signifiers from one metonymic context are appropriated by and inscribed into another, now similar but not identical, context. Identity is produced from difference, but the identity is not isomorphic. Identity first appears as analogue evidenced at the limits of signifying possibilities. For example, the elaboration of information theory and technology is metonymic development in the engineering sciences but is metaphoric evolution for rhetoric and communication. Metaphoric movement is generated from inarticulateness; analogues, thus, are seams of articulability.

In the production of differences, contexts of signifiers, as texts, recontextualize by appropriating texts as analogues. In metaphor's appropriating movement, one discourse comes to be inscribed in another, articulating new possibilities, thereby elaborating the now transmuted discourse along analogous seams. I propose the analogue of improvising as a way of understanding the dialectical movements of metonymy/metaphor.

IMPROVISING/MODULATING

Ramos (1974, p. 1) has fashioned an analogue of music for speech in terms of improvisation and modulation:

> I will view conversants as improvisors, conversations as extemporaneous compositions, and topic changes within a conversation as modulations. Thus, I suggest that conversations can be seen as extemporaneous compositions analogous to the compositions produced by musicians when they improvise jazz, a contemporary form of improvisation, and that the process conversants use to make topic changes within a conversation can be seen as being analogous to the modulation process musical composers use to make key changes within a musical composition.

Ramos is concerned with the methods by which conversing's production is inscribed in the practical affairs of everyday living.

The Harvard Dictionary of Music (1969, p. 404) defines improvisation as "the art of performing music spontaneously, without the aid of manuscript, sketches, or memory." This does not imply, however, that it is done with no training or prior mastery of technique. Improvising is the art of extemporaneous composition, but it presupposes highly sophisticated skills. As Evans (n.d.) notes, improvising dissolves the possibility of erasing/correcting mistakes. Consequently, the improvising player, quite literally, must know what he or she is about. According to Coker (1964), knowing what you are doing if you are improvising jazz entails knowing the general framework of the base of the piece, including the length, the thematic and harmonic structure, the length of the different movements of the tune, whether there are modulations to other keys, the chord progression, and the emotional quality or mood of the tune. Ramos (1974, p. 9) summarizes: "The jazz musician, then, develops harmonic, rhythmic, and thematic strategies to weave into an ongoing process the motif or idea he is going to express."

For a textually produced subject, the utterance, "I know what I want to have said by the time I finish talking to you," evidences these principles of improvising. When I begin to speak I know what I am doing, where I am going, and how to get there in general structural terms. But I can, on the base of my communicative experience, fill in, elaborate, punctuate, accentuate, and temporarily re-form the extemporaneous composition in the process of production. I do not know all the production requirements before I begin, but because I know generally what I am doing and where I am going I can detail it as I am composing it.

The analogue of musical/conversational improvising is as follows. When people gather and talk, they have a more or less clear sense of how to talk to one another as well as what will be appropriate possibilities for topics (that is, the assumption of foundational competence). When musicians gather and play they have a more or less clear sense of the thematic and harmonic structures founding their improvising. Conversing subjects, like playing musicians, know when talking is in and out of tune and when the course of talking needs a turn. Like a musical composition, a conversation can be structurally complete insofar as it has a beginning, middle, and end, and at the same time can be part of a larger conversational composition. Finally, as with a musical production, a conversational production is part of past and future conversations; conversing, like playing music, is a demonstrating of traditional competences (that is, knowledge of the tradition and a level of skill for accessing and reforming traditional practices). Improvising music and talk, then, are hermeneutic compositions; history is re-membered and the future, as possibility, is adumbrated.

Modulation — the change from one key or tonality to another by means of a regular melodic or chord progression — has four functions: to intensify harmonic motion, to underscore change, to produce mood contrasts, and to emphasize structural divisions (Siegmeister 1965, p. 37). A smooth modulation is produced in four stages: a home key is established, a pivot chord is produced, a new key is entered, and that new key is established. Importantly for the proposed conversational analogue, the pivot chord belongs to both keys of the modulation and thereby bridges the two keys.

> The modulating phrases contain the melodic line of the composition and the melodic line generally consists of pivot notes which form part of the pivot chords. Thus, for the listener, everything that he hears is within the normal course of the old tonality until he discovers there has been a change of key. This discovery, if it occurs, generally comes after the new key is well established (Ramos 1974, pp. 13,14).

Ramos then proposes that keys in music are analogous to topics in conversation and that new topics are modulated smoothly through the production of pivot words, phrases, and clauses. This accounts for the adumbrative capabilities of utterances; they contain units of talk relevant to the established topic and at the same time are adumbrative of new but not yet established topics.

There is, however, a critical difference in the analogue. When improvising, a musician does not change keys privately; the other musicians know and expect the modulations. A conversing subject, however, frequently modulates without telling other conversants for the strategic purposes of concealing and revealing. "The conversant withholds information in much the same way a composer withholds certain aspects of the composition until it fits in with his ideal of what is to go on" (Ramos 1974, p. 15). The extemporaneous composing of conversing subjects strategically insinuates itself into the pragmatic affairs in a world apart from yet intimately connected with the conversation being composed. The turning movement of conversing's modulating is the material evidence of social pragmatics. Producing varying levels of intensity of motion, dramatic changes, mood contrasts, and structural divisions are vital signifying practices in the production of discourse.

FAITH/HISTORY

Conversing, as improvising, then, is neither predetermined performance nor happy accident; to improvise is to play at a level of skill beyond mere performance. Plan is discursive; its structure materializes temporally. As play, improvising relies as much on faith as on history; expectation and memory are the corresponding structures on the interpersonal level. Faith is foundational for improvising inasmuch as play simultaneously produces and presupposes possibility. Possibility, as that moment when absence makes itself evident in presence as opportunity, rests on the belief in absence. Such faith, however, does not materialize as opportunity until present action discloses itself as its possibilities. In this way, conversing presupposes faith in the possibility of understanding and in understanding's product —

rationality. That subject listens to a present utterance is material evidence of such faith inasmuch as listening is listening for possibility, without which there would be no reason to listen. When faith in conversing's presupposed promise of possibility is fraudulent, when one suspects conversing's play to be rigged, one loses faith in its play. The play is not legitimately improvisational if done in bad faith.

Faith also presupposes history; the past produces possibility as present actuality. Present possibility presupposes prior actuality. Faith in present action thereby produces the presupposition of temporality. Without faith, conversing — or any temporally articulated play — collapses in on itself. Temporality collapses and, with it, memory and opportunity. Catatonia is one clinical label for such evisceration of signifying.

INDEXICALITY/REFLEXIVITY

Conversing, as an improvising activity, is the turning of indexical metonymy and reflexive metaphor. Subject, as text, is articulated in the turning from metonymic to metaphoric consciousness. Subject is formulated reflexively as the generative locus of experience and meaning. The subject is the text in whose terms the sense of signifying practices is made. Subject is a temporarily stable and centered text for which other texts are significantly contextualized. Although modifiable through such appropriating, subject is not deconstructed.

Conversing's utterances articulate difference from identity. Simultaneously, of course, identity is the product of articulated difference. An utterance, thereby, produces the identity of subject and the difference of temporality; an historical subject/object is inscribed in space/time. Reflexive practices produce subject-reference; to be reflexive is to be subject-conscious; to be indexical is to lose the centeredness of subjectivity in the metonymic immediateness of play and its production of possibility. Reflexive practices, such as erasures and corrections, punctuate discourse by locating difference in identity.

Consider the play of basketball as an analogue for conversing's turning. In the discursive play of basketball, referees' practices are reflexive; so are those of the coaches. They halt the metonymic drifting of fluent discursive play, thereby articulating two modes of consciousness — time-in and time-out — by means of correcting and compensating, and a signifying relation is marked as a difference that makes a difference. Such practices formulate metaphor from metonymy; a present similarity is differentiated by indexing signs from different spatiotemporal texts. The referee's practices call consciousness from play to subject; attention is taken away from play and focused on subjects/objects. Such practices problematize the contemporaneity of metonymic significations and produce the presence of past and the possibility of future.

PLAYING/WORKING

One of the primal pleasures of play is the temporary suspension of self-consciousness, and with it conventional structures of reflexive spatiotemporality. In fact, to be self-conscious is to play less competently; it is to work at playing. To the extent corrections are needed, subject must be identified as object, thereby directing consciousness to subjectivity as a metaphoric production and away from play as a metonymic production.

Reflexivity produces not only consciousness of subject but simultaneously consciousness of object and of activity. The intentionality of play's consciousness is the totality of activity and the deconstructed indexicality of subjectivity; subject is not experienced separately from action as object but rather as productive of and simultaneously produced by activity.

> Each form of play, if my view is correct, should contain within it a moment when possibility can be acutely felt by the player . . . . To the player, the game, if properly constructed, presents not so much a challenge — in the usual sense of the word — as an opportunity to experience possibility (Esposito 1974, p. 141).

Plessner (1970, p. 77) argues that "play is always playing with something that also plays with the player . . . . " Inasmuch as consciousness's intentionality is the individual player as subject/object as opposed to the possibilities of the entirety of play, the playing is distorted and neurotic; it is work, not play. Self-conscious reflexivity is what becomes evident in the place of metonymically produced possibility.

As play becomes conventionalized, as play becomes bounded by explicit rules defining consequences of play, play is transformed into game. Playing a game need not involve players other than self; in primordial game-playing the child plays against self. As games come to be transformed from conventional play into institutional play, games become sports. For sport, not only are the game's rules made explicit but also its history comes to be materially inscribed. As rules and history are explicated, sport, as work for the players, is insinuated into the domain of everyday, mundane existence.

Each movement of reflexivity — from the undifferentiated reality of Piaget's infant as __hommelette,__ to play, to game, to sport — is an articulating of actuality and possibility from identity. In their primal, undifferentiated state, actuality is infused with possibility. It is only later, developmentally, that a child separates playing from working, thereby producing the possibility of game and sport and of observing another's work as play — that is, as a fan or spectator. For gambling–playing, the sport becomes an object of a meta–game with rules and players of its own.

The common property of play, game, and sport, then, is the production of the experience of possibility. In each of its structures, the possibilities produced entail risk; however, as play is transformed into work, the risk of possibility becomes a risk to subject/object. The risk is to subject's identity; play is experienced less as the liberating of possibility and increasingly as consciousness of identity separate from play.

Improvising is characteristic of much, but certainly not all, social activity, whether that activity is experienced as play or work. The metonymic elaborating of turning's play is punctuated by its metaphoric inmixing in its own history. The discursive locations of such reflexive punctuation of indexicality are of interest. Any and all forms of play are more than pure improvising; reflection alters the intentionality of consciousness from the totalizing experience of play to the fragmentary experience of subject as separate from object, and play itself, for that matter. It is how and where such transitions of consciousness materialize that are of critical interest.

IMPROVISING/APPROPRIATING

For Greenblatt (1980, p. 60), improvisation is "the ability to both capitalize on the unforeseen and transform given materials into one's own scenario." Greenblatt's analysis of improvisation is helpful insofar as he emphasizes its relations to power. Thus far, I have considered improvisation as an element of play without considering the power of appropriation inherent in playing as improvising. "The 'spur of the moment' quality of improvisation is not as critical here as the opportunistic grasp of that which seems fixed and established" (Greenblatt 1980, p. 60). This opportunistic grasping presupposes the ability first to recognize possibility and then to appropriate that possibility as an opportunity to transform it into a homologous discursive structure. In the language of earlier sections, metaphoric movement is just such an opportunistic grasping of possibility.

From the metonymic elaboration of incremental differences within a discourse, metaphoric similarities between discourses are appropriated as opportunities for identity. Greenblatt uses the verb "to insinuate" for such appropriating of similarity from dif-

ference. Of sixteenth-century European imperialism he says:
"What is essential is the Europeans' ability again and again to
insinuate themselves into the preexisting political, religious, and
even psychic structures of the natives and to turn those structures to their advantage" (p. 60).

Greenblatt is clear that improvisation is not necessarily an
act of imaginative generosity; a sympathetic appreciation of the
situation of the other fellow. When I think of improvising in
music's discourse and I hear Oscar Peterson quote a phrase of
Duke Ellington's "Satin Doll," I hear Peterson's appreciation of
Ellington; I hear it as quote rather than as plagiarism (that is,
naked appropriation). Greenblatt (1980, p. 61) is examining the
other side of the phenomenon, the side on which improvising is
deception's resource:

> It [deception] depends first upon the ability and willing-
> ness to play a role, to transform oneself, if only briefly
> and with mental reservations, into another. This necessi-
> tates acceptance of disguise, the ability to effect a
> divorce, in Ascham's phrase, between the tongue and the
> heart. Such role playing in turn depends upon the trans-
> formation of another's reality into a manipulable fiction.

The key phrase here, for purposes of my argument, is
"manipulable fiction." Greenblatt (1980, p. 62) elaborates.

> If improvisation is made possible by the subversive percep-
> tion of another's truth as an ideological construct, that
> construct must at the same time be grasped in terms that
> bear a certain structural resemblance to one's own set of
> beliefs. An ideology that is perceived as entirely alien
> would permit no point of histrionic entry; it could be
> destroyed but not performed.

The perception of "a certain structural resemblance," that
perception of homology, is what I have been calling metaphoric
movement; it is perception of similarity across differences. Given
that the similarity is just that and is not isomorphism, the
emphasizing of similarity and the suppressing of difference is the
act of insinuating. To insinuate by improvising presupposes the
ability to read a prior truth as present ideology, fiction or
story. If a truth were apprehended as Truth rather than as one
more ideological narrative among the world's variety of ideological narratives, to improvise that discursive structure would be to
profane it, to treat it relatively rather than absolutely, to see it
as resemblance rather than reality.

At the level of interpersonal conversing rather than at the
level of institutional conversing, speaking is an opportunistic

grasping, of appropriating subjectivity. The concept of power, on the interpersonal level, is inherent in the turning of metonymic and metaphoric movement. The heuristic paradox is that to move metaphorically desacralizes the discourse appropriated as homological fiction and at the same time strengthens the discourse being insinuated. At the institutional level, by treating the truth of a culture as primitive ideological fiction, missionaries and governments strengthen their own imperialistic discourse as the more powerful, the more legitimate truth.

Greenblatt (1980, p. 63) calls improvising "a central Renaissance mode of behavior." He attributes its cultivation, in large part, to the characteristic forms of rhetorical education that emphasized two fundamental operations of improvisation: displacement and absorption. Displacement is "the process where a prior symbolic structure [that is, a discourse] is compelled to coexist with other centers of attention that do not necessarily conflict with the original structure but are not swept up in its gravitational pull" (p. 64). Absorption is "the process whereby a symbolic structure is taken into the ego so completely that it ceases to exist as an external phenomenon" (p. 64). What is displacement for Greenblatt is the metonymic marking of difference; absorption is metaphoric appropriation of homologous structure of a different discourse.

To the extent that the cornerstone of the classical humanist project was a rhetorical education (Jaeger 1939), and to the extent that such education rested on arguing persuasively for diametrically opposed positions, such education fostered a facility for fictionalizing, for transforming "a fixed symbolic structure into a flexible construct ripe for improvisational entry" (Greenblatt 1980, p. 69). Greenblatt calls this mode of consciousness a "submission to self-fashioning" (p. 69). To be persuasive, a Renaissance rhetor was to construct narratives into which others were inscribed. Conceiving of one's historical life as a story is a response to public inquiry; self-fashioning narratizing is the persuasive accounting of reasons and motives, hence, the intimate tie between rationality and narrativity as ethnoepistemology. The storyteller is constantly formulated as subject/object of the story. The paradox is that one can be persuasive only by becoming a tale of oneself, and hence by ceasing to be oneself" (p. 73). Lacan (1977, p. 106) makes a similar point in arguing that psychoanalysis "manipulates the poetic function of language," which becomes sometimes a lyric statement and sometimes a narrative account of origins and understandings. One's identity is a story and, of course, an identity fashioned as a story can be unfashioned and refashioned in different narrative formats. Thus, the more imaginatively the stories are improvised, the more possible identities there are for a rhetor.

The deceptive, appropriative character of the improvisational process depends upon concealing its center; for appropriation to work, the center of the appropriating discourse must be asserted implicitly to be the center of the structure being appropriated. The persuasive rhetor, having the talent for entering into the consciousness of another, perceives its deepest structures as a manipulable fiction and inscribes it in one's own narrative form. As such, improvisational success is a matter of concealment as much as of disclosure. This was Ramos's (1974) insight about interpersonal conversing; given larger practical concerns, conversing subjects conceal and disclose strategically.

NARRATIZING/EXPERIENCING

For Labov (1972, p. 360), a minimal narrative is "a sequence of two clauses which are temporally ordered." Rayfield (1972) adds that a story must have a minimal degree of complexity, the focus should be on a single character, and the incidents should logically flow one to the other. Specifying the nature of complexity and logical flow, of course, remains problematic in the study of conversationally produced stories. Labov does specify the following six elements of a story told in conversation (or, for Labov's work, in interviews):

abstract: a brief resumé of the completed action, used as an introduction
orientation: time, place, occasion, personnel involved
complicating action: the minimal narrative spun out
evaluation: markers by which the value orientation of the speaker is reminded
result: in terms of events
coda: the way out of the story and back into the conversation by way of generalization, later doings of characters involved, and so on (pp. 362-66).

Roger Abrahams (1977, p. 1) says of stories: "So much of our intense involvement with life we seem to find ourselves doing not so much for the experience itself but for the possibilities that kind of experience represents and — even more — because we know that if something significant comes of the involvement we can talk about it afterward." Victor Frankl (1959) makes a very similar argument for understanding how some Jewish prisoners survived the Nazi concentration camps and others, seemingly younger and physically stronger, did not. He claims that for those who experienced life and death in the camps as experiences for telling to others, survival chances were stronger than for those who did not. It is the "afterward" expectation, the faith that there is a future at which time the experience can be told as a story, that sustained the survivors. The possibility of telling the experience later as a story also provided the survivors with a narrative structure for the experience itself as it was being lived. The expectation of telling a story in the future shapes how the experience is experienced during the experiencing. Either because one believes there is no one to tell the experience to or, as profoundly, because one no longer believes in an afterward — a future — one ceases to experience narratively. Without the expectation of retelling experience, the experience has no point and the subject becomes lost from the meaning of experience.

Abrahams argues that stories are products of a culture's useful fictions — or what Greenblatt calls ideologies. It is these manipulable fictions that organize our experiences as particular kinds of experiences. The rationality of our experience inheres in the narrative structure giving it form. Telling stories formulates and positions the subject/object as central to the experience being told. In this sense, stories are metaphoric moments of conversational movement; a moment of self-conscious formulation of identity but simultaneously a moment when analogous but different discourse is inscribed into the metonymic development of conversation. Stories, as metaphoric movement, insinuate (that is, turn into and against) analogous structures to shape metonymic articulating. Stories are but one device of making retrospective sense of prior metonymic elaboratings.

Conversing entails the alternating articulation of dialogue from monologue and the periodic reinstatement of monologue for a variety of pragmatic purposes. Among those purposes is the telling of a story. The relationship between dialogue and monologue can be characterized as a dynamic polarity in which sometimes dialogue and sometimes monologue gains the upper hand according to the discursive context. In more semiotic terms, a monologue is conversing's metaphoric movement and dialogue in its metonymic movement. Telling a story usually is a one-speaker phenomenon and is the metaphoric pointing of prior metonymic dialogue. Realize, here, that self-identity, as such, is not explicitly formulated in metonymic dialogue; in metaphoric narratizing, teller as subject is identified and located as a subject. Conversing is a dialectic of monologue/dialogue, dialogue is articulated from monologue, metaphoric movement insinuates metonymic movement, stories focus information flow, and conversing iteratively turns consciousness from identity to discourse.

The argument I am making presupposes that ideologies, personal or cultural, are enacted metaphorically; narrative structures (that is, kinds of stories) appropriate experience either during the experiencing itself or retrospectively. This is one important connection of improvising and narratizing; a particular ideology is only as powerful as its capacity to appropriate experience in its narrative forms. Thus, a powerful ideology is one that provides its members narrative forms for remembering values; the stories point experience toward particular ideological significances. Stories, from this vantage point, formulate moral texts and conversing is the discursive context in which stories are embedded and to which they land their ideological significance.

As structures that organize, shape, and point experience, stories not only focus their conversational contexts but have an integrity of their own. They are capable of being removed from their discursive context of production and inscribed into other contexts. It is their discursive transplantability that gives them their ideological power. Unger (1975, p. 143) argues that the universal and the particular constitute a dialectic and are not mutually exclusive phenomena; the universal properties become evident only in the particular case that discloses what it is not — that is, possibilities — in the details of what it is — that is, particularities. Stories are universal in their particularity; the more successful a story is in organizing varieties of recurrent situations, the more it acquires an independent moral and rational status of its own. As its appropriateness to particular contexts increases, so does its validity.

Stories are paradoxical in another way; they are presumed to be monologic, yet they are produced for dialogic use. Dialogue, according to earlier terminology, is metonymic and indexical in production and is, thereby, relatively unself-conscious. Monologue, on the other hand, formulates the identity of the subject as either the subject of the experience or the object of its retelling. Conversing is the medium for negotiating how exclusively self-conscious the subject's identity is formulated. When a speaker tells a story, the conventions of conversing's production are temporarily bracketed such that the story may be produced more or less uninterruptedly. It is presumed, however, that the storyteller will maintain conversational fluency and relevancy.

A story either points the conversing produced to the discursive location of its telling or it elaborates a point already in conversational evidence. If the story has no recognizable point or is not consonant with the point of the developing conversation, the teller is vulnerable to sanctions. Grice's (1975) cooperative principles apply to both monologically produced stories as well as dialogically produced conversation. Yet, "our abilities to entertain, persuade, even translate each other between our various worlds of value and significance emerge more through the deflected development of the 'good example' and the 'representative anecdote' than any other single expressive device" (Abrahams 1977, p. 7).

TEXT/CONTENT

A story's point or moral or lesson is what ties text to context; discourse to discourse. The story's point is the locus at which individual experience and actions are aligned with socially and culturally significant activities. In this integrative and remembering capacity, stories are everyday, implicit theories of rational/pragmatic action. Alternatively formulated, the argument is that one's commonsense knowledge of the world, the ethnoepistemology of mundane reality, is narrative in form. Stories, as ideological structures, organize experience and locate the value of what now appear to be recurring actions. Stories recount, relive, and appreciate values inasmuch as a story's point or moral is its value; the pointing of experience is the punctuating of experience's flow into recognizable lessons.

The more unplanned the discourse, the easier it is to produce a story. "To appropriately introduce a narrative or anecdote, a speaker needs only the most tenuous links with previous discussion precisely because of the semi-autonomous and detachable character of stories" (Pratt 1977, pp. 144-45). The dialectical play of monologue and dialogue is greater in unplanned, informal discourse, which is where many stories can be monologically inscribed because of the ease of the improvising play.

The more formal and planned the discourse, the more stringent are the expectations of appropriateness for stories and the more they are assessed on performative criteria. What is at issue in conversings has to do with what kinds of stories are appropriate for telling (that is, stories as metaphoric movements, appropriate analogous discourse structures, and what range of discourse is appropriate as appropriatable is ever at issue and to be articulated metonymically if necessary) and how much elaboration of the story is to be allowed prior to interruption.

Abrahams (1977, p. 17) points out that telling a story "is likely to alter the definition of the scene by the participants. We have a wide range of named interactional scenes clustering around the term conversation, and each scene-type entails slightly different means of organizing the interaction." Discursive structures of speech such as variety and register, pitch and tone of voice, rhythm and duration, are the evidential organizing features of scene-types (that is, discursive contexts). Abrahams notes the metaphoric movement of stories as modulating devices: "Thus a getting-together to have a chat with someone turns without design or forethought into a discussion, a really deep talk, a tiff, an argument, or even a lecture or sermon" (p. 18). He is articulating what I have been calling the improvising nature of conversing; conversing turns from context to context and the turning device frequently is a story or some form of narratizing. Each discursive context is a metonymic elaborating and stories are the metaphoric movements for modulating.

As a culture's useful fictions, stories, as metaphoric devices, constitute a finite and usually modest ensemble for which conventional modes of attending are sufficient for selecting an appropriate story to tell. As contexts become more formal, the expectation that stories have points is relaxed and in some instances even ignored. Style is the expected point as the story's context becomes more self-reflexively performative (that is, self-conscious); meaning is the expected point as the story's context becomes more indexically casual. It is important to note in making this distinction, however, that stories do not have implicit, inherent points, messages or morals, although stories are detachable, transplantable, and reinscribable. As shifting or modulating devices, stories move the organization of discourse by means of their appropriateness to analogous discursive contexts.

Stories, as the metaphoric appropriating of analogous discourse, are the points of contact between varieties of universes of discourse.

> We make distinctions, for instance, between news, gossip, rumor, examples, reminiscences, anecdotes and legends. We do this not only by having these generic names, but by employing conventional place and time-markers that indicate what kind of story we propose to tell. "Have you heard the latest about . . . " differs from "That reminds me of the one about . . . " as it does from "Once upon a time" with regard not only to time but to the kinds of reported actions one expects, the relative specificity of character and the amount of instruction between story-teller and listener, and how much the story will surge ahead and how much time will be given to the direction of the sentiments of teller and listener alike (Abrahams 1977, p. 28).

Distance markers also articulate social position, location, and relationship inasmuch as distance can be marked in social, geographical, or temporal terms. Inasmuch as stories articulate social typologies, stories typify who we are, to what communities we are members, and what our identities and values are. It is the stories, as metaphors connecting disparate discourses, that bind different personal worlds into increasingly dimensionalized relationships that most effectively articulate our presuppositions of self and social structure and what is of primordial constitutive importance are the conventions of their conversational production rather than their content per se. In experiencing narratively we do not so much confuse reality with fiction as much as acknowledge the continuity of their relationship. It is the subjunctive (that is, the "as-if" or metaphoric) status of stories that gives them their power and resiliency as just stories on the one hand and truthful insights on the other.

Living and reliving are so intricately bound up with each other, and storytelling is so central to the related process of remembrance that we find ourselves not only telling and listening to stories constantly, but also checking up on each other's abilities to tell stories well and truthfully (Abrahams 1977, p. 30).

In art as in life, however, some stories are all of a piece and completable whereas other stories are sagas that may never end or end only in the distant future.

10
INDIVIDUAL RESPONSIBILITY IN RELATIONAL COMMUNICATION
William K. Rawlins

Recent critiques suggest that an ideology of intimacy has permeated the literature on interpersonal communication and undermined essential attitudes toward interacting in society at large (Parks 1981; Sennett 1977). The nub of the philosophy, according to Sennett, is that "social relationships of all kinds are real, believable and authentic the closer they approach the inner psychological concerns of each person" (1977, p. 259). Corresponding to this ideology is a belief in the desirability of "open communication" in personal relationships, the idea that increasing disclosure and candor facilitates attraction and greater intimacy between people (Parks 1981).

This orientation to relational communication lately has undergone sharp criticism (Bochner 1981; Parks 1981; Rawlins 1981, 1983). After a comprehensive examination of the research on self-disclosure in close relationships, Bochner (1981) offered four speculative conclusions:

- People believe it is appropriate to engage in high amounts of self-disclosure with others whom they like (p. 118).
- People overestimate the extent to which they self-disclose to others whom they like (p. 118).
- Self-disclosure does not cause liking (p. 119).
- Liking inhibits self-disclosure (p. 119).

Also, Parks (1981) reported little support in the literature for self-disclosure's purported salubrious effects on interpersonal attraction, empathy and accuracy, or mental health.

Meanwhile, several writers have documented the widespread emergence of narcissistic tendencies in the United States (Nelson 1977; Lasch 1979; Engel 1980; Sennett 1977; and Boyd 1968). Engel holds, for example, that "narcissism has been proclaimed the essential social and psychological characteristic of our times . . . " (1980, p. 79). Some scholars argue that the ideology of intimacy reflects certain narcissistic impulses (Sennett 1977; Boyd 1968). As an ideal type the narcissistic individual is described as unwilling to accept personal limits and desiring ties with others as extensions of the self (Boyd 1968; Sennett 1977). Consequently, narcissists typically view others as "mirror-like reflections of [their] own needs for symbiotic self-completion" (Boyd 1968, p. 274). In such a vision intimacy is conceived as a blurring of borders between persons, a mutual indwelling. Nothing better facilitates this process than unrestricted interpersonal communication.

I am not necessarily assuming narcissistic tendencies in all people developing relationships in this culture. Nevertheless, the above surveys of research results indicate that full and open communication does not guarantee lasting or satisfying intimacy even though many people believe that it should. Moreover, various thinkers have argued for the importance of individuals establishing certain limits in their interactions with others, including those closest to them (Sennett 1977; Sisk 1972; Boyd 1968; Rawlins 1983; Hart and Burks 1972; Wilshire 1982; Mayer 1957; and Bensman and Lilienfeld 1979). Bensman and Lilienfeld lament the lost boundaries of the self while Wilshire maintains that individual identity is so uncertain in everyday life that "we slip into aggressive or submissive fusion at the merest breath" (1982, p. xv).

This chapter considers communication practices for preserving individuality and self-responsibility in ongoing interpersonal relationships. I hold that disclosing personal thoughts and feelings and speaking freely in a relationship are rights, not obligations. To allow viable associations to develop, intimates should acknowledge limits in their communication and respect each other's separateness (Boyd 1968). Such interaction emphasizes self-conception rather than self-consumption in enduring bonds. According to Eric Bentley, "like other forces of freedom, spontaneity operates within limits, i.e., within an iron ring of unfreedom, of unspontaneity" (quoted in Sisk 1972, p. 253). For there to be freedom to converse intimately with another person, each party must take responsibility for communicative behavior. Individual responsibility means being self-conscious and monitoring the effects of one's messages on self and other as autonomous beings. In part, self-oriented communicative responsibility involves structuring messages that preserve personal privacy and shield self's vulnerabilities. Responsible other-directed communication fosters individuality by respecting other's privacy and protecting other's sensitivities. In attempting to mediate the concerns of self and other through strategic communication, an individual may have to suppress personal beliefs and/or deceive the other. As a result, both parties should remain wary of producing bad faith through duplicity, no matter how worthy their intentions may be. Let us turn to a cornerstone of responsible relational communication, individuation and self-consciousness.

INDIVIDUATION AND SELF-CONSCIOUSNESS

In **Self and Others** R.D. Laing states: "The amount of 'room' to move a person feels that he has is related both to the room that he gives himself and the room he is given by others" (1971, p. 135). To gain "room" for oneself in a close relationship thus requires both personal initiative and mutual negotiation. Individuation results from active self-definition and self-regulation. Conscious, intentional choices characterize an individuated person's endeavors and communication, and these acts are recognized as emanating from the self, not as caused by the other (Scoresby 1977; Bugental 1965; Sisk 1972). Such effort "secures the self as an enclave of awareness and purpose from the sheer process and welter of existence in which it would otherwise be unselfconsciously lost" (Sisk 1972, p. 254). In so doing, the person also accepts responsibility for choosing and helping to create interaction contexts.

Self-consciousness produces distance from immediate experience. It can foster constructive detachment, which allows for "the power to monitor and moderate our own impulses rather than being engulfed in them" (Wilshire 1982, p. 285). Stein contrasts this human option with her cat's predicament:

She is always immediately there. She has no center apart from her momentary involvement. She _cannot_ stop and reflect on what she is doing or feeling, and so she cannot feel her way of being threatened . . . she cannot help being transparent because she lacks the capacity to act from a center (1975, p. 76).

Stein asserts that people are capable of disciplined spontaneity based upon learning, choice, and emotional priorities. The result is an ability to regulate one's emotional and cognitive reality and one's responses to others.

Sennett (1977) also argues strenuously for self-conscious presentation of self. Reminiscent of Hart and Burks (1972), he holds that the unreflective representation of or "sheer recounting" of experiences is often less _effective_ than presenting or stylizing them. In the latter option a speaker, adapting to the needs of the listener, can mold the account by emphasizing or suppressing certain details. Both Hart and Burks (1972) and Sennett (1977) suggest that this rhetorical composition of messages is often necessary for civilized behavior.

Moreover, joining "the question of effective expression to the issue of authenticity of expression," according to Sennett (1977, p. 267), produces people who are preoccupied with their own motives and reluctant to experiment with different ways of presenting their feelings. Communication thereby is stifled, not enhanced, because it "is made contingent upon authentic feeling, but one is always plunged into the narcissistic problem of never being able to crystallize what is authentic in one's feelings" (Sennett 1977, p. 267).

Sennett decries the loss of self-distance implied by questions like, "Is what I'm showing really me?" Wedding one's communication too closely to one's feelings prevents functional adaptations to emergent individual or social objectives. Similar to Wilshire and Stein, Sennett (1977) believes that self-distance preserves personal freedom by allowing for self-observation, self-criticism, and ultimately the ability to change. Thus, the exigencies of the moment and the needs of the other person are examined in light of an individual's purposes before communication is attempted.

Some authors might argue that the previous discussion reduces interaction to cognition and that thinking undermines feeling in personal relations (Bugental 1965; Morgan 1976; Maslow 1968). Conscious aims, including prior knowledge of one's message and concern with one's speaking effectiveness, are inimical for mutually beneficial dialogue (Buber 1965). In such views feeling has positive connotations and thinking negative ones; feeling is seen as arising "from the dynamic core of being while thinking is an acquired process detached from and antithetical to the reality of self" (Miale 1973, p. 55).

Yet, a view that feeling contains genuine meaning and thinking, merely rationalizations, is open to question (Miale 1973). Actually, responding as a whole person to another individual involves both thoughts and feelings (Friedman 1976). One can insult another's intelligence and elicit an emotional response like hurt or anger. Conversely, someone who is emotionally distraught or ecstatic might be unable to think clearly. Friedman (1976) warns that emphasizing feelings too much causes a loss of respect for language and its capabilities. Miale (1973) in turn indicates that a compulsion to mirror or vent feelings may derive from confusing the easy rendering of feelings with the integrity of their experience.

Sennett (1977) argues that at present people are less concerned with their actual behaviors than with their feelings about them. However, regardless of one's feelings while communicating, such behavior has consequences for self and other (Scult 1981). Thus, relationships may often be better served if participants compose caring and responsible messages "irrespective of how they might be feeling at a given time" (Scult 1981, p. 12).

Friedman (1976) reinforces such a conception by noting the paradox that when we consciously respond to another person, rather than concentrating on our own feelings, the deepest sentiments emerge.

THE RESPONSIBILITY OF STRUCTURING MESSAGES IN RELATIONSHIPS

Close relationships are not immune to the "central problem of interaction" identified by Weinstein in his early essay on interpersonal competence, that of "pursuing personal purposes while still keeping the other bound in the relationship" (1969, p. 769). I have emphasized self-conscious individuation, the avoidance of engulfment with another. Nevertheless, individual well-being and relational viability are not mutually exclusive; concern for self and regard for the other comprise a figure/ground relationship. One satisfies one's needs while honoring relational commitments. Conversely, as one facilitates the other's and superordinate goals, one is mindful of the personal repercussions.

In the communicative arena of relationships, each party must assume the responsibility for asserting personal interests while acknowledging the restrictions imposed by an autonomous, yet interdependent, other. Renouncing or downplaying self's interests and merging with someone else is fertile ground for martyrdom; self may later expect extensive obligations from other in return for a previous period of exaggerated selflessness. On the other hand, attempting to administer to the other's interests without recognizing self's own gains may result in mystification (Laing 1965).

Responsible communication preserves the rights of self and other; there exists the freedom to be open without the compulsion to be "transparent." One avoids truth-dumping and burdening another with personal affairs, which reduce the other's freedom by thrusting emotional and cognitive work and/or requirements of confidence upon that person. Self-disclosure, for example, may threaten the other's choice in responding by occasioning the perceived duty to reciprocate (Derlega and Chaikin 1977). Moreover, blanket honesty evades personal responsibility for the effects of one's statements. Eck (1970, p. 28) notes that "total frankness could in reality be aggressive and sadistic on the part of someone who uses a concern for the truth as a pretext to express his antisocial attitudes with a good conscience."

Indeed, self-regulation may be necessary in circumstances like personal relationships where society provides few, if any, strictures (Simmel 1949; Paine 1969). Commitments to self and other beget practical exigencies that must be managed appropriately in order to preserve the relationship. The freedom to speak comparatively openly and spontaneously is a privilege associated with intimacy in contrast to interaction in more impersonal realms. Yet this liberty experienced in close relationships is often limited by other individual rights. I will consider two prerogatives that are theoretically vital in preserving a sense of individuality and well-being: the right to privacy and the right to protection from undue pain. To sustain these privileges for self and other often requires the prudent composition of messages, both in self-disclosing and in commenting to another.

THE RIGHT TO PRIVACY

In a close relationship two individuals escape from the superficiality of role-related interaction in the public sphere. It is a context in which subjective experience can be confirmed as "real" by another and a person can be made to feel significant (Berger and Kellner 1964; Askham 1976). Nevertheless, intimacy is not privacy. There are many thoughts, feelings, perceptions, memories, and activities that belong solely to the self. When they are voiced to or apprehended by a close associate, they are no longer private in a strict sense, but intimate. Because someone's private concerns can be burdensome, they may be revealed to a familiar and trusted other. But this process socializes the private and at times may overly tax the other and violate that person's privacy (Bensman and Lilienfeld 1979).

Individual privacy appears essential in interpersonal bonds; it involves the right to exclude other and recognition of the other's respective right (Bates 1964). Kelvin (1977, p. 366) stipulates that "the limits of information available to others about ourselves, as we perceive these limits, constitute the core of our subjective sense of privacy." Accordingly, the self-conscious differentiation of significant from immaterial personal data and the decision to reveal or conceal such matters are requirements for privacy (Bates 1964). Individual integrity and responsibility for one's behavior are experienced only to the degree that one can control personal accessibility (Kelvin 1973). When privacy is negligible, independence and individuality are greatly reduced or destroyed (Jourard 1971; Kelvin 1973).

Privacy between relational partners therefore both promotes and results from responsible communication. Restricting self-disclosure is necessary to preserve self's and other's evolving ideas and actions. For despite the fact that it opens one to another's validation, disclosure also objectifies and reifies half-formed images and plans for action (Laing 1971). To reveal aspects of oneself can limit individual growth and imprison one in the "said" of a given relationship (Geertz 1973; Askham 1976) by prematurely concretizing emergent personal and interpersonal potentials. Further, though relationships need a certain amount of predictability and reliability, an excess of transparency can rob actions of surprise and vitality (Kelvin 1977; Bolton 1961; Simmel 1949).

If self-consciousness is necessary to individuate oneself during the "heat" of interaction, privacy serves the same function in a conceptual, almost scheduled sense. A person's private moments provide the opportunity to synthesize the historical progression of one's life, the chance to celebrate one's singularity and distinctiveness, and a sanctuary to rejuvenate self-esteem (Bensman and Lilienfeld 1979; Bates 1964). Askham states: "I need my privacy in order to reflect upon past interaction and behavior and upon potential future behavior, and in order to produce order out of what may be conflicting, identities" (1976, p. 536). These processes of self-definition occur when one is free from any social demands.

Ironically, a distinctly interdependent aspect of a dyad may be the rules that are mutually developed for protecting the privacy and individuality of each person (Schwartz 1968). As more matters are enacted within a relationship, the aspects that remain private concerns for each person compose a pattern contrasting with the areas of open disclosure, observation, and commentary. The fact that persons can recognize each other's crucial private issues is a privilege of intimacy that must be responsibly handled. Violating an implicit agreement to respect another's privacy regarding a particularly touchy concern can be experienced by the other as a hostile act that may even signify a desire to end the relationship (Bensman and Lilienfeld 1979).

It is important, however, to distinguish privacy from secrecy in a relationship. While both concepts refer to control over other's observation of and access to self, there is a moral distinction between them (Warren and Laslett 1977). Warren and Laslett argue that secrecy usually hides something viewed negatively by self and others. Self may deny harboring a secret that is illegitimate and possibly harmful to other. Privacy, in contrast, "protects morally neutral or valued behavior" (Warren and Laslett 1977, p. 44). It justifiably screens out other since the concealed information does not affect that person. As a result, a "right to privacy" is commonly accepted whereas a "right to secrecy" is not (Warren and Laslett 1977).

When self exercises the legitimate right to privacy and other treats such actions as attempts at secrecy, a moral judgment of self thereby is implied that may be unfair. Attributions by other may compel self to deceive other on critical issues in an aggressive maneuver to protect self's privacy (Derlega and Chaikin 1977). In contrast, the acknowledgment of "constructive privacy" (Fischer 1975) is advocated here for intimate relations; it constitutes the opportunity for partners to be insulated from each other without being isolated (Wilshire 1982).

THE RIGHT TO PROTECTION

It is commonly held that individuals strive to maintain a sense of well-being (Becker 1962; Sullivan 1954). Freud (1961) argues that people generally prefer the absence of pain over its presence, while Sullivan (1954) theorizes that persons are motivated to avoid anxiety and seek security. Feeling personally secure facilitates achieving social objectives and constitutes "in itself, one of the main goals of the interpersonal relationship" (Swensen 1973, p. 42). Not surprisingly, Becker (1962) considers it a fundamental social function to protect personal self-esteem and that of the other. Self is well cared for, Sullivan (1954) observes, when someone believes self merits the conscious effort to protect self's feelings of personal worth and security.

The right to protection is closely associated with the right to privacy because people tend to conceal matters that make them feel vulnerable. As intimates become aware of each other's private areas, they often simultaneously gain knowledge of sensitive, hurtful issues. Much is learned simply by passing time together and monitoring how the other experiences certain events. By observing a person's nonverbal reactions to situations or comments, self obtains an impression of what other regards as potentially stressful or threatening. The other in turn achieves similar insights about self.

In short, people become aware of each other's everyday insecurities. After all, in addition to a partner's unintentionally nonverbal cues, a person is privy to the other's spoken interpretations of and reactions to the smallest details of mundane experience as well as significant, pivotal occurrences and decisions. An individual's most casual avoidance of certain issues may in time be revealing if it is a consistent tendency. Isolated bits of such "knowledge of the other" are, for the most part, innocuous and can be gleaned during a chance encounter with anyone. In an ongoing relationship, however, the tiniest insecurity can be festered inadvertently, thereby potentially threatening someone's self image. More crucial are the various configurations of such trivial details that may eventually coalesce into one person's realization of another individual's patterns of vulnerability.

Thus, protectiveness is essential for individuals to tolerate the vulnerability accompanying intimacy (Henry 1965; Kelvin 1977; Rawlins 1983; Bochner 1981). There are various strategies for guarding self and other. Self limits personal vulnerability by discriminating self-disclosure. Self protects other by preserving any confidences that other has revealed and avoiding any issues that aggravate or hurt other (Rawlins 1983). Bensman and Lilienfeld (1979, p. 103) suggest that a basic requirement of intimacy is "turning a blind eye" to the flaws of another. They remark:

> Each party must be able to have noted, in previous situations, the taboos, avoidances, values, and sources of trauma and outrage in the other, and, having internalized such images of the other, cut for himself what emerges as a clear but dangerous path. This is because the patterns of avoidance coexist with intense social communication, often intimacy, on other topics . . . The avoidance of communication in such situations may be one of the highest forms of communication behavior . . . (1979, p. 71).

Scoresby (1977, p. 180) terms such selective attention and comment "benevolent blindness." Whatever the purpose of or reason for a relationship's existence, if the partners deliberately or repeatedly hurt one another and abandon sensitivity to each's respective vulnerabilities, then the relationship is not likely to endure.

Excessive protectiveness between intimates, however, may be as dysfunctional as "total" expressiveness. Laing (1967, p. 59), criticizing overprotectiveness in a relationship, likens it to "gangsters offering each other mutual protection against each other's violence." Ambivalence is present in all relationships; caring and affection seldom completely eliminate latent hostility and aggressiveness (Freud 1961; Brain 1976). Rituals of enmity and friendship probably inhere in most intimate bonds and people are bound to feel these emotions at various points in an encompassing relationship (Harré 1977).

If "dark" feelings cannot be expressed openly, self will find other ways. One method is communicating nuances of irritation in otherwise pleasant statements. Yet a tradition of self's polite but cryptic revelations of anger or dissatisfaction may produce an habitual search on other's part for veiled antagonism in the most innocent remarks. As Speier (1977) has indicated, whenever the freedom of expression is limited, people increase their sensitivity to allusions.

Protective communication strategies should not function as rain checks on hostility that are stored up and cashed in all at once. Certain painful observations are necessary to foster the clear perception of negative messages in a specific relational context but not as tips of an unspoken iceberg of resentment. Self's hurtful candor offers other known pain, which may be preferred in many cases by other over apprehension about the extent of self's misgivings or disdain. Moreover, rejection can be confirming; it communicates that a person is worth the trouble of disagreement (Laing 1971); it is easy to validate an opinion that is not taken seriously (Friedman 1976). In short, too much protectiveness may prevent a partner from testing the reality of tacitly experienced fears.

As familiarity between intimates increases through mutual disclosure and observation, areas of privacy and vulnerability are recognized. Such knowledge provides each person with the capacity to publicize other's weaknesses, hurt other via well-targeted comments, and control other by the ability to predict behaviors and reactions to persuasive messages (Kelvin 1977; Rawlins 1981). However, information that an individual can employ to exploit another also can be used to protect that person (Kelvin 1977).

At times, a person needs another's straightforward opinion even at the risk of offense. Yet it is when self protects other and feels that that person will protect self that vulnerability is tolerable and intimate expressiveness is functional. Thus, the tension between candor and restraint must be managed consciously in responsible relational communication. While revealing personal information enables other to know self better, telling everything degrades self's privacy and makes self excessively vulnerable. Similarly, self must be candid in order for other to trust in self's honesty; but self cannot be too blunt or other's privacy and/or feelings may be threatened, thereby diminishing other's trust in self's protection. Consequently, self must be selective about disclosures without being viewed as too secretive, and self must be discreet in remarks about other without being perceived as too polite.

Admittedly, benevolent intentions are likely to make the most painful comments bearable if a partner senses a more encompassing good will behind the statements. Even so, caring and affection must be communicated somehow to establish such a perception, and they typically are not maintained by unremitting threats to privacy and well-being. As a result, two individuals must negotiate the areas of their interaction in which exercising restraint preserves trust in other's protectiveness and the topics about which being candid maintains trust in that person's honesty. As two individuals become better acquainted, they are likely to be routinely more expressive regarding some issues while remaining protective concerning others (Rawlins 1983).

RISKING BAD FAITH THROUGH DECEPTION

The challenges embraced by responsible communication in relationships can be formulated using H.W. Simons's (1970, 1982) "requirements-problems-strategies" model. Considerable openness and

honesty usually are expected of individuals in ongoing relationships, but so are the requirements of respecting privacy and
protecting self and other from undue harm. These coexisting
demands for expressiveness and protectiveness present certain
problems for intimates (Rawlins 1983). For example, self may
violate other's privacy in an effort to protect that person or
self may risk other's trust in self's restraint in order to remark
frankly about an issue. Such ongoing situational exigencies
necessitate various communicative strategies in mediating the
needs of self and other. These tactics may involve the subtle
concealment of certain perceptions or sentiments by avoiding
comment or by carefully composing messages. Strictly speaking,
such maneuvers constitute deception if they misrepresent an individual's "true" thoughts and feelings or delude the other.

Of course, there is a root sense in which all verbal messages
are transformations of a person's experience. Burke (1969a)
observes that in trying to provide a linguistic reflection of
reality, one makes a selection from it that is ultimately a
deflection. The same limitations apply in making one's inner
truths known. No matter how genuine self's intentions are to be
open and expressive with another, the statements made to that
person involve punctuating self's thought processes. It is
impossible to report the actual content and sequence of one's
cognitive processes in any situation. At most self relates
isolated portions of self's stream of consciousness to other. As
Simmel (Wolff 1950, p. 312) notes, "what is more, these fragments
are not a representative selection, but one made from the standpoint of reason, value and relation to the listener and his
understanding." In the very act of revealing even one's deepest
thoughts in an intelligible form to a close associate, one commits
a de facto concealment.

Beyond this basic selection and composition of thoughts for
utterance is the purposeful act of misleading another person via
message design or silence. This is the realm of intentional deception. Developing this ability to deceive, according to Eck
(1970), implies individuality in relation to others and the world
and the freedom to employ this self-consciousness as one
chooses. Reality does not constrain individuals in any way to
provide accurate descriptions of it dealing with others. Thus,
after Sartre, Eck (1970, p. 20) argues that "lying poses the
problem of the 'for oneself' and the 'for the other.'" What
objectives are an individual's deceptive messages designed to
achieve?

There is a basic distinction between duplicity as a fundamental social experience and deceit that is unethical or bad. Unless
one adopts a formalistic ethical stance wherein all deception is
wrong, the principal criterion for evaluating an instance of deception is the intentions motivating the behavior (Nilsen 1966;

Eck 1970; Knapp and Comadena 1979). Henry stresses: "Social life compels deception . . . . Though even the innermost circle of relationships is not free of deception and fear — not free of sham — there is an enormous difference between these white deceptions and the massive black sham practiced in the outer world" (1965, p. 99).

One can hide and/or misrepresent thoughts and feelings through active or passive strategies and for benevolent or malevolent reasons. Lying by commission is an active strategy for expressing formulations other than the truth. Henry calls this "sham" the "concealment of how we really feel and the pretence of feeling something different" (1965, p. 99). In most relationships, benign or white sham is at times necessary to protect others and to allow us to get along with them (Henry 1965). In contrast, "black sham," exploitative and destructive fakery used to take advantage of others, undermines relationships (Henry 1965).

Lying by omission characterizes the passive strategies for veiling the truth. One may considerately sidestep the opportunity to make a hurtful remark or to probe another's privacy by engaging in "diplomatic silence" (Speier 1977). On the other hand, strategic exclusions from one's comments may misdirect other, obscure necessary information and/or falsify perceptions, all of which might threaten that person's well-being. Moreover, the "silent treatment" isolates and puts another person on "hold" so that the individual is incapable of responding (Johnstone 1981). All things considered, Knapp and Comadena (1979, p. 271) suggest: "Deception, like truth, is relative. Everything that can be true can also be false — given the right people and circumstances. What is a vicious, harmful lie for one person may be an act of loving concern for another." However, an individual is responsible for communicating beneficially or harmfully when that person consciously misleads an intimate.

It is necessary to consider honesty with oneself in examining one's probity with another. Sincerity describes a reflexive conception of honesty, the personal conviction that actions provide an authentic reflection of one's actual feelings and thoughts, a belief in one's communication (Goffman 1959; Eck 1970). Its opposite is hypocrisy, in which one consciously acts in contradiction to one's true views, often to achieve personal gain or to avoid disapproval. Such a manipulative orientation suggests interpersonal cynicism and gives strategic conceptions of interaction inimical connotations (Hart and Burks 1972; Jones and Baumeister 1976).

Yet, as our discussion of the communicative requirements of intimacy demonstrates, the matter is not clear-cut. The cross-pressures of concern for self and regard for other may lead an individual consciously to communicate in ways that fall short of honesty without necessarily being hypocritical. Part of the protective function of communication is that truth may dictate untruth. One's knowledge of another demands the deception of that person.

However, drawing upon Sartre's ideas, Eck (1970) warns that lying, even with good intentions, risks developing bad faith, "the absence of sincerity" (p. 3). At the outset one retains some good faith to the degree that one is aware of lying to oneself and to another (Eck 1970; Laing 1971). However, if an individual unknowingly tells a falsehood because of misinformation, that person is only mistaken; deception arises with awareness. However, when pervasive or fundamental lies are required to preserve a relationship or another's feelings, self-delusion may be necessary to present a sincere appearance in deceiving the other.

A primary quality of bad faith emerges when "one lies oneself so subtly that gradually the lie becomes a new truth" (Eck 1970, p. 50). Bad faith is thus a state of mind in which sincerity imperceptibly vanishes. Whereas lies are conscious actions, bad faith envelops consciousness; one is unaware that it has supplanted sincerity. As with sincerity, a person in bad faith believes in the veracity of certain messages, but they are, nevertheless, false. So an individual in bad faith contributes to a relational context where deception of self and other is experienced as the normal state of affairs. There are few footholds in authentic self-awareness or validation by other. Laing (1971) describes a similar shared process called collusion, in which each partner is required to confirm the other's "false self."

Deception appears unavoidable in ongoing close associations because of the contradictory communicative requirements of intimacy and the resultant problems that must be strategically handled; but remaining conscious of and responsible for the extent of deception occurring in a relationship is also essential. Even if one has the best intentions in deceiving another, Eck advises that "the road to good conscience at the price of lying passes through bad faith" (1970, p. 70).

CONCLUSION

A basic assumption of this chapter is that people may have high-minded or abstract expectations of their intimate relationships. They may desire the personal confirmation, security, or fulfillment of "true love" or "real friendship." But these grand purposes actually are achieved by making behavioral choices in concrete interpersonal situations, and accepting certain personal limitations is essential for relationships to prosper. A recent trend veers away from the romanticism and idealism characterizing earlier writings on open interpersonal communication, the expressive flavor of which is still found in many textbooks (Parks 1981). Beginning with Hart and Burks's (1972) highly influential article, a diverse array of thinkers have suggested more instrumental, rhetorical, strategic, and otherwise realistic appraisals of the challenges and decisions facing those who would intentionally communicate in goal-oriented ways with other people, including and in some cases highlighting intimate partners (Hart and Burks 1972; Sisk 1972; Snyder 1974; Friedman 1976; Phillips 1976; Phillips and Metzger 1976; Bochner 1981; Parks 1981; Rawlins 1982, 1983). Such an attitude toward communication has been variously termed "rhetorical sensitivity" by Hart and Burks (1972), "sensibility" by Koch (1971), "self-monitoring" by Snyder (1974), combining "principled commitment with flexibility" by Sisk (1972), and indicating the courage to respond coupled with the courage not to respond by Friedman (1976).

Thus, the degree of openness occurring in most ongoing relationships is considered here as a negotiated, practical matter. What is said to those who are close to an individual involves conscious choice-making, strategy, and concern for shared consequences. Responsible relational communication mediates the rights of self and of other. It requires self-conscious, autonomous individuals who are willing to be accountable for their self-revelations and their comments regarding others. Communicative responsibility does not necessarily mean responsibility for another individual, only for one's messages and the anticipated effects of those messages upon self/or other based upon relational precedents, unspoken accords regarding discretion, and prior knowledge of that person.

Individuated persons are necessary for responsible interaction. Individuation implies some cognitive distance from immediate experience; an individual is not "fused" with another person or unself-consciously immersed in present circumstances. Thus, self-awareness secures personal boundaries for an individuated person's existential involvements. As a result, such an individual is liberated from momentary impulses and responses to perceived urgencies. Self-consciousness allows one to consider a larger picture, including the implications and probable outcomes of one's statements. In fact, a person is individuated by becoming mindful of the impact of one's own actions and communication and acknowledging them as coming from the self as a primarily self-defined and motivated agent.

The autonomy of the responsible communicator is consistent with individuation. Autonomy arises from accepting and respecting self's as well as other's separateness and personal concerns. Individual freedoms and privileges experienced within an ongoing relationship are dependably handled to preserve the relational context in which they occur. Thus, the limits of each person's freedom are the rights of the other individual.

Three communicative rights and examples of their potential contradictions and interdependencies were discussed here: the privileges of openness, privacy, and protection. Close relationships typically provide one with the right to be more spontaneous and less encumbered by social restraints, to express oneself more freely, to self-disclose and make oneself known, and to feel less concerned with objective evaluations of personal messages. I argue that this right need not be experienced as an obligation because of other conflicting prerogatives.

For example, both self and other also have the right to privacy in ongoing associations. An individual consciously preserves one's own and respects anther's privacy in communicating with another. The opposition between privacy and openness thus constitutes a strategic challenge. Violating self's or another's privacy threatens individuality. Being too private, however, may communicate a lack of trust by self in the other or the suspicion of harmful information hidden by self. Preserving the right to privacy depends upon responsible communication by both parties and simultaneously enhances self-responsibility by reinforcing personal boundaries and sustaining each's opportunity for individual reflection, assessment, and planning.

Lastly, there is a right to protection from undue harm. An individual defends self and other from threats to well-being by discriminating self-disclosure and discretion in commenting to others. This right is frequently fostered in conjunction with the preservation of privacy but as often may be at odds with the desire or necessity for unburdening self or making frank observations. There is thus an implicit tension between candor and restraint in ongoing relationships, and excessive protectiveness can be a problem if it subverts someone's faith in the other's honesty.

To preserve self's and/or other's privacy or sense of individual worth, select portions of various personal disclosures or remarks to other may be deleted or worded differently. The perceived need for such strategic communication or message design in relationships may result in passive or active forms of misleading another, in short, of deception. Ironically, deceptiveness exhibits some of the identical personal qualities as are often found in responsible communication, that is, the self-conscious doctoring of message content by an autonomous individual with an eye to the interpersonal consequences. Thus, deceptive practices comprise the dark side of responsibly strategic communication in relationships, the morally questionable underbelly. They represent what Hammerskjöld (1955, p. 147) once observed: "The most dangerous of all moral dilemmas: when we are obliged to conceal truth in order to help the truth to be victorious."

Another peril of using deception, however broadly defined, as a protective tactic is the risk of slipping into bad faith. In bad faith the awareness of one's deception of self and/or of other is radically dimmed. As self-consciousness fades with repeated deceitful efforts, one's responsibility for them also deteriorates. The primary antidote for bad faith is heightened mindfulness of one's duplicitous acts, their purposes, and their potential for creating utterly false images of self and other that are mutually nourished by gliding together into bad faith. To retain such awareness is to rescue partially the capacity for responsible communication.

A person experiences freedom and individuality in a relationship by maintaining a measure of distance from one's actions and avoiding engulfment with the other person. Indeed, these are potentially dangerous fissures, too easily filled with fakery and alienation. But what of personal creativity and "genuine seeming" (Buber 1965)? What of aspirations to transcend an undesirable past or relational ruts? What of innovation and improvisation in communicating? Intimates can trust in, promote, and respect each other's self-awareness, independence, and personhood. Relational partners can constrain each other's freedom unnecessarily and avoid responsibility for their actions by lock-step intimate communication, unreflective commentary, and merging. An individual limits oneself in becoming cognizant of one's communication, in making commitments to another, and in assuming responsibility for one's own actions. It requires conscious effort to rein in one's vagaries. If other duplicates this responsibility, one's own rights and freedoms are safeguarded. Thus, Wilshire (1982, p. 54) maintains: "At the heart of love is distance, reverence, shame in the face of the other's precarious sanctity and individuality, not shame as disgrace but shame as reverence."

11
THE ROLE OF COMMUNICATION IN DECISIONMAKING GROUPS: A FUNCTIONAL PERSPECTIVE

Dennis S. Gouran and Randy Y. Hirokawa

INTRODUCTION

In formulating his oft-cited equation ("actual productivity = potential productivity - losses due to faulty processes"), I. D. Steiner (1972, p. 9) implicitly, though nonetheless clearly, suggests that communication is one of the crucial determinants of how successfully the members of a group will be able to perform a task. Other scholars, particularly concerned with decisionmaking groups, similarly have acknowledged the central role that group interaction plays in determining whether a group will arrive at a low- or high-quality decision (Fisher 1970; Gouran 1973, 1981; Hackman and Morris 1975; Hirokawa 1982; Mortensen 1970; Seibold et al. 1981).

Although there appears to be substantial agreement among many small-group scholars that communication plays a key role in determining whether a group will arrive at a low- or high-quality decision, research to date ironically has contributed little information with which to describe the precise nature of that role. The fact is that despite the attempts of a number of researchers (for example, Bayless 1967; Brilhart and Jochem 1964; Hackman and Morris 1975; Harper and Askling 1980; Hirokawa 1980; Katzell et al. 1970; Landsberger 1955; Lanzetta and Roby 1960; Larson 1969; Leathers 1972; Maier and Maier 1957), we still possess a very limited understanding of how group communication functions to affect the quality of a group's decision. At best, the results of previous investigations merely confirm what

---

Authors are listed alphabetically.

most of us already assume to be true — that is, a systematic relationship exists between group communication and group decisionmaking performance.

THE PROBLEM

It is our general belief that an important reason why the findings of previous investigations have failed to provide us with a better understanding of the role that communication plays in successful and unsuccessful group decisionmaking is because they have tended to be <u>atheoretical</u> in nature. That is to say, they have not been guided by an adequate theoretical conceptualization of how group communication functions to affect group decisionmaking performance. We contend that because previous researchers failed to possess a better theoretical understanding of how group communication might affect group decisionmaking performance, they frequently focused their attention on communication variables that proved to be of little value in accounting for the role of communication in successful and unsuccessful group decisionmaking. From our perspective, then, there is little doubt that the findings of previous investigations would have been far more fruitful had researchers been guided by a viable frame of reference for viewing communication in groups that clarified its role in the group decisionmaking process.

PURPOSE

The purpose of this chapter is to provide future researchers with such a frame of reference. Specifically, it attempts to develop a theoretical framework that suggests how group communication functions to affect the quality of group decisions. In developing this theoretical conceptualization of the role of communication in the group decisionmaking process, it is hoped that future researchers will possess both a "stimulus" for future research and a "catalyst" for synthesizing the findings of past and future investigations.

A CRITICAL ASSUMPTION

The theoretical framework proposed in this chapter is based upon an important assumption regarding the impact of group communication on group decisionmaking performance: Simply stated, we assume that group decisionmaking performance is not affected by the production of certain types of communicative behaviors, per se, but rather by the extent to which those communicative behaviors allow group members to satisfy certain underlineword{preconditions} for successful group decisionmaking. In other words, we believe that simply "asking questions" or "introducing ideas" will not necessarily affect the quality of a group's decision, unless the production of such behaviors allows group members to satisfy the requisite conditions for successful group decisionmaking. In essence, we assume that the role of communication in the group decisionmaking process is best viewed as an "instrumental" one — that is, it represents the means by which group members attempt to meet the requisites for successful group decisionmaking. What the requisites of successful decisionmaking are, and how communication can affect their fulfillment in group settings, are the topics to which we now direct our attention.

REQUISITES OF EFFECTIVE DECISIONMAKING

Before we adequately can discuss the types of influence that communication exerts on a decisionmaking group's ability to perform effectively, we must first consider the requirements that decisional tasks impose. Of course, these requisites vary from situation to situation and are affected by a number of different variables, including the type of question a group is discussing (Gouran 1982), the risks or consequences associated with the decision (Janis and Mann 1977), the relative possibilities for pursuing, maximizing, optimizing, and satisficing strategies (March and Simon 1958; Simon 1976), the degree of crisis present in the situation prompting a decision (Head, Short, and McFarlane 1978; Stein and Tanter 1980), knowledge and the possibilities for acquiring relevant information (Braybrooke and Lindblom 1963), and the importance of the issue (Janis 1982).

In spite of variation in the conditions necessary for making effective decisions, one can identify general requirements common to a substantial array of specific situations. From an examination of the sources referred to above and others concerned with decisional choices (Bayless 1967; Brilhart and Jochem 1964; Dewey 1910; Gulley and Leathers 1977; Hoffman 1965; Katz and Kahn 1966; Larson 1969; Maier and Maier 1957; Phillips, Pedersen, and Wood 1979; Scheidel and Crowell 1979), we have distilled a list of needs that any decisionmaking group should meet in order to maximize the chances of choosing appropriately. More specifically, within the limits imposed by available resources and environmental constraints, the members of a decisionmaking group need to:

● understand the type of answer for which the issue under consideration calls;

- determine the characteristics of an acceptable answer;
- marshal a realistic range of alternatives among which an acceptable answer is presumed to exist;
- critically examine every alternative in relation to each criterion used to define an acceptable answer;
- select the alternative that best conforms to the characteristics of an acceptable answer.

Although most decisionmaking tasks encountered by groups involve questions of policy or finding solutions to problems, our list of requirements encompasses a broader spectrum of the issues that decisionmaking groups (and individuals, for that matter) may confront. A jury, for instance, must try to resolve questions of innocence and guilt, whereas a group involved in community planning would be more likely to deal with some matter requiring a projection of a desired outcome in community development.

The phrasing in our list of requirements reflects an effort to avoid describing the needs to which decisional activity is directed in a manner that is peculiar to only one embodiment of the task. With this explanation in mind, the reader may better appreciate the subsequent discussion of the requisites identified.

Understanding the Type of Answer for Which
the Issue under Consideration Calls

Although most decisionmaking groups ostensibly would be aware of the type of answer the question being discussed implies, their behavior does not always appear to be consistent with this expectation. The nature of the answer to a discussion question and, hence, the decision that a group will reach, vary as a function of the classification to which the question is assigned (see Bormann 1975; Gouran 1982). Therefore, it is important that decisionmakers understand the principal characteristics of the various kinds of questions they may be called on to discuss.

Four commonly recognized categories of issues that often require group decisions are: questions of fact, questions of conjecture, questions of value, and questions of policy. Questions of **fact** call for answers that specify what is true or false in a given case or that otherwise provide descriptions of reality. For example, "Are nuclear power plants safe?" is an example of a question of fact. A question of **conjecture**, on the other hand, requires an answer that makes some claim about what is probable or improbable in respect to events that have not yet occurred. "Will President Reagan seek reelection?" is an example of a question of conjecture, insofar as the issue does not focus on a present or past reality. The answer to a question of **value** represents a choice among preferences concerning what constitutes an appropriate opinion, belief, attitude, or mode of behavior. "What should be society's obligation to its poor?" is one such question. Finally, an issue necessitating that one select a course of action aimed at achieving some desired state of affairs (for instance, "What can be done to reduce unemployment in the United States?") is what we typically refer to as a question of policy.

Because the answers to the aforementioned questions have unique defining qualities, what an individual or group does in making a choice entails different considerations in each case. In short, each classification imposes a qualitatively distinct problem. The failure to understand this can do much to promote unwise or unsound decisions.

As an illustration, consider a state budget committee whose responsibility is to recommend to the legislature appropriations for given categories of state services. One of the questions implicit in formulating such recommendations is, "At what level will projected revenues enable us to support state services?" (question of conjecture). To confuse the answer to this question with a related one, say, "At what level should state services be supported?" (question of value), could result in funding recommendations far above or below what is realistically possible. In either case, the interests of effective decisionmaking would not be served. At one extreme, action based on the recommendation could leave the state in an untenable economic position. At the other extreme, important services might suffer unnecessarily from a group's confusion of what is possible with what the members happen to think is desirable. Whether or not such confusion could persist throughout the course of a discussion, of course, would depend heavily on what those who understand the kinds of answer for which the question calls say to those who do not.

Determining the Characteristics of an Acceptable Answer

A second requisite of effective decisionmaking involves determining the characteristics of an acceptable answer to the question an individual or group is addressing. In other words, the selection of the "best" available option requires that one have some clear idea of the criteria the choice should satisfy. Every problematic situation or undesirable state of affairs suggests standards that must be met by an ideal or satisfactory solution. These standards — which can range from political and legal concerns, to the rights and preferences of those directly being affected by the alternative selected — dictate what kind of answer to the questions being pursued is appropriate. To make a "sound" choice, then, it is essential that an individual or group articulate the criteria by which the merits of competing positions are to be judged.

Since the criteria for evaluating alternatives differ according to the issue being decided, the decisionmaker needs to be alert to this aspect of informed choice (Gouran 1982; Hempel 1964). For instance, whereas the criteria for assessing acceptable answers to **questions of fact** focus on the determination of truth and falsity among competing claims, the criteria for assessing an acceptable answer to **questions of conjecture** focus on certain tests of probability. Similarly, in selecting the answer to a **question of value,** a decisionmaker tests alternatives against criteria that assess the consistency of each alternative with other values that are not in dispute. In the case of **questions of policy,** a decisionmaker tests alternatives in light of the consequences that any enacted alternative is expected to have. Communication aimed at making group members aware of the criteria peculiar to the type of question they are discussing can do much to increase the likelihood that the right decision will be reached.

Marshaling a Realistic Range of Alternatives among Which an Acceptable Answer Is Presumed to Exist

Because the quality of a decision depends on the options that are available to the decisionmaker, it is vital that one have a realistic range of alternatives to consider. Unless the alternative that best satisfies the established set of criteria is among those under consideration, the decisionmaker obviously cannot choose it. Hence, it becomes crucial to generate as broad a range of possibilities as is both appropriate and realistically feasible.

As in the situation involving the selection of criteria, the number of options as an individual or group considers is affected by the type of question raised. Answers to questions of fact, for instance, typically reduce to only two alternatives: "Yes" and "No." Within these general categories of affirmation and negation, however, the range of specific factual claims may be rather considerable. For example, suppose a group were discussing whether or not foreign economic aid has improved the image of the United States among Third World countries. A negative answer in this case could imply several particular positions: the U.S. image has remained unaffected by its foreign aid policy; the U.S. image has deteriorated in spite of its foreign aid policy; or although the U.S. image has improved in some areas as a result of its foreign aid policy, it has grown worse in other areas, with the net effect being no perceptible overall improvement.

Similarly, an affirmative answer to the question could imply anything from slight to substantial change. In either case it would be important for the group to know what a general answer represents and to have devised means for assessing which of the various representations of its answer best captures the reality of the situation to which it applies. How thorough a group is in identifying the range of options it wishes to examine depends heavily on how communication functions. If no one calls attention to the need for generating as many alternatives as is realistically possible, then relatively few may be introduced, and the corresponding probability of finding an acceptable answer will be low.

Critically Examining Every Alternative in Relation to Each Criterion Used to Define an Acceptable Answer

Understanding the type of answer for which a question calls, formulating evaluative criteria, and identifying possible options that can be examined in relation to the criteria, although necessary, are not sufficient to assure that one will make a good decision. A fourth requirement for successful decision-making is that one critically evaluate the relative merits of each alternative in relation to the previously established character-istics of an acceptable answer. Pedagogical and research-oriented scholarship suggests that individuals and groups have the best chance of making appropriate decisions when they follow this practice (see Gouran 1982; Janis 1982; Janis and Mann 1977; Phillips, Pedersen, and Wood 1979; Scheidel and Crowell 1979).

Applying criteria to alternatives, of course, assumes skills, knowledge, and a highly developed sense of objectivity. If one is ill-equipped to draw correct inferences from the information he or she consults, has inadequate information, or deliberately ignores relevant information, then the testing of alternatives will be of no particular value in increasing the likelihood of intelli-gent choice (see Hogarth 1980; Nisbett and Ross 1980; Wallsten 1980; Wyer and Carlston 1979).

Even in situations where decisionmakers possess the necessary skills, knowledge, and inclinations to make correct inferences about how well various alternatives satisfy their criteria, social and cognitive forces may conspire to create erroneous or other-wise indefensible judgments (Gouran 1981). One needs to be alert to these possibilities and not fall prey to the notion that assessing the relative strengths and weaknesses of alternative positions in decisional acts is some sort of cybernetic process — that is, sound judgment **automatically** follows from a perfunctory matching of criteria with different options. The requirement calls for rigor and detachment in the evaluation process. In group situations, when communication is functioning effectively, the probability of such a pro forma approach to this aspect of decisionmaking is low — but it nonetheless needs to be guarded against.

Selecting the Alternative That Best Conforms to the Characteristics of an Acceptable Answer

Once a decisionmaker understands the type of answer for which a question calls, has formulated a set of appropriate evaluative criteria, has identified the possible range of options that can be examined in relation to the criteria, and critically has evaluated each alternative in light of the previously established characteristics of an acceptable answer, that individual or group is well on its way to making a high-quality decision. However, one final requirement for successful decision-making still needs to be met. Specifically, the decisionmaker must select from among the alternative possibilities that which most clearly satisfies the criteria previously established in the decisionmaking process. Unless the decisionmaker is able properly to identify the alternatives that best conform to the characteristics of an acceptable answer, the satisfaction of all of the previous requirements are meaningless. In short, the decisionmaker needs carefully and systematically to compare the relative strengths and weaknesses of each of the alternatives, and to identify that alternative that appears to be the most desirable and appropriate choice.

Although this final requirement seems intuitively obvious and not worth mentioning, it is unfortunately the case that some individuals and groups, upon reaching this point in the decision-making process, somehow back away from the option that appears to be the most desirable in light of their previous analysis and, instead, follow some intuitive hunch. For example, a television executive council may meet to decide which new television series will be allowed on the air. In trying to make this decision, the decisionmakers may satisfy all of the previous four requirements for successful decisionmaking. However, instead of selecting the series that best conforms to their criteria for a "good" series (that is, one with a high probability of success), the group may choose a new series on a "hunch" that it will work. Sometimes, of course, their "hunches" pay off; but in many instances they later discover that their analysis was far more accurate than their intuition. In general, we suggest that probability favors choice based on what one's analysis implies — assuming, of course, that all of the other requirements have been satisfied.

In those instances where intuitively based choices prove to be good ones, or where rationally derived ones turn out to be wrong, at least two explanations can be offered. First, the task requirements leading up to the choice were not satisfactorily met. For example, the individual or group may not have identified the most appropriate criteria, or the decisionmaker may have evaluated incorrectly the alternatives in light of those criteria. Second, the criteria used in evaluating alternatives were improperly weighted — that is, a criterion that was more important than another was somehow given a lower value in the evaluation process. In the case of the television council, for example, the executives may have put too much importance on the past ratings of similar series and not enough importance on other criteria like the quality of production, the quality of the scripts, or the capabilities of the actors and actresses. In short, then, while we do recognize that occasional successes do accrue from ignoring the alternative that appears to follow logically from our analysis, we still maintain that if the analysis is error-free, habitually following such a practice is likely to result in more poor decisions than good ones.

COMMUNICATIVE INFLUENCES ON DECISIONMAKING IN GROUPS

Earlier in this chapter we pointed out that the theoretical framework developed here is based on the assumption that communication serves an "instrumental" role in the group decisionmaking process — that is, it represents the means by which group members attempt to meet the requisites for successful group decisionmaking. Having identified what these requisites are, we are now able to specify how communication functions to affect the quality of a group's decision. Although in identifying the requisites of successful decisionmaking we already have hinted at some of the ways that communication can affect the quality of a group's decision, we shall now discuss the relationship more systematically.

We believe that communication functions to affect the quality of a group's decision in three major ways: communication may facilitate the execution of the requisite condition; communication may inhibit the execution of the requisite conditions; and communication may serve to overcome the obstacles created by inhibitory influences. We have chosen to call these functions of communication promotive, disruptive, and counteractive influences. We suggest that both promotive and counteractive influences are conducive to successful group decisionmaking, while disruptive influences generally lead to unsuccessful group decisionmaking. Thus the communicative behaviors of group members are likely to result in a high-quality decision if they function as either promotive or counteractive influences, while their communicative behaviors are likely to result in a low-quality decision if they function as disruptive influences.

Communication as a Promotive Influence

The communicative behaviors of group members function as a promotive influence when they serve to help the group satisfy one of the requisites for successful group decisionmaking. Stated another way, if we think of a decisionmaking group as traveling from a starting point to a destination along a path defined by the requirements of the task, then any communicative behavior that contributes to progressive movement along that path functions as a form of promotive influence in that context. For example, suppose in suggesting a particular idea, a group member helps the group to recognize a realistic alternative available to them. In that context, the act of suggesting an idea functioned as a form of promotive influence because it contributed to the execution of a requisite condition — that is, marshaling a realistic range of alternatives. In short, any exchanges between group members that call attention to and fulfill any of the five requisites for effective decisionmaking identified in this chapter can be said to function as a promotive influence because they essentially help the group to arrive at a high-quality decision.

Communication as a Disruptive Influence

Unfortunately, promotive influence is usually not the only kind present in a decisionmaking discussion. Communication also functions to create obstacles that can prevent the group from arriving at a high-quality decision (Gouran 1983). The communicative behaviors of group members function as a disruptive influence when they serve to prevent the group from satisfying any of the requisites for successful group decisionmaking. In terms of our goal-path analogy, then, any communicative behavior is said to function as a form of disruptive influence if it retards progressive movement along the path, or diverts the group from that path in a direction away from their desired destination. For example, suppose the members of a group are brainstorming for possible alternatives, and one member of the group introduces an idea that causes the group to reject a viable alternative. The utterance of that member in that particular context functions as a form of disruptive influence because it acted against the group's efforts to satisfy a requisite condition — that is, marshaling a realistic range of alternatives. Similarly, suppose the same group is engaged in a discussion of possible criteria

178 / Communications in Transition

for evaluating alternatives available to them, and the same member introduces another idea that causes the group to eliminate an important criterion from their list of evaluation criteria. Here again, the communicative utterance of that member functioned as a form of disruptive influence because it again prevented the group from satisfying a requisite condition — in this case, the determination of the characteristics of an acceptable answer. In short, any communicative act that functions to diminish a group's capacity for dealing with the requisites of a decisional act is said to represent a form of disruptive influence.

Communication as a Counteractive Influence

Despite the presence of disruptive influences in virtually all decisionmaking groups, we know that many perform exceptionally well. Usually this success is a result of the existence of communicative acts that function to counteract disruptive influence. The communicative act functions as a form of counteractive influence when it serves to negate or neutralize a communicative act that functioned as a disruptive influence. In terms of our goal-path analogy, any communicative act is said to function as a form of counteractive influence if it permits the members of a group to resume progressive movement along the goal-path when such movement has been halted or shifted in a faulty direction by the communicative act(s) of another member. For example, suppose the members of a group are examining the relative strengths and weaknesses of various alternatives, and a member of the group says something that leads the group improperly to evaluate the strengths or weaknesses of a particular alternative. Now suppose another member recognizes the "problem" and immediately offers a counterargument that causes the group to recognize the actual strengths or weaknesses of the alternative. The communicative act of the second member is said to function as a form of counteractive influence because it led the group toward the satisfaction of a requisite condition — that is, the proper evaluation of each alternative in light of the established criteria. In short, any communicative behavior that functions to help the group resume its efforts to satisfy a requisite condition after such effort was halted or prevented by the communicative act(s) of another member is said to represent a form of counteractive influence.

AN EXTENDED ILLUSTRATION OF COMMUNICATION AS A PROMOTIVE, DISRUPTIVE, AND COUNTERACTIVE INFLUENCE

To appreciate the senses in which we are viewing the promotive, disruptive, and counteractive functions of communication, consider the following hypothetical situation. A group, consisting of several students and faculty members, has been asked by the dean of the college to discuss the question, "To what extent does grade inflation exist on this campus?" The answer conceivably would have later policy implications. Although the question is one of fact, a legitimate answer can range from "Grade inflation does not exist on this campus" to "The amount of grade inflation on this campus is substantial." Determining where in that range the most acceptable answer lies presupposes a clear conception of what grade inflation is.

Assume now that one of the students begins by observing: "Before we can answer the question intelligently or with any degree of confidence in our position, I think we must specify what we mean by the term <u>grade inflation</u>." Another student responds: "In economics, inflation refers to an increase in money and, hence, prices, that is not matched by a corresponding increase in productivity. By analogy, then, grade inflation would refer to an increase in the number of high grades being given without a corresponding increase in the actual level of achievement of students. In other words, today's B is yesterday's C." The two students, in their effort to define a critical term, have been exercising promotive influence.

Now further assume that a faculty member joins in and says: "All I know is that when I came here 20 years ago, the campus grade point average (GPA) was 2.0, and today it is 3.0. That's all the proof I need to suggest that we have a serious problem here. Standards quite obviously are slipping." Scarcely three comments into the discussion, communication is functioning disruptively. Not only has the focus of the issue been shifted, but the faculty member is implying prematurely what the group should conclude.

Before our contentious professor has the chance to go any further, suppose that a fourth participant jumps in and points out: "While a change in GPA over a base period like the one you have mentioned would surely be consistent with the possibility that we are inflating grades in the sense described, I believe it would be helpful if we first make sure that we are all using the term in the same way. Then we can go on to determine whether or not an increase in GPA is necessarily symptomatic of grade inflation. Personally, I think the definition previously offered is a good one. What do the rest of you feel?" The combined acknowledgment of the possible merit in the professor's position and the subtle nudge to return to the original point in this comment represent an instance of attempted counteractive influence. How successful one might be in such an effort is difficult to gauge. The point to be emphasized, however, is that the person making the request is trying to offset the impact of a disruptive influence before it and others like it draw the group's attention away from an essential consideration. If successful, the members could resume their forward progress. If not, then some stronger initiative would have to be taken; otherwise they might well continue discussing the wrong point at the wrong time.

ADVANTAGES OF THE PROPOSED PERSPECTIVE

Given the taxonomy of functions we have been describing, it would be well to reflect briefly on some of the possible advantages in conceiving of the role of communicating in decision-making groups as the exercise of promotive, disruptive, and counteractive influence. First, approaching the communication/decision outcome relationship from this perspective should enable us to compile a more meaningful inventory of extant scholarship. If nothing else, we could clarify what we actually know about communication in decisionmaking groups and, perhaps more importantly, what we still need to know. In the absence of such a framework, we are not convinced that anyone adequately can answer these questions. An outgrowth of this kind of development could be the targeting of research areas that can be more profitably explored.

A second advantage of organizing and expanding knowledge within the framework suggested is that we may better equip ourselves to respond to and to overcome many of the criticisms advanced about the study of decisionmaking as a whole. For example, such frequent criticisms as the capriciousness in variable and question selection, the use of ad hoc groups, and the lack of generalizability in laboratory findings, may be better dealt with using our proposed framework. To illustrate our point, consider the frequently voiced criticism that the type of subject employed in the typical laboratory investigation is unrepresentative of the members of so-called real groups. In some instances this is undoubtedly true, but if the purpose of our inquiry is to identify relationships between functions of communication and outcomes, there is no justifiable reason to assume that such relationships are necessarily unique to the laboratory experience or to the type of subject studied. For example, if we were to discover that expressions of congeniality serve the function of building cohesiveness within the group, one would have no justifiable reason for arguing that such a pattern is only a characteristic of groups composed of college sophomores. On the other hand, we could appreciate the possibility that expressions of congeniality manifest themselves differently among other types of people, but that would in no way negate the principle. In short, the proposed framework should encourage development of generalizations at a level of abstraction sufficient to apply to many and varied contexts.

A third way in which the perspective presented in this chapter may benefit scholarly inquiry lies in its potential for stimulating theory building and development. For every communication/requirement relationship we identify, the question, "Why should this be so?" would be an appropriate one to raise. With this concern pervading our scholarship, we can begin to do much more to generate theoretical explanations for our observations. At this point, such activity would be both useful and desirable for improving our understanding of decisional processes in ways that are comprehensible to scholar and practitioner alike.

A final, and possibly the most important, advantage of working within the sort of framework proposed is that we shall have better bases for synthesizing knowledge, comparing research findings, developing meaningful criticism, and constructing methodological tools necessary for conducting investigations in a rigorous and systematic fashion. That our scholarship has suffered in these respects is well attested, particularly in assessments by Miller (1981) and Seibold (1979).

Identifying the collective contribution of individual studies, determining whether observed relationships are probable or improbable in light of competing evidence, ascertaining the deficiencies in a line of research, and improving our methods of investigation would each be facilitated by our ability to fit research findings into a structure of general questions addressing the ways in which communication affects the performance of decisionmaking groups. In the absence of such a structure, we can see little hope of ever fully understanding what scholarship reveals or of advancing it in any appreciable way.

DIRECTIONS FOR FUTURE RESEARCH

In spite of the advantages we foresee, the merit of the proposed conceptualization and the framework it embodies will be determined by what future research reveals. The value of our framework, at this stage, is largely heuristic; that is, it suggests a number of questions that must be addressed before we clearly can envision the full potential of the perspective advanced.

First, is the fulfillment of the five requisites identified sufficient to ensure group members of making consistently good decisions, or are there other essential requirements to which they must attend? This question is important to the comprehensiveness of our conception of decisionmaking tasks. Since we have argued that the role of communication is an instrumental one, an adequate description of that role is obviously contingent on our ability to identify all of the requisites on which good decisions depend.

A second question in need of exploration concerns the strategic nature of communicative behavior. Specifically, what means of exercising influence — particularly promotive and counteractive influence — have the greatest impact on how well a decisionmaking group performs its task? Because our perspective is based on the assumption that influence is often deliberate, it seems clear that we should try to develop a better understanding of the characteristics of behavior that produce intended consequences. At least some of our future research, then, should attempt to identify which strategies of influence are most effective and what accounts for their relatively greater impact on the direction in which a group moves. Differences in sensitivity to the peculiar circumstances in which a group is functioning probably hold the key, but at present we are largely ignorant of what specific capabilities enable some group members to exercise influence more effectively than others.

In recommending that future research focus primarily on the promotive and counteractive functions of communication, we do not wish to imply that the continued study of disruptive influence is somehow unimportant. However, a review of the extant literature (for example, Buys 1978; Gouran and Fisher 1983; Hoffman 1965; Shaw 1981) suggests that we have substantially greater knowledge of disruptive influences than we do of the means by which members of decisionmaking groups prevent or effectively combat their intrusion. In terms of priorities, then, we believe that there is a greater need to understand the promotive and counteractive functions that communication serves.

We also do not wish to imply that communication that functions incidentally rather than intentionally to influence a group's progress toward its goals is unworthy of investigation. The inroads to improved understanding may be much less cumbersome, however, if we concentrate on deliberate influence attempts. On the other hand, what we discover from the incidental impact of communication on the performance of decisionmaking groups may be of value in the later construction of particular strategies. As a result, we would not discourage research that focuses on nonintentional influence. In the long run, it might prove to be extremely useful.

A third question that we believe needs to be addressed in future research is the following: What are the characteristics of the behavior and the producers of that behavior that determine the extent to which particular functions are served?

In our efforts to distinguish the "communicative approach" to small-group research from that of other disciplines, some of us may have gone too far in ignoring the characteristics (for example, attitudes and personality traits) of message producers. Although the trend has been healthy in certain respects, it may have outlived its usefulness. We know, for example, that a superior making a request of a subordinate is more likely to elicit compliance than another subordinate making exactly the same request. Some of our more recent research appears to discount the importance of this type of factor in the overall behavior of a group. (See Hewes 1979 for an excellent critique of research on sequential interaction having the kind of focus mentioned.) As a result, we are at a loss to explain substantial irregularities in the sequence or flow of communication in groups and instead retreat to the comparative safety of probabilistic interpretations. Our point is that in cases like the one cited, it is the combination of characteristics of the source and the manner in which the influence attempt is made that determines effectiveness. To disregard the agents in any such transaction could result either in the inappropriate identification of an act/function relationship or in many erroneous predictions about what kinds of behavior have what specific consequences for the performance of decisionmaking groups.

From the first three questions and the directions in which they take us comes a fourth: How are the functions of communication affected by the context in which they are performed? It appears that in some instances the functions that communication serve in decisionmaking groups are relatively free of contextual influences, while in others they are significantly affected by context. For example, we might predict that the statement, "Why don't you come down off your high horse?" would function as a disruptive influence because it would create ill will within a group, possibly instigate an argument, and most likely retard the progress of the group. In most situations that is probably true. On the other hand, the very same utterance might function to silence a member who had been disrupting the progress of the group, and in this instance it would serve as a form of counteractive or promotive influence.

That act/function relationships should vary as a consequence of contextual variables is an intuitively sensible proposition to most people who have much experience participating in decisionmaking groups. We are afraid that in research, however, variations in the effects of given classes of behavior all too frequently are dismissed as anomalies, inconsistencies, or statistical artifacts when, in fact, they may be attributable to contextual influences. As an illustration, a consistently high level of cooperativeness might be characteristic of communication that enables a decisionmaking group to resolve an issue to its members' satisfaction; but in a situation necessitating the negotiation of a disputed point, displaying a high level of cooperativeness could result in a very poor disposition of the issue under consideration. Should this type of possibility go unrecognized, a researcher might be inclined to consider the evidence as merely inconsistent with the general proposition that cooperativeness promotes effective decisionmaking. If we become more concerned with contextual influence, however, there will be much less likelihood of attributing to error or random factors variations that actually may be explainable in terms of contextual variations.

SUMMARY AND CONCLUSIONS

In this chapter we have attempted to present a unified perspective from which we believe the study of communication in decisionmaking groups can be advanced profitably. At the base of our perspective is a distinction between task requirements and the functions communication serves in their fulfillment. Essential task requirements, we have suggested, entail understanding the type of answer for which the issue under consideration calls; determining the characteristics of an acceptable answer; marshaling a realistic range of alternatives among which an acceptable answer is presumed to exist; critically examining every alternative in relation to each criterion used to define an acceptable answer; and selecting the alternative that best conforms to the characteristics of an acceptable answer.

In the group context, we contend that communication is the vehicle by which participants progress in meeting the requirement of their task. As a form of influence, communication functions promotively, disruptively, and counteractively. Communication as promotive influence consists of contributions that specifically focus on task requirements and represent efforts to see that they are fulfilled. As disruptive influence, communication may be viewed as any act that interferes with the execution of task requirements. Finally, communication functions as counteractive influence when it enables a group to redirect its attention to meeting task requirements in the face of disruptions.

Among the advantages of the framework proposed in this chapter are the possibilities that it will enable us to compile a more successful inventory of extant scholarship, better equip us to deal with many of the deficiencies noted by critics of small group research, create a greater potential for theory construction and development, and improve the bases for synthesizing knowledge, comparing research findings, developing meaningful criticism, and constructing methodological tools for conducting investigations in a rigorous and systematic fashion.

For the anticipated utility of our functional perspective to come to fruition, however, future research will have to supply answers to several questions. Specifically, it is important that we determine whether all of the essential requirements of effective decision making have been identified; what means of exercising influence have the greatest impact; the nature of the interaction between messages and message producers in their effects on the probability of a given function's being served; and how the functions of communication are affected by the context in which they are performed.

With answers to the sorts of questions raised in the chapter, we feel that the study of communication in decisionmaking groups can come to occupy a conspicuous and major position in the larger realm of interpersonal influence. In addition, it is our belief that the perspective offered has the potential for creating a genuine partnership between theory and practice in the enterprise of group decisionmaking.

12
STRUCTURAL PARADIGMS AND THE STUDY OF GROUP COMMUNICATION
Marshall Scott Poole

Structure is one of the most important — and problematic — terms in modern social science. Its dictionary definition, "the configuration of elements, parts, or constituents in a complex entity; organization; arrangement," accurately reflects the role structure plays in social scientific theories. Structure refers to the organizational and ordering principles in social phenomena. The way in which a theory defines structure determines not only its research strategy and the types of explanations it can offer but also its practical applications. Structural analysis has been applied to subjects as diverse as entire societies, decisionmaking groups, and the psychological dynamics of motivation. Across this whole range of applications a consistent set of theoretical tensions arise, tensions (1) between the researcher's emphasis on structural stability or structural change, (2) between a conception of structure as a framework external to the actor or a conception of structure as produced by actors, and (3) between a causal analysis of structure as a force determining actors' behavior or an analysis that treats structures as patterns to be used to gain an interpretive understanding of human action (Skidmore 1979). Structural theories must make choices among these tensions, and the choices they make determine their character. The character of structural theories — the choices they make and the strengths and limitations these imply — is the subject of this chapter. Its purpose is to evaluate four prominent approaches to the study of structure, with particular em-

I would like to thank Bob McPhee and Dean Hewes for their helpful comments.

phasis on their implications for group communication research. It attempts to provide an analysis of how far structural analysis has come and of where it might go in the future, its problems and potential.

Task-oriented groups are the ideal subject for the analysis of structural paradigms. The need to study the group as a social formation vis-a-vis its members makes structure an indispensable element of group theories. Groups exhibit many different ratios of structural stability and change and therefore are amenable to the entire range of structural perspectives. Moreover, interaction has immediate effects in groups, so the influence of individual action relative to enduring, "external" structures can be directly considered. Finally, groups are important social institutions in their own right. A good argument can be made that the work group is _the_ fundamental unit in organizations (Sayles 1957), and Lewin (1947), among others, has noted that most interpersonal processes occur in group, not dyadic, contexts.

This chapter is organized into two major sections. In the first, I consider the two traditional conceptions of structure that dominate past research, the Deterministic and Emergence perspectives. Both, I will argue, have serious problems that are insurmountable within present frameworks. The second section discusses two new conceptions, the Generative and Structurational perspectives, which attempt to resolve the problems in traditional views of structure. Neither is sufficiently developed to warrant a conclusive evaluation, but this analysis raises a number of issues that must be addressed in developing two paradigms. For each perspective an effort is made to distill its spirit and to spell out its implications for conceptualization and research strategy. It is hoped that this chapter can array the options available to group and organizational researchers so as to encourage the move from traditional modes of analysis toward new integrative frameworks.

TRADITIONAL CONCEPTIONS OF STRUCTURE

The Deterministic View of Structure

In the Deterministic perspective, structures are regarded as stable (sometimes institutionalized) patterns of relationships that shape and condition group activities. The formal theories most often associated with this perspective are exchange theory (for example, Thibaut and Kelley 1959) and structural-functionalism (for example, Bales 1953). Almost all quantitative research on small groups falls within this position, and the structures studied include communication networks, norms, and leadership hierarchies (Fisher 1980; Shaw 1981). These structures are treated as "given" aspects of the group and members are assumed to work within and adapt to them. In this sense, structures are construed as the internal environment of the group.

As such, structures exert causal influence on member behavior and group activities: for example, members' actions are explained as conformity to norms; likewise, the quality of group decisions has been explained in terms of the adequacy of group communication networks. Both explanations require the static structure to enter into group behavior; this is accomplished by incorporating the complementary term "process." For the Deterministic perspective, the critical feature of process is that it involves structure-in-action (Fisher 1980, p. 16). Structure is a framework that constrains and shapes interaction processes, thereby influencing outcomes: To return to our earlier examples, members are attentive to one another <u>because</u> a norm governs their interaction; likewise, a group's decision is bad <u>because</u> an inefficient communication network inhibits member input.

A concrete example will illustrate these points. I have chosen Fisher and Hawes's (1971) Interact System Model, because it represents an important research tradition and because it attempts to deal with the complex role of structure in group interaction. Fisher and Hawes distinguish two concerns in group research: the Human System Model (HSM) takes group members as components of the structure, while the Interact System Model (ISM) takes "codable units of verbal and nonverbal communication" as components of structure. Thus there are two genres of group structures: structures of interpersonal relations (for example, status hierarchies) and interaction structures. In the study of the ISM the researcher identifies "recurrent patterns" of acts and interacts in group discussions, isolating different phases of group activity and cycles of phases over time. Thus Fisher (1970) discovered four phases of group decisionmaking by identifying the distinctive patterns of acts and interacts at different points in group discussions. The orientation phase, for example, was characterized by more clarifications and ambiguous behavior than other phases. Fisher attributed these patterns to the tentative, exploratory process of orientation, in which the group initially defines and clarifies its task.

Once the recurrent patterns in the ISM have been identified, the researcher then turns to the task of specifying the relationship between the ISM and various structures of interpersonal relationships in the HSM (including power, leadership, composition, group size, and task commitment). In particular, the researcher is enjoined to determine the "reciprocal impact" of HSM and ISM. HSM structures are expected to have direct causal effects on ISM interaction patterns, while the behavioral forms available in the ISM structure constrain the operation of HSM structures. For example, in groups with high cohesiveness and an authoritarian leader, we might expect the orientation phase to be shorter and less ambiguous than in groups with lower cohesiveness and an undetermined leadership hierarchy. At the same time, we might also expect the leader's control over the group to be exerted in terms of clarification and elaboration of ideas — the controlling acts that are "normal" or "expected" during orientation periods.

The ISM assumes that both interaction and interpersonal relationships have more or less stable structures and that the relationships among these structures explain group activity. Characteristic of all research in the Deterministic perspective, there is a presumption that structure is there, ceteris paribus. Group processes put structures into action, but at any given moment the structure exists as a determinant entity, conditioning and constraining member behavior: ideally, a group's progress could be dissolved into a series of "snapshots," each depicting the structure at successive moments. The ISM also makes another feature of the Deterministic view apparent: It relies on the notion of function to give structures coherence. Function, the contribution a structure makes to a social unit (Skidmore 1979), is associated with structural-functionalism, but it is implicit in all Deterministic notions of structure. Without some notion of function or effect, the definition and identification of structures is problematic; function provides that the coherency principle is needed to place boundaries on what features constitute the structure. The act ad interact patterns in Fisher's orientation phase are coherent because of the assumption that they function to orient members to the task. Identification of a leadership hierarchy usually presumes a controlling and motivation function for leadership; indeed, a different hierarchy would result if leadership is assumed to meet different functions, for example, support and nurturance.

The connection between structure and process implies that structures change. For example, structural features of the HSM are translated into interact correlates in the ISM, and this constrains and can eventually change the form that HSM structures take. However, structural change in the Deterministic view is construed in a restricted sense, as inherently orderly. Change is ordered on several levels. Individual members are, of course, the initiators and motivators of structural change, because their actions are the group's process; but the influence of their actions on group structures is assumed to be channeled and mediated by other structures. For example, when a member's nonconformity alters a norm, the change may be explained as a product of the member's power or legitimacy in the eyes of the group (Shaw 1981, p. 272). Even when a "purely processual" variable like argumentative force is used to explain changes in the norm, it is assumed to operate in the confines of other structures and to exert a definite causal force on the structure (Moscovici 1976). Moreover, members do not have complete knowledge of structures, partly because the relationships among structures are simply too complex and partly because these relationships often remain hidden. As a result, members' actions have unintended consequences that escape from their control. For example, a democratically oriented leader of a traditional, hierarchical group may attempt to increase participation by suggesting formal rules for decisionmaking (on the assumption that knowing the rules will enable members to exert control over the process). However, because of the strongly entrenched hierarchy, this may in fact increase the group's reliance on her, as members turn to her for interpretation and enforcement of the rules. The leader's helping activity thus unintentionally reinforces the very hierarchy she seeks to change: Structures transcend individuals and individual actions have limited scope to affect them.

The research strategy fostered by the Deterministic view explicitly recognizes that the separation of structure and process is a methodological move that does not reflect the complex "reality" of groups. In line with this methodological "bracketing," structures and their properties are treated as variables that can be decomposed and studied independently of each other. For example, power and normative structures are often separated and studied independently. As the ISM model illustrates, interaction itself is assumed to have structural properties, and these are studied both as dependent and independent variables (compare the long tradition of "sequential structure" studies summarized in Cragan and Wright 1980). Deterministic studies attempt to uncover the causal influence of structures on group behavior and outcomes, as well as the causal forces that shape structures.

The predominance of the Deterministic perspective in small group research can be traced to several strengths. First, the Deterministic view decomposes structures into numerous variables, each of which can be studied independently. These structural variables are granted equivalent status in Deterministic theories; findings from disparate studies can then be linked into a common integrative framework, such as an input-process-output model. This perspective is ideal for the small-scope, variable-oriented research characteristic of most laboratory and field studies of small groups. It offers hope of "exhaustive" knowledge through accumulation (see Hare 1976 and Shaw 1981). Second, the Deterministic perspective emphasizes generalizable causal explanations and predictions of concrete outcomes. This greatly enhances the power and scope of Deterministic theories. Researchers and practitioners alike can "see" (or at least think they can see) their theories work in many contexts. Third, the Deterministic view can account for the continuing existence of structures over time. We are intuitively aware of the presence of norms, power structures, and so on, that shape and constrain our actions; in accord with this awareness, the Deterministic view depicts these as concrete entities, with a reality all their own. It recognizes the force of social structure in human existence. Along the same line, the notion of unintended consequences offers a plausible and appealing explanation for how social institutions escape their members' control and often come to dominate them.

These strengths notwithstanding, the Deterministic perspective faces two serious problems. The first concerns the "weak" role it assigns to human action. The Deterministic view emphasizes structure as an internal environment, influenced by, but essentially independent of, members' activities. Activities are part of "process," and structure is conceptually distinct from process. Certainly Deterministic theorists cannot be charged with ignoring the "real" linkage between action and structure, because they explicitly recognize that this separation is for conceptual and methodological convenience only. The mistake they make is in assuming that the study of structures as static entities, divorced from interaction, can yield an adequate grasp of the nature of structure. I believe that it cannot. The "Emergence" theorists described next have shown that an inherent feature of structures is their production and realization through members' actions. Given its conception of structures as fixed patterns, the Deterministic perspective cannot encompass this continual process of use and renewal.

Second, the notion of structure as a fixed pattern is itself problematic. Giddens's (1979, 1981) well-known critique of structural-functionalism illustrates this clearly:

> The structure of society is like the anatomy of a body, so the reasoning runs: it is the morphology, or "patterning of parts." If we inject the "functioning" — if, in other words, we think of a living body — we have a system. A system is a "functioning structure." But however valid this may be in the case of a biological organism, it is inapplicable to a society. While one might (perhaps) accept that the anatomy of a body can be examined independently of its "functioning" — as in the case of dissecting a corpse, which has stopped "functioning" — such a separation has no sense when applied to a society. A society which ceases to "function" . . . ceases to be [and, hence, has no remaining structure] (1981, p. 169).

Although the Deterministic separation of structure and process is initially appealing, it does not hold when pushed to the limit. It is difficult to see how there could be structure without process.

The Emergence View of Structure

This perspective developed alongside the Deterministic view through the theoretical traditions of symbolic interactionism (G. H. Mead 1934) and some forms of phenomenological sociology. In recent years it has gained prominence through its opposition to the Deterministic view; instead, this perspective analyzes structures as emergent properties of group interaction. On this view structures are actively accomplished by members; they do not exist apart from the negotiations, presentational efforts, accounting practices, and other methods members use to structure the social world (or give it the appearance of structure). Whereas the Deterministic view turns on causal explanation, the Emergence perspective emphasizes what has been called the "action approach" (Toulmin 1969; Giddens 1979, chap. 2). This approach argues that human behavior cannot be explained adequately by reference to causal forces, but instead must be understood in terms of actors' intentions and knowledgeability.

The intentional nature of action implies that actors "could have done otherwise" and have some volitional control over their activity; in turn, this implies that no strict causal explanation of human behavior is possible (Toulmin 1969). The emphasis on knowledgeability refers to the assumption that action is guided by the actor's interpretation of the situation, which is grounded in her or his knowledge of its workings. As Giddens (1981, p. 163) notes, "knowledge" here does not refer only to conscious knowledge, but also to a "vast variety of tacit modes of awareness and competence" that cannot be consciously formulated or verbalized. Hence, the Emergence perspective puts great emphasis on the situated nature of action. It is the actor's ability to recognize and diagnose the context, bring his or her stock of knowledge to bear, and draw on the resources provided by contexts that make action and structuring possible. Research in the Emergence perspective focuses on these aspects of members' behavior to give an account of "situated action" in groups.

Certainly the most famous examples of Emergence research are the studies conducted by Strauss, Stelling, Bucher, and others on the "negotiated order" of psychiatric clinics (see Strauss 1978). In one study Bucher and Schatzman (1964) observed the emergence of division of labor in experimental psychiatric wards. They explored the negotiations among psychiatrists, social workers, and nurses in five wards concerning how patients should be cared for and who should undertake various tasks. They found that each ward developed different systems of treatment and divisions of labor and that these depended on several critical features of the negotiation process. Among these were members' ideologies regarding psychiatric treatment, their definitions of what work members of various occupational groups could be held responsible for, and the formation of alliances.

Bucher and Schatzman depict the division of labor as a continual process, in which earlier agreements are constantly being called into question and renegotiated.

Barbara Sharf's (1978) study of leadership emergence in groups employed a more explicit theoretical framework — Burke's dramatistic theory. Sharf traced leadership emergence to the rhetorical strategies members use to transcend inherent divisions among members and to create or capitalize on members' sense of hierarchy and identification with each other in order to obtain their cooperation. Her method of analysis consisted of: identifying members' use of divisions, hierarchy, and identification to create a unifying vision of the group; tracing others' reactions to these rhetorical efforts; and interpreting leadership emergence based on the dynamic between rhetoric and reactions. Sharf demonstrated clear distinctions between rhetorical transactions in groups with "stabilized" and "nonstabilized" leadership.

Emergence research emphasizes the role of members' actions in the creation and maintenance of structural properties. Structures are assumed to have no impact or existence without the sustaining activities of members. This process is analyzed in terms of members' creation and use of meanings and symbolic systems. The coherence provided by the notion of "function" in the Deterministic view is here replaced by concepts such as interpretive schemes, symbolic orders, and accounts. Each serves to organize the group's interaction and make it understandable for members and for researchers. Preexisting structures enter into this understanding, but always as a backdrop or resource used by members in their structuring activities. Sharf refers to structural features such as members' educational levels and class rankings and Bucher and Schatzman refer to education and occupational groups, but both treat them simply as resources for their central concern: how members negotiate and define their place in a group. "Given" structural features remain unelaborated concepts in Emergence research; they are essentially one-dimensional and figure mainly to contextualize members' actions.

Change is part and parcel of the Emergence perspective. Because members' actions bear structure, when members' activities change, so do structures. Bucher and Schatzman found that even "tasks backed by law and constitutional authority were called into question" in their study (Strauss 1978, p. 112). Change is not chaotic in the Emergence perspective; it is shaped by symbolic orders and interpretive schemes. However, this view of change is much more fluid than the orderly process envisioned by the Deterministic view.

There is also a sharp contrast between Emergence and Deterministic research strategies. The Emergence perspective stresses qualitative, on-site research aimed at gaining an interpretive grasp of members' action.   In opposition to the Deterministic perspective, Emergence researchers resist decomposing social processes into variables;   instead they attempt to grasp the entire situation, insofar as that is possible.   Moreover, the keystone of Emergence research is not causality, but interpretive understanding.   This interpretive turn leads Emergence researchers to emphasize individual resources such as memory, practical reasoning, and negotiative skills rather than the group-level structures advanced by the Deterministic view.

The greatest strength of the Emergence perspective is its emphasis on the creative role of human action in the evolution and maintenance of structures.   It brings members back into the picture as competent, knowledgeable actors rather than as carriers and pawns of obdurate, overarching structures.   In so doing the Emergence perspective compensates for the overstructured, deterministic "blind spot" in the Deterministic perspective. The emphasis on action and actors produces careful, focused research on how group processes work and how they generate and utilize structures.   This research illuminates group processes "from the inside," in terms of what they mean to members and how structures actually figure in group activities.   It explicitly attacks the problem of the linkage between structure and process, an issue the Deterministic view glosses.

The strengths of the Emergence perspective carry with them a major problem: the Emergence perspective cannot deal with the persistent structures in group life.   I do not mean to deny that Emergence research often refers to preexisting structures. Maines (1977) and Strauss (1978) clearly show that symbolic interactionist research does not ignore the contextualizing properties of structure.   However, simply referring to structures does not give them "body":   Emergence research focuses on situated action and is not much concerned with context except insofar as it figures in action per se.   "Given" structures are regarded as markers for other processes that need not be explicated for the current analysis (but could be).   The requirement to explicate every structure, it is obvious, could very easily turn into an infinite regress that makes research impossible.   This problem is solved by researchers in the same way members solve it, that is, by taking certain structural features as "givens."   I believe, however, that there is more to this than simply an expedient to solve a maddening infinite regression.   Members often take structures as "givens" because they are institutions, stable features that can be expected to persist.   In some groups, for example, leadership hierarchy may be so stable that it goes unquestioned and unchanged for years.   Members' actions play a role in sustaining this hierarchy, but there is also no question that the hierarchy is a stable institution.   More important, because it is stable and taken for granted, the hierarchy often exerts a "negative" causal influence on group behavior; it limits the options members have or can even envision and the issues that can be raised in negotiation. This "negative" structural determination is one of the unintended consequences of structure the Emergence perspective cannot handle.

A related problem, which need be mentioned only briefly here, is the difficulty this perspective has in explaining how structures continue to exist over time. This problem is solved "automatically" in the Deterministic perspective, because structures are assumed to be stable entities. It is much more difficult to explain how an emergent, ephemeral structure that is continually "in process" can have any coherence over time (Garfinkel 1967), and, as far as I know, no explanation has been advanced by Emergence theorists. An adequate integration of stability and production can be achieved only by moving to the dual-level analyses considered in the next section.

NEW DIRECTIONS

Deterministic and Emergence perspectives have complementary strengths and weaknesses, yet as they stand they are fundamentally irreconcilable. Each implies different assumptions about structure and radically divergent research and explanatory strategies. Indeed, the two positions stand at opposite poles of several antinomies basic to the study of groups or any other social formation; the tensions of determinism versus agency, permanence versus change, causal explanation versus interpretive understanding. To cut through these antinomies we must move to wholly different explanatory frameworks, perspectives capable of encompassing both poles of these oppositions. In this section we will consider the two possible responses to the traditional perspectives: the study of deep structures that determine the pattern of contingent, observable activities and structures; and the analysis of structuration, in which observable activities and underlying structures continuously codetermine each other. It is noteworthy that both responses emphasize a clear distinction between observable, surface activity and underlying structural features and explain group activity in terms of the relationship between the two; this represents a decisive break with traditional views — which neither differentiate the two levels nor consider the relation between them problematic — and is necessary in order to resolve the antinomies they embody. The deep structure and structurational perspectives differ primarily in the degree of importance they attach to surface activity and underlying structure, respectively; the contrasting strengths and weaknesses of the two views stem largely from the particular form of interlevel relationships they posit. Neither perspective has been developed completely, so this discussion focuses on their basic moves and potential, rather than offering a final verdict.

The Generative Perspective: Deep Structure

This perspective posits a radical split between "surface" activities and the "deep" structures that underlie them. The surface level consists of the contingent features of particular interaction contexts — observable group activities and structures (for example, norms). The deep level consists of stable structures that generate surface features. Several Generative theories, including Cicourel's cognitive sociology, Lidz's transformational functionalist perspective, and Habermas's universal pragmatics, are catalogued in Lidz (1981). Chomsky's (1965) transformational generative grammar serves as the model for these attempts, so it will be discussed first in order to illustrate the ideal pattern. Generative theorists depart from Chomsky's model in the specifics of deep and surface constituents, but Chomsky's logic and explanatory mechanism is the paradigmatic case for Generative theories.

For Chomsky, a transformational grammar has two syntactic components that explain an individual's linguistic competence: a base component and a transformational component (Newmeyer 1980). The base component is made up of phrase structure rules and lexical rules that determine the deep structure of each sentence. The transformational rules convert the deep structure into various surface structures. Both base and transformational components are formal systems; there is no claim that they correspond to features actually in subjects' heads. Since more than one formal grammar can be developed, Chomsky suggests two tests of adequacy for evaluating proposed grammatical elements. At the level of descriptive adequacy a generative grammar should be able to account for linguistic forms that native speakers would consider proper usages and should "specify the observed data (in particular) in terms of significant generalizations that express underlying regularities in the language" (Chomsky cited in Newmeyer 1980, p. 83). To satisfy the stronger criterion, explanatory adequacy, the theory should be able to specify the principles underlying the native speaker's intuition.

Like Chomsky, the Generative perspective presumes there is structure underlying particular, contingent events and observations. It looks for order under changing events and in deep structures finds an analog to the Deterministic view's stable structures. However, the Generative perspective does not regard structures as "automatic" determinants of group activity: Actors apply the generative rules and draw on their knowledgeability in creating surface features, so the action emphasis of the Emergence perspective is also incorporated.

Cicourel's (1974) study of the negotiation of status and role uses transformational rules to explain how actors determine whether status categories or norms apply in particular situations. For Cicourel, the norms and status categories that make up common knowledge are surface rules. In the process of generative behavior from the deep structures that formulate their intentions, actors use transformational rules "to recognize the relevance of surface rules and convert them into practiced and enforced behavior" (1974, p. 51; see also pp. 33-38). These transformational rules represent the member's "sense of social structure" and include features such as "the reciprocity of perspectives" — which enjoins members to assume they share a common perspective and temporarily disregard any differences — and "normal forms" — typifications of social structure or utterances that provide models for behavior. These rules are advanced as "invariant properties" that pertain to the practical reasoning involved in acting and in understanding others. Ideally, researchers could identify a set of transformational rules sufficient to explain how a basic set of normative and status categories could be employed across the whole range of group activities.

Lidz's (1981) attempt to translate Talcott Parson's functionalist sociology into a transformational framework suggests an important alternative to Cicourel's approach. Lidz argues that Parsons's four families of circulating social media — money, power, influence, and value-commitments — and the four general action media — intelligence, affect, collective sentiment, and collective representations — can be interpreted as both deep and transformational components. The forms these media take and the processes governing their circulation (which are socially defined) determine the forms social action can take. In effect, the media are generative rules that shape deep structures and their transformation into particular activities. The forms power can "normally" take in a group (for example, the legitimate authority of the chairperson) limit the ways in which power can be exercised and transform members' impulses to control the group into particular forms of behavior (for example, making a motion within the rules set down by the chair). Lidz's analysis assumes that social structures can act as generative rules and the same structures serve both as deep and transformational rules. This is in sharp contrast to Cicourel, who clearly separates deep and transformational levels and argues that generative rules are cognitive, not social, properties.

Because it is social, Lidz's generative framework is open to change: when members alter social structures, so too they alter generative rules. This contrasts with Cicourel's transformational system, whose rules are presumed to be invariant (with the possible exception of normal forms). At base, however, both genres of generative theory are conservative; deep structures are viewed as stable and fundamental, as fixed explanatory principles underlying contingent behavior. If the social structures in a generative framework change, they are assumed to change slowly; they bias the system toward their own preservation.

Whether deep structures are cognitive or social, both causal and interpretive elements combine in Generative explanations. The causal aspect is explicit in the generative mechanism: base and transformational rules determine surface behavior. Moreover, the Generative perspective also allows for causal effects of unintended consequences through the complexities of generative rules. These causal effects operate through the active process of production of surface structures: actors' intentionality is assumed to drive the generative process, and their interpretations of both context and rules guide their use of generative frameworks. Hence group activity is explained as an active process strongly conditioned by the generative rules.

In general outline, the research strategy implied by the Generative perspective is similar to that of the transformational linguists: specify a system of deep and transformational rules, collect instances of observable behavior, and test the rule system by ascertaining whether it can generate surface patterns. The deep and transformational rules are generally worked out during observations of group behavior; they represent an interlocking set of "basic" rules that can be used to explain members' adaptation to particular contexts (Cicourel 1974, p. 46). These rule systems can be evaluated at both of Chomsky's levels of adequacy. At the level of <u>descriptive</u> adequacy the system ought to be able to motivate an interpretive account of members' practical reasoning and use of surface structures such as Cicourel (1974, chap. 5) provides. At the level of <u>explanatory</u> adequacy the system should imply general explanatory principles that are both usable in qualitative accounts <u>and</u> empirically testable. For example, assume we are studying the transformational properties of Lidz's "power" medium. Assume further that legitimate authority and the rules, procedures, and so on, involved in using it constitute <u>the</u> accepted form of exercising power in decision-making groups. If this "legitimate authority complex" serves as a transformational principle, all attempts to exercise power should be translated into legitimate terms, a prediction that is, in principle, testable.

Perhaps the greatest strength of the Generative principle is the systematic and parsimonious explanation it gives for members' ability to adapt to a great range of contexts. It melds recognition of the importance of human action with a powerful generative logic, providing a resolution of the antinomies inherent in the Received view and the Emergence perspective. The Generative perspective also has a satisfying explanation for how structures can persist over time: The level of deep structure provides continuity, while the surface level exhibits contingency and change. The operation of this generative system offers a penetrating explanation of the order underlying members' production of group structures, while at the same time allowing members an active role in this process.

Generative explanations also face several problems and limitations. It is hard to determine if these are inherent or surmountable, because generative theories are still largely undeveloped, but they do suggest concerns for future work. First, the Generative theories thus far developed are seriously incomplete, as the two examples show. Cicourel presents only half a system — he specifies transformational rules, but no base rules. Lidz, on the other hand, is unclear as to which aspects of social structures are transformational and which are base features. In view of the difficulties the transformational linguists had in specifying the base component (Newmeyer 1980, chaps. 5 and 6), this is not just an issue of completeness; at issue here is the ability of the generative system to support detailed, powerful explanations rather than speculative accounts. Unless the workings of both transformational and base components are identified, detailed explanation is impossible; if either is left vague, it can be stretched to fit whatever happens and a throughgoing evaluation of the system becomes impossible.

Second, even though the Generative perspective attempts to incorporate human action, its theory of action may be too weak. The degree of constraint imposed by invariant cognitive rules or social structures is in danger of overwhelming the role of individual actors. In essence, it can be argued that Generative theories replace members by a set of base and transformational rules and employ intention or impulse as an unanalyzed "motor" to drive the generative process. The Generative model of the actor is certainly more complex than that implied by the Deterministic perspective, but whether the two differ in their essentials is open to question.

Finally, like transformational linguistics, Generative theories may be open to the charge of circularity. Searle (1972) notes that transformational linguists must refer to some notion of the use terms and statements have in ongoing practices to account fully for the meaning of surface statements. Although the generative grammar can account for the syntactic form of statements, it cannot account for their specific meaning without invoking information from the surface level — in effect, the surface level must be consulted to explain the surface level. Newmeyer (1980, chaps. 5 and 6) notes a similar problem with syntactic rules themselves: To specify rules disallowing certain nonsense transformations requires linguists to import information about the sense of statements on the surface level. Both objections suggest that it may be impossible to develop a generative system that is not circular at some level. This, in turn, implies that a generative explanation in the strong sense may not be possible; both surface rules and deep structures may be needed to explain surface behavior. If this problem applies to social as well as linguistic Generative theories — and there is no reason to believe that it does not — it may not be possible to achieve the power promised by the Generative approach.

The Theory of Structuration

Like Generative theories, the theory of Structuration distinguishes the observable surface level from underlying structures. However, unlike the Generative perspective, it assumes surface and structure interpenetrate and codetermine each other. Several social theorists, including Barthes, Giddens, Althusser, and Gurevitch, have developed structurational theories (see Giddens 1979 and Coward and Ellis 1977), and these have been applied to groups and organizations in recent research (Poole, Seibold, and McPhee 1982; Ranson, Hinings, and Greenwood 1980; see also Garfinkel 1967).

The theory of structuration makes a distinction between sys-tem and structure. Structures are the rules and resources people use in interaction. Systems are the observable outcomes of the applications of structures, "regularized relations of interdependence between individuals and groups" (Giddens 1979, p. 66). A group's status hierarchy is a system property; the structure of this system consists of rules, such as the norms governing superior-subordinate interaction and resources, such as superiors' control over the budget and subordinates' evaluations. The status system exists through a process of structuration — the production and reproduction of the system via actors' application of these rules and resources. Members use rules and resources to create and maintain status relationships, and their hierarchical pattern can be explained by differences in the rules and resources available to different members. The analysis of structuration underscores the dual nature of structure as both the medium and outcome of interaction (Giddens 1979). They are its medium because members draw on rules and resources to act within and produce the status structure. They are its outcome because rules and resources exist only by virtue of being used and acknowledged in the interaction system; whenever the structure is employed, the activity reproduces it by tacitly displaying and confirming it as a meaningful basis for action.

Structuration emphasizes a conception of action as a continuous flow of intentionality and conduct that actors "reflexively monitor" and change at intermittent points. The process of reflexive monitoring depends on members' knowledgeability, in the sense employed by the Emergence perspective. Their structures of explicit and tacit knowledge, skills, experience, and so on, enable members to use other rules and resources and thus contribute to the system's structuration. At the same time members actively use the group's rules and resources, they reconstitute and reproduce them. Since members adapt structures to particular contexts and exigencies, they can introduce innovations in the system, changes that may be reproduced in the structure if sustained for a period of time. For example, a member's challenge to a leader may enable other members to "see through" the leader; if the other members sustain this challenge they may undermine the leader's authority and change the group's hierarchy.

Action is not completely "free," however. It is constrained and conditioned by several factors, themselves products of structuration. First, structuration is conditioned by the system's history. Members act in the context of preexisting structures; with the exception of occasional innovations, they can only invoke the particular rules and resources that have evolved in the system. Previous structures thus constrain later ones and perpetuate themselves, limiting actors' ability to alter or adapt them. Second, actors are constrained by differential distributions of knowledge and resources. Those members who "know the ropes" and have power in a work group will do better than novices or outcasts. These differential distributions are hard to overcome because they are often reinforced by structuration. Kanter (1977), for example, discusses a case where low-ranking members' sense of powerlessness is maintained and reinforced by repeated failures, setting up a self-sustaining cycle. Third, action is conditioned by its unintended consequences. However, whereas the Deterministic analysis of unintended consequences traces them to the complexities of stable structures, here unintended consequences are a product of the recursive nature of structuration — they "loop back" through the complexities of evolving systems and reinforce or undermine later action. Each of these three classes of conditioning processes is assumed to exert a causal or "causelike" effect on member action.

The Structurational perspective assumes that interaction organized around a practice such as group decisionmaking is the locus of structure. Practices are "forms of life" (Wittgenstein 1958) that organize and give coherence to interaction and hence are the starting point of all structurational analysis. In any practice, rules and resources operate in three modalities of structuration: structures serve as interpretive schemes, which enable and constrain communication and understanding, as facilities, which enable and constrain members' attempts to wield power in the group, and also as norms, which enable and constrain actors through evaluative sanctions. Although it is possible to identify social institutions that appear to be primarily associated with a single modality (for example, language with communication and religion with norms), all structures can and do participate in all three modalities (compare the use of language as a tool of domination and religion as a symbolic system).

Research on group decisionmaking by McPhee, Poole, and Seibold takes the Structurational approach (see Poole, Seibold, and McPhee 1982). One structural feature they chose to focus on was group decision rules, such as majority vote. They recast previous Deterministic analyses of decision rules (K. Davis 1973) into a Structurational framework and attempted to compare how well the two frameworks "fit" observed decision processes. On the assumptions of the Structurational perspective: (a) decision rules should exist in group interaction rather than as the external norms described by Deterministic models; (b) the key feature of the operation of decision rules should be their production and reproduction in group interaction; and (c) decision rules should function not just as norms, but also as facilities and interpretive schemes. In an empirical study of the role of message valence (the positive or negative affect a comment expresses toward a proposal) in group decisions, Poole, McPhee, and Seibold (1982) found support for assumption (a). Their Valence Distribution model, which assumed decision rules based on interaction, explained group decisions better than Davis's (1973) Social Decision Scheme model, which assumed decision rules were norms external to interaction.

To fully establish the viability of the Structurational model it is also necessary to establish assumptions (b) and (c). The researchers are presently conducting a study of the production and reproduction of preference distributions and decision rules. It is designed to use qualitative methods to track valence "accumulation" and the evolution of preference distributions through various episodes in group discussions. In particular, the study will focus on the structural features (for example, power differences) entering into the production and reproduction of preference orders. At the same time, it should also be possible to track the production and reproduction of structures. Processes contributing to the introduction of structural elements through "rule-bids" and to the reproduction (or rejection) of these structures are of interest here. Poole et al. also outline several proposals for exploring the operation of decision rules in other modalities (assumption [c]). Although the brevity of this chapter does not permit elaboration, these proposals involve incorporating symbolic and power structures into the analysis.

Structurational explanations combine action-based and causal elements. The process of structuration is driven by members' active production and reproduction of structural elements; this process is, in turn, conditioned by other structural features, which exert causal influence on the effects of members' actions. To study this necessitates an interlocking series of studies, each of which gets at a few aspects of the whole. Once interaction-based decision rules are identified, the structural constraints governing their production and reproduction must be traced out, and once this is done the structuration of the constraints and the operation of rules in other modalities becomes of interest. At each new stage the theory grows by increasingly encompassing the practice in question; a web of explanations based on both quantitative and qualitative data is necessary to understand adequately decisionmaking practices.

When researchers initially have explored the interaction system they can move to the final layer of explanation, the analysis of the relationships among structural features themselves. These relationships can take two forms. One structure mediates another when its production and reproduction influences the reproduction of the other. For example, the economic metaphor, in which choices are based on rationalistic cost-benefit calculations, often mediates decision rules in groups. Those rules that support the metaphor are given preferred status and reproduced while the many other possible rules (for example, ethical standards) go by the board. A contradiction exists when two structural features influence each other's reproduction but at the same time contravene one another and create strains in the system. For example, numerous investigators have reflected on the contradiction between the social, collegial nature of group action and members' individualistic striving for control and rewards in the group. This contradiction in organizing principles, each of which conditions the other, can produce serious problems in a group; when these problems mount, the group may use time and energy to cope with them or it may change to "reprioritize" the organizing principles. The analysis of mediations and contradictions is quite complex and specifics are beyond the scope of this chapter (see Poole et al. 1982). It is sufficient to note that it adds another dimension to Structurational theories by accounting for change and influence within and between the generative structures themselves.

The Structurational perspective offers several important advantages:

It provides an orderly frame of reference that incorporates causal forces, yet also recognizes the critical role of action in structuring. The concept of structuration guards against the reduction of structures either to unanalyzed, given features of action or to a fixed framework. It treats structure as a "permanent process," the medium and outcome of continuous action.

Because Structurational analysis focuses on ongoing practices, it also sets limits on what aspects of a phenomenon are relevant for the researcher. For every practice (for example, decision-making) there are certain processes or features critical either to doing or to understanding it (for example, decision rules); these are part of "what everyone knows" about the practice. These processes or features form the core of what is important for structurational analysis; they signal "what is of interest" and "what is not" to the researcher. This diverges significantly from the Generative view, which would, in principle, be satisfied with a generative system developed solely through the researcher's analytic deductions (that is, one that was not related to members' schemes).

The Structurational perspective also avoids the difficulties inherent in the Generative perspective's radical separation of surface and deep structures. Since interchange between system and structure is an essential aspect of structuration, the articulation of the two levels does not present a problem and is, in fact, a strength when we try to come to grips with structural change.

At least two key problems confront the Structurational perspective. First, there is the problem of accounting for the persistence of structures over time. Although the notion of continual production and reproduction admits the causal force of structure into the equation, what is, in effect, an instantaneous renewal of the structure at each successive instant can very easily dissolve into a chaotic Heracleitean process of continual flux. Various answers to this problem have been advanced, including grounding structure in the extension of practices over time, tying it to the physical world, and incorporating a different conception of time. At present, however, these answers are not sufficiently developed to determine if they will overcome the problem.

The second problem relates to the great reliance placed on the system's history by Structurational explanations: How are we to determine exactly what elements of the group's vast historical corpus are relevant? The Structurational framework narrows the field considerably: It specifies a model of action, three particular types of conditioning factors, and definite genres of relationships between structures. Combined with knowledge of a particular practice, this enables us to rule out a good deal of the historical corpus. However, within these elements we are still faced with the problem of determining which particular historical features are important: For example, which is more critical to sustaining a group's majority vote procedure: members' voting behavior or the group's adoption of <u>Robert's Rules of Order</u> a year ago? In some cases the specific context may provide the answer; it may also be possible to use hermeneutic methods to sort through the group's history. However it is addressed, the issue of historical analysis is a critical one in structurational theory.

CONCLUSION

This chapter has explored the two traditional approaches to the study of group structures and two new perspectives designed to resolve problems in the traditional analyses. The new perspectives attempt to broaden the analyst's focus to encompass both poles of tensions between determinism and agency permanence and change, causal explanation and interpretive understanding, dualities that the earlier perspectives split. Whereas the Deterministic perspective focuses on <u>situated</u> action, and the Emergence perspective centers on situated <u>action</u>, both the Generative and Structurational perspectives try to account for <u>situated action</u>. In focusing on the "spirit" rather than the details of each position, this chapter traces a shift toward more sophisticated models of structure. These models have great promise, but they also raise a number of complex questions. Whether these (and other) questions can be resolved will ultimately determine whether group research moves to new levels of complexity or retreats to the limited but firmly grounded traditional views.

13
A CRITICAL REVIEW OF RESEARCH TRADITIONS IN ORGANIZATIONAL COMMUNICATION
Linda L. Putnam and George Cheney

Our beliefs about social reality underlie the way we "think" about organizations. For the social scientist, these beliefs undergird definitions of organizations, problems, and issues worthy of study, and methodological tools for conducting research. For the practitioner, beliefs about reality shape organizational choices that range from making sense of daily activities to making decisions on product diversification, layoffs, or closing of plants. Likewise, each organizational action rests on theory (Albrow 1980). Just as social scientists establish communities based on "bodies of thought," organizational members rely on cognitive schema to analyze situations. The difference between the two, as Weick (1979) points out, is that social scientists are more detached and objective about their theories.

In effect, social scientists and organizational practitioners "are placed in the role of mutual assistance in thought and action" (Albrow 1980, p. 296). This relationship springs from university training of practitioners and social science involvement in organizational problem solving. These alliances, in turn, account for the charge of "managerial bias" frequently aimed at organizational theorists. In most cases, however, this bias is implicit in the concepts and propositions of organizational theory. Although recent essays in organizational communication have attempted to uncover such basic premises underlying our research (Deetz 1982; Putnam 1982a; Redding 1979), they do not address the knowledge claims that form inseparable bonds between theory and practice.

One theorist, Jürgen Habermas, espouses a philosophy of science based upon an integral linkage between theory and social life. This chapter employs Habermas's (1971) three modes of scientific inquiry to critique the knowledge claims and interests of dominant research traditions in organizational communication. In particular, it applies the empirical-analytic, historical-hermeneutic, and critically oriented forms of science to four research domains in organizational communication: communication channels, climates, networks, and superior-subordinate communication. Our aims are to critique the research traditions and to illustrate how each might be transformed when cast in uncharacteristic modes of inquiry. Throughout this analysis we hold to the assumptions that theory and practice are tightly coupled and that multiple theoretical perspectives are a necessary "quality of social life" (Bernstein 1978, p. 194).

HABERMAS'S TYPOLOGY OF INQUIRY

Habermas (1971) is one of the foremost figures in contemporary intellectual history. With the goal of outlining a comprehensive critical theory, Habermas posits three modes of scientific inquiry: the empirical-analytic, the historical-hermeneutic, and the critically oriented. He contends that while the three modes are linked together through cognitive strategies, each offers an autonomous schema for discovering and validating knowledge claims in a distinct dimension of human social life. Thus, Habermas sets forth what Brown (1977) calls for in his critique of social science: an embracing perspective that synthesizes potentially irreconcilable theoretical positions.

In this chapter we employ Habermas's typology as a framework for describing and reconstructing dominant traditions in organizational communication research. We treat the three modes of inquiry as "ideal" types of knowledge. Further, we realize that a given research tradition rarely adheres to all the characteristics of any one mode and that the boundaries that separate the three modes merge to some extent. Some theorists may be offended by the use of Habermas's framework to classify and reconstruct research traditions. Following Bernstein (1978), we would respond that Habermas's schema functions more effectively in posing salient questions than it does in providing definitive answers. In effect, it provides a compelling model for analyzing organizational communication. Through our application, we aim to reconstruct research traditions and to suggest new domains of knowledge, ones grounded in a comprehensive view of society and social inquiry.

Habermas's typology employs four primary characteristics to differentiate among the three modes of inquiry. The first characteristic, dimension of social existence, centers on the nature and function of action — specifically on the way work, interaction, and power supply us with skills, norms, and types of relationships. The second characteristic refers to knowledge-constitutive cognitive interest. It focuses on the motivational forces of knowledge creation and knowledge use and it also embodies assumptions about social reality. Habermas (1971) distinguishes among the technical, the practical, and the emancipatory interests of human existence. Dimensions of social existence and cognitive interests inform the methods of inquiry. In Habermas's framework, methodology refers to theory construction, measurement, the role of data, and verification. The final characteristic is the ultimate goal or the general use society makes of knowledge — specifically control, understanding, and change. These four characteristics structure our overview of each mode of inquiry and its implications for organizational theory in general and organizational communication research in particular.

Empirical-Analytic Inquiry

Habermas's (1971) discussion of the empirical-analytic mode of inquiry centers on the way science and technology have become dominant forms of knowledge in modern society. In fact, Habermas laments the way philosophy itself purports to be a science, a merger that has led to the apparent dissolution of epistemology (Held 1980). Work as purposeful-rational action emerges as the dominant factor of social existence in this mode of inquiry (Habermas 1970). Work supplies us with instrumental reasoning, problem-solving skills, and technical rules for structuring and evaluating human behavior. It depends on a rational process in which rules, decision procedures, and goals govern action (Habermas 1970). Action and meaning then operate as outcomes of rational choice, outcomes derived from correctly deducing the preferred rules.

The knowledge claims of the empirical-analytic mode concern technically useful data. Social reality is treated as objective, materialistic, and subject to prediction and technical control. Both the researcher and the practitioner turn to instrumental activity as a source of data and as a filter for understanding events. In research, this mode of inquiry is best exemplified by the positivist tradition where methodological tools are borrowed from the natural sciences and are aimed at constructing lawlike hypotheses. Concept formation occurs in abstraction, two steps removed from ongoing social events. Theories are constructed deductively from the lawlike hypotheses. Hypotheses are verified through empirical testing under objective and carefully controlled research conditions.

This form of inquiry aims at comprehending reality, predicting behavior, and thus exerting technical control. Through the use of experimentation, theory becomes detached from communicative action in a way that "objectifies reality" within a "restricted mode of experience" (Held 1980, p. 305). Even though Habermas criticizes the restrictiveness of the empirical-analytic mode, he recognizes that it is appropriate for certain types of research. However, he points to its narrowly defined purview and he challenges the use of it as the "only type of legitimate knowledge" for understanding social reality.

This mode of inquiry dominated the study of organizations for decades. Beginning with the work of Taylor (1947), American social scientists strived to develop a positivistic science of administration. Taylor's scientific management was designed to direct work-related processes through the manipulation of tangible incentives and task segments. Such scientific approaches merged with models of rational authority in an effort to map out the most efficient and effective way of organizing (Zey-Ferrell and Aiken 1981). Bureaucracy represented an outgrowth of rational models of organizing, one in which technical control was exercised through "recruitment, selection, appraisal, decision making, information flow, and uncertainty reduction" (Thompson 1980a, p. 16). The claim to rationality manifested in these functions became an ideology in itself, one that was legitimated by treating values and choices as mere technical decisions (Thompson 1980a; Ellul 1964). Through adoption of purposeful-rational models, social scientists demonstrated the usefulness of knowledge in mastering the techniques of work (Albrow 1980).

Interestingly, assumptions of rationality and technical control also inform the basic tenets of the human relations, the systems, and the contingency schools of organizational thought. The human relations school, while shifting the focus from authority and structure to the needs of organizational members, essentially maintained the goal of meshing individual needs with organizational objectives. Motivational theories, then, served as managerial tools to aid instrumental action. Similarly, systems and contingency theories stressed uncertainty reduction and adaptation to the environment. Ultimately, these approaches attempted to harness human resources for rational action and technical control. Research within these traditions typically ignored the intersubjective meanings linked to organizational events and focused primarily on discovering relationships among objectively defined variables.

Historical-Hermeneutic Inquiry

Interaction, as constituted by communicative action and language, comprises the dimension of social existence in the historical-hermeneutic sciences (Bernstein 1978). Interaction, however, becomes intertwined with shared experiences and consensual norms that emerge and evolve over time. Habermas (1970) contends that individuals form a dialogic relationship in which each recognizes the other as sharing meanings. When there is a breakdown in expectations, a hermeneutic procedure is required to rebuild mutual consensus through reference to social sanctions (Held 1980, p. 314). The cognitive interest of the historical-hermeneutic sciences is practical. People depend on linguistic skills and shared expectations for successful social action (Held 1980). Moreover, the ongoing process of understanding contributes in a practical way to self-formation. Language is the medium in which meanings are realized; social reality is defined through "a specified grammar of world-apprehension and of action" (Habermas 1971, p. 195).

Methodology in the historical-hermeneutic sciences works from integrating parts to achieve a conjectural whole. Through an inductive process, interpretations of texts are continually revised by reexamining the parts in light of the whole (Held 1980). The social scientist must learn the language and historical purview of his or her subjects, a process that makes the researcher an integral part of the study. Concept and theory formation evolve from the way individuals structure their social world rather than from preselected, abstract categories. Interpretations are verified through logical consistency, consensus of meanings among subjects, and dialogue between the researcher and the subjects.

Understanding is the goal of the historical-hermeneutic sciences. Grounded in anthropological modes of inquiry and biblical text analysis, hermeneutics aims to disclose the intersubjectivity of meanings evident in social action (McCarthy 1979a). As conceptualized by Dilthey (1976) and Gadamer (1975), the construct that guides hermeneutic inquiry is <u>verstehen</u>, a form of empathy and dialogic understanding: empathy in the sense of reconstructing the psychological states of others and dialogic understanding in terms of the meanings individuals ascribe to historically framed actions (McCarthy 1979b). Habermas criticizes this mode for its treatment of tradition and context as neutral phenomena, irrespective of sources of domination and distortion. When evaluation is divorced from description and understanding, the thread that ties theory to practice is broken (Held 1980).

Only a few organizational theorists adopt the historical-hermeneutic mode of inquiry. Weick (1979), for example, features the process of <u>organizing</u>: a means of reducing equivocality through the use of interlocked behaviors governed by a consensual grammar. That is, organizing involves commonsense agreement about ways to achieve certain goals through coordinated action. Thus, Weick emphasizes the socially constructed aspect of organizational life, including language, meaning, retention or memory, and the "loose" relationships that exist among organizational units. Johnson (1977) and Hawes (1974) offer a communicative slant to Weick's notion of organizational sense-making. A second organizational theory that adheres to the tenets of the historical-hermeneutic mode is Silverman's (1970) social action model. He outlines an organizational sociology based upon the way meanings define social reality, the way they become institutionalized as social facts, and the way they are transformed through daily interactions. In effect, he advocates a process of understanding organizations through a focus on the context-bound interactions that emerge from the symbols and meanings of organizational members.

Critically Oriented Inquiry

Unlike the other two modes of inquiry, critically oriented science strives for autonomy and responsibility through self-reflection, self-formation, and a critical understanding of our historical situation (Habermas 1971). The salient dimension of human existence in the critical perspective is power, specifically the way unwarranted power relationships restrict public communication by using language as a medium of social domination (Held 1980). Moreover, these power relationships often distort reality by dominating consciousness and imprisoning behaviors in an ideology that remains inaccessible to the individual and removed from public criticism. The critical perspective embraces an "emancipatory" interest, one aimed at dissolving barriers of false consciousness and establishing processes of self-reflection (McCarthy 1979a). Thus, self-reflection leads to self-formation through gaining insights previously removed from one's consciousness. In this sense, self-reflection coincides with knowledge; the two become one (Habermas 1971). The act of knowing merges with self-reflection in achieving the goals of autonomy and responsibility — an emancipation from constraining power relationships. Self-reflection, then, links theory to practice and knowledge to emancipation (Held 1980).

Methodology in the critically oriented sciences is a type of depth hermeneutics that resembles Freudian psychoanalysis. Through dialogue, the subject reconstructs his or her life history, bringing to consciousness "original scenes" and latent content previously repressed (Held 1980). The meanings of symbols and observed behaviors surface through a dialogue of constructing and testing interpretations. Hence, theories are constructed by merging understanding with causal explanation. They are tested by reconstructing individual case histories in terms of their "capacity to reveal and dissolve distortions of communication" (Held 1980, p. 324). Verification in the critical mode hinges on acceptance and successful continuation of the self-formative process — the emancipation achieved through understanding one's life history (Bernstein 1978). In Habermas's theory of social evolution, the ultimate goal is change: the reconstruction of society's history to dissolve ideologies and open up public discourse (Held 1980).

Organizational theorists who espouse Habermas's view of critical theory are rare, but investigations that expose oppressive and alienating aspects of organizational life are evident in research on organizational dialectics (Benson 1977); control patterns of "dominant coalitions" (Thompson 1980a); Zey-Ferrell and Aiken 1981); technological ideology (Bendix 1970); and corporate political language (Pfeffer 1981; Thompson 1980b). Coleman (1974) describes how corporations initially emerge as "juristic persons" to protect individual interest and how they end up exerting power over the individuals that they once served. Similarly, Galbraith (1979) traces the evolution of organizational power from land to technical expertise, and the corresponding shift in work motivation from pecuniary rewards to the adoption of organizational values. Finally, Scott and Hart (1979) take an even more critical posture in arguing that the values of large corporations have replaced the American value system. These theorists depict contemporary organizations as limiting individual choice and restricting public debate over collective values and goals.

In short, we find in Habermas's work a schema for examining the goals, knowledge claims, and methods of different types of scientific inquiry. Knowledge, according to Habermas (1971), is formed through three interests: information that enhances technical control, interpretations that lead to historically bound actions, and analyses that free consciousness from the domination of power relationships. The three interests and their corresponding forms of scientific inquiry (empirical-analytic, historical-hermeneutic, and critical) emanate from the way knowledge is used.

Interestingly, though, we identify three senses in which Habermas treats each cognitive interest: the social scientist's way of knowing, the social scientist's application of research findings, and the practitioner's ongoing production and consumption of knowledge. These perspectives are implicit throughout Habermas's (1971) discussion of the modes of scientific inquiry. We note that one cognitive interest, say technical, may inform a particular research tradition; yet the tradition may not develop all of the ways that technical control can be exercised. In the critically oriented sciences, distinctions among the three perspectives become blurred, if not entirely erased. In this way, the emancipatory interest holds a different status than the other two interests (Bernstein 1978). It is derivative in that it is inspired by systematically distorted communication; it is the "first among equals" in that it provides for self-reflection, the closest association between theory and practice. This built-in "bias" has far-reaching implications, implications the critical theorist must consider.

TRADITIONS OF ORGANIZATIONAL COMMUNICATION RESEARCH

Through applying Habermas's typology to the four dominant areas of research, we intend to show how these traditions can evolve from an empirical-analytic science to hermeneutic and critical modes of inquiry. This evolution necessarily entails a transformation of assumptions, issues, and terminology to "recast" research into "new" modes of inquiry. The four domains — communication channels, climate, networks, and superior-subordinate interaction — have dominated organizational research since the early 1950s. They represent our discipline's struggle to establish the boundaries of organizational communication and their development parallels our field's move from a preoccupation with sender-oriented transmission effects to a focus on communication process and meaning (Fisher 1978).

Since they grew out of the empirical-analytic sciences and the human relations school of organizational theory, the traditions share a concern for technical efficiency, productive employee interaction, use of objective measurement tools, and generally a "managerial bias." Moreover, communication concepts in a particular tradition overlap to some extent with those of other domains. For example, communication channels are essential components of both an organization's network and its climate. Also, some investigators frequently treat organizational networks as antecedents to communication climates. In effect, the four research domains are not discrete areas, but they represent significant concentrations of organizational communication research. The following sections present a brief synopsis and analysis of each research tradition, drawing from selected studies in each area. We regret that spatial constraints preclude a comprehensive critical review of the literature in each domain.

Organizational Communication Channels:
The Message Flow Approach

Channel research was the first identifiable "tradition" of organizational communication study. As the product of an early effort to define the concept of "organizational communication," channel research focused primarily on the flow of information as it "moved" in three directions: upward, downward, and horizontally. In his review of organizational communication research,

Richetto (1977) noted that studies on message flow attracted great interest in the 1950s and 1960s. Investigators reported that lower-level employees tended to distort messages that they initiated upward (Read 1962). K. Davis (1953), following Jacobson and Seashore (1951), developed a research technique (ECCO: Episodic Communication Channels in Organizations) to examine the spread of rumors through the informal networks of the employee grapevine. J.G. Miller (1960) and O'Reilly (1980) observed the effects of "information overload" on organizational members. All of these research interests have continued to be pursued. Katz and Kahn (1978), while offering explanations for the types of information most likely to "move" in particular directions, bemoaned the lack of attention to message content in channel research.

It is this criticism that provides the most potent argument for placing channel research in the empirical-analytic category. Channel research, as its name suggests, has been characterized largely by a mechanistic, flow-oriented approach to communication. The literature on organizational communication features such concepts as "by-passing," "chain of command," and "criss-crossing," suggesting a linear view of communication rooted in the "conduit" or the container metaphor (Axley 1982). The goal of channel research reflects technical control, the need to redirect information to aid managerial practices. For example, the International Communication Association (ICA) Audit, which includes measures of information flow, is aimed at helping managers improve communication practices that enhance organizational effectiveness (Goldhaber 1976). Moreover, "behind" the audit is an "accounting" metaphor that reinforces the technical interest.

Even though the cognitive interest of channel research reflects an emphasis on technical control, the methods for study are generally more diverse. In a "classic" study of upward message distortion, Read (1962) uses a topically ordered questionnaire with categories derived from the concerns of middle-level executives. Thus, the meanings of at least one group of organizational members play a role in the research. Most channel studies, however, employ experimental or questionnaire designs that utilize researcher-derived constructs. Our criticism of this overemphasis on the technical interest is tempered by an awareness that researchers in an emerging area of study tend to focus on the most easily measured aspects of a phenomenon. Quantity, directionality, and symmetry of information flow are structural dimensions that one readily observes when trying to describe communication in an organization.

However, for channel research to move into the historical-hermeneutic realm, it must display far greater concern for the socially created meanings of organizational actors. Davis (1978), for example, writes of using a variety of methodologies to capture the informal communication flow in an organization, but he does not go far enough in discussing the potential richness of channel data. We suggest that surveys, such as the ECCO technique, can account for interpretations of organizational members through a linguistic emphasis. In this way, the perspectives of actors at different levels of the organization can transform such concepts as "timing," "transmission," and "accuracy" that traditionally have been conceived only in objective terms.

Interestingly, studies in the late 1950s and early 1960s adhere in part to the "practical" interest of historical-hermeneutic sciences. C.H. Weaver (1958) attempts to capture the "semantic profiles" of labor and management groups and the effects of these profiles on message flow. Similarly, Tompkins (1962) assesses what he terms "semantic information distance," the gap in information and understanding that exists between organizational levels. As Jablin (1979, p. 1208) notes, studies in this area yield some of the "most consistent conclusions of any topic of study in organizational communication." For any study to truly manifest Habermas's practical interest, however, it must use research findings to enhance the understanding of organizational members. Motivated in part by such an interest, Tompkins (1977) employs interview-derived data to recommend the establishment of new lines of upward communication in NASA's Marshall Space Flight Center. The new system proves remarkably effective in keeping administrators apprised of and open to the suggestions of engineers.

To embody the emancipatory interest of the critically oriented sciences, channel research must open up dialogue between levels of the organization, not just in terms of the quantity of information flow, but also with respect to the opportunities for self-reflection and mutual understanding. Although channel researchers aim to improve communication effectiveness in organizations (Brooks, Callicoat, and Siegerdt 1979), managers typically reap the dividends of such changes. This is not to minimize the value of such change-oriented research; however, critically oriented channel research must treat the aims of organizational elites as potentially shaping an oppressive reality. The critical researcher should uncover the factors that inhibit communication, such subtleties as interdepartmental and interlevel competition and differences in conflict strategies. Even though researchers have answered Redding's (1966) call for more studies on upward communication, they generally have abandoned interest in the downward flow of messages. In the critical spirit, we challenge researchers to explore <u>downward</u> as well as upward distortion. For we expect many downward messages to be characterized by omission and protection of information.

Organizational Communication Climate:
The Psychological Approach

As previously noted, channel and climate research overlap to some extent, particularly since each area targets the "flow" of communication in an organization. However, they differ conceptually in that channel research adopts a mechanistic view of communication, while climate studies display a psychological, perceptual perspective.

As Jablin (1980a) points out, the first explicit linkage of psychological climate to organizational behavior appears in the work of McGregor (1960), who explains that "many subtle behavioral manifestations of managerial attitude create what is often referred to as the 'psychological climate' of the relationship" (p. 134). Researchers use the term "climate," in the broad sense, to refer to perceptions of such organizational factors as structure, individual responsibility, rewards, job challenges, and tolerance (Litwin and Stringer 1968). More specific to our purposes, climate is associated with such communicative dimensions as those comprising the Ideal Managerial Climate (IMC): supportiveness, participative decisionmaking, trust, openness, and high performance goals (Redding 1972). Although Redding (1972) acknowledges the "slippery" nature of the climate construct, he observes that most researchers echo McGregor's (1960) concern for the way employees perceive the "subtle behavioral manifestations of managerial attitude" (Redding 1972, p. 112). Moreover, "the climate of the organization is more crucial than are communication skills or techniques (taken by themselves) in creating an effective organization" (Redding 1972, p. 111).

Jablin (1980a) observes that most researchers view climate as a relatively persistent, molar attribute shared by organizational members but affected by individual perceptions. Yet, at the same time, researchers disagree about the way to define and measure the construct. One school of thought treats climate as a psychological attribute of individual members, a "summary evaluation of events," derived from actual occurrences and perceptions of those occurrences (James and Jones 1974). Studies that adopt this approach use self-report questionnaires and multivariate statistics to indicate how members feel about particular climate dimensions. The second approach treats climate as an organizational attribute determined by member perceptions. These perceptions are influenced by such organizational characteristics as size and structure and by such individual experiences as interpersonal communication and managerial style. Researchers who operate from this perspective aim to validate self-report measures through objective indexes (for example, grievances and turnovers) or through a high degree of consistency among scores on a questionnaire. Most communication researchers pursue the first avenue and report individual differences in perception of climate (Jablin 1980a; Muchinsky 1977; Roberts and O'Reilly 1974).

The technical interest of the empirical-analytic sciences dominates research on organizational communication climate. This conclusion, however, is tempered by early "hints" of a phenomenologically informed theory of climate, namely, the idea that climate represents a compilation of the meanings and the interactions between members. For the most part, researchers consistently locate climate externally to the individual. Climate is frequently treated as having an objective "life" of its own, a reality assessed through summaries of individual perceptions. These perceptions are measured through the use of questionnaires devoid of member interpretation of climate dimensions (Roberts and O'Reilly 1974; Goldhaber et al. 1978).

The conceptual slippage associated with the term "climate" contributes to this confusion. "Individual and organizational attributes are often confounded . . . when the individual is used as the unit of analysis and the research conclusions are drawn at the organizational level of analysis" (Falcione and Werner 1978, p. 14). Moreover, not only are climate researchers torn between "subjective" and "objective" perceptions and between individual and organizational units of analysis, they are unable to choose between description and evaluation (Jablin 1980a).

The source of this difficulty may lie in the fact that "climate" suggests a meteorological metaphor or organizations (Tompkins 1984). Even when researchers aim to focus on interactions and meanings, the climate or atmosphere metaphor directs them to look "outside the individual." Moreover, managerial control of climate becomes a desirable, but elusive goal. When and if climate can be controlled, it will affect all organizational members.

The problems with climate research and with its underlying metaphor call for new labels to recast this construct in the historical-hermeneutic and the critical perspectives. These new conceptualizations would treat "climate" as a phenomenon "constituted by communication" (Hawes 1974) and created through intersubjective understanding. We offer Pacanowsky and O'Donnell-Trujillo's (1982) notion of "organizational culture" as a way to recast "climate" into an interpretive mode. A cultural perspective centers on the interaction and meaning systems previously ignored in traditional climate research. As Pacanowsky and O'Donnell-Trujillo (1982, p. 122) suggest, "we are interested in the workways, folktales, and ritual practices of an organization." These features embody many of the attitudinal dimensions that typify climate studies. Other investigators express similar interest in explaining organizations through the use of culture (Pettigrew 1979), symbolism (Dandridge, Mitroff, and Joyce 1980), stories and myths (Mitroff and Kilmann 1976), and symbolic convergence (Bormann 1982).

In the critical mode, climate research entails both description and evaluation. That is, a climate researcher with an emancipatory interest seeks openness when it is absent and criticizes the oppressiveness of an organization's "atmosphere." Redding's (1972) IMC manifests a change-oriented perspective, but it adopts an "ideal" managerial view that is problematic for researchers (Tompkins 1984). Poole and McPhee (1983) offer a theoretical foundation for critical work on climate. They introduce an intermediate level of analysis — one between objective and subjective variables. Further, they employ a "structurational" model to examine the way climate is produced and reproduced and the way it inhibits or enhances organizational self-reflection. In a similar vein, Koch and Deetz (1981) detail how analysis of organizational metaphors can uncover prevailing and constraining practices (for example, the military metaphor and its restrictions). This analysis "not only shows the current reality of the organization but also the other possibilities open to it" (Koch and Deetz 1981, p. 13). We believe that metaphor analysis provides a methodology for recasting critical research on communication climate.

Organizational Communication Networks: The Structural Approach

The origins of "network analysis" can be traced to early sociometric studies (Moreno 1953), small-group research (A. Bavelas 1950), information diffusion work (Rogers 1962), and specific mass communication investigations (Lazarsfeld, Berelson, and Gaudet 1948). Simply put, "a network consists of interconnected individuals who are linked by patterned communication flows" (Rogers and Agarwala-Rogers 1976, p. 110). Organizational network researchers typically employ a systems approach (Katz and Kahn 1978). From this perspective the social network comprises the total set of linkages among all organizational members. Members appear as "nodes" in a larger structure composed of dyadic linkages (Farace, Monge, and Russell 1977). Richards (1974) suggests four key characteristics of linkages: symmetry, strength, specificity, (the uniqueness of the linkage's function), and transitivity (consistency of linkages): "If I like A, and A likes B, I should like B." Other linkage properties include centrality, connectedness, reachability, density, and range (Farace, Monge, and Russell 1977; Tichy Tushman, and Fombrun 1979).

Some researchers posit that an organization is composed of a number of interrelated and often overlapping network structures, rather than a unitary network (Redding 1972). For example, Katz and Kahn (1978) identify five "substructures" that approximate communication networks: production; support, concerned with environmental interaction, for example, "disposal activities"; maintenance, concerned with insuring system inputs and allocating rewards and punishments; adaptive, concerned with organizational change; and managerial, concerned with control, coordination, and direction of subsystems. As Jablin (1980a) observes, most investigators use variations of these network types in their research.

Network analysis adheres to assumptions of the technical cognitive interest. This appears in the rigid reification of "clique," "liaison," and "isolate," concepts that are treated at an abstract structural level far removed from the communication that they aim to describe. Researchers often use such labels to prescribe network restructuring, independent of the "meanings" of organizational actors, for example, their interpretations of the relative power of these linkages.

In particular, the knowledge claims of network research embody the technical interest. First, there are difficulties with the notion of a "linkage." While network analysts aim to study the dyad, their frequent failure to account for asymmetry (that is, unreciprocated links) raises questions as to whether researchers are treating the dyad or the individual as the unit of analysis (Jablin 1980a). Moreover, the meaning of a communication "link" has yet to be defined, conceptually or methodologically. Second, as noted, the concepts of network research (for example, "liaison," "bridge," "isolate," "integration," "connectedness") attempt to describe interaction patterns, yet they do so in a way that is detached from the content, meaning, and dynamics of communicative relationships (Putnam 1982b).

The methods of network analysis also manifest a technical orientation. Most network methods gather data through self- report instruments and analyze it with sociograms, matrix methods, or multidimensional scaling. The most popular network analysis technique in speech–communication is Richards's (1974) NEGOPY, which aims to analyze a set of systematic relationships. Techniques such as NEGOPY, while useful in depicting communication structures at a point in time, overemphasize the frequency of communication and give little or no attention to content and meaning.

Interestingly, network techniques are deficient in describing actual communicative behavior (Bernard and Killworth 1977). Specifically, perceived frequency of communication with others does not reflect, with any accuracy, the actual frequency of these contacts. Thus, network techniques represent abstract communication structures by relying on perceptual data loosely tied to objective dimensions. A more important and more serious limitation is that network research is largely method–driven. "Network analysis has been dominated in the past by tool–makers rather than tool-users. The field has been characterized by sophisticated methodologies looking for theoretical problems to answer" (Rogers and Kincaid 1981, p. xii). Stohl (1982) notes that network research has been largely atheoretical until the recent work of Rogers and Kincaid (1981). In a similar vein, Monge, Edwards, and Kiriste (1978) call for a priori hypotheses to guide network research. This preoccupation with method suggests a technical orientation, one that features the re-searcher's control to the relative exclusion of both deductive and inductive theorizing.

Consistent with Habermas's pluralistic view, researchers should avoid casting networks in exclusively technical terms by focusing on message flow and ignoring the dimensions of meaning and time. An approach to network analysis that adheres to the "practical" interest of the historical-hermeneutic sciences highlights relational meanings of organizational actors and uses network findings to enhance intersubjective understanding of roles and relationships. Even though some network researchers, particularly users of the ICA Audit, inform organizational members about their respective "place" in the emergent, communi-cation structure, such feedback often merely caricatures organi-zational roles and relationships. "Practically informed" network research should be meaning-grounded and meaning-directed. More specifically, network analysts should target actors' inter-pretations of such dimensions as the strength of linkages, salient or "memorable" messages (Knapp, Stohl and Reardon 1981), the nature of power relationships, dimensions of social context, and changes over time. As Albrecht and Ropp (1982) argue, network contexts are best examined with such qualitative methods as nondirective interviews and constitutive ethnography, while such factors as contact frequency and channel use are best assessed with quantitative measures.

A critically oriented network researcher treats communication structures and relationships as potential inhibitors or facilitators of self-reflective communication. In the process, the researcher focuses on mutual understanding and on the material constraints imposed on interaction. An "emancipatory" interest can motivate the examination of strong ties and the exploitation of weak ones. "Strong" ties often appear as dominant coalitions that influence the day-to-day dynamics of an organization's network structure. Awareness of such relationships may help the re-searcher and the organization members locate "necessary" (that is, demanded by situational constraints) and "unnecessary" commu-nication restrictions. Moreover, researchers can use the rich in-formation potential of "weak" ties (Granovetter 1973) to increase a member's organizational sources and his or her access to ideas. Tichy (1981) suggests this strategy for increasing inputs from the environment to the organization. In sum, the critical researcher who expresses concern for "strong" or "weak" ties aims to provide greater communication opportunities for members at all organizational levels.

Superior-Subordinate Communication: The Dyadic Approach

As climate research demonstrates, effective communication with one's superior is essential to employee job satisfaction (Goldhaber et al. 1978). Superior-subordinate communication encompasses both upward and downward flow, but it centers on the superior-subordinate dyad rather than on the transfer of information across organizational levels. Jablin (1979, p. 1202) defines superior-subordinate communication as "those exchanges of information and influence between organizational members, at least one of whom has formal . . . authority to direct and evaluate the activities of other organizational members." Jablin (1979) and Kelly (1982) present comprehensive literature reviews on superior-subordinate communication. They concur that most research focuses on perceptions of the amount, frequency, and mode of interaction; upward distortion; upward influence; openness; feedback; communicator style; and effectiveness of superior-subordinate relationships. Both reviewers also lament the neglect of systemic variables that affect dyadic relationships and both urge researchers to adopt situational and developmental approaches to the study of superior-subordinate relationships. Situational variables moderate the impact of type and quality of communication, while developmental approaches uncover the evolution and stability of these interaction patterns. Although Jablin (1979) acknowledges the importance of informal communication, most research on superior-subordinate communication focuses on the task dimension of interaction. Research orientations and general conclusions of these seven areas of study reveal implicit assumptions of technical control and purposeful rational action that characterize this task domain.

Openness, feedback, and upward distortion are areas that grew out of climate or channel research. Openness refers to message sending and receiving in terms of "candid disclosure of feelings" and "a willingness to listen to discomforting information" (Redding 1972, p. 330). Research on upward distortion shows that subordinates frequently filter and conceal valuable information from their superiors (Jablin 1979). However, subordinates who receive positive feedback from their superiors are less likely to distort information than are subordinates whose superiors send negative messages (C.D. Fisher 1979). Evidence of upward distortion also appears in research on perceptual congruency, effectiveness of relationships, and communicator style. Superiors and subordinates generally disagree over the nature of their jobs (Boyd and Jensen 1972); the amount of communication between them (Webber 1970); and personality traits of each (Infante and Gordon 1979). Effective supervisors bridge these status and perceptual gaps through a relaxed, attentive style (Bradley and Baird 1977) and through asking, persuading, and passing along information (Redding 1972). The final area, upward influence, focuses on a superior's influence in the organization at large and on this person's influence with his or her subordinates. Jablin's (1980b) study reaffirms the "Pelz Effect" that subordinates interact more and are more satisfied with their boss if the superior has substantial upward influence.

At first glance, the superior-subordinate literature seems directed toward emancipation of subordinates from ineffective superiors. Even though some studies reflect this orientation (Redding 1972), most are preoccupied with making superiors more effective. Effectiveness, in this sense, refers to technical control and rationality. That is, superiors who use positive feedback and open communication attain greater compliance and higher job performance than do ineffective superiors (Fodor 1974; Hegarty 1974); or as Greene (1975) notes, subordinates who comply with their superior's expectations show higher job satisfaction than those who deviate from the technical rules. In effect, the ultimate goal of research on superior-subordinate communication is helping superiors control their work environments (Redding 1979).

Some degree of upward distortion, perceptual incongruence, and gaps in semantic distance exist despite a superior's communicative effectiveness. Perhaps as Sussman (1975) contends, perceptual incongruence and upward distortion are inevitable outcomes of status differentials between superior and subordinate. Moreover, most superior-subordinate studies employ self-report questionnaires, rarely matched for dyadic analysis. This practice overlooks the possibility of reciprocal influences between superior and subordinate (Greene 1975). Smircich and Chesser (1981) examine reciprocity in their study of metaperspectives of subordinate performance. They argue that a critical factor in perceptual congruence is whether both parties share interpretations of their realities. In actuality, a superior's communication may grow out of a unique relationship with each subordinate, the interpretations each person holds for that relationship, and the context in which it exists.

Some researchers, however, focus on the interaction dimension of the historical-hermeneutic mode by examining managerial work as a communicative performance (O'Donnell-Trujillo 1983). These performances differ in that managers adapt their behaviors to their settings, their audiences, and their functions (Mintsberg 1973). Moreover, as managers interact, they construct a symbolic world complete with grammars for action and shared meanings (Pfeffer 1981). Effective leaders give others a sense of this reality by providing shared visions and shared interpretations of organizational experiences (Pondy 1976). Here the goal of superior-subordinate communication is to enhance understanding of organizational processes.

From a critical perspective, research on superior-subordinate communication could examine the way superiors manage organizational realities and the way subordinates handle the exercise of technical control. Current work on bargaining (Putnam and Jones 1982); organizational politics (Jablin 1981); superior-subordinate conflict (Putnam and Wilson 1983); and relational control (Watson 1982), though largely shaped by the technical interest, holds promise for discovering how these activities lead to organizational reflection and increased autonomy. Further, Tompkins and Cheney's (1982) theory of unobtrusive control can aid in uncovering the subtle decisional premises that superiors employ with subordinates. Thus, examining superior-subordinate communication from an historical-hermeneutic or a critical perspective may lead to new insights about reciprocity in this dyadic relationship, the "staging" of managerial performances, and the ways subordinates can transform systems of unobtrusive control into processes of self-reflection.

CONCLUSION

In sum, we offer Habermas's typology of scientific inquiry as a useful way to characterize past research traditions and to generate new ones. in reviewing organizational theory in general and domains of organizational communication in particular, we find that an interest in technical control dominates research traditions and overshadows work on intersubjective understanding and critical self-reflection. We challenge scholars to embody a healthy pluralism, with a critical bent. Such a perspective could focus on human understanding, while recognizing material constraints, in examining ideological distortions that inhibit communication between and within organizations.

With this in mind, we hope that researchers seek to revitalize the "traditional" areas of research and vigorously pursue emerging areas. Many new foci for research are appearing on the scene. These include, in addition to organizational culture, conflict and negotiation (Donohue, 1981; Putnam and Jones 1982), decision making and information processing (Penley 1982; Poole 1978; Putnam and Sorenson 1982), power and politics (Conrad 1983; Gandz and Murray 1980), socialization/learning/competence (Feldman 1981; Louis 1980), boundary-spanning/organizational- environment interface (Caldwell and O'Reilly 1982; Tushman 1977), unobtrusive organizational control (Cheney 1983; Tompkins and

Cheney 1983), technology and communication (Fowler and Wackerbarth 1980), and organizational deviance/dissent (Stanley 1981; Stewart 1980). It will be interesting to track the development of such areas — especially in light of the "interests" that shape and infuse them.

We close by echoing Habermas's (1973) call for the integration of theory and practice. In organizational communication, as in other forms of social scientific inquiry, theory is best conceptualized as a process by which a person cultivates a thoughtful and enlightened way of life. With such a goal uppermost in mind, one's research should never be far removed from the social life that it is intended to explain.

14
THE INTERPRETATION OF ORGANIZATIONAL CULTURES
Nick O'Donnell-Trujillo and
Michael E. Pacanowsky

The Valley View Police Station, Saturday morning, 7:00
a.m. Two patrol officers — Robert Hancock and Richard
Christiansen — are sitting at a long table in the staffing
room. They are filling out their incident reports for the
just completed graveyard shift. Hancock grumbles about
how relatively uneventful the shift was, and then begins
talking about the night's only action. At 6:15 a.m., he
backed Christiansen up in dealing with a man who became
excessively rowdy celebrating his 26th birthday.

Hancock:	I wished he invited me to that party. I heard you (over the radio) say, "He's thinkin' about swingin'," and I'm sayin' to myself, "swing asshole swing."
Christiansen:	I may not have looked ready, but I was kinda hoping he'd try something.
Hancock:	I'da liked to see what a flashlight woulda done right between his eyes.
Christiansen:	I'd've had to pick him out of the grille of my car first. That's where he was heading.1

As communication researchers who have naively made our way
into various organizations, we have found that the actual communication in those organizations — like this conversation between
two Valley View officers — often does not "fit" well with many
traditional notions of organizational communication. In part, this
lack of fit between actual communication in organizations and
our ways of thinking about organizational communication reflects
the fact that most organizational communication researchers do

not examine communication per se, but instead manipulate numbers that are supposed to represent prepackaged attitudes about, or reflections on, or aggregations of actual communication activity. When confronted with conversational data taken from organizations, we asked ourselves the fairly obvious (and to us more fundamental) question: What is going on here? In piecing together an answer for that question, we find ourselves working through the corpus of conversations we have from any organization, threading our way from comments overheard here, to jokes and stories told there, to staff meetings, incident reports, and lunchtime chats.

For example, when we look at the conversation in the staffing room between Hancock and Christiansen and ask ourselves "What is going on here?" we see a similarity in this behind-the-scenes interaction with many other backstage occasions where the Valley View police "talk tough." For these policemen, talking "tough" is an important social ritual — it's a time to swear, tell "disgusting" jokes, and brag about one's invincibility as a fighter and virility as a lover. As we look through our data, we find that Officer Hancock is particularly inclined to be a "tough" talker. On one occasion, he claimed that when he gets to handle a traffic fatality, he's in "fifth heaven," though he matter-of-factly admits "it does get bad, like when there's a little boy and his bones are all broke and every time his heart beats, blood rushes out of his head." On another occasion he allows he does not like to write traffic tickets when he's in a bad mood,

> cause if somebody tried to push me, I may hurt 'em. I don't wanna hurt 'em. Cause I'm capable of being a very efficient killer, no ifs, ands, or buts about it. I can just see myself explainin' to the Chief [in a louder, high pitched voice], "Well, Chief, this guy pushed me to the point where we ripped his jug'lar veins out." [Now smiling] Or, "He pushed us to the point where we broke his throat or crushed his esophagus."

There is a problem, however, in accepting too quickly the simple assertion that what is going on here is "tough" talk. For that same corpus of conversation used to establish that the Valley View police do talk "tough" and that Hancock is a preeminent "tough" talker can also be used to show that Christiansen, normally, is anything but a "tough" talker. In fact, quite to the contrary, Christiansen admits to having been on the police force for 18 months and never yet having been in a fist fight. Moreover, he is willing to confide to one of us researchers that he's not sure he's looking forward to that first fist fight either. Belittling his tough-talking comrades, he says that "they watch too much 'Starsky and Hutch'"; downplaying physical bravado, he prefers instead to "reason with a guy"; and he describes being a Valley View officer, all in all, as a "meet-the-mortgage-payments type of job." Furthermore, Hancock who <u>knows</u> these things about Christiansen, characterizes him as a uniquely "mellow" guy and accounts for his differentness by the fact that Christiansen grew up in a "good LDS [Mormon] family." So, if Christiansen is not given to talking "tough," and if Hancock knows this, why does Hancock nonetheless initiate an episode of talking "tough"? And why does Christiansen respond?

Again, we turn to the data for an answer. What we discover is a nagging doubt that Hancock harbors about Christiansen. "Christiansen's a mellow guy," he confided, "but you go into a situation, you really got to watch for him. You really don't know if he's gonna stand with you or he's gonna back down." What Hancock is doing in initiating this "tough" talk with Christiansen is subjecting him to a social test, inviting him to talk in a way that displays his apparent readiness to "stand with" a fellow policeman, rather than "back down."

But there is more. Another comment by Hancock reveals an even richer notion of the "tough" talk as the social test. The trust that Hancock seeks is not simply trust that Christiansen will <u>physically</u> "stand with" him, he wants to know that Christiansen will "stand with" him in other ways. Hancock explains:

You can't really trust the guys until you get to know 'em and what they'll do in a crisis situation. Cause we're only human, you know. We may have someone out here in handcuffs and they haul off and kick the shit outa you and you pop 'em in the mouth. Well, that's illegal — there's no way you can legally knock the shit outa some-one in handcuffs. But it's gonna happen, somebody kicks you and it hurts like hell and you end up poppin' the sonovabitch before you really realize that you've knocked the shit outa him. Hell, everybody's done that — there isn't an officer here that hasn't. And you worry about things like that 'cause you don't know if the new guy's gonna rat on you or what.

The social test of "tough" talk is not simply to feel out Christiansen's physical readiness to "stand with" a fellow cop, it is a test to feel out more directly Christiansen's <u>verbal</u> readiness to "stand with" a fellow cop. In this case, Christiansen seems to have passed the test, matching Hancock's "flashlight between the eyes" with visions of flesh mashed into the "grille of my car." Indeed, merely to express a desire for action is evidence of one's readiness; to exhibit eagerness and dramatically depict the outcome is all the more convincing.

Lest we get too carried away with the conversation and mistake it for some swaggering brutality on the part of these two officers, we need to consider what happens next, as Christiansen walks to the bulletin board (out of Hancock's earshot) and a rookie asks him, "So Officer Christiansen almost mixed it up last night?" Christiansen replies, "Not really. I didn't give the guy a chance to get mad at me." Christiansen's interaction with the rookie is a metacommunicative commentary that instructs the rookie not to take the prior exchange with Hancock as an endorsement of fighting. As the rookie observes more instances of this behind-the-scenes "tough" talk, he comes to understand it as an enjoyable social ritual and an important social test.

In working our way back and forth from the conversational episode to the various bits and pieces of conversational data we have from the Valley View police, it should be clear that what we have done is provided an <u>interpretation,</u> an account that makes sensible not only the speaking event itself but also the content of that event as well. We have done this by playing out the meanings and significances of the talk, and by so doing we have embedded them within some incipient notions of the overall "culture" of these Valley View police officers. If we pieced together more interpretations of still more episodes, we would construct an interpretation of the culture of the Valley View police in all its fullness. We would argue, for any "chunk" of conversational data taken from any organization, a full answer to the question "What is going on here?" requires nothing less than an explication of the "culture" that surrounds it.

Our particular attachment to the metaphor of "culture" is by no means unique. In recent years the concept of culture has enjoyed a growing interest among many organizational research- ers (Pacanowsky and O'Donnell-Trujillo 1982; Pettigrew 1979). As anthropologists have studied myth, folklore, and symbolism in different societies, these organizational researchers are studying myth, folklore, and symbolism in different organizations (DeWine and Wagner 1981; Kreps 1983; Dandridge, Mitroff, and Joyce 1980; Peters 1978). Although these researchers tread a common path guided by the same metaphor of "culture," their notions of culture and their notions of the most appropriate ways to study it are vastly different.

For many researchers, "culture" is something an organization <u>has</u> — a variable like "climate," the particular value of which can spell success or doom. To study "culture" in this way, the researcher classifies it, or at least classifies its manifestations in various myths or stories or jokes, and then links it in various ways to organizational effectiveness (Burrell and Morgan 1979).

For us, however, this functionalist orientation trivializes "cul- ture" and robs the metaphor of its potential richness for studying organizational communication. We prefer to adopt an interpretive approach toward organizational "culture" for organizational analysis. We refuse to consider culture as one of several variables that can be found and measured in an organization like the Valley View Police Department. We prefer to consider the Valley View Police Department and other organizations as cultures, as systems of socially created meanings. Thus our research interest seeks not to "list" or "document" the symbolic aspects of organizational life, but to understand how that organizational life is meaningful to organizational members. To put it simply, we want to make sense of how they make sense of their organizational experiences.

In the remainder of this chapter, we hope to more clearly articulate this form of scholarship by outlining the relevant intellectual traditions and research practices that underlie an interpretive approach toward organizational culture: semiotics, hermeneutic phenomenology, ethnomethodology, and hermeneutics. These traditions are not rigid perspectives into which organizational culture research should be pigeon-holed, but are useful frameworks for displaying some of our own theoretical and methodological assumptions about the nature of organizational life. We conclude this chapter with a discussion of some of the problems and potentials of taking an interpretive approach to the study of organizational communication.

ORGANIZATIONAL CULTURE AS SEMIOTIC

For anthropologist Clifford Geertz (1973), culture is semiotic. Geertz invites us to consider cultures as "webs of significance" that members spin as they go about participating in their culture. These "webs," or patterns of significant symbols, are the conventionalized structures by which members orient themselves toward one another. Symbols stand as things not because of any necessary relationship to those things, but because of an underlying convention that is revealed and constituted as members make sense of their culture. Unfortunately, many organizational communication researchers have forgotten this basic assumption that symbols have arbitrary meaning. For these researchers, communication in organizations does not have arbitrary meaning — its meaning is determined by a presumed necessary relationship with organizational goals.

A semiotic stance toward organizational life reinforces the position that communication has conventional meanings. This stance encourages us as organizational researchers to come up with alternative meanings, multiple meanings of communicative events. Culture, after all, is no simple matter. In Geertz's (1973, p. 10) terms, culture is a "multiplicity of complex conceptual structures, many of them super-imposed upon or knotted into one another, which are at once strange, irregular, and inexplicit" — webs spun on webs spun on webs. The purpose of organizational inquiry from a semiotic perspective, thus, is to uncover some of the richness embedded in those interconnected symbolic structures.

For example, reconsider the opening episode involving the two Valley View officers. As an instance of backstage staffing room talk between officers, it is relatively simple to say their talk stands as a "tough" display of physical prowess and verbal up-manship. After all, the officers regularly participated in these staffing room exchanges, depicting themselves as invincible fighters and incredible lovers. But this episode of "tough" talk involves two particular policemen, Hancock and Christiansen. The episode stands as a social test, initiated by Hancock, of Christiansen's physical readiness. As we suggested, the episode stands as a test of Christiansen's verbal readiness to support a fellow cop as well.

The view of organizational culture as semiotic is influenced by the work of Charles Peirce. For Peirce (1955a), semiotic was established in a triadic relationship between a sign (something that stands as something else), an object (that which is identi-fied by the sign), and an interpretant (the context of signs that renders the sign/object relationship culturally meaningful). Unlike Ferdinand de Saussure, the French structuralist, Peirce suggested a processual account of semiotics, highlighted in his discussion of "semiosis." Peirce described this process of semiosis in terms of an ongoing dialectic between the inter-pretant and the sign. As Umberto Eco (1976, p. 68-69) elab-orated:

> In order to establish what the interpretant of a sign is, it is necessary to name it by means of another sign which in turn has to be named by another sign and so on. At this point there begins a process of unlimited semiosis, which, paradoxical as it may be, is the only guarantee for the foundation of a semiotic system capable of checking itself entirely by its own means.

Peirce epitomized this notion of "infinite semiosis" when he iden-tified the sign as "anything which determines something else (its interpretant) to refer to an object to which itself refers (its object) in the same way, the interpretant beginning in turn a sign, and so on ad infinitum" (1955b, p. 300).

This process of semiosis makes for a more precise reading of the "webs of significance" invoked by Geertz. The strength of Geertz's web metaphor is its implication that spiders continually reshape and expand old webs in spinning new webs. Peirce's notion embellishes the web metaphor with analytical texture, as semiosis has a weblike quality in which interpretants and signs dialectically elaborate each other. Such a processual view of semiotics does not, however, lead the researcher to an infinite regress insofar as plausible descriptions of cultural structures can be posited. The important insight is that such interpretations as the social test initiated by Hancock are not deterministic explanations that fully exhaust cultural meaning but are partial interpretations subject to change as organizational members go about spinning their webs of significance.

Several criticisms have been leveled against semiotics on philosophical grounds, two of which seem particularly relevant to the organizational culture approach. First, as Leo Pap (1979) has suggested, a semiotic focus on sign systems has led some theorists to a reification of signs — the world is divided into things that are signs and things that are not signs. Pap cautioned that signs have no inherent meaning but become meaningful when they are subject to interpretation. For Pap, it is this interpretation or sense-making by cultural members that is the focus of analysis and he redefined semiotics as the "study of patterns of interpretive behavior" (1979, p. 338). We endorse Pap's reformulation of semiotics as it emphasizes the processual aspects of meaning in the sense-making behavior of organizational members.

A second criticism of semiotics, raised by phenomenologists such as Merleau-Ponty (1964) and Sartre (1966), is that some semioticians lose sight of language use in their analysis of linguistic structure. This criticism is directed toward those "radical structuralists" such as Levi-Strauss (1963) who follow the lead of Saussure (1959). For Saussure, the distinction between langue (language) and parole (speaking) was a crucial one. Langue was described as an unconscious a priori code that underlies all communicative activity and parole was characterized by the conscious individual act of using language. Saussure argued that langue was the most fundamental system of signs and that linguistics, as the scientific study of language, was the most appropriate model for semiotic analysis. The criticism of this argument is that langue becomes all encompassing while parole drops entirely out of analysis and is viewed merely as a predetermined manifestation of linguistic structure. Levi-Strauss, for example, epitomizes the Saussurian type of semiotic inquiry in his attempt to deduce the linguistic structures that constitute a deterministic and universal grammar of culture.

Clearly, semiotic structures provide constitutive and regulatory contours that shape communicative behavior, but such structures are not deterministic nor all encompassing. Moreover, as implied in the process of semiosis, symbolic structures are continually reinforced as modified in the very communicative behaviors they serve to structure. As Giddens (1976, p. 121) has pointed out, "social structures are both constituted by human agency and yet are the very medium of this constitution." The recognition of this insight encourages us to adopt a more phenomenological semiotics. Such an orientation presupposes the influence of semiotic structures on language use but invites us to pay critical attention to the process of how culture is constituted in the act of speaking. This invitation to attend to communicative behavior is grounded in the work of Martin Heidegger and it is to his writings that we now turn.

THE LINGUISTICALITY OF ORGANIZATIONAL REALITY

The claim that communicative activities are constitutive of organizational reality has its philosophical roots in the hermeneutic phenomenology of Martin Heidegger. Heidegger (1959) argued that being in a world presupposes the interpretation or meaningfulness of that world. One does not perceive a reality and subsequently import meaning to that reality. Instead, one experiences an already meaningful, preconsciously interpreted world. To see things in the world is to take them for granted as things; to see them, as Heidegger proposed, as "thematized." For Heidegger, language provides the medium by which meaningfulness is made manifest, by which "being becomes thematized." "Language," as Heidegger's (1962, p. 252) familiar axiom stated, "is the house of being." More specifically, "Words and language are not wrappings in which things are packed for the commerce of those who write and speak. It is in words and language that things first come into being and are" (1959, p. 13). Thus, the linguisticality of being is at the same time its ontology, its "coming into being."

For Heidegger, the foundation of the linguisticality of being was the phenomenon of speaking. It is in speaking that being is made manifest. As Palmer (1969, p. 128) suggested, "[speaking] is not really a power given to language by its user but a power which language gives to him, a means of being seized by what is made manifest through it." This "power" given to an individual in language is no less than access to a social reality, a social reality constructed in that language. It is the act of speaking that provides the sole medium for participating in that social construction of reality. As Hawes (1977, p. 31) has offered, "a hermeneutic phenomenology of communication ultimately becomes a theory of ontological disclosure insofar as studying communication both as a theme and as a medium discloses the constituting of social worlds." The research challenge, thus, is to take speaking events, like the exchange between Hancock and Christiansen, and explore and explicate the constitutive features of those events as well as the social reality those events disclose.

The directive of a hermeneutic phenomenology is clearly implicated in an interpretive approach to organizational culture. Organizational members participate in an already meaningful, preconsciously interpreted, social world. The Valley View police do not experience their world tabula rasa and then make sense of it; they simply go about their everyday communitative activities already making sense of those activities. We seek to explicate this taken-for-granted reality; that is, to make sense of their organizational sense-making. Our interpretations of their reality, however, are not dependent on establishing a psychological rapport with the members we observe. Organizational sense-making has its locus in communicative behavior (Wittgenstein 1969; Schrag 1980). As Bauman (1978, p. 179) has suggested, "the fact that dialogue took place shows that the conversationalists understood each other; otherwise they would not know 'how to go on,' and dialogue would not be possible." Thus, research from an organizational culture position seeks to reconstruct the constitutive, taken-for-granted, features of organizational talk and explicate the sense of organizational reality made and displayed in that talk. Specifically, organizational culture research from an interpretive perspective attempts to answer two questions: What are the key communicative behaviors that evidence that organizational sense-making is being accomplished? and What is the sense that members of a particular organization make of their organizational experience? These two questions may be fruitfully approached through the interrelated perspectives and practices of ethnomethodology and hermeneutics.

THE COMMUNICATIVE ACCOMPLISHMENTS
OF ORGANIZATIONAL LIFE

In his articulation of the ethnomethodological perspective, Garfinkel (1967) encouraged the presumption that social facts are accomplishments. Where others see, or more frequently assume, the existence of "real things," the ethnomethodologist attempts to reconstruct the process by which these things become real. "Reality," for the ethnomethodologist, does not determine a priori the behaviors of persons nor is that reality merely a place in which behaviors occur. Rather, reality exists for the persons only as they "accomplish" it in their behaviors.

An ethnomethodological orientation toward organizations renders organizational reality problematic and in need of thorough explication, not gloss by assumptive fiat. "Tickets" and "accidents" and "false alarms" are entities not independent of the communicative activities of the Valley View police but constituted in and by those activities. "Standing with" another officer acquires meaning only when the officer physically or verbally supports another officer at the scene or, as we saw earlier, when the officer is able to talk "tough." The ethnomethodologists would say that the ontological status of "standing with" another officer is accomplished in its use.

The concept of "accomplishment" directs organizational researchers to consider the process, the "doing," of organizational life. These researchers, as Weick (1979, p. 44) would have it, "are generous in their use of verbs." The methodological directive is to explicate these verbs, to articulate how members accomplish their organizational lives in their talk.

These ongoing accomplishments of organizational reality are embedded in the very reality they create. Garfinkel used "indexicality" to convey this sense of embeddedness. "Indexicality" refers to the inherent contextual nature of any communicative activity. Words have meaning only in a context or, as Palmer (1969, p. 203) wrote, "one only uses the words already belonging to the situation." This situation includes such things as who the participants are (for example, "Hancock" and "Christiansen"), where the activity took place (for example, "in the staff room"), and on what occasion the activity occurred (for example, "the change of shifts"), but these constituents of context do not determine meaning. Rather, communicative behavior and context mutually elaborate each other, a characteristic known as "reflexivity." Leiter (1980, p. 139) concluded: "The setting gives meaning to talk and behavior within it, while at the same time, it exists in and through that very talk and behavior." So the social test of Christiansen's readiness is meaningful not in the talk nor in the context but in the texture of the talk in the complexity of the context.

Our ethnomethodological interest in understanding accomplishments as indexical constituents of organizational culture encourages us to observe and record occasions of naturally occurring talk in organizational settings. We are simply not content with accounts of organizational reality acquired in questionnaires and interviews. Rather, we take extensive notes of, and tape record whenever possible, the conversational activity of organizational members, for it is in these contextually embedded interactions that members accomplish and disclose a sense of organizational culture.

In order to get a sense of the culture disclosed in organizational talk, researchers may attend to a variety of constitutive indicators of organizational sense-making (Pacanowsky and O'Donnell-Trujillo 1982). First, each organizational culture has its relevant constructs (objects, individuals, processes), such as "radar units," "rookies," and "false alarms" for a Valley View policeman, that identify the global aspects of organizational membership. The constructs serve as general indicators of how members structure their experience. Second, each organizational culture has its <u>facts</u> that members use to explain the way the organization operates. For example, Valley View policemen's view of "the city" as "more interested in the money than in the people" is used to account for their having to spend more time "selling tickets" than "fighting crime." Third, each organizational culture contains the <u>practices</u> for accomplishing organizational activities, for "getting the job done." Practices known as "tasks" are often expressed formally by supervisors but come to be realized informally as one "learns the ropes." Thus, Valley View police come to "sell tickets"; they offer a "break" to a violator by writing the ticket for five miles an hour less than the "actual" speed. Fourth, each organizational culture has specialized <u>vocabularies</u> that reveal features of a member's sense-making. Police in Valley View maintain a suspicion about the citizens they deal with, and this suspicion is reflected in the words they use to label these citizens. The "regular" people are "assholes," but most others are "scrotes," "dirtbags," "creeps," and "maggots." This vocabulary, though often used kiddingly, serves as a daily conversational reminder that the Valley View police see themselves as dealing with the "negative" element of society. Fifth, each organizational culture contains <u>stories</u> that members exchange on a regular basis. These stories typify and anonymize organizational experience because they reveal that, in principle, the experience could be duplicated by another organizational member (Berger and Luckmann 1966). Thus, stories about "close calls" are not merely titillating narratives but are possible future scenarios. Finally, each organizational culture develops various <u>rites and rituals</u> that orient members temporally and serve as occasions for sense-making. "Shooting at the range," "shift changes," and "daily 7-11 breaks" all constitute organizational rites and rituals in which Valley View officers regularly participate. Participation in such events provides access for members to a particular sense of shared reality.

In summary, the ethnomethodological directive considers these aspects of organizational culture by treating them not as objects that reflect and regulate organizational life but as accomplishments in their own right. The preliminary task in organizational culture research, then, is to explicate how constructs, facts, practices, vocabularies, stories, and rituals come to be socially constructed or accomplished. This explication focuses on the "doing" of these aspects as their ontological status is their use.

At the same time members constitute their relevant constructs, practices, and rituals, they are also constituting parts of their organizational culture. These constructs, practices, and rituals are, if we may, miniaccomplishments embedded in the larger ongoing accomplishments of organizational culture. As Weider

(1974, p. 161) formulated it, these miniaccomplishments represent "indexical expressions which operate as 'parts' of a Gestalt-contextual." That is, each part, each accomplishment, is one constitutive indexical "piece" of the larger contextual whole of organizational culture. Thus, a <u>reflexivity</u> is implicated in which these indexical accomplishments and the context of organizational culture mutually elaborate one another. It is this reflexive character of an organizational culture and the constitutive elements of that culture that mandate that we embrace a hermeneutic stance in our research.

HERMENEUTICS AND ORGANIZATIONAL CULTURE RESEARCH

In "Blurred Genres," Clifford Geertz (1980, p. 167) quips that the label "hermeneutics" frightens some scholars, "conjuring up images of biblical zealots, literary humbugs, and Teutonic professors." There are others, less frightened but equally pessimistic, who view hermeneutics as little more than academic bemusement. It is our belief that a hermeneutic orientation is neither frightening nor trivial but can lead to an insightful understanding of organizational communication.

Hermeneutics refers to the interpretation, the making sense, of a text-analogue. It is an analytic mode of inquiry, with roots in biblical and literary explication, which seeks to bring to light the underlying coherent features of a particular text. As Schrag (1980, p. 98) recently elaborated, this "text" need not be limited to a literal text but may refer to everyday behavior:

> Although we might be straining the metaphorical reach of "text," we would not, I think, be stretching it beyond its elastic limits by using the term as an oblique designator of the <u>texture</u> of lived-through world experience. It is this texture of everyday life that becomes the "text" in our extended hermeneutic.

Thus an interpretive approach to organizational culture seeks to explicate the text of everyday organizational life as constituted in the members' communicative activities and accomplishments.

The hermeneutic implications of organizational culture research are perhaps best highlighted in the so-called hermeneutic circle. The essential idea behind the hermeneutic circle — that context and talk mutually elaborate each other — has already been hinted at in the concept of reflexivity. The context, the whole of organizational culture, receives its definition from talk, its parts, and, reciprocally, the parts can be understood only in reference to the whole. Thus every organizational accomplishment is meaningful only in relation to other accomplishments.

In closely analyzing these interacting accomplishments, we begin to construe an interconnectedness or a particular configuration of "webs of significance." At the moment we get this sense of an interconnected whole, an analytic dialectic is set in motion. Geertz (1979, p. 239) explains: "Hopping back and forth between the whole conceived through the parts which actualize it and the parts conceived through the whole which motivates them, we seek to turn them, by sort of intellectual perpetual motion, into explications of one another.

This perpetual motion that Geertz speaks of is more conventionally considered a "hermeneutic spiral." As we observe, describe, and explicate additional instances of organizational talk, we are able to make sense of larger segments of the culture, in increasingly wider hermeneutic circles. Thus we can take the single exchange between Hancock and Christiansen and, by observing more and by digging into our notes, we can work through the backstage banter of physical bravado and verbal upmanship to the social testing of Christiansen's readiness to physically and verbally "stand with" Hancock. The longer we analytically observe this talk, of course, the better we are able to make sense of episodes that seemed enigmatic or make textured sense of episodes that seemed self-evident. This hermeneutic spiral is sustained because every communicative activity has a retrospective feature (Mehan and Wood 1975). That is, past episodes make sense in light of what is disclosed in present episodes. Organizational activities, then, are always open to reinterpretation in the light of subsequently observed activities.

The hermeneutic spiraling of organizational culture research does not result in the discovery of causal laws. Culture is not a "cause" but a "context." Culture is amenable not to causal analysis but to interpretation or "thick description," which reveals organizational sense-making displayed in the discourse of members. By the same token, organizational culture research is not condemned to an infinite hermeneutic regress. Bauman (1978, p. 31) explained: "The process goes on, in even wider circles, until we are satisfied that the residue of opacity still left in our object does not bar us from appropriating its meaning." In other words, we admit that interpretive analysis is inherently incomplete and thus do not suggest the "exhaustiveness" of our interpretations. Rather, we attempt to present a plausible account of the organizational culture that captures much of the nuance of sense-making. The reader must ask: Have we offered an account that takes you to the heart of the culture?

INSCRIBING INTERPRETATIONS OF ORGANIZATIONAL CULTURES: PROBLEMS AND PROMISES

Much of what we have discussed so far in this chapter has been the scholarly traditions from which our notions of organizational culture flow, but there is one more issue we feel we must address. It is an issue often perceived as irrelevant to or is overlooked in most calls for new theoretical or methodological approaches to the study of communicative phenomena. We are referring to the activity of the writing of the research report, or, in this case, the inscribing of an interpretation. We contend that an interpretive approach to organizational culture is not only theoretically and methodologically unique as an approach to studying organizational communication, but it ought to be presentationally different as well. As Victor Turner (1978, p. xi) has said, "new theoretical wine requires new presentational bottles." What we are arguing for are presentational bottles more art-like than science-like in shape and form.

This notion that the form of writing is an issue worth bothering about may seem strange, even preposterous to some. Training and practice have taught us that social scientific research is, fundamentally, the application of social scientific methods. Of course, we accede (sometimes grudgingly) to the need to write up our research "clearly," lest we obscure the beauty of our methods or diminish the impact of our conclusions. But writing remains essentially an adjunct activity, what we do after we've completed the study (as in, "I finished the study last quarter, I'm just waiting to find some time to write it up"). From this point of view, the form of writing really neither adds to nor detracts from the already completed research. Competent writing is simply a matter of competent translation, of transferring our knowledge and insights onto the page.

Such a notion of writing, however, may be simplistic. Daft and Wiginton (1979), working from Ashby's Law of Requisite Variety, posit that our forms of discourse are variously capable of capturing and displaying the equivocality of phenomena. More to the point, they argue that mathematical symbols and social scientific writing may be appropriate to describe the simple relations within organizations but inappropriate to describe more densely interrelated, contingent, and evanescent aspects of organizations (and, surely, an organization's culture is just such an interrelated, contingent, and evanescent aspect of an organization). Although they themselves do not make the point, their argument logically extends to the claim that those most equivocal forms of discourse (poetry, dance) would be most appropriate for registering the most equivocal aspects of organizations.

Quite a few years ago, Gregory Bateson (1958) made the similar observation about the methods of presentation of anthropological data. For Bateson, the task of the anthropologist was to render the details of a culture as sensible to the reader as they are to the natives who have lived their whole lives within the culture. Bateson could see two ways of attempting this — through scientific modes of expression or through artistic modes of expression — and he noted that art permits a writer

> to describe culture in such a manner that many of its premises and inter-relations of parts are implicit in his composition. He can leave a great many of the most fundamental aspects of culture to be picked up, not from his actual words, but from his emphasis. He can choose words whose very sound is more significant than their dictionary meaning and he can so group and stress them that the reader almost unconsciously receives information which is not explicit in the sentences and which the artist would find it hard — almost impossible — to express in analytic terms (1958, p. 1).

There are two features of Bateson's ideas that seem particularly relevant to us. The first is the recognition that the task of cultural description is not simply the detailing and documenting of observations, but of rendering those sensible. The second is that sensible renditions are not necessarily ineluctably linked to the details of observation. That is, although in scientific exposition the observations or facts constitute the "truth," in artistic expositions this is not necessarily the case. Instead, the truth is a gestalt, arising from facts, surely, but arising also from "implicit premises," "emphasis," even the "sound" of words. Thus, the crucial distinction between science and art: In science, truth resides in the methods one uses to establish fact; in art, truth resides in the writing (Pacanowsky 1981).

There is an implication of this conclusion, often raised as an objection to art-like writings, that seems to us a red herring. It has to do with the ultimate irrelevance of art to social science because of our inability to train or evaluate artistic talent. Dorothy Walsh (1969, p. 104), for example, has written: "Mere fluency in the language is adequate for informational reports, but talent is necessary for the imaginative evocation of vicarious experience." Peggy Sanday (1979) uses a similar logic in explaining why Geertz's notion of thick description has produced more interesting discussion than actual research. Sanday both praises Geertz and damns his approach by saying it requires "artistic imagination," a commodity presumably in short supply among social scientists. We think that words like "talent" and "artistic imagination" do more to mystify than usefully to describe. Surely, great science, like great art, is the product of talent and imagination as well; yet although we do not all pretend to be great scientists, we do feel we can, in our fash-ion, produce useful scientific descriptions. In the same way, we would argue, we can produce useful artistic descriptions without pretense of great art.

We are not claiming that all organizational communication scholars should begin writing fiction (although, we would hasten to add, a novel may be an appropriate way of rendering organi-zational life sensible and should be taken seriously). We are, however, claiming that our interpretations of organizational cul-ture will profit from art-like exposition. What we mean by this is not that we need to cultivate artistic talent and imagination so much as acquiesce to the demands of artistic writing as a form — with all its divergence, potentiality, and absence of lists.

Herein lies the true promise of an interpretive approach to organizational culture. Our interpretations, more art-like than science-like, should strive not to eliminate all other claims about organizational life but should instead strive to open up as many rich and plausible claims as we can. This elaboration of our understanding of organizational life made possible by our inter-pretations will lead to a by-product of research typically over-looked by those with a strict social scientific orientation — that of the appreciation of organizational experience. We mean by appreciation not some self-serving enthusiasm for organizations, but an increased discernment and subtle sense of what goes on in organizations. In this way, an interpretive approach to orga-nizational culture is a true complement to other ways of study-ing organizational communication. It does not intend to answer the same kinds of questions that have been traditionally asked. It is not a "triangulating" methodology that gives us another fix on the same phenomenon. It is not redundant. Instead, it invites us to ask new questions and, we hope, come up with broader answers. Weick's (1979, p. 234) comments on this sense of complementarity seem an apt point for closing: "Organiza-tional theorists bite off too little too precisely and we've tried to encourage them to tackle bigger slices of reality. And, if poetry, appreciation, and the artistry of inquiry need to be coupled with science to produce those bigger bites, so be it." Organizational culture research from an interpretive position encourages the development of this art-like potential in our scholarly research, and holds the promise for an increasingly subtle appreciation of the richness of organizational life.

NOTE

1. This conversation passage is taken from a four-month field study of a small urban police force, fictitiously named the "Valley View Police Department." At the time the study was

conducted, the community was offering a ride-along program. Thus, members of the research team accompanied the officers as they cruised the streets and responded to calls. Structured interviews were not conducted. Rather, we watched, listened to, and made written note of their behaviors. The names of all patrolmen referred to in this episode have been changed.

15
HOW CHILDREN READ
TELEVISION: THE LEVELS
OF THE GAME
Peter G. Christenson

There recently has been a strong surge of interest in investigating the many different ways children interpret and attempt to make sense of television programs. From where we sit today, it seems altogether obvious that these issues are important in determining the impressions television leaves with children. However, as Dorr (1980) has noted, much of the earlier research on children and television notably was unconcerned with what goes on in the child's mind during viewing. Instead, early studies focused on the correspondence between TV messages — or certain characteristics of them — and such outcomes as learning, attitudes, and behavior. The implicit assumption was that children were blank slates upon which television was free to write almost at will.

There are at least two reasons why this assumption is inappropriate. First, though the cognitive maps of children may be more sparsely settled and less integrated than those of adults, they certainly have habits, attitudes, predispositions, preferences, patterns of thought, and so on, that predate any particular session with a television set. Second, the assumption fails to capture the essential fact that when we are considering the potential impact of TV it is <u>precisely</u> the blank slate upon which it is impossible for a message to "write" <u>anything</u>. A child must have certain basic cognitive skills, a certain knowledge of the world, in order to make any sense at all of television.

I would suggest in passing that the simple cause–effect model in communication research perhaps always has been more a way of framing certain research questions — especially those with pressing policy implications — than the true intellectual philosophy or "theory" of any researcher. I think it would be difficult to find a serious scholar who would support the notion

242

that any message or set of messages would be likely to have uniform and completely predictable effects on everybody who is exposed to it. The "early period" of research on children and television (if a field with a history of roughly 20 years could be said to have earned an early period) was concerned primarily with a very serious social issue, that is, whether televised portrayals of violent and aggressive behavior might lead to more violence and aggression in the young viewer. The direct approach was the logical first step, and indeed the many studies of children's reactions to TV violence have established a basic effect — in many circumstances, violent/aggressive content does produce more violent and aggressive tendencies and behavior in some children (see, for example, Comstock et al. 1978; NIMH 1982).

It has become apparent, however, that although television programs have been shown in experimental studies to produce reliable differences on certain measures between those who have seen them and those who have not, a great deal and usually most of the variance in criterion measures is not accounted for in any obvious way by content variables. In fact, one scholar has arrived at the general conclusion that "content is a poor predictor of effect" (J. Anderson 1981b, p. 21). Like any strong generalization, this forces us to think. It leads naturally to a consideration of the network of factors that might explain this lack of correspondence between the kinds of effects a message logically ought to have and the kinds of effects, or lack of effect, it in fact does have. From here we are led of necessity to a consideration of the kinds of processes subsumed under the general term "comprehension."

Children, like adults, are not passive conduits of information but processors and shapers of meaning, and to the extent that different children process a message in different ways we could expect them to react differently to it. There are reasons, certainly, to study children's comprehension of television for its own sake, but the primary status of comprehension processes in mass communication research is that of an intervening variable. Conceptually and temporally, these processes occur between the production and presentation of a TV message and the measurement of some dependent variable that we expect might somehow be influenced by it. By looking more closely at how children interpret and make sense of television or the products of any other medium, we are in principle better able to predict just how the message will translate into knowledge, attitudes, or behavior — or to put it another way, we should better understand why what comes out is not necessarily what goes in.

In sum, then, our field has discovered that an investigation into issues of sense-making and comprehension is indispensable to a thoughtful study of children's interactions with media. The next few pages are devoted to an exposition of some of the important questions involved. After a brief attempt to define the notion of comprehension within the current context, the chapter will organize the research into three levels or types of comprehension and summarize the state of our knowledge within each. Finally, some general suggestions will be made concerning the ideal shape of the future.

DEFINING COMPREHENSION

The dictionary on my desk defines the verb "to comprehend" thus: "To grasp mentally, to understand fully." This definition implies strongly that there is generally a <u>correct</u> way to understand something, that comprehension is an all-or-none phenomenon. Either one comprehends — understands — or one does not. This is, of course, the way the terms are used normally. For instance, if somebody says something to us and we do not think we are receiving the meaning they intend to send, we are apt to say "I don't understand you." Once we are fairly certain we are getting the message, we say "O.K., now I understand." In this formulation, then, comprehension is seen as an ideal state, one in which the meaning received corresponds to the meaning intended. This is frequently the way the concept is applied in the literature on children and television. That is, the assumption is made that there is a "proper" or "correct" way to interpret a program (that is, the adult way) and children who do not interpret it in this way are characterized as having "failed" to comprehend or understand it.

> The fundamental goal of most symbolic messages is to elicit in the receiver a mental image similar to the one intended by the sender. Hence most studies of comprehension attempt to compare what is grasped by the receiver either to what was intended by the sender or to what is deemed by some third party to be evident in the message (Comstock et al. 1978, p. 271).

This approach is appropriate and useful in many situations. However, when left as it is, it can fail to capture the essential active, constructive, and processual nature of comprehension. When we focus on the way children fail by adult standards, we may lose sight of what they accomplish — namely, to make some sense of the message in their own terms in order to meet their own current needs (J. Anderson 1981c). In recognition of this, comprehension currently is conceived in the literature on children's television interpretive processes not so much as an end state but as a sense-making <u>activity</u> that embraces a variety of cognitive skills and styles.

Thus, comprehension is best seen as a complex of processes through which children interpret and make sense of television. We are warned that by describing their readings as more or less "in deficit" — that is, as falling short in various ways of mature, adult standards — we may lose sight of how their modes of information processing help them to function within their own environments (J. Anderson 1981c; Comstock et al. 1978; Dorr 1980).

Should we completely abandon this "deficit view" as being somehow ontogenetically ethnocentric and treat children's perceptions and interpretations with perfect relativity, as if they formed their own culture? No, for two reasons. First, children are not from another culture. We should try to understand to the extent possible the way they think and respond; on the other hand, children in any society have one cardinal business: to grow up in that society. Thus, while it would be wrong to characterize children as failures because they do not fully comprehend a program, there is some utility in comparing their readings of it to the adult standards of their own society. (This strategy is very seldom truly followed in the sense of asking the same questions of adults that are asked of children. Rather, an adult mode of responding is generally constructed in hypothetical form and then applied as a gauge to the actual responses of children.) Hence the term "developmental psychology" as opposed to the "psychology of children" (as if they were a distinct tribe of small, young humans).

Second, and of perhaps more real significance, is that from the very beginning much — and by middle childhood most — of the television programs children watch are not "children's" programs at all but are aimed for the adult audience (Banks 1980). By early grade school, virtually all of children's radio and popular music listening is to material directed to adolescents and adults (Christenson and Lindlof 1982). I call this process "developmental eavesdropping," and it is obviously a rich source of information about the world outside and about the roles to which children aspire in that world.

This process is by no means limited to media, of course. Children are always listening in on conversations and events that were not intended for them. When that happens, parents, recognizing that a child may understand things the "wrong way," generally do one or more of three things: first, they may debrief the child, or interpret the event in such a way that it helps the child make sense of it in his own terms; second, they attempt to instill general modes of responding so that the child will be able to interpret in the future similar or analogous events; and third, parents will try to censor the environment so that the child is not exposed, to the extent possible, to confusing or distressing events.

Each of these intervention strategies is applied to children's televiewing. Many parents try to censor their children's viewing, and social action groups long have urged that some form of censorship be imposed on children's programming on a general basis. Many parents interpret television programs for their children (Messaris and Sarett 1981); both parents and an increasing number of schools, churches, and other community groups are involved in the cultivation of general information processing strategies in children (see, for example, Ploghoft and Anderson 1981).

Beneath these quite reasonable strategies lies the essential assumption that, though children indeed may be making sense of what they see, their comprehension may be inadequate to cope with what they overhear. Just as a child may be upset by the most trivial quarrel between his parents, so he may be upset by a verbal or physical conflict on television that an adult would read in a "proper perspective." In any case, it is virtually impossible to avoid characterizing children's comprehension evaluatively, as, for instance, when one speaks of receivership skills (J. Anderson 1981b), effective processing of content (Collins 1981), increasingly better understanding with age (Wartella 1981).

THE LEVELS OF COMPREHENSION

In the next few pages I will summarize some of the current knowledge and issues surrounding children's interpretations of television. This section is divided into three parts, corresponding to three conceptually distinct (though not hermetic) areas of concern: comprehension of television stories and the people in them, comprehension of television form and "grammar," and "meta-comprehension," which includes global concepts of the nature of the media, their economic purpose, and their social and cultural context.

The Story and the People In It

Here we are talking about the sense children make of the shows they watch, how well they seem to grasp the action, the plot, the motivations for and the consequences of actions, and the internal feelings of the characters. There are certainly various levels of this sort of comprehension, but the ideal is well defined by Comstock et al. (1978, p. 270): ". . . comprehension refers to a viewer's understanding and integration of the various parts of a program into a meaningful whole. It implies not only a grasping of the specific actions portrayed, but also of the conditions and contingencies, both explicit and implicit, surrounding whatever actions are portrayed."

At the simplest level, one could consider the sheer amount of discrete bits and pieces of information and action that are understood and recalled. Even preschoolers and kindergartners can encode and remember visual information remarkably well (Entwisle and Huggins 1973) and visual memory may not improve much with age past the first four years of life (Mowbray and Luria 1973). It is worth noting that in the case of certain types of television presentations — for instance, children's commercials — the simple storage of a few visual details may be a quite adequate level of "comprehension" from the standpoint of the originators of the message (Christenson 1980). In any case, the amount of other types of information learned from film or television narratives does increase with age (Comstock et al. 1978).

The true measure of comprehension is not the extracting of bits and pieces of information but the reconstruction of those bits and pieces into a unified, coherent story. Here we find a steady increase from preschool through the grade school years in not only the sheer amount of information learned but more importantly in the amount of information that is considered essential or central to the plot (Christenson 1982a; Collins 1975; Hale, Miller, and Stevenson 1968). During the same years there is a rapid development of the ability to reconstruct the proper sequence of central events: preschoolers have a great deal of trouble doing this, but by late grade school children seem to have no trouble with the task (Leifer et al. 1971).

Recalling the central elements in their proper order is necessary for a thorough, integrative comprehension, one involving an awareness of the cause-effect relationships among the plot elements. By middle grade school children may have developed a schema of an "ideal plot line" (Dorr 1980), in which events generally proceed from beginning to resolution in a certain predictable way, and this schema may act as an aid in making sense of the narrative. This notion is supported by the finding that older children fare worse on tests of story recall when the original order of scenes is scrambled than they do when the order is logical, while young children recall the story in much the same fashion (that is, confused) regardless of the order of the scenes (Collins 1979). In any case, the abilities accurately to describe (again, by adult standards) the causal relationships among scenes (Flapan 1968) and the motives behind the consequences of characters' actions (Collins, Berndt, and Hess 1974; Leifer et al. 1971; Leifer and Roberts 1972) are virtually nonexistent at preschool or kindergarten but quite solid by late grade school.

It is also crucial to be able to read the internal emotional states of the characters who participate in television events.

Most motives for action (for example, anger, love, jealousy) and many consequences of actions (for example, grief, disappointment, joy) consist of emotional and psychological states that must be inferred from what social cues are available — primarily characters' words, deeds, and facial expressions. As noted above, young children do not understand motives well. They do judge characters, but primarily on the basis of whether the consequences of their actions are bad or good, regardless of their motives (Collins, Berndt, and Hess 1974; Leifer and Roberts 1972).

In general, as children grow older they base their understanding of real people less on surface features and more on inner qualities (Delia and O'Keefe 1979), and there is evidence of a similar developmental trend in their descriptions of television people (Wartella and Alexander 1978). Reeves and Greenberg (1977) report that children use different dimensions to differentiate among TV characters than they use with real people. Humor is the most salient dimension applied to TV characters at each of three age levels (third, fifth, and seventh grade), but this dimension did not emerge in the top ten dimensions for real-life people.

In apparent contradiction to the general finding in the developmental literature that advancing age brings more complex and variegated person perception, Reeves and Greenberg found that older children's perceptions of TV characters were actually simpler than those of younger children. In other words, older children concentrated more exclusively on humor than younger ones. In a later discussion of this finding, Reeves (1979) makes the case that, since it is illogical to suppose that third graders are cognitively simpler than seventh graders, the relative unidimensionality of their perceptions of TV people may stem from a more abstract awareness of the nature of the television medium. Thus it may take a complex cognitive structure to understand that TV people are simple. In other words, general concepts of the medium ("metacomprehension") interact with perceptions of media people.

Yet another essential ingredient in thorough comprehension is the ability to go beyond the explicit information in the story and arrive at what that information implies. One expression of this ability is to be able to deduce assumed, off-screen story elements on the basis of what is depicted on-screen to fill in the gaps in the story. Looking at second, fifth, and eighth graders, Collins et al. (1978) found that even when second graders could remember explicit scenes, they were unable to use them to arrive at implied information. Fifth and eighth graders, however, were able to answer questions concerning implied information at a rate much better than chance.

An even higher level of story comprehension, and one that assumes competency at lower levels, is the ability to view a program in its totality and then abstract from it an underlying moral or lesson — the "message." Not all TV shows have a message or moral, of course, but many do, and it is of interest to know to what extent children are able to perform the abstraction and synthesis necessary to arrive at the "moral of the story." I recently conducted a study (Christenson 1982a) aimed at this issue. Respondents at three age levels — kindergarten/first grade, third/fourth grades, and sixth grade — were shown one of four prime-time situation comedies that had been produced with the intent of conveying a moral lesson, and that adult viewers agreed did so.

Kindergarten and first-grade children had virtually no detectable comprehension of even the central elements of the plot, and absolutely no awareness of the lesson or moral of the story, on either an open-ended or a multiple- (three) choice item. Third and fourth graders, on the other hand, had a very thorough knowledge of the central events and concepts in the programs, and a significant minority — about 29 percent — were able to supply in the open-ended format either a variant of the "ideal" lesson or some other that plausibly could have been synthesized from the program as a whole. Finally, while there was no further improvement at sixth grade on measures of central elements (there was really very little room for it), sixth graders were better at abstracting lessons from the programs. Thirty-nine percent gave an "adequate" response to the open-ended item. These results suggest two things. First, since comprehension of central plot elements peaks at the third/fourth grade level while lesson comprehension continues to improve through sixth, the latter is probably a superordinate mode of processing. Second, while many of the older children were able to extract a plausible moral from the programs, by far the majority even at sixth grade were not. This result was surprising to me; the programs seemed sufficiently simple that sixth graders would have hit near the ceiling on the task.

The results at sixth grade, that is, a 39 percent success rate, even coupled with some reasonable extrapolation beyond that age, call into serious question the assumption that a solid majority of televiewing **adults** would have "got" the messages in these shows. While we may find it useful in certain cases to apply adult standards to children's performances, we ought not to assume that adults are generally processing television at the highest possible level (Dorr 1980). In any case, it may have been an oversight not to have included adult viewers in the sample, though I derive some solace from the fact that in the commission of this flaw in design I am in good company.

The Grammar of Television

The stories that television tells are in many ways similar in form to any prose story, and one factor that must certainly figure in television comprehension is the possession of a set of schemata concerning the ways stories are structured in general. Yet television is a different medium from print or speech, and so has its own set of forms and conventions. In recognition of this fact, some research energy has been spent lately in elucidating the role that television's production codes, its audiovisual "quasi grammar" (Dorr 1980), play in children's processing of TV content. The general notion here is that one would expect, ceteris paribus, that those who are "media literate," that is, understand the grammar of television (or its close relative, film), ought to be more efficient interpreters of television programs that those who are not.

A distinction can be made between two types of formal features relevant to television programs. One type consists of a set of dimensions, usually perceptual, along which media messages may vary in "style" somewhat independently of their "content," or the stories they tell. For instance, Huston et al. (1981) talk about such variables as the pace of a show, the level of physical activity present, the variability of characters, and the presence of loud music as being formal dimensions that could be applied to any program no matter what its plot or story line. Watt and Krull (1974) refer to "form complexity," or the degree to which occurrences in a program are predictable, and "visual-verbal interaction," the extent of congruence or independence between what is seen and what is heard. These stylistic features have been shown to have strong effects on children's attention to programs and perhaps even on their social behavior (Huston, Wright, and Potts 1982). They do not, however, constitute the audiovisual grammar. Rather, they overlay it in the same sense that the style of Shakespeare and the style of a Harlequin novel both overlay the grammar of English, or the most abecedarian advertiser's jingle and the most harmonically and rhythmically complex jazz composition both overlay the rules of Western music and its notation.

The second class of formal features consists of the system- or media-specific and language-like rules and conventions that govern the encoding and decoding of symbols, both in terms of how the symbols relate to their referents and how they relate to one another. Television language, if it is a language at all, is a lingua franca. It obviously is based heavily in verbal language, in fact so heavily that most television stories (especially news) can be followed quite well with the ear alone. It is also music, photography, and theater and incorporates in varying degrees their conventions as well.

Furthermore, as Salomon (1979) has noted, the television/film language is of a different nature than, for instance, spoken languages and music. These latter are both semantically and syntactically "articulate" — their symbol-referent and symbol-symbol relationships are spelled out lawfully and relatively unambiguously. In comparison, the audiovisual grammar is both semantically and syntactically more flexible and vague. Yet hybrid or not, ambiguous or not, it is a <u>symbol system</u>. Its material may be real life or fiction, but in either case the messages it presents are encoded according to certain rules, procedures, and assumptions with which the viewer must be familiar in order to decode the message properly, to make sense of it. (I say "familiar" because, as the briefest talk with a three year old will establish, it is quite possible to be fluent in a language without being able to describe its grammar.)

Of the two types of formal features identified here, much more is known about the first, the stylistic features. These have been considered primarily in terms of how they determine children's attentional patterns (Watt and Krull 1974; Anderson et al. 1979) and how they may influence behavior directly through, for instance, modeling processes or heightened states of arousal (Huston, Wright, and Potts 1982). It may also be important to know how children deal with the audiovisual symbol system, what role their conversance with the quasi-linguistic representational code of the screen plays in their interpretations of TV programs. About this we know very little.

As with written language, children are not born with a facility for "reading" television. Rather, it develops through use and begins with a great deal of confusion about the meaning of various conventions and structures. In support of this notion one finds, for instance, Dorr's (1980) observation that children of five to seven years fail to interpret Steve Austin's slow-motion "bionics" in the "Six Million Dollar Man" as a symbol of power and speed, but give it a literal meaning, leading to the quite logical misapprehension that he will never catch up or escape, whichever applies.

It is unclear to what extent television comprehension depends on familiarity with media-specific forms and conventions. If the criterion is the thoroughness of a child's understanding of the plot or story line, it may not be very important at all. First, many (if not most) of television's visual representations are either literal pictures of real life or analogs of real-world mental operations (Rice, Huston, and Wright 1982). In such cases, specialized media literacy may not serve a very large role in the extraction of knowledge from the piece. Second, the visual component of television frequently may add very little plot-related information over what is supplied by verbal language in the forms of narration and dialogue. In many instances, the story line or even the moral of the story is quite accessible to any viewer who is fluent in English, has certain minimal relevant "world knowledge," and has a general understanding of the way stories of any kind are put together (Collins 1981).

The importance of specialized media literacy probably depends on the nature of the material shown and the sort of cognitive impact one seeks to find. Story comprehension of dramatic programs may not require much familiarity with the unique elements of screen language; on the other hand, this fluency may be a very important factor in the extraction of other kinds of information from other kinds of fare. For instance, Salomon's (1979) work on the introduction of "Sesame Street" into Israel found a strong relationship among consistent second- and third-grade viewers between the mastery of skills closely related to filmic codes (such as close-ups and changing angles of view) and the extraction of certain types of knowledge. Furthermore, it was the heaviest viewers among whom the correlation between skill mastery and knowledge extraction was the highest. This is at least indirect evidence that, as one might expect with any "language," increased use leads to greater fluency, which in turn leads to more efficient information processing.

Metacomprehension: Concepts of the Medium

Many cognitive skills and processing modes are subsumed in metacomprehension; what they all seem to have in common is that they are grounded in the awareness that television programs are symbolic messages sent from somebody to somebody with some purpose; in other words, that the nature of television as a medium and as an industry has some bearing on the way its messages should be construed. Some of the elements of metacomprehension — such as the perceived reality of TV — might fit as well under the "grammar of television" or "visual literacy" headings. However, the concept of visual grammar as defined here does not entail the perception of the medium as object. The rules of the grammar are used to link message segments in certain lawful ways so that the message may be interpretable by a viewer who understands them. The King James version of the Bible is "accessible" in this sense to anybody who can understand and read the English language. Whether one takes the Bible as the literal truth, the figurative truth, or as an interesting piece of literature has nothing to do with fluency and literacy in English. The same laws of English grammar are internalized and applied, usually unconsciously, in the same way by the fundamentalist Christian as by the avowed atheist.

In the same sense, then, there is a level on which one can "read" a television program or a film that corresponds to the way one reads something written in English; and there is another level of "reading" analogous to the different interpretations of the believer and the nonbeliever. Metacomprehension, then, has to do not with one's mastery of the audiovisual symbol but with one's view of the nature of the people and institutions that use it, as well as the economic and social contexts of that use.

It also happens that what are generally thought to be the "mature" forms of metacomprehension are more skeptical, more critical, than the "immature" modes. In contradistinction to the cognitive skills involved in the mastery of the audiovisual "language," which generally act in the service of "effective" communication (communication in which the mental image received is similar to the one intended), metacomprehension skills frequently act as cognitive filters, guarding the viewer from certain impacts and impressions (presumably the unhealthy ones) whether these impacts and impressions are intended by the program's source or not. Thus, the primary thrust of most of the recent school curricula in TV viewing is in fact to demystify television, to inculcate a mode of cognitive processing that involves an awareness of the "hidden agenda" of television and an active criticism of content.

What are the dimensions of metacomprehension and what is known about them? I have mentioned perceived reality already, and it is a logical starting point here. Whether one understands a television story qua story or not, there are various degrees to which that story may be interpreted as being or mirroring real life. As one might expect, age generally is related inversely to how real programs and characters are seen to be (compare Comstock et al. 1978). Children under four years of age tend to believe that the television world is the real world in a literal sense, that the "little people" on the screen can be spoken to and can hear. For children of this age, TV is a "magic window" on reality (Hawkins 1977). Somewhat later, perhaps about the age of five or six, children adamantly will maintain that the TV world is "just pretend," that TV people are not real. However, as Dorr (1980, p. 199) has remarked, these verbal protestations may not be entirely heartfelt: "Fundamentally . . . children at this age are still uncertain. The concrete, visual representation of a television program is difficult to override with cognitive controls."

By late grade school there is a thorough and more or less universal awareness that television stories and characters are fabricated and there is a heightened sense that the stories and characters are not true-to-life (Lyle and Hoffman 1972; Dorr 1980; Hawkins 1977). It is clear, however, that the question of TV's reality is complex. While a sophisticated perception of television's reality certainly must include the fundamental notion that the screen event is not literal reality, it must also allow for the possibility that certain stories, characterizations, and episodes may be realistic, and must be considerably flexible in application to different types of programming, ranging from cartoons through hard news.

Perceptions of reality probably depend on one's picture of how and why programs are produced and delivered. If a child is aware that TV dramas, for instance, are created by production teams and actors from written scripts in order to entertain an audience, this might say something to the child about the relationship of the TV image to the real world. In any event, many of the elements of metacomprehension revolve around the viewer's concepts of the source of programming, the motivation behind it, and the relationship between the television industry and society as a whole.

One key set of source-related concepts is composed of those that contribute to an awareness of who puts television programs on the air and why. If the "correct" answer to this question is something like "TV shows are put on by networks and stations to make money by selling advertising," then we find, not surprisingly, that young children do not understand the system. Dorr (1980) reports that no children in a sample of kindergarten through sixth grade had an accurate understanding of the economic system that supports commercial television. There did seem to be some age-related development in the awareness of why programs are broadcast, but even by sixth grade only 25 percent of Dorr's sample could even say that programs were there to make money. These sixth graders said that programs were there to "tell the truth," to entertain or to inform; younger children gave either these sorts of answers or had no idea at all.

This trend parallels the research on children's perceptions of the intent and nature of television advertising. However, by sixth grade virtually all children seem to understand the essential persuasive/selling intent of commercials (Adler 1977; Christenson 1980; Ward and Wackman 1973), compared to the minority who understand the rudiments of television's economic structure. This is logical, of course, in that the latter is a much more complex concept that, unlike the intent of advertising, is not immanent in the messages themselves. In either case, attributions of intent potentially are related to the believability of both sources and messages. Dorr (1980) has proposed that the basic awareness of television's money-making objective is a necessary condition for the ability to "question" television. However, as I have suggested elsewhere (Christenson 1982b), the link between awareness of intent and persuasibility in children is problematic, since awareness of intent may serve to clarify the desires of an attractive source just as much as it calls into question the purity of the source's motives.

There are important source perceptions other than those concerning economic motives. One such is the knowledge that a message (or the people who send it) may have a <u>symbolic intent</u> in addition to a literal meaning. Worth and Gross (1974) hold that whereas a "real" event is interpreted in terms of one's knowledge of the "real world," a symbolic event is assessed and construed in recognition that there is "somebody out there who is trying to tell us something." Here a certain recursivity of thought is required. One's reading of the events in a story cannot be formed as if she or he were witnessing the events on the street. Rather, a truly sophisticated strategy of interpretation must account for the fact that screen images are put there by somebody and that somebody "means something" by them. The available evidence is that the use of this strategy is strongly age-related — it seems to be available by fifth grade but not at second grade (Murphy 1973).

Thus, we see a greater awareness with advancing age that there is a source "out there" who may be trying to tell us something. It is also likely that age brings an improving sense of what kinds of messages are likely to emanate from a given source (see Christenson 1982a). Older children bring with them to a viewing situation some relatively valid notions about the sorts of lessons or messages one is likely to find in a TV program, and so they have a significant head start when it comes to the actual process of viewing, interpretation, and systhesis. In this way, as in many others, as children get older they learn to learn.

This development could be the result of increasingly more sensitive and diagnostic source perceptions, that is, better theories about the kinds of lessons television producers might want to convey to kids. Or it could be the result of a simple inductive process: A fourth or fifth grader has seen a lot of television and may be aware of some patterns in programming that converge on a fairly good rule of thumb. Either of these scenarios, or both, might also fit the Reeves (1979) finding that children's perceptions of television characters become in some ways simpler and more unidimensional with increasing age. His own explanation coincides with the induction notion. He proffers the hypothesis that children may be learning from repeated viewing that television does not require fine distinctions, that by its very nature the medium levels differences and creates stereotypes. Whichever mechanism explains these particular results, we see that the sense made of TV content depends on global concepts of the medium and, more specifically, that increasingly complex cognitive structures may make the interpretive process simpler and more streamlined.

Other components of metacomprehension include most of the information-processing modes associated with "critical viewing skills" or "receivership skills." Anderson (1981b, p. 23), for instance, defines "receivership skills" as "those skills related to the assimilation and utilization of communication messages for some purposeful action." His gazetteer includes these abilities: to understand our own motives for use; to understand how those motives influence the sense we make of messages; to grasp not only the overt meanings of messages but also the "hidden" ones; to comprehend audiovisual languages and symbols discriminately; to identify source and intended audience; to evaluate fact, opinion, types of persuasive appeals, and stylistic devices; to understand "the sources of bias inherent in the medium of pre-sentation"; to recognize intended affective reactions and motives; to "relegate personal value" to messages; to identify how messages lead to "emotional satisfaction"; to relate the messages to the rest of life; and, finally, to draw conclusions and establish predictions on the basis of messages (Anderson 1981b, p. 23).

This recipe for the accomplished viewer could be added to in various ways (Lloyd-Kolkin 1981; Hawkins and Pingree 1982). We might even require that a sophisticated viewer understand the fundamentals of television electronics (Singer, Zuckerman, and Singer 1981). Overall, in virtually every case where data have been gathered — mirabile dictu! — older children more closely approach the avatar of the critical viewer, though in some ways younger ones can be moved toward it through training and in-struction.

WHY DO WE CARE WHAT WE DO?

To many, the process of investigating the way children inter-pret television is intrinsically interesting. There are few pursuits more entertaining, for those with the proper inclination, than talking to young children about what they have seen on television. If the comprehension process is important, though, it is important because it is a potent determinant of the impacts of television content on the young viewer. The current wave of interest in interpretive processes is but one manifestation of what could be viewed as Phase II of research on television and children. Phase I established effects, particularly of violent content, on groups. However, we also were forced to admit that the effects were frequently not there, or were weak, or appeared only in certain subgroups. In other words, we were forced to admit that the world is a complicated place and that children are complicated people. Now a phase has begun that is primarily concerned with explicating the many conditions and processes that mediate children's uses of and responses to television. There is a virtual galaxy of such conditions and processes (see Hawkins and Pingree 1982 for a discussion of many of them).

It is probably in the very nature of mass communication research in general and children-and-media research in particular to be involved with questions of application to real-world social problems. Ours is a "variable field" — one that isolates a certain set of phenomena, a certain set of institutions, and then studies them at various levels of social abstraction. As such, mass communication research inevitably is drawn into relationships with the communication industry and with those who would make policy with regard to it (McLeod and Reeves 1980). Many researchers and scholars entered this area of endeavor not purely out of curiosity but also out of a general concern about the role mass media might play in the development of children.

It is debatable whether researchers ought to be completely dispassionate in their work, even if they could be. It is fairly clear, though, that the cognitive skills and information processing modes that have been discussed here under the banner of comprehension mediate television's influence in such complicated ways that even the most passionate meliorist with the strongest mandate to promote social good would be hard pressed to settle on a strategy of intervention. Another way of putting this is to say that there is no particular configuration of comprehension "skills" that systematically will promote "prosocial" learning and behavior and suppress "antisocial" effects.

An example from my own work might serve to illustrate the point. The study (Christenson 1982b) concerned children's responses to TV commercials, specifically whether it might be possible to "protect" them from being easily influenced by inserting, into the normal flow of programs and commercials, messages concerning the selling intent of commercials and recommending a skeptical, critical attitude toward them. The work derived from the general concern from a policy standpoint about the basic unfairness of a persuasive situation in which the persuader has such tremendous sophistication and resources while the viewer is naive and trusting (Federal Trade Commission 1978; Roberts, Bachen, and Christenson 1978).

The treatment did "take" — that is, children were made more aware of intent and more skeptical of commercials in general and, to some extent, this general attitude seemed to be applied to product evaluation. Since the product in question was a sugared snack food, and since we are all in favor of healthy teeth, we might all applaud this result. However, there is a sense in which this success might backfire. Not all persuasive messages sent to children, on TV or through other media, are for bad causes. Certainly a young child (and the effects of the announcements were especially strong on first and second graders) might apply the same skepticism to any message that resembled a commercial, including public-service announcements for balanced meals, bicycle safety, racial tolerance, and so on. Thus the teaching of one aspect of metacomprehension — the nature of the source — may be misapplied because of a remaining deficit in another area, in this case the ability to differentiate between apparently similar messages. A parallel scenario could be built around the recent attempts to teach young children "critical viewing skills," in that any set of heuristic principles developed by a child for dealing with prime-time drama or Saturday morning cartoons may be applied to presentations that do not have quite the same hidden agenda, for example, news, educational programs, films shown in school, rented videotapes brought home for family viewing.

On a more global level, one may question the broad effects on a young child's world view when a large part of his world is demystified, when magical special effects are explained, when the Six Million Dollar Man is defrocked and what remains is Lee Majors in slow motion over a slick synthesized audio track. Maybe early childhood is a time when having confidence in one's beliefs makes a lot more difference in the long run than the hard substance of those beliefs. In any case, our thinking in the future must recognize the organic essence of the young viewer, who is of course not a "viewer" but a person. As with any system, we cannot consider one part of a child's life — for example, media use — without looking at the rest; we cannot intervene in one cognitive skill without anticipating the reverberations of change throughout the organism. The imperfect or "naive" sense-making abilities of the six or seven year old may articulate elegantly with the rest of his cognitive structure to serve current needs in a current environment. Induced acceleration in one isolated realm may not, on balance, be adaptive.

One studies comprehension processes primarily because they mediate social impact. One must also recognize that these processes interact in complex ways and are an integral part of a larger cognitive structure. Future studies of the sense-making process will inform us about the media's role in social learning only inasmuch as they explore the interrelationships among the ingredients of comprehension and the relationship between his gestalt and the totality of children's psychological and physical environments. In other words, any significant improvement in insight requires a more ecological approach than we have seen to date.

Of course such an approach is demanding. It is made much more so by the volatility of the communication environment. The research agenda in mass communication long has been heavily skewed toward television, to the point where it would be easy to get the sense that children do not listen to radio or popular music, do not go to movies, do not read magazines or newspapers. Not only has the field been blinded to television's historic competitors, but it really has not come to grips with the shape of television today. Depending on how we choose to define it, "television" now means much more than ABC, NBC, CBS, and "Sesame Street." It means cable systems with 12, 20, 40, 100 channels, with offerings ranging from all-children's programs to the hardest porn. It means direct broadcast from satellite to home. It means videocassettes and discs bought or rented for home use. It means computer-interactive informational "programs" in school and at home. It means, if we care to stretch the definition, video games, with their uniquely strong grip on many children's attention.

A recent critique of the kid-vid research posed this irreverent question: "How would we be poorer if we simply threw out the literature to date?" (Anderson 1981c, p. 395). It is hard to avoid a wince of agreement with the implied answer. The corpus gives very little by way of a unified impression. Rather, one sees a rampant eclecticism, hundreds of bits and pieces with almost no vertical development. Indeed the question is unavoidable: How can so much data reveal so little? If our magpie science is to transcend this criticism, it must improve in its ability to integrate children's media experiences with the conduct of the rest of their lives, and it must make a better effort to do this in the technological present with an eye on the future.

16
MEDIATED COMMUNICATION IN FAMILIES: NEW THEORETICAL APPROACHES

Thomas R. Lindlof and Paul J. Traudt

Since the study of media audience behavior became a systematic pursuit, it has become apparent that much of the social activity of families, peer groups, and other collectivities is constituted and regulated by the use of mass media. The view that mass communication begins with content production and ends with individuals' reception of that content is clearly a myopic one for understanding the character of symbolic exchange in advanced-technology cultures. That view, we might add, has taken as its warrant a model of human behavior as a syndrome of mechanistic response to structured environments, including media products. The legacy of behaviorism persists as a ghost in the machines of many empirical efforts claiming "active audience" orientations. Conspicuously absent from most studies of media and social behavior up to the present day are considerations of how humans make media the loci of joint actions, how interpretive procedures for "making sense" of television and other media develop from intersubjective sources of validation. At least as absent as these in the research literature are thoroughgoing critiques of methods, instruments, and subjects' perceptions of the researcher's task demands. In place of naive operationalism, we need, in Luckmann's (1973, p. 180) words, "the guarantee of continuous epistemological reflexivity, which is an essential condition of the philosophical foundation of social science."

This chapter outlines the usefulness of new theoretical approaches for the empirical problems of mediated communication in

---

Authors are listed alphabetically.

families: symbolic interactionism, ethnomethodology, and rules theory. What is "new" about these approaches for mass communication concerns is their focus on the patterns of families' negotiations with media. Although disparate in some of their assumptions, they share a basic phenomenological foundation: Social reality-making is a tenuous and variable undertaking and is held together by humans' interpretations, plans, goals, and orientations to social settings (M. Morris 1977).

As a point of distinction, the predominant paradigm in studying mass-mediated social behavior thus far — social learning theory — has based its procedures on the effects of reinforcement contingencies (in media stimuli) on such criteria as attitudinal or behavioral outcomes. The objective of social learning theory is a set of covering laws that permit universal explanation and prediction. Among the major criticisms of this approach relevant to the impact of mass media is that learning theory relies on the experimental or statistical control of those "person parameters" (Harré and Secord 1973) — individual differences of meaning attribution — that, when randomized in treatment groups, appear to isolate causal relations. Yet, as Harré and Secord have pointed out, randomization of person parameters results in correlational relations only in an actuarial sense; a true causal explanation would require that person parameters and their functional relationships become the prime variables of investigation. The celebrated equivocation of media research — "television portrayals of violence cause aggressive behavior in some children under certain circumstances" — represents to some a pretheoretic statement in need of more research of intervening and conditional variable. If we look upon human behavior, however, as manifest choices that are rational in terms of the social actor's ongoing constructions of reality, then the research experiment itself is only one situation where the actor has defined personal interests at that biographical point in time. Evidence of significant differences between treatments tells us little of the subjects' understandings of audiovisual sequences or their construals of the normative televiewing settings where such sequences might be encountered.

For the family household where most televiewing and other media use occasions are enacted there is a poverty of evidence regarding the forms of interpersonal adjustment that family members construct and their paths of development. For many of the central theoretical and policy questions to be satisfactorily framed, let alone answered, a number of prerequisite questions concerning what the act of television viewing entails for all family members need to be posed and investigated. James Anderson (1980, p. 2) has noted the lack of concern about questions of What (ontology) and How (praxiology) in the mass communication field:

The emphasis on experimentalism in communication studies has resulted in a fundamental imbalance in our discipline — nowhere more apparent [than] in studies using mass communication. We have approached questions of why to the exclusion of what and how. We have attempted to describe causes and consequences of televiewing without an adequate understanding of what it is and how it gets done. This imbalance has littered our field with hypotheses of little utility.

Thus, the prerequisite questions we are suggesting here are ontological in nature, in which "studying communication both as a theme and as a medium discloses the constituting of social worlds — being-in-the-world" (Hawes 1977, p. 31).

The first section of the chapter introduces some notions of the family's institutional development in this century as radio and television became installed in the household domain; some reasons for our state of ignorance regarding family-media processes will be suggested. Next, the perspectives of symbolic interactionism and ethnomethodology, and their roles in the research of mass communication processes, will be described. Although this chapter is not meant to demonstrate field research practices, examples of ethnographic studies of media audiences have been interwoven with the theoretical discussion to illustrate the applications of each approach. The interested reader is encouraged to consult a number of useful guides to qualitative research (Bogdan and Taylor 1975; Denzin 1978; Lofland 1976; Lull 1982; Meyer, Traudt, and Anderson 1980). Finally, rules theory will be reviewed both as it extends ethnomethodological inquiry to substantive areas of family structure and as it applies to the cognitive components of social conduct.

THE CHANGING FAMILY AND MASS MEDIA

Characteristic of many media scholars' work in the area of television and childhood socialization has been the tendency to view use of the medium as supplanting family functions. While the introduction of electronic media obviously has led to major shifts in time allocations to other activities (McDonagh 1950; Robinson 1977; Schramm, Lyle, and Parker 1964), concomitant changes in family norms, such as value clarification, that are directly attributable to new media use patterns are difficult to document. As with other types of mass communication research, it is fairly easy to find variables that "wash out" the direct media effect; where the media effect does hold up in statistical controls, the direction of effect is often in doubt. If we analyze changes in family structure and functions since the advent of industrialization, however, a more holistic thesis that media resources are adapted to families' economic and person-ality-development needs becomes probable.

One theme that pervades much of the historical literature of family structure concerns the increasing isolation of the family from other, more public concourses. The Western nuclear family, including the recent variants of single-parent and multiple caretaker units (Bronfenbrenner 1982), is the paradigm of most social analysis. Many phenomena are related to the change from extended kinship structures to the self-contained modern family, including: changes in both the length and status of childhood (Aries 1962; Saal 1982); fewer opportunities for children to observe workplace or other societal and political activities (Bronfenbrenner 1970; Mead 1949; Saal 1982); the increasing extension of children's primary relationships to contemporaries, whether through peer groups or vicarious identifications with media figures (Bowerman and Kinch 1959; Bronfenbrenner 1970; Faber, Brown, and McLeod 1979); and increasing privacy rules and controls over behavior displays among family members (Laslett 1973; Sennett 1978).

Of particular interest to this discussion is the latter phenom-enon: the evolving differentiation of family roles evidenced in privacy norms. For Laslett (1973, p. 481), privacy means "the structural mechanisms which prohibit or permit observability in the enactment of family roles." She notes that spatial and temporal separations among family members have the effect of reducing possible conflicts over role expectations. In other words, social controls weaken when fewer family "audience members" are present for rewarding and maintaining normative behavior. In further exploring the historical circumstances for this claim, Laslett found that the dominant American family structure had in fact been nuclear since the colonial period; she also found that the number of children per family had been in steady decline and, central to her thesis, the proportion of grown children remaining in their parents' household decreased substantially from 1940 to 1960. Because children are presumed to function as contributors to intrafamily controls as they ap-proach adulthood, the effect of these demographic shifts is to shorten the period of the family life cycle in which children can "serve as meaningful sources of social control" (p. 483). Recent evidence indicates that spatial privacy correlates with family size in a curvilinear pattern, with low- and high-density families incorporating more privacy rules (Parke and Sawin 1979); in higher-density families, however, television viewing may function as a way of avoiding conflicts or lessening tensions in lieu of spatial privacy (Rosenblatt and Cunningham 1976).

In a similar vein, Richard Sennett's (1978) social history of public behavior suggests that by the nineteenth century the family home was already evolving toward its present "purpose": a domain where stable, well-ordered personality development could be accomplished by reducing the number of role combinations available for observation. Sennett argues that the family was not actually a refuge from the anonymous role relations being experienced in the public life of the new industrial world, but instead presented organized idealizations of behavior to children. In accomplishing such appearances, privacy plays a crucial role:

> Each adult need have only two [roles], spouse and parent: with no grandparents in the house, the child will never see them as someone else's children. The child himself will have only one image of adult love and adult expectation before him; he will not have to sort out what is different about the way you are supposed to behave in front of parents from the way you behave in front of grandparents or uncles. In other words, the nuclear form permits orderly human appearances to resolve into a matter of simplified human relationships (p. 180).

Electronic media arrived in the American household at a time not only when the American family was becoming self-contained but also as the nascent study of "normative" child development was having a material impact on the design of school curricula, social welfare, and other family support systems (Boorstin 1973, pp. 227-37). The key role of radio in bringing attractive programming reconstructed from other media together with consumer goods advertising, and making the entire package freely available at the center of family activity, has been noted by broadcast historians (Barnouw 1975). Yet the received histories of the adoption and expansion of radio offer few indications of how the medium was integrated at the level of the family unit.

Williams (1975) coined the term "mobile privatization" to describe the dual tendencies of radio in furthering both the self-sufficiency of the nuclear family and the needs of family members for orientation to rapidly developing consumer markets. In this analysis, industrialization eliminated the need for the economic benefits of extended families. With the withdrawal of the workforce from manufacture in the home and the appearance of child labor laws, childhood became a protracted, protected condition. Not only were many child-rearing tasks farmed out to external agencies, but children themselves became popular culture idealizations in the advertising of the 1920s (Ewen 1976). According to Williams (1975, p. 27), the smaller family, now privatized,

> carried . . . an imperative need for new kinds of contact. The new homes might appear private and "self sufficient"

but could be maintained only by regular funding and supply from external sources, and these, over a range from
employment and prices to depressions and wars, had a decisive and often a disrupting influence on what was nevertheless seen as a separable "family" project. This relationship created both the need and the form of a new
form of "communication": news from "outside," from otherwise inaccessible sources.

The small family apparently provided the means for stable,
simplified role relationships, made possible by the greater opportunities for family members' behavioral privacy in the home. At
the same time, the _individual_ family member's contacts with the
world outside the household increased so that the dependence on
orienting information sources became a critical matter. The
distinctive form of electronic media programming — a sequential,
time-based "flow" of content — had the effect of creating diverse settings of audience reception. Radio, and television, programming did not so much intrude on existing family activities as
provide organizing centers for new types of communicative contexts. Thus it is not surprising that a major popular argument
regarding the negative influence of radio and other household
media is that they "[disrupt] household routines and family relationships" (Davis 1976, p. 460). Media provided family members
with differential schedules for gathering; they also provided
acceptable zones for private pursuits. Where "disruptions" are
perceived to occur — such as fewer opportunities for other
activities, the appearances of undesirable media role models, and
so on — parents generally cite their lack of control over not
only the content but also the fact of its universal accessibility
(Bower 1973; Comstock et al. 1978).

We can get a rough sense of the new types of communicative
contexts in the pictures of rich profusions of behavior that
occur in normal televiewing settings when documented by observers or recording devices (Bechtel, Achelpohl, and Akers 1972;
Csikszentmihalyi and Kubey 1981; Lull 1980a). Family members
eat and drink with their television viewing, engage in con-
tent-related and content-unrelated talk, iron clothes, study,
dress, undress, daydream, and so on. Yet our knowledge of how
programming flows create communication patterns in different
kinds of families has been limited in past research by the usual
treatment of television viewing as a molar behavior — that is, as
a variable that "predicts" outcomes. In discussion new approaches to empirical research of the family-media interact, our
foremost concern is with the discovery of the interactive _pro-
cesses_ of media use. These processes, we will argue, cannot be
defined a priori but emerge through researchers' involvement in
the worlds of audiences.

RECONCEPTUALIZING THE STUDY OF FAMILIES AND MASS MEDIA

Media behaviors may be viewed phenomenologically to the extent that people use the media for successful social interaction and to establish their own sense of "what is." The fundamentals of phenomenological methods are situated in the observation and analysis of the empirical world. The growth and development of the electronic media have created commonplace situations suitable for empirical examination in natural settings. Of great import are the two primary distinctions that media provide in the individual's maintenance of social reality. First, the environmental opportunities provided by the mass media that make up the many options of commonplace activity; second, and more individualistic, are the content uses of media that provide meaning for integration into everyday interactions.

By adopting phenomenological perspectives, the media researcher is necessarily concerned with the individual's view of the mass media environment. For symbolic interactionists (Blumer 1969; G.H. Mead 1934), this view is best understood from within the experiential realm of the individuals under study. When examining the family, and its relationship to mass media, it becomes necessary to enter the small and sensitive domain of the family in order to become acquainted with and, when possible, integrated in daily life patterns. Of import for ethnomethodologists (Garfinkel 1967; Mehan and Wood 1975; Turner 1974) are the interactive components integral to the ongoing construction of this everyday reality.

The forms and scenarios for mass media are many, but nowhere are they better examined than from within the family unit. The coexistence of daily life and the media is universal, spanning all conceivable family typologies. Social activities within this setting provide, through systematic study, greater understanding of the process of coexistence between social behavior and the media — mediated communication.

The Mass Media and Symbolic Interactionism

Symbolic interactionism focuses on the meanings generated in communication exchange as well as the self in social interaction. Persons are seen as actors, defining reality by means of internal-interpretive structures. Within this perspective, human meaning is largely dependent upon the experiential occurrences of the individual, including meanings gained directly from encounters with media presentations. Faules and Alexander (1978) elaborated on this notion and suggest that, as facilitators of indirect experience, the media contribute substantially to the individual's constructs of social reality. The notion of reality constructs takes on an important dimension when one is addressing issues regarding mass communication. Some theorists suggest that social reality is highly dependent upon the cultural reality indigenous to a particular group or population. Youngblood (1977, p. 12) is such a proponent:

> When we say "media" what we really mean is "culture." And that culture is the single most important factor in the orientation of human behavior — especially that primary behavior called consciousness — is beyond dispute. Any anthropologist will agree that reality is a function of the culture in which one lives; this is true on the physiological level as well as the psychological plane. And in any advanced industrial nation, in any politically relevant sense, the mass media are the culture. That is, the product of their functioning is the common cultural reality.

The mass media, seen as participants to this cultural reality, are best viewed within the symbolic interactionist perspective at the level of personally shared meanings. Useful explication on the role of the mass media within this perspective is found in Blumer (1969, pp. 187-88), who provides a scenario for the interpretive procedures between the individual user and the mass media:

> Their interests, their forms of receptiveness, indifference, or opposition, their sophistication or naivete, and their established scheme of definition set the way in which they initially receive the presentation. Usually there is a further intervening stage before the residual effects of the presentations are set in experience and behavior. This additional stage is an interpretive process which through analysis and critical judgment reworks the presentations into different forms before assimilation into experience. This process of interpretation in the individual is markedly guided by the stimulations, cues, suggestions, and definitions he secures from other people, particularly those constituting his so-called reference groups. Account must be taken of a collective process of definition which in different ways shapes the manner in which individuals composing the "audience" interpret and respond to the presentations given through the mass media.

Blumer suggests that symbolic mediation by individual media users is processual rather than static, and that the interpreter's definitional process is continually being updated with new information. For the symbolic interactionist, the interest is in the meaning of the "same event" shared between communicating participants. How does this happen when we are examining the process of mass communication and social behavior?

For Blumer, the process of media usage is two-staged. First, the individual's predispositions determine the nature of the receptive stage of information from media to user. Second, but more fundamental to our concerns, is the interactionist's scheme for interpretive processes that color the nature of social behavior and individual experience; over time, such processes are dependent on "fine-tuning" by immediate others located in the actor's social arena. Again inherent within the symbolic interactionist's perspective is the interpretive enactment of individuals on the information provided by mass media outlets. The unit of analysis, however, holds at the level of subgroup or individual: "The essence of symbolic response is centered in the connotative dimensions of meaning which rests with the receiver (perceiver) of the message rather than the sender; and the associational meanings one develops and uses vary from individual to individual" (Meyer, McIntyre, and Baran, in press). Individual meanings, then, are universally independent for media users, although commonalities will be found across groups to the extent that aspects of the symbolic culture are actively shared. The unit of examination, as Blumer also suggests, is the collectivity of meanings derived by interaction networks for the media user. Social reality for media processes is the media user's definition of that reality.

In a distinctively symbolic interactionist frame, Frazer (1976) and then Reid (1978) have pursued an examination of the relationship between family interaction and mediation of televiewing processes. Reid has investigated the structure of parental rules in their mediation of children's response to television advertising (1979a) and the more indirect impact of family-group interactions on the child's understanding of commercials (1979b). Reid and Frazer (1979) explicated a symbolic interactionist approach to conceptualizing and observing children's interactions with commercials.

In more recent research, Reid and Frazer (1980) performed naturalistic inquiry into the nature of children's television play, within the larger order of play and its importance to overall child development: "Play [was] undeniably part of the co-viewing setting, involving the interactions (which need not be face to face) of children orienting their cognitive, physical, and symbolic behaviors toward themselves, one another, or animate or inanimate objects" (p. 67). Of particular import was the social interaction among siblings and influences on the televiewing setting.

The authors also demonstrated through the children's discourse evidence for how play shifts in focus from program-oriented to free-form inprovisational play; in this case, they found that "viewing that occurred with parents tended to be more of the former type [program-oriented], while viewing with siblings only was more often of the latter type" (Reid and Fraser 1980, p. 71). Siblings also appeared to exercise control over the tuning and selection of the television receiver, but also displayed tendencies to exercise control over proximal environs, including play, by involving the content of television within other activities.

Ethnomethodology:
An Interpretive Framework for Mass Media Inquiry

Ethnomethodologists are concerned with explaining how persons exercise reflexivity in the accomplishment of everyday life. The focus, as with symbolic interactionists, is on natural settings and the participants within those settings, but the ethnomethodologist must always retain a certain element of distance from the people being studied in order to recognize these everyday, taken-for-granted behaviors. Data for the ethnomethodologist are primarily talk, the study of discourse, in the examination of people's methods for creating and sustaining reality, not the substance or meaning of the reality itself.

The fundamental components of Garfinkel's ethnomethodology are the individual's: use of reflexive methods, based on reactions to rules or norms with indexical properties sensitive to situated activities. Our application of these concepts to mass communication will reverse the present order and begin with the last component first.

A host of typified settings for media-related activity seem ideally suited for classification as situated activities. When brought closer to home — the U.S. family and television — the concrete parameters of analysis become clear. Ethnographic procedures have proven adaptable to a host of topics, including the village, the tribe, the union, the organization, and the institution. All have proven accessible as units of study given ethnographic procedures. Though smaller in definitive scope, the nuclear family has also proven accessible to observation and study through ethnographic means (Bryce 1978; Lull 1976; 1980b; Meyer, Traudt, and Anderson 1980; Traudt 1979).

Situated activities can be separated conceptually when viewed from the television-as-setting viewpoint. There is the reality of the viewing setting, where a great many routinized behaviors are directly or indirectly implicated as part of the situated activity. Human interactions with television and other participants become one of the settings for analysis.

Independent in approach, but just as important, are the situated activities the content of which is inherent to viewer-selected televised material. Talk about television, apart from watching television or "sitting around the TV," can be integrated easily in the passing conversations and other acts of the moment. (See Blum [1964] for some interesting evidence of lower-class urban blacks' conversational exchanges "with" white television performers.) These interactions on the part of family members represent indirect uses of media for informing, underlining, or even correcting their sense of how the world is ordered. When applied to the U.S. family, considerations about where to conduct research requires two paths or directions in technique. The television set, the physical source of television programming — the information/symbol resource — is for most families located in one or more static locales in the household. Variations in the physical character of viewing environs can be observed, recorded, and, if need be, participated in by the researcher visiting the household. There are a number of ways to do this, but the combining of participant-observation techniques, such as observation, with forms of record-keeping and temporal indicators of the flow and composition of the family's audience patterns can be compatible with the goals of "thick description."

Of primary interest to the ethnomethodologist, however, is examination of people's successful interaction of a larger order within these settings. Parenthetically, we might note that a large measure of the success of some interactions lies precisely in making them routine, or forgettable to the participants; among the tougher tasks of the ethnographer is that of bringing into sharp relief the developmental logics of these interactions. Again, the topic of concern for the ethnomethodologist is not the content of these activities but the reflexive work performed by the participants in their discursive and manipulative treatment within reality-sustaining situations. What, then, is the reflexive work performed within family discourse attributable to the mass media? Again, two related arguments present themselves.

The mass media can be seen as both the cause and outcome of social activities. This has dual ramifications when applied to the family setting. Perhaps a better way of describing this process is to say that mass media both provide media-based ethno-methods and are the goal for other family ethnomethods. James Lull (1978, p. 5) has referred to the media scheduling and consequent ordering of other activities as "audience ethno-methods."

The methods of audience members (not to be confused with scientists' methodology) are, first and foremost, socially interactive practices that are made real in talk, nonverbal and elocutionary acts, and objects:

They are handy expedients which can be exploited by individuals, coalitions, and family units to serve their personal
needs, create practical relationships, and engage the so-

cial world. Television and other mass media, rarely mentioned as vital sources in the construction or maintenance
of interpersonal relations, can now be seen to play a central role in the methods which family members and other
social units employ purposefully to interact normatively
within their own special everyday realities (Lull 1978,
p. 5).

These are practical accomplishments, then, often concurrent
with or attributable to television content, but nonetheless independent of its content. Further, television programming may
provide contextual meaning to encounters among individuals, with
content merely serving as the common experiential ground for
prosperous interactions. In these instances, television is used
for other than entertainment functions. They serve as forms —
methods for the successful engagement of social interaction. No
doubt televiewing-as-ethnomethod also serves the individual in the
accomplishment of nonsocial goals. Televiewing as normally accomplished activity can serve the functions of communication
avoidance, individual or subgroup isolation, or task procrasti-
nation.

It is also legitimate to assume that part of the ethnomethod
repertoire will include content attractions for the social actor's
private goals. Some show remarkable strategizing. Consider this
example: Children are known to feign homework or reading to
retard parental exercise of bedtime rules. Parents, upon observing their children's late-night behavior, are impressed with the
child's diligence (a display of prosocial behavior) and condone
the flexibility of family rules. The child then engages in
late-night televiewing alone in the family den (Traudt 1979,
p. 148). Ethnomethods for televiewing might be examined for
their temporal predictability. Do families schedule other events
around televiewing to facilitate group activities? Patterns of
family and individual activity would provide resourceful indicators
as would the identification of norms, rules, or maxims constructed
by family members as components of media-based ethnomethods.
Of particular interest would be the examination of ethnomethods
of televiewing relative to the ethnomethods of other household
behaviors. Does televiewing dominate other ethnomethods? What
is the hierarchical distribution of the ethnomethods of television
compared to others?

The third component of Garfinkel's ethnomethodology is indexicality, a malleable, situation-specific form of prescribed expression that corresponds to societal (external) norms, rules, and
terms. By speculating further on the two forms of media-related
reflexivity, we can begin to sort out the indexical arenas for
media study that become the natural settings in which to pose
questions. The distinction between reflexive activity that uses

television to accomplish everyday activities (media-based ethno-methods) and efforts to accomplish the desired goal of doing media (ethnomethods of mass media) require concurrently independent scenarios for indexicality. Consider the following.

It is reasonable to suggest that most households have fairly well-established patterns of activity, either implicit or explicit formative rules, agreements, or operating procedures performed by family members within a general sequencing of time, whether externally or internally geared. This is also true for the use of television. Though the content of interactions per se is different, the cause is the same. The structure of programming, its temporal predictability (whether that means time of day, week, or season is irrelevant for this discussion) helps to determine its viability when incorporated as an ethnomethod.

Ethnomethodological Studies of Family-Media Use

James Lull has systematically developed research programs for the collection of data from families. His adaptation of ethnographic procedures for investigating media-related ethnomethods corresponds to the view that the mass media are important expedients for social interchange. Lull identified two typologies of audience ethnomethods: structural and relational. Structural units in the typology are the environmental (proximal) and regulative components of family use of television. Relational aspects were examined through four constructs: communication facilitation, affiliation/avoidance, social learning, and competence/dominance (Lull 1978; 1980a). The typologies drawn by Lull have provided a guide for later field study. To insure empirical validity, the typologies were confirmed by preliminary observations, reporting, and discussions with natural audience members.

More recently, Lull broadened his theoretical outlook to include ethnographies of mass communication and integrated communication rules, interpretive paradigms for field research, and ethnomethodology as it advances the enterprise of qualitative study. Lull's development in procedural design is founded in: a modification of the rules approach in communication theory (Lull 1982b); an interpretive framework for data analysis; and a dependency on conversation/discourse as data and, therefore, "grammar" for lexical use and support for data claims (Lull 1979, pp. 5-11).

The second operational tenet above clearly addresses methodological concerns. The form of the argument follows the adoption of methodology couched in an open, inductivist frame or system of analysis. Here, rather than employ normal appeals to objective validity, the researcher's analysis tends to operate in a more hermeneutic mode in which adequacy of explanation is gained by coherence in "texts." (The issue of establishing criteria for assessing data-based claims in qualitative studies of communication is given a provocative treatment by Anderson [1981a].)

Also specific to methodological concerns, Lull's third feature distinguished perspectives for data collection and analysis, and was clearly in keeping with fundamental tenets of humanistic understanding. That man is deterministic and manages his own interaction arena propels the researcher to those scenes where people do their interacting. As a consequence of this process of personal management, Lull argues, individuals develop rules-based choices (manifested in action repertoires) applicable to any number of social encounters. It may be that these repertoires, though varied in number and combination, may be limited so as to be manageable for most persons. Such subsets of behavior, of interest to various social science disciplines, have included many of the rituals of daily interaction and, as a result, we have seen the examination of ritual in talk — and for Lull's purposes — of doing television and other mass media for social mediation. Ethnographic data, according to Lull (1979, p. 11), "are retrieved by intensive, careful scrutiny of social units over time. They include detailed, first-hand observations of social life, insights provided by informants, and information gathered by in-depth interviewing of social actors."

Rules Theory and Media Use in Families

We have argued so far that much media use seems to evolve from individuals' strategizing for both content-bound and content-free purposes. The third approach, rules theory, is concerned with the production of behavioral regularities in social action (that is, conduct), and also seeks to locate systematic sources of control that guide conduct. Rather than being a substantive theory for a specific genre of human behavior, notions of "rule" have been appropriated by many disciplines and seem to represent more of a philosophical stance in opposition to nomothetic science; the following, from Collett (1977, p. 4), provides a taste of these differences:

It has been pointed out that rules have no truth value, and that they are conditional and prescriptive. There are various types of rules, and these may be distinguished from scientific "laws," in that laws have truth value and are not prescriptive. More importantly, laws cannot be violated, whereas it is a fundamental requirement of a rule that it can be broken. This is the condition of breach.

Another more contentious requirement is that rules be capable of change. This is the condition of <u>alteration</u>.

Like ethnomethodology, rule-governed regularities are built on complexes of information that are "taken-for-granted": that is, "messages not actualized in physical speech, but nevertheless ordinarily understood in-common" (Hopper 1981, p. 196). The idea of taken-for-granted in all its forms — frames, schemas, presuppositions, commonsense constructs, and so on — is fundamental to the phenomenological outlook and to rules that "govern" interactions. Alfred Schutz (1967) has proposed that humans, in their dynamic streams of consciousness, question neither the appearances nor the regularities of their daily physical and social worlds. In the natural attitude, humans understand the features of the social world as given, or a priori, and suspend doubt in the reality of its existence. Such beliefs are stocks of commonsense knowledge that are, however, socially distributed.

Most rules theorists do not treat individuals' stocks of knowledge as static but rather as <u>conventional</u> and <u>prescriptive</u> rule organizations for getting things done in a culture. The element of choice in following a rule (observable in verbal and nonverbal behavior) always implies a standardized usage. The employment of a rule for successfully completing a communication task is potentially open to criticism by that "community" which upholds the rule. Even in nonserious play among children, where the rules are made up on the spot, noncompliance by another child or adult is reprimanded (Millar 1968). In other words, rules cannot be idiosyncratic; however, it may be that individuals can internalize contradictory rules for the "same game," as Bateson (1972) explained in his double-bind theory of schizophrenia. Disagreement within the community as to what performance can count as an enactment of the rule can occur, and if consensus is arrived at, the rule itself may eventually change. (In the area of televiewing interpretive processes, it is conceivable that people's concepts of what counts as "acceptable acts of civil disobedience" have substantially changed following innumerable viewings, and interpersonal discussions, of television coverage of certain groups' and individuals' acts.) Yet such changes in turn imply changes in the social structure; changes in the cognitive "horizon" of the rule-upholding community (Cicourel 1970). The concept of rules goes beyond ethnomethodology in its concern with the cognitive considerations of action, especially in terms of: levels of awareness of the rules of "other minds" (Toulmin 1974); awareness of cues that invoke different orders of rules (Bateson 1972); and awareness of self in following a rule, whether habitual unfoldings of behavior occur out of conscious direction or the role perceptions of self in a rule-governed episode are not recognized as incongruent with others' expectations (Cronen and Pearce 1981). Generally, a behavior cannot be considered rule-governed if no verification of the actor's "knowing the rule," usually in the form of verbal evidence, can be had. On the other hand, some theorists hold that knowing the rule is not enough — that without a record of behavioral regularity on the part of the actor, verbalization of a rule merely evidences an attitudinal or world-view disposition (Sigman 1980). The issue of actor knowledge of rules is theoretically controversial, and the discussion of explicit and implicit media use rules will refer back to it.

The social-scientific interest in rules is recent and follows the work of sociolinguists and philosophers of linguistic acts in analyzing how meaningful utterances are performed. In reaction to Chomsky's idea that transformational rules operate at the syntactic level and that such rules are both potentially innate and universal, others have focused on the problem of deviant sentence production as a way of expanding rules formulations to include the performative constituents of speech. In other words, a user's competence level (knowledge of grammatical "rightness") does not account for the variances in actual discourse contributed by contextual and social-structural features. (For analytic discussions of this change in thinking, refer to Cicourel 1970; Gumb 1972; Searle 1968.)

Raymond Gumb (1972) argues that all linguistic rules have a prescriptive, normative force and can simply be considered social rules, since sanctions regarding their use are coextensive with those regulating communicative acts in general. Like Collett (1977), Gumb counts among the five essential "marks" of social rules the possibility that a rule may be misapplied or performed incorrectly. Most social rules do allow some latitude for judging correct performance by an actor, with varying levels of success in meeting prescriptive requirements. But success in "bringing off" a piece of behavior in which a rule has been applied depends in large part on the actor's ability to self-criticize the performance. Rules theory's allowance of incorrect performance entails other "marks" for identifying a social rule: they must be reflected in the behavioral regularities of the community; more mature agents of the community must be able to cite the rules in criticizing rule-governed behavior; and there must be enabling conditions — physical, legal, moral, and so on — that permit persons to conform to rules (Gumb 1972, pp. 37-44). A community, then, is defined by those rule organizations that guide the goal-oriented behavior of its members.

In application to media use in families, rules have generally referred to social controls of media operation and content by one or more family members. Rules can define limits on viewing time or duration, acceptable ranges of program content, program selection, and prescribed or proscribed media-linked activities

(Barcus 1969). The direction of influence in the development and maintenance of rules is invariably from parents to children. The types of rules that parents devise appear to be based on socialization concerns. For example, Bower (1973) found that parents reported that controls on specific content rise between ages 7-9 and 10-12, while controls on viewing time show a slight decrease between those ages. The inference is that controls over content become more necessary as children begin to view media models for guidance in making future role decisions.

Most of the media rules in the literature are actually family media policies, in the sense of verbalized intentions or goals, rather than the kind of behavioral negotiation in specific contexts that characterize rules. The requirement that social rules must be reflected in the behavioral regularities of the group that upholds them is ordinarily missing from research descriptions of televiewing rules. Without behavioral criteria, it also becomes difficult to document the manner in which rules are misapplied. The predominant research method in media rules studies has been the sample survey where one family member respondent, usually one parent, represents the family unit's rules articulation. In addition to the overestimation bias that may be present in parents' rules reports (Rossiter and Robertson 1975), there may also be differences between marriage partners in their formulations of rules (Lindlof and Copeland 1982).

In a recent review of interpersonal communication research, Bochner (1978) questioned the empirical study of rules on grounds that rules are rarely explicitly stated and that the identification of implicit rules is confounded with problems of definition and order of complexity. This objection seems central to rules conceptions of media use since those social behaviors are so highly ingrained in routinized, taken-for-granted patterns of action. The implicit rules that Bochner questions, that is, "metarules" like those that regulate what rules will be in force at a particular time, may not be rules as we have treated them to this point, but rather norms. Whereas rules are the "relationship agreements" (Jackson 1965) aimed at achieving a stable system within the family unit, norms are value baselines around which family behaviors will fluctuate over time. Family members may not be able to state their norms, since they are analytical constructs, but the rules for interactions in specific household regions (including media use regions) should be readily available upon interrogation and corroborative observation. The reasons given by social actors for their behavior should not be construed as "rational" or as corresponding to a scientific theory of causes of behavior; a rule's rationality lies in its consistency with the cultural system as it is conceived by the actor (Toulmin 1974, p. 193).

The exceptions, deviations, mistakes, and misapplications of social acts are part of any description of social rules. Such "special" cases provide evidence of the consensual practices of participants (in the ethnomethodological sense), and also reveal the interpretive procedures of a community. In other words, rules provide information about how so-called content should be interpreted (Jackson 1965; Reusch and Bateson 1951; Wilder 1979). Although rules theory as an empirical endeavor is still in a primitive state, it does hold promise for considering the levels of meaning by which human interpreters normally put together the sequences of behavior called acts. Pushed even further, it is possible to envision the use of rules concepts in postulating the patterning of social-structural ideology at the micro level of individuals' incorporation of television. Evidence that social class seems to predict the numbers and types of televiewing rules for children (Blood 1961; Messaris 1982; Rossiter and Robertson 1975) indicates that different values are placed on how a child interprets programming. Here, the object of interest is not so much what the child interprets, but rather the fact that some parents attribute heavy developmental outcomes to the child's interpreting activity. The application of ethnographic research methods can provide useful information regarding the complexity of viewing rules and how they are communicated differently in terms of speech communities.

CONCLUDING THOUGHTS

At the outset of proposing new approaches to any type of problem, it is often the case that more is promised by proponents than can ever be realistically delivered. We have presented these new orientations to the research of families and mass media in a positive light; our expectations for theoretical advance in this area are modest. Not only do individual research programs take much longer to complete than more tradtional approaches, but the ontological stance resists the rapid construction of general theory.

Because these reconceptualized approaches to mediated communication deal explicitly with **processes** of behavior, their most productive application may be in those areas of family functioning where change is either imminent or already underway. The advent of new communications media to augment the present receive-only devices may portend major effects on the family. A research orientation that remains flexible and able to document the subjective worlds of its subjects is well-suited to the task of investigating the social impact of new technologies. Similarly, changes in the life cycle that may involve new clusterings of media use activities are amenable to these approaches. At present we know very little about the manner in which changes in family composition over time is accompanied by shifts in media use among family members. As we suggested earlier in this chapter, the family is probably comprised of spatial and temporal zones where identities are organized and rehearsed. Media may play integral parts in those ongoing enactments.

BIBLIOGRAPHY

Abrahams, Roger D. 1977. "The Play of Worlds in Story and Storytelling." University of Texas at Austin. Mimeographed.

Adams, Parveen. 1978. "Representation and Sexuality." _M/F_, no. 1, pp. 65-82.

Adler, R., ed. 1977. _Research on the Effects of Television Advertising on Children._ Washington, D.C.: U.S. Government Printing Office.

Albrecht, T. L. and V. A. Ropp. 1982. "The Study of Network Structuring in Organizations Through the Use of Method Triangulation." _Western Journal of Speech Communication_ 46 (2):162-78

Albrow, M. 1980. "The Dialectic of Science and Values in the Study of Organizations." In _Control and Ideology in Organizations,_ ed. G. Salaman and K. Thompson, pp. 278-96. Cambridge, Mass.: MIT Press.

Althusser, Louis. 1970. _For Marx._ Trans. Ben Brewster. New York: Vintage.

_____. 1971. "Ideology and Ideological State Apparatuses." In _Lenin and Philosophy and Other Essays,_ trans. Ben Brewster, pp. 127-86. New York: Monthly Review Press.

"American Indians and the Media: Neglect and Stereotype." 1979. _Journalism History_ 6 (2).

Anderson, Daniel R., L. F. Alwitt, Elizabeth P. Lorch, and Stephen R. Levin. 1979. "Watching Children Watch Television." In _Attention and Cognitive Development,_ ed. Gordon A. Hale and Michael Lewis, pp. 331-61. New York: Plenum.

Anderson, James. 1980. "An Agenda for the Social Sciences and the Study of Mass Communication." Paper presented to the Speech Communication Association, New York.

_____. 1981a. "Evaluative Principles for Naturalistic Inquiry, Or: How Do I Know That You Know What You're Talking About?" Paper presented to the International Communication Association, Minneapolis.

_____. 1981b. "Receivership Skills: An Educational Response." In _Education for the Television Age,_ ed. Milton E. Ploghoft and James A. Anderson, pp. 19-27. Springfield, Ill.: Charles C. Thomas.

_____. 1981c. "Research on Children and Television: A Critique." _Journal of Broadcasting_ 25 (4):395-400.

280 / Communications in Transition

Anderson, P. 1976. Considerations on Western Marxism. London: New Left Books.

Arendt, Hannah. 1958. The Human Condition. Chicago: University of Chicago Press.

_____. 1977. Between Past and Future. Enlarged ed. Baltimore: Penguin.

Aries, P. 1962. Centuries of Childhood: A Social History of Family Life. New York: Knopf.

Arnold, Carroll C. 1968. "Oral Rhetoric, Rhetoric, and Literature." Philosophy and Rhetoric 1 (4):191-210.

Aronowitz, S. 1981. The Crisis in Historical Materialism: Class, Politics and Culture in Marxist Theory. New York: Praeger Publishers.

Ashby, W. Ross. 1956. An Introduction to Cybernetics. London: Chapman and Hall.

Askham, J. 1976. "Identity and Stability within the Marriage Relationship." Journal of Marriage and the Family 38 (August):535-47.

Axley, S. R. 1982. "Saying That It's 'Difficult' — But Really That It's 'Easy': Managerial and Organizational Communication in Terms of the Conduit Metaphor." Paper presented at the annual meeting of the Speech Communication Association, Louisville.

Ayer, A. J. 1935. Reprinted 1952. Language, Truth, and Logic. New York: Dover.

Bailyn, Bernard. 1960. Education in the Forming of American Society. Chapel Hill: University of North Carolina.

Bales, R. F. 1953. "The Equilibrium Problem in Small Groups." In Working Papers in Social Action, ed. T. Parsons, R. F. Bales, and E. Shils, pp. 111-62. New York: The Free Press.

Banks, Seymour. 1980. "Children's Television Viewing Behavior." Journal of Marketing 4 (2):48-55.

Barcus, F. E. 1969. "Parental Influences on Children's Television Viewing." Television Quarterly, no. 3, pp. 63-73.

Barnouw, E. 1975. Tube of Plenty. New York: Oxford University Press.

Barthes, Roland. 1967. Elements of Semiology. Trans. Annette Lavers and Colin Smith. New York: Hill and Wang.

_____. 1974. S/Z: An Essay. Trans. Richard Miller. New York: Hill and Wang.

_____. 1978. A Lover's Discourse: Fragments. Trans. Richard Howard. New York: Hill and Wang.

Bartley, William W. III. 1962. The Retreat to Commitment. New York: Knopf.

Barton, Allen H. 1979. "Paul Lazarsfeld and Applied Social Research." Social Science History 3 (3-4):4-44.

Barton, Richard and R. Gregg. 1982. "Middle East Conflict as a TV News Scenario: A Formal Analysis," Journal of Communication 32 (2):172-85.

Bates, A. P. 1964. "Privacy — A Useful Concept?" Social Forces 42 (4):429-34.

Bateson, Gregory. 1958. Naven. 2d. ed. Stanford, Calif.: Stanford University Press.

_____. 1972. Steps to an Ecology of Mind. New York: Ballantine.

Baudrillard, Jean. 1978. "Requiem for the Media." In Language, Sexuality and Subversion, ed. Paul Foss and Meaghan Morris, pp. 83-96. Darlington, Australia: Feral Publications.

_____. 1980. "Forgetting Foucault." Humanities in Society 3 (1):87-111.

Bauman, Z. 1978. Hermeneutics and Social Science. New York: Columbia University Press.

Bavelas, A. 1950. "Communication Patterns in Task-Oriented Groups." Acoustical Society of American Journal 22 (6): 727-30.

Bavelas, Janet Beavin. 1983. "Situations that Lead to Disqualification." Human Communication Research 9:130-45.

Bayless, O. L. 1967. "An Alternative Pattern for Problem Solving Discussions." Journal of Communication 17 (3):188-97.

Bechtel, R. B., C. Achelpohl, and R. Akers. 1972. "Correlates Between Observed Behavior and Questionnaire Responses on Television Viewing." In Television and Social Behavior, Vol. 4: Television in Day-to-Day Life: Patterns of Use, ed. E. A. Rubenstein, G. A. Comstock, and J. P. Murray, pp. 274-344. Washington, D.C.: U.S. Government Printing Office.

Becker, E. 1962. The Birth and Death of Meaning. Glencoe, Ill.: The Free Press.

Bell, Daniel. 1979. "The Social Framework of the Information Society." In The Computer Age, ed. Michael L. Dertouzos and Joel Moses, pp. 163-211. Cambridge, Mass.: MIT Press.

Bendix, R. 1970. "The Impact of Ideas on Organizational Structure." In The Sociology of Organizations: Basic Studies, ed. O. Grusky and G. A. Miller, pp. 529-36. New York: The Free Press.

Bensman, J. and R. Lilienfeld. 1979. Between Public and Private: The Lost Boundaries of the Self. New York: The Free Press.

Benson, J. K. 1977. "Organizations: A Dialectical View." Administrative Science Quarterly 22 (3):1-21.

Berelson, B. 1959. "The State of Communication Research." Public Opinion Quarterly 23 (1):1-16.

Berger, P. and H. Kellner. 1964. "Marriage and the Construction of Reality." Diogenes, 36:1-24.

Berger, P. L. and T. Luckmann. 1966. The Social Construction of Reality. Garden City: Doubleday.

Berlin, Isaiah. 1976. Vico and Herder: Two Studies in the History of Ideas. London: Hogarth.
_____. 1981. Concepts and Categories. New York: Penguin.
Bernard, H. R. and P. D. Killworth. 1977. "Informant Accuracy in Social Network Data II." Human Communication Research 4 (1):3-18.
Bernstein, R. J. 1978. The Restructuring of Social and Political Theory. Philadelphia: University of Pennsylvania Press.
Bitzer, Lloyd F. 1968. "The Rhetorical Situation." Philosophy and Rhetoric 1 (1):1-14.
_____. 1978. "Rhetoric and Public Knowledge." In Rhetoric, Philosophy, and Literature, ed. Don M. Burks, pp. 67-93. West Lafayette, Ind.: Purdue University Press.
Bitzer, Lloyd F. and Edwin Black, eds. 1971. The Prospect of Rhetoric. Englewood Cliffs, N.J.: Prentice-Hall.
Bleyer, Willard Grosvenor. 1927. Main Currents in the History of American Journalism. New York: Houghton-Mifflin.
Blood, R. O. 1961. "Social Class and Family Control of Television Viewing." Merrill-Palmer Quarterly of Behavior and Development 7 (3):205-22.
Blum, A. 1964. "Lower-Class Negro Television Spectators: The Concept of Pseudo-Jovial Skepticism." In Blue Collar World, ed. A. B. Shostak and W. Gomberg, pp. 437-43. Englewood Cliffs, N.J.: Prentice-Hall.
Blumer, H. 1969. Symbolic Interactionism: Perspective and Method. Englewood Cliffs, N.J.: Prentice-Hall.
Bochner, A. P. 1978. "On Taking Ourselves Seriously: An Analysis of Some Persistent Problems and Promising Directions in Interpersonal Research." Human Communication Research 4 (2):179-91.
_____. 1981. "On the Efficacy of Openness in Close Relationships." In Communication Yearbook 5, ed. M. Burgoon, pp. 109-24. Beverly Hills: Sage Publications.
Bogdan, R. and S. J. Taylor. 1975. Introduction to Qualitative Research Methods. New York: John Wiley.
Bolton, C. D. 1961. "Mate Selection as the Development of a Relationship." Marriage and Family Living 23 (August):234-40.
Boorstin, D. 1973. The Americans: The Democratic Experience. New York: Random House.
Booth, Wayne C. 1974. Modern Dogma and the Rhetoric of Assent. Chicago: University of Chicago Press.
Boraiko, Allen A. 1982. "The Chip: Mini-Marvel that is Changing Your Life." National Geographic 162 (4):421-56.
Bormann, E. G. 1972. "Fantasy and Rhetorical Vision: The Rhetorical Criticism of Social Reality." Quarterly Journal of Speech 58 (4):396-407.

_____. 1975. _Discussion and Group Methods: Theory and Practice_. 2d ed. New York: Harper and Row.

_____. 1980. "The Paradox and Promise of Small Group Research Revisited." _Central States Speech Journal_ 31 (3):214-20.

_____. 1982. "Symbolic Convergence Theory of Communication: Applications and Implications for Teachers and Consultants." _Journal of Applied Communication Research_ 10 (1):50-61.

Bourdieu, Pierre. 1980. "The Aristocracy of Taste." _Media, Culture and Society_ 2 (3):225-54.

Bower, R. T. 1973. _Television and the Public_. New York: Holt, Rinehart and Winston.

Bowerman, C. E. and J. W. Kinch. 1959. "Changes in Family and Peer Orientation of Children Between the Fourth and Tenth Grades." _Social Forces_ 37 (3):206-11.

Boyd, B. B. and J. M. Jensen. 1972. "Perceptions of the First-Line Supervisor's Authority: A Study in Superior-Subordinate Communication." _Academy of Management Journal_ 15 (3):331-42.

Boyd, H. 1968. "Love Versus Omnipotence: The Narcissistic Dilemma." _Psychotherapy: Theory, Research and Practice_ 5 (4):272-77.

Boyd-Barrett, Oliver. 1977. "Media Imperialism: Towards an International Framework for the Analysis of Media Systems." In _Mass Communication and Society_, ed. James Curran et al., pp. 116-35. London: Edward Arnold.

_____. 1982. "Cultural Dependency and the Mass Media." In _Culture, Society and the Media_, ed. M. Gurevitch et al., pp. 174-95. London: Methuen.

Bradley, P. H. and J. E. Baird, Jr. 1977. "Management and Communicator Style: A Correlational Analysis." _Central States Speech Journal_ 28 (3):194-203.

Brain, R. 1976. _Friends and Lovers_. New York: Basic Books.

Braithwaite, R. B. 1953. _Scientific Explanation_. Cambridge: Cambridge University Press.

Braudel, Fernand. 1969. _On History_. Trans. Sarah Matthews. Chicago: University of Chicago Press.

Braybrooke, D. and C. E. Lindblom. 1963. _A Strategy of Decision_. New York: The Free Press.

Brilhart, J. K. and L. M. Jochem. 1964. "Effects of Different Patterns on Outcomes of Problem-Solving Discussion." _Journal of Applied Psychology_ 48 (2):175:79.

Brinton, Alan. 1982. "William James and the Epistemic View of Rhetoric." _Quarterly Journal of Speech_ 68 (2):158-69.

Brockriede, Wayne. 1975. "Where is Argument?" _Journal of the American Forensic Association_ 11 (3):179-82.

Bronfenbrenner, U. 1970. _Two Worlds of Childhood: U.S. and U.S.S.R._ New York: Russell Sage Foundation.

_____. 1982. "New Images of Children, Families, and America." _Television and Children_ 4-5 (Fall 1981/Winter 1982):3-15.

Brooks, K., J. Callicoat, and G. Siegerdt. 1979. "The ICA Communication Audit and Perceived Communication Effectiveness Changes in 16 Audited Organizations." _Human Communication Research_ 5 (2):130-37.

Brown, R. H. 1977. _A Poetic for Sociology: Toward a Logic of Discovery for the Human Sciences._ Cambridge: Cambridge University Press.

Brummett, Barry. 1976. "Some Implications of 'Process' or 'Intersubjectivity': Postmodern Rhetoric." _Philosophy and Rhetoric_ 9 (1):21-51.

Brunsdon, Charlotte and David Morley. 1978. _Everyday Television: "Nationwide."_ London: British Film Institute.

Bryce, J. W. 1978. "Television Use and the Family: A Proposal for Exploratory Research." Doctoral dissertation prospectus, Columbia University.

Buber, M. 1965. _The Knowledge of Man,_ ed. M. Friedman. New York: Harper and Row.

Bucher, R. and L. Schatzman. 1964. "Negotiating a Division of Labor Among Professionals in the State Mental Hospital." _Psychiatry_ 27 (3):266-77.

Bugental, J. F. T. 1965. _The Search for Authenticity._ New York: Holt, Rinehart and Winston.

Burke, Kenneth. 1950. _A Rhetoric of Motives._ New York: Prentice-Hall.

_____. 1954. _Permanence and Change._ 2d rev. ed. Los Altos, Calif.: Hermes.

_____. 1969a. _A Grammar of Motives._ Berkeley: University of California Press.

_____. 1969b. _A Rhetoric of Motives,_ 2d ed. Berkeley: University of California Press.

Burrell, G. and G. Morgan. 1979. _Sociological Paradigms and Organizational Analysis._ London: Heinemann Press.

Buys, C. J. 1978. "Humans Would Do Better Without Groups." _Personality and Social Psychology Bulletin_ 4 (2):123-25.

Caldwell, D. F. and C. A. O'Reilly III. 1982. "Boundary Spanning and Individual Performance: The Impact of Self-Monitoring." _Journal of Applied Psychology_ 67 (1):124-27.

Campbell, Paul N. 1973. "Poetic-Rhetorical, Philosophical, and Scientific Discourse." _Philosophy and Rhetoric_ 6 (1):1-29.

_____. 1975. "The Personal of Scientific Discourse." _Quarterly Journal of Speech_ 61:391-405.

Carey, James W. 1974. "The Problem of Journalism History." _Journalism History_ 1 (1):3-27.

——————. 1975a. "Communication and Culture." Communication Research 2:173-91.

——————. 1975b. "A Cultural Approach to Communications." Communication 2 (1):1-22.

——————. 1977. "Mass Communication Research and Cultural Studies: An American View." In Mass Communication and Society, ed. James Curran, Michael Gurevitch, and Janet Woollacott, pp. 409-26. London: Edward Arnold.

Carleton, Walter M. 1978. "What is Rhetorical Knowledge? A Response to Farrell — and More." Quarterly Journal of Speech 64 (4):313-28.

Carnap, R. 1935. Philosophy and Logical Syntax. London: Keegan, Paul, Trench, Trubner.

Casey, Ralph D. 1944. "What Lies Ahead in Education for Journalism?" Journalism Quarterly 21 (1):55-60.

——————. 1965. "The Scholarship of Frank Luther Mott." Journalism Quarterly 42 (1):81.

Cassirer, Ernst. 1953. Language and Myth. New York: Dover.

——————. 1955. The Philosophy of Symbolic Forms. 3 Vols. Trans. Ralph Manheim. New Haven, Conn.: Yale University Press.

Cawelti, John G. 1976. Adventure, Mystery and Romance: Formula Stories as Art and Popular Culture. Chicago: University of Chicago Press.

Chaffee, S. H., J. M. McLeon, and C. K. Atkin. 1971. "Parental Influences on Adolescent Media Use." American Behavioral Scientist 14 (3):323-40.

Chambers, Iain. 1981. "Pop Music: A Teaching Perspective." Screen Education 39:35-46.

Chaney, David. 1981. "Public Opinion and Social Change: The Social Rhetoric of Documentary and the Concept of News." In Mass Media and Social Change, ed. E. Katz and Tamas Szecsko, pp. 115-36. Beverly Hills: Sage Publications.

Chase, Stuart. 1938. The Tyranny of Words. New York: Harcourt.

Cheney, G. 1983. "The Rhetoric of Identification and the Study of Organizational Communication." Quarterly Journal of Speech 69 (2):in press.

Cherry, Colin. 1957. On Human Communication. Cambridge, Mass.: MIT Press.

Cheseboro, J. W., J. F. Cragan, and P. McCullough. 1973. "The Small Group Techniques of the Radical Revolutionary: A Synthetic Study of Consciousness Raising." Speech Monographs 40 (2):136-46.

Chomsky, N. 1965. Aspects of the Theory of Syntax. Cambridge, Mass.: MIT Press.

Christenson, Peter G. 1980. "The Effects of Consumer Information Processing Announcements on Children's

Perceptions of Commercials and Products." Ph.D. diss., Stanford University.

_____. 1982a. "Prosocial Themes in Prime Time: Are the Kids Getting the Message?" Unpublished manuscript, Department of Speech Communication, The Pennsylvania State University.

_____. 1982b. "Children's Perceptions of TV Commercials and Products: The Effects of PSA's." Communication Research 9 (4):491-524.

Christenson, Peter G. and Thomas R. Lindlof. 1982. "Children and Audio Media: What's Going on When the TV's Turned Off?" Paper presented to the annual conference of the Popular Culture Association, Louisville.

Christians, Clifford and James W. Carey. 1981. "The Logic and Aims of Qualitative Research." In Research Methods in Mass Communication, ed. Guido H. Stempel III and Bruce H. Westley, pp. 342-62. Englewood Cliffs, N.J.: Prentice-Hall.

Cicourel, A. V. 1970. "The Acquisition of Social Structure: Toward a Developmental Sociology of Language and Meaning." In Understanding Everyday Life, ed. J. Douglas, pp. 136-68. Chicago: Aldine.

_____. 1974. Cognitive Sociology. New York: The Free Press.

Clanchy, Michael T. 1979. From Memory to Written Record: England, 1066-1307. Cambridge, Mass.: Harvard University Press.

Cody, Michael J., Mary Lou Woelfel, and William J. Jordan. 1983. "Dimensions of Compliance-Gaining Situations." Human Communication Research 9:99-113.

Coker, Jerry. 1964. Improvising Jazz. Englewood Cliffs, N.J.: Prentice-Hall.

Coleman, J. S. 1974. Power and the Structure of Society. New York: Norton.

Collett, P. 1977. "The Rules of Conduct." In Social Rules and Social Behavior, ed. P. Collett, pp. 1-27. Totowa, N.J.: Rowman and Littlefield.

Collins, W. A. 1975. "The Developing Child as Viewer." Journal of Communication 25 (4):35-44.

_____. 1979. "Children's Comprehension of Television Content." In Children Communicating: Media and Development of Thought, Speech, Understanding, ed. E. Wartella, pp. 21-52. Beverly Hills: Sage Publications.

_____. 1981. "Recent Advances in Research on Cognitive Processing of Television Viewing." Journal of Broadcasting 25 (4):327-34.

Collins, W. A., T. J. Berndt, and V. L. Hess. 1974. "Observational Learning of Motives and Consequences for Television Aggression: A Developmental Study." Child Development 45

(4):799-802.

Collins, W. A., H. Wellman, A. H. Keniston, and J. D. Westby. 1978. "Age-related Aspects of Comprehension and Inference from a Televised Dramatic Narrative." Child Development 49 (3):389-99.

Compaine, B., C. Sterling, T. Guback, and J. Noble. 1982. Who Owns the Media? Concentration of Ownership in the Mass Communications Industry. White Plains, N.Y.: Knowledge Industry Publications.

Comstock, G., S. Chaffee, N. Katzman, M. McCombs, and D. Roberts. 1978. Television and Human Behavior. New York: Columbia University Press.

Conrad, C. 1983. "Toward a Symbology of Organizational Power." In Communication in Organizations: An Interpretive Approach, ed. L. L. Putnum and M. E. Pacanowsky, in press. Beverly Hills: Sage Publications.

"A Conversation with Edwin Emery." 1980. Journalism History 7 (1):20-21.

Cooper, Martha. "A Foucaultian Critique: The Neutron Bomb Issue." Paper read at the Sixty-Seventh Speech Communication Association Meeting, November 12-15, 1981, Anaheim, Calif. Mimeographed.

—————. "Michael Foucault's Study of Discourse: Implications for Rhetoric." Paper read at the Sixty-Eighth Speech Communication Association Meeting, November 4-7, 1982, Louisville. Mimeographed.

Corcoran, Paul E. 1979. Political Language and Rhetoric. Austin: University of Texas Press.

Corrigan, Philip and Paul Willis. 1980. "Cultural Forms and Class Mediations." Media, Culture and Society 2:297-312.

Coward, Rosalind. 1977. "Class, 'Culture and the Social Formation.'" Screen 18 (1):75-105.

Coward, R. and J. Ellis. 1977. Language and Materialism: Developments in Semiology and the Theory of the Subject. London: Routledge and Kegan Paul.

Cowell, C. 1972. "Group Process as Metaphor." Journal of Communication 22 (2):113-23.

Crable, Richard E. 1982. "Knowledge-as-Status: On Argument and Epistemology." Communication Monographs 49:249-62.

Cragan, J. F. and D. W. Wright. 1980. "Small Group Communication Research of the 1970's: A Synthesis and Critique." Central States Speech Journal 31 (3):197-213.

Croasmun, Earl and Richard A. Cherwitz. 1982. "Beyond Rhetorical Relativism." Quarterly Journal of Speech 68 (1):1-16.

Cronen, V. and W. B. Pearce. 1981. "Logical Force in Interpersonal Communication: A New Concept of the 'Necessity' in Social Behavior." Communication 6 (1):5-67.

Cronkhite, Garry and Jo Liska. 1977. "Introduction." Western Journal of Speech Communication 41:3-8.

Crosson, Frederick J. and Kenneth M. Sayre, eds. 1967. Philosophy and Cybernetics. New York: Simon and Schuster.

Csikszentmihalyi, M. and R. Kubey. 1981. "Television and the Rest of Life." Public Opinion Quarterly 45 (3):317-28.

Curran, James, Michael Gurevitch, and Janet Woollacott. 1982. "The Study of Media: Theoretical Approaches." In Culture, Society and the Media, ed. M. Gurevitch et al., pp. 11-29. London: Methuen.

Czitrom, Daniel J. 1982. Mass Media and the American Mind: From Morse to McLuhan. Chapel Hill: University of North Carolina Press.

Daft, R. L. and J. C. Wiginton. 1979. "Language and Organization." Academy of Management Review 2 (2):179-91.

Dahlgren, Peter. 1981. "TV News and the Suppression of Reflexivity." In Mass Media and Social Change, ed. E. Katz and Tamas Szecsko, pp. 101-13. Beverly Hills: Sage Publications.

Dandridge, T. C., I. I. Mitroff and W. F. Joyce. 1980. "Organizational Symbolism: A Topic to Expand Organizational Analysis." Academy of Management Review 5 (6):77-82.

Darnton, Michael. 1979. The Business of Enlightenment: A Publishing History of the ENCYCLOPEDIE, 1775-1800. Cambridge, Mass.: Harvard University Press.

David, J. H. 1970. "Group Decision and Social Interaction: A Theory of Social Decision Schemes." Psychological Review 80 (2):97-125.

Davis, K. 1953. "Management Communication and the Grapevine." Harvard Business Review 31 (5):43-49.

_____. 1978. "Methods for Studying Informal Communication." Journal of Communication 28 (1):112-16.

Davis, R. E. 1976. Response to Innovation: A Study of Popular Argument about New Mass Media. New York: Arno Press.

Deetz, S. A. 1982. "Critical Interpretive Research in Organizational Communication." Western Journal of Speech Communication 46 (2):131-49.

Deleuze, Gilles and Felix Guattari. 1977. Anti-Oedipus: Capitalism and Schizophrenia. Trans. Robert Hurley, Mark Seem, and Helen R. Lane. New York: Viking Press.

_____. 1981. "Rhizome." Ideology and Consciousness 8:49-71.

Delia, J. and B. O'Keefe. 1979. "Constructivism: The Development of Communication in Children." In Children Communicating: Media and Development of Thought, Speech, Understanding, ed. E. Wartella, pp. 157-85. Beverly Hills: Sage Publications.

Denzin, N. K. 1978. The Research Act. 2d ed. Chicago: Aldine.

Derlega, V. J. and A. L. Chaikin. 1977. "Privacy and Self-Disclosure in Social Relationships." Journal of Social Issues 33 (3):102-15.

Derrida, Jacques. 1973. Speech and Phenomena: And Other Essays on Husserl's Theory of Signs. Trans. David B. Allison. Evanston, Ill.: Northwestern University Press.

_____. 1976. Of Grammatology. Trans. Gayatri Chakravorty Spivak. Baltimore: Johns Hopkins University Press.

_____. 1981. Dissemination. Trans. Barbara Johnson. Chicago: University of Chicago Press.

Dewey, John. 1910. How We Think. Boston: Heath.

_____. 1922. Human Nature and Conduct. New York: Henry Holt.

_____. 1938. Logic: The Theory of Inquiry. New York: Henry Holt.

_____. 1939. Theory of Valuation. Chicago: University of Chicago Press.

_____. 1948. Reconstruction in Philosophy. Enlarged ed. Boston: Beacon Press.

_____. 1954. The Public and Its Problems. Chicago: Swallow Press.

DeWine, S. and R. Wagner. 1981. "The Study of Myths: An Alternative Way of Understanding Organizations." In Proceedings of the Conference on Interpretive Approaches to Organizational Communication. West Lafayette, Ind.: Department of Communication, Purdue University.

Dickinson, Burrus. 1929. "A German Text on Journalism." Journalism Quarterly 6 (2):9-11.

Dilthey, W. 1976. Selected Writings. Ed. H. P. Rickman. London: Cambridge University Press.

Dizard, W. 1982. The Coming Information Age: An Overview of Technology, Economics and Politics. New York: Longman.

Donohue, W. A. 1981. "Development of a Model of Rule Use in Negotiation Interaction." Communication Monographs 49 (2): 106-20.

Dorr, Aimee. 1980. "When I was a Child I Thought as a Child." In Television and Social Behavior: Beyond Violence and Children, ed. S. B. Withey and R. P. Abeles, pp. 191-230. New York: Erlbaum.

Duhamel, P. Albert. 1949. "The Function of Rhetoric as Effective Expression." Journal of the History of Ideas 10 (3):344-56.

Eck, M. 1970. Lies and Truth. London: Macmillan.

Eco, H. 1976. A Theory of Semiotics. Bloomington: Indiana University Press.

Eisenstein, Elizabeth. 1979. The Printing Press as an Agent of Change. 2 Vols. London: Cambridge University Press.

Ellul, J. 1964. The Technological Society. New York: Vintage Books.

Emery, Edwin and Michael Emery. 1978. The Press and America: An Interpretative History of the Mass Media. Englewood Cliffs, N.J.: Prentice-Hall.

Endres, Fred. 1978. "Philosophies, Practices, and Problems in Teaching Journalism History." Journalism History 5 (1):2.

Engel, S. 1980. "Femininity as Tragedy: Re-examining the 'New Narcissism.'" Socialist Review 53 (1):77-104.

Entwisle, D. and W. Huggins. 1973. "Iconic Memory in Children." Child Development 44 (2):393-94.

Ernst, Martin L. 1982. "The Mechanization of Commerce." Scientific American 247 (3):133-44.

Esposito, Joseph L. 1974. "Play and Possibility." Philosophy Today 18 (Summer):137-46.

Esslin, Martin. 1982. The Age of Television. San Francisco: Freeman.

Evans, Bill, n.d. "Improvisation in Jazz." Liner notes on Miles Davis record, Kind of Blue, Columbia Records, no. CL1355.

Ewen, S. 1976. Captains of Consciousness. New York: McGraw-Hill.

Faber, R., J. D. Brown, and J. M. McLeod. 1979. "Coming of Age in the Global Village: Television and Adolescence." In Children Communicating, ed. E. Wartella, pp. 215-49. Beverly Hills: Sage Publications.

Falcione, R. L. and E. Werner. 1978. "Organizational Climate and Communication Climate: A State of the Art." Paper presented at the annual meeting of the International Communication Association, Chicago.

Farace, R. V., P. R. Monge, and H. M. Russell. 1977. Communicating and Organizing. Reading, Mass.: Addison- Wesley.

Farrell, Thomas B. 1976. "Knowledge, Consensus, and Rhetorical Theory." Quarterly Journal of Speech 62 (1):1-14.

Farrell, Thomas B. and G. Thomas Goodnight. 1981. "Accidental Rhetoric: The Root Metaphors of Three Mile Island." Communication Monographs 48 (4):271-300.

Faules, D. F. and D. C. Alexander. 1978. Communication and Social Behavior: A Symbolic Interaction Perspective. Reading, Mass.: Addison-Wesley.

Federal Communications Commission (FCC). 1980. New Television Networks: Entry, Jurisdiction, Ownership and Regulation. Final Report. Network Inquiry Special Staff. Washington, D.C.: U.S. Government Printing Office.

"Federal Integrity, Dead Sheep and a Very Angry Judge." New York Times, August 8, 1982, p. 6E, Section 4.

Federal Trade Commission (FTC) 1978. FTC Staff Report on Television Advertising to Children. Washington, D.C.: U.S. Government Printing Office.

_____. 1979. Proceedings of the Symposium on Media Concentration. Bureau of Competition. Washington, D.C.: U.S. Government Printing Office.

Feibleman, James. 1968. The Theory of Human Culture. New York: Humanities Press.

Feldman, D. C. 1981. "The Multiple Socialization of Organizational Members." Academy of Management Review 6 (2):309-18.

Finley, M. I. 1965. "Myth, Memory, and History." History and Theory 4 (3):281-302.

Fischer, C. T. 1975. "Privacy as a Profile of Authentic Consciousness." Humanitas 11 (1):27-43.

Fisher, B. A. 1970. "Decision Emergence: Phases in Group Decision-Making." Speech Monographs 37:53-66.

_____. 1978. Perspectives on Human Communication. New York: Macmillan.

_____. 1980. Small Group Decision-Making. 2d ed. New York: McGraw-Hill.

Fisher, B. A. and Lloyd G. Drecksel. 1983. "A Cyclical Model of Developing Relationships: A Study of Relational Control Interaction." Communication Monographs (in press).

Fisher, B. A. and L. Hawes. 1971. "An Interact System Model: Generating a Grounded Theory of Small Groups." Quarterly Journal of Speech 57 (4):444-53.

Fisher, C. D. 1979. "Transmission of Positive and Negative Feedback to Subordinates: A Laboratory Investigation." Journal of Applied Psychology 64 (5):533-40.

Flapan, D. 1968. Children's Understanding of Social Interaction. New York: Teacher's College Press.

Fodor, E. M. 1974. "Disparagement by a Subordinate as an Influence on the Use of Power." Journal of Applied Psychology 59 (5):652-55.

Foucault, Michel. 1972. The Archaeology of Knowledge. Trans. A. M. Sheridan Smith. New York: Harper & Row.

_____. 1978. The History of Sexuality: An Introduction. Trans. Robert Hurley. New York: Pantheon Books.

_____. 1981. "Questions of Method: An Interview." Ideology and Consciousness 8:3-14.

Fowler, G. D. and M. E. Wackerbarth. 1980. "Audio Teleconferencing Versus Face-to-Face Conferencing: A Synthesis of the Literature." Western Journal of Speech Communication 44 (3):236-52.

Frankl, Victor E. 1959. Man's Search for Meaning. New York: Pocket Books.

Frazer, C. F. 1976. "A Symbolic Interactionist Approach to Child Television Viewing." Doctoral diss. University of Illinois, Urbana.

Frazer, C. F. and L. N. Reid. 1979. "Children's Interactions with Commercials." Symbolic Interaction 2 (2):79-96.

Frech, H. E. and Nielsen, L. n.d. "Competition, Concentration and Public Policy in the Media: A Survey of Research." Working Papers in Economics, No. 145, University of California, Santa Barbara.

Freud, S. 1961. Civilization and its Discontents. Trans. J. Strachey. New York: Norton.

Friedman, M. 1976. "Aiming at the Self: The Paradox of Encounter and the Human Potential Movement." Journal of Humanistic Psychology 16 (2):5-34.

Frye, Northrop. 1957. Anatomy of Criticism. Princeton, N.J.: Princeton University Press.

_____. 1971. The Critical Path. Bloomington: Indiana University Press.

Gadamer, Hans-Georg. 1975. Truth and Method. Ed. Garrett Barden and John Cumming. New York: Seabury.

Galbraith, J. K. 1979. The New Industrial State. 3rd ed. Boston: Houghton Mifflin.

Gandz, J. and V. V. Murray. 1980. "The Experience of Workplace Politics." Academy of Management Journal 23 (2):237-51.

Gans, Herbert. 1972. "The Famine in American Mass Communications Research." American Journal of Sociology 77 (January):697-705.

Garfinkel, H. 1967. Studies in Ethnomethodology. Englewood Cliffs, N.J.: Prentice-Hall.

Garnham, N. 1979. "Contribution to a Political Economy of Mass Communication." Media, Culture and Society 1 (2):123-46.

Gass, William H. 1971. Fiction and the Figures of Life. Boston: Nonpareil Books.

Geertz, Clifford. 1973. The Interpretation of Cultures. New York: Basic Books.

_____. 1979. "From the Native's Point of View: On the Nature of Anthropological Understanding." In Interpretive Social Science, ed. P. Rabinow and W. M. Sullivan, pp. 225-41. Berkeley: University of California Press.

_____. 1980. "Blurred Genres: The Refiguration of Social Thought." American Scholar 39 (Spring):165-79.

Gerbner, George and Larry Gross. 1976. "Living with Television: The Violence Profile." Journal of Communication 26 (2):173-99.

Gergen, Kenneth. 1973. "Social Psychology as History." Journal of Personality and Social Psychology 26 (2):309-20.

Giddens, A. 1976. New Rules of Sociological Method. New York: Basic Books.

_____. 1979. Central Problems in Social Theory. Berkeley: University of California Press.

_____. 1981. "Agency, Institution and Time-Space Analysis." In Advances in Social Theory and Methodology: Toward an Integration of Micro- and Macro-Sociologies, ed. K. Knorr-Cetina and A. V. Cicourel, pp. 161-74. Boston: Routledge and Kegan Paul.

Goffman, E. 1959. The Presentation of Self in Everyday Life. Garden City, New York: Doubleday.

Goldhaber, G. H. 1976. "The ICA Communication Audit: Rationale and Development." Paper presented at the annual convention of the Academy of Management, Kansas City.

Goldhaber, G. H., M. P. Yates, D. T. Porter, and R. Lesniak. 1978. "Organizational Communication: 1978." Human Communication Research 5 (1):76-96.

Golding, Peter and Graham Murdock. 1978. "Theories of Communication and Theories of Society." Communication Research 5 (3):339-56.

Goody, Jack and Ian Watt. 1968. "The Consequences of Literacy." In Literacy in Traditional Societies, ed. Jack Goody, pp. 27-68. Cambridge: Cambridge University Press.

Gordon, George N. 1977. The Communications Revolution: A History of Mass Media in the United States. New York: Hastings House.

Gordon, K., J. D. Levy and R. S. Preece. 1981. FCC Policy on Cable Ownership. Staff Report, Office of Plans and Policy, Federal Communications Commission. Washington, D.C.: U.S. Government Printing Office.

Gouran, D. S. 1973. "Group Communication: Perspectives and Priorities for Future Research." Quarterly Journal of Speech 59 (1):22-29.

_____. 1981. "Cognitive Sources of Inferential Error and the Contributing Influence of Interaction Characteristics in Decision-Making Groups." In Dimensions of Argument: Proceedings of the Second Summer Conference on Argumentation, ed. G. Ziegelmueller and J. Rhodes, pp. 728-48. Annandale, Va.: Speech Communication Association.

_____. 1982. Making Decisions in Groups: Choices and Consequences. Glenview, Ill.: Scott, Foresman.

_____. 1983. "Principles of Counteractive Influence in Decision-Making and Problem-Solving Groups." In Small Group Communication: A Reader, ed. R. S. Cathcart and L. A. Samovar, 4th ed. Dubuque: William C. Brown.

Gouran, D. S. and B. A. Fisher. 1983. "The Functions of Communication in the Formation, Maintenance, and Performance of Small Groups." In Handbook of Rhetorical and Communication Theory, ed. C. C. Arnold and J. W. Bowers. Boston: Allyn and Bacon.

Graff, Harvey J., Ed. 1981. _Literacy and Social Development in the West._ Cambridge Studies in Oral and Literate Cultures. Cambridge: Cambridge University Press.

Gramsci, Antonio. 1971. _Selections from the Prison Notebooks._ London: Lawrence and Wishart.

Granovetter, M. S. 1973. "The Strength of Weak Ties." _American Journal of Sociology_ 78 (6):1360–80.

Grassi, Ernesto. 1976. "Rhetoric and Philosophy." _Philosophy and Rhetoric_ 9 (4):200–16.

Greenblatt, Stephen J. 1980. "Improvisation and Power." In _Literature and Society,_ ed. Edward W. Said, pp. 57–99. Baltimore: Johns Hopkins University Press.

Greene, C. N. 1975. "The Reciprocal Nature of Influence Between Leader and Subordinate." _Journal of Applied Psychology_ 60 (2):187–93.

Gregg, Richard B. 1978. "Kenneth Burke's Prolegomena to the Study of the Rhetoric of Form." _Communication Quarterly_ 26 (1):3–13.

_____. 1981. "Rhetoric and Knowing: The Search for Perspective." _Central States Speech Journal_ 32 (3):133–44.

Grice, H. P. 1975. "Logic and Conversation." In _Syntax and Semantics: Speech Acts,_ edited by Peter Cole and Jerry L. Morgan, pp. 41–58. New York: Academic Press.

Griffith, William E. 1973. "Communist Esoteric Communications: Explication De Texte." In _Handbook of Communication,_ ed. Ithiel de Sola Pool et al., pp. 512–20. Chicago: Rand McNally.

Gronbeck, Bruce E. 1981. "Qualitative Communication Theory and Rhetorical Studies in the 1980s." _Central States Speech Journal_ 32 (4):243–53.

Grossberg, Lawrence. 1978. "Dialectics and Rhetoric: An Effort at Definition." Paper presented to the Speech Communication Association Convention, Minneapolis.

_____. 1979. "Marxist Dialectics and Rhetorical Criticism." _Quarterly Journal of Speech_ 65 (3):235–49.

_____. 1983a. "Experience, Signification and Reality: The Boundaries of Cultural Semiotics." _Semiotica,_ in press.

_____. 1983b. "The Politics of Youth Culture: Some Observations on Rock and Roll in American Culture." _Social Text,_ in press.

Groth, Otto. 1928. _Ein System der Zeitungskunda._ Vol. 1, pp. 21ff. Mannheim: J. Bernsheimer.

Gulley, H. E. and D. G. Leathers. 1977. _Communication and Group Process: Techniques for Improving the Quality of Small- Group Communication._ 3rd ed. New York: Holt, Rinehart and Winston.

Gumb, R. 1972. _Rule-Governed Linguistic Behavior._ The Hague: Mouton.

Habermas, Jürgen. 1970. Toward a Rational Society: Student Protest, Science and Politics. Trans. J. J. Shapiro. Boston: Beacon Press.

_____. 1971. Knowledge and Human Interests. Trans. J. J. Shapiro. Boston: Beacon Press.

_____. 1973. Theory and Practice. Trans. J. Viertel. Boston: Beacon Press.

_____. 1979. Communication and the Evolution of Society. Trans. Thomas McCarthy. Boston: Beacon Press.

Hackman, J. R. and C. G. Morris. 1975. "Group Tasks, Group Interaction Process, and Group Performance Effectiveness: A Review and Proposed Integration." In Advances in Experimental Social Psychology, Vol. 8, ed. L. Berkowitz, pp. 1-55. New York: Academic Press.

Hale, G. A., L. K. Miller, and H. W. Stephenson. 1968. "Incidental Learning of Film Content: A Developmental Study." Child Development 39 (1):69-77.

Hall, Stuart. 1973. "Encoding and Decoding in the Television Discourse." Paper prepared for the Centre for Contemporary Cultural Studies, University of Birmingham, England.

_____. 1977. "Culture, the Media and the 'Ideological Effect'." In Mass Communication and Society, ed. James Curran, Michael Gurevitch, and Janet Woollacott, pp. 315-48. London: Edward Arnold.

_____. 1980. "Cultural Studies and the Centre: Some Problematics and Problems." In Culture, Media, Language, ed. Stuart Hall, Dorothy Hobson, Andrew Lowe, and Paul Willis, pp. 15-47. London: Hutchinson.

_____. 1982. "The Rediscovery of 'Ideology': Return of the Repressed in Media Studies." In Culture, Society and the Media, ed. M. Gurevitch, T. Bennett, J. Curran, and J. Woollacott, pp. 56-90. London: Methuen.

Hall, Stuart, Dorothy Hobson, Andrew Lowe, and Paul Willis, eds. 1980. Culture, Media, Language. London: Hutchinson.

Hallaron, J. n.d. "The Context of Mass Communication Research." Document prepared for UNESCO, International Commission for the Study of Communication Problems.

Halley, J. A. 1981. "Culture in Late Capitalism." In Political Economy: A Critique of American Society, ed. S. G. McNall, pp. 137-55. Glenview, Ill.: Scott, Foresman.

Hamelink, C. J. 1983. Finance and Information: A Study of Converging Interests. Norwood, N.J.: Ablex Publishing Corp.

Hammarskjöld, D. 1955. Markings. New York: Knopf.

Handlin, Oscar. 1979. Truth in History. Cambridge, Mass.: Harvard University Press.

Handlin, Oscar and Mary Handlin. 1964. "Mobility." In American History and the Social Sciences, ed. Edward Saveth, pp. 215-30. New York: The Free Press.

Hanson, Norwood Russell. 1958. *Patterns of Discovery: An Inquiry into the Conceptual Foundations of Science*. Cambridge: Cambridge University Press.

Hare, A. P. 1976. *Handbook of Small Group Research*. 2d ed. New York: The Free Press.

Harper, N. L. and L. R. Askling. 1980. "Group Communication and Quality of Task Solution in a Media Production Organization." *Communication Monographs* 47 (2):77–100.

Harré, R. 1977. "Friendship as an Accomplishment: An Ethogenic Approach to Social Relationships." In *Theory and Practice in Interpersonal Attraction*, ed. S. Duck, pp. 339–54. London: Academic Press.

Harre, R. and P. F. Secord. 1973. *The Explanation of Social Behavior*. Totowa, N.J.: Littlefield, Adams.

Hart, R. P. and D. M. Burks. 1972. "Rhetorical Sensitivity and Social Interaction." *Speech Monographs* 39 (2):75–91.

Hartley, R. V. L. 1928. "Transmission of Information." *Bell Systems Technical Journal*:7.

The Harvard Dictionary of Music. 1969. Edited by W. Apel. Cambridge, Mass.: Harvard University Press.

Haslett, Betty J. 1983. "Communicative Functions and Strategies in Children's Conversations." *Human Communication Research* 9:114–29.

Hauser, Gerard A. 1979. "Searching for a Bright Tomorrow: Graduate Education in Rhetoric During the 1980s." *Communication Education* 28:259–70.

Hauser, Gerard A. and Carole Blair. 1982. "Rhetorical Antecedents to the Public." *Pre/Text* 3 (2):139–68.

Hauser, Gerard A. and Donald P. Cushman. 1973. "McKeon's Philosophy of Communication: The Architectonic and Interdisciplinary Arts." *Philosophy and Rhetoric* 6 (4):211–34.

Havelock, Eric. 1967. *Preface to Plato*. New York: Grosset and Dunlap.

_____. 1978. *The Greek Concept of Justice: From Its Shadow in Homer to Its Substance in Plato*. Cambridge, Mass.: Harvard University Press.

_____. 1982. *The Literate Revolution in Greece and Its Cultural Consequences*. Princeton, N.J.: Princeton University Press.

Hawes, Leonard C. 1974. "Social Collectivities as Communication: Perspectives on Organizational Behavior." *Quarterly Journal of Speech* 60 (4):497–502.

_____. 1977. "Toward a Hermeneutic Phenomenology of Communication." *Communication Quarterly* 25 (3):30–41.

Hawkins, R. 1977. "The Dimensional Structure of Children's Perceptions of Television Reality." *Communication Research* 4 (3): 299–320.

Hawkins, R. and S. Pingree. 1982. "T.V. Influence on Social Reality and Conceptions of the World." In Television and Behavior: Ten Years of Scientific Progress and Implications for the Eighties, ed. National Institute of Mental Health. Washington, D.C.: U.S. Government Printing Office.

Hayakawa, S. I. 1941. Language in Action. New York: Harcourt, Brace.

Head, R. G., F. W. Short, and R. C. McFarlane. 1978. Crisis Resolution: Presidential Decision Making in the Mayaguez and Korean Confrontations. Boulder, Colo.: Westview Press.

Hebdige, Dick. 1979. Subculture: The Meaning of Style. London: Methuen.

_____. 1981a. "Towards a Cartography of Taste 1935–1962." Block 4:39–56.

_____. 1981b. "Object as Image: The Italian Scooter Cycle." Block 5:44–64.

_____. 1982. "Posing . . . Threat, Striking . . . Poses: Youth, Surveillance and Display." Unpublished manuscript.

Hegarty, H. W. 1974. "Using Subordinate Ratings to Elicit Behavioral Changes in Supervisors." Journal of Applied Psychology 59 (6):764–66.

Heidegger, M. 1959. An Introduction to Metaphysics. Trans. R. Manheim. New Haven, Conn.: Yale University Press.

_____. 1962. "Letter on Humanism." In Philosophy in the 20th Century, ed. and trans. W. Barrett and H. D. Aiken. New York: Random House.

Held, D. 1980. Introduction to Critical Theory: Horkheimer to Habermas. Berkeley: University of California Press.

Hempel, Carl. 1942. "The Function of General Laws in History." Journal of Philosophy 39 (1):35–48.

_____. 1964. Aspects of Scientific Explanation. New York: The Free Press.

Henry, J. 1965. Pathways to Madness. New York: Vintage Books.

Hewes, D. E. 1979. "The Sequential Analysis of Social Interaction." Quarterly Journal of Speech 65 (1):56–73.

Higham, John and Paul K. Conklin, eds. 1979. New Directions in American Intellectual History. Baltimore: Johns Hopkins University Press.

Hirokawa, R. Y. 1980. "A Function–Oriented Analysis of Small Group Interaction within Effective and Ineffective Decision-Making Groups: An Exploratory Investigation." Doctoral diss., University of Washington.

_____. 1982. "Group Communication and Problem-Solving Effectiveness I: A Critical Review of Inconsistent Findings." Communication Quarterly 30 (1):134–41.

Hirsch, E. D. 1968. "Literary Evaluation as Knowledge." In Criticism, ed. L. S. Dembo, pp. 45–57. Madison: University of

Wisconsin Press.

_____. 1976. The Aims of Interpretation. Chicago: University of Chicago Press.

Hoffman, L. R. 1965. "Group Problem Solving." In Advances in Experimental Social Psychology, Vol. 2, ed. L. Berkowitz, pp. 99–132. New York: Academic Press.

Hofstadter, Richard. 1968. The Progressive Historians: Turner, Beard, and Parrington. Chicago: University of Chicago Press.

Hogarth, R. 1980. Judgement and Choice. New York: John Wiley.

Hoggart, Richard. 1958. The Uses of Literacy. London: Penguin Books.

_____. 1970. "Contemporary Cultural Studies: An Approach to the Study of Literature and Society." In Contemporary Criticism, ed. M. Bradbury and D. Palmer. London: Edward Arnold.

Hopper, R. 1981. "The Taken-for-Granted." Human Communication Research 7 (3):195–211.

Howard, H. H. 1982. "Television Station Group Ownership and Cross-Media Ownership: 1982. "Renaissance Rhetoric and Modern Rhetoric: A Study in Change." In The Rhetorical Idiom, ed. Donald C. Bryant, pp. 53–71. Ithaca, N.Y.: Cornell University Press.

Hur, K. Kyoon. 1982. "International Mass Communication Research: A Critical Review of Theory and Methods." In Communication Yearbook 6, ed. Michael Burgoon, pp. 531–54. Beverly Hills: Sage Publications.

Husserl, Edmund. 1970. Logical Investigations. Trans. J. N. Findlay. London: Routledge and Kegan Paul.

Huston, A. C., J. C. Wright, and R. Potts. 1982. "Television Forms and Children's Social Behavior." Paper presented to the annual meeting of the International Communication Association, Boston.

Huston, A. C., J. C. Wright, E. Wartella, M. L. Rice, T. Campbell, and R. Potts. 1981. "Communicating More than Content: Formal Features of Children's Television Programs." Journal of Communication 31 (3):32–48.

Hymes, Dell. 1967. "The Anthropology of Communication." In Human Communication Theory, ed. Frank E. X. Dance. New York: Holt, Rinehart and Winston.

_____. 1974. Foundations in Sociolinguistics: An Ethnographic Approach. Philadelphia: University of Pennsylvania Press.

Infante, D. A. and W. I. Gordon. 1979. "Subordinate and Superior Perceptions of Self and One Another: Relations, Accuracy, and Reciprocity of Liking." Western Speech 43 (3):212–23.

Innis, Harold A. 1950. *Empire and Communications.* New York:
Oxford University Press.
_____. 1951. *The Bias of Communication.* Toronto:
University of Toronto Press.
_____. 1972. *Empire and Communications.* 2d ed.
Toronto: University of Toronto Press.
Jablin, F. M. 1979. "Superior-Subordinate Communication: The
State of the Art." *Psychological Bulletin* 86 (6):1201-22.
_____. 1980a. "Organizational Communication Theory
and Research: An Overview of Communication Climate and
Network Research." In *Communication Yearbook 4,* ed. D.
Nimmo, pp. 327-47. New Brunswick: International Communica-
tion Association/Transaction Books.
_____. 1980b. "Superior's Upward Influence,
Satisfaction, and Openness in Superior-Subordinate Communica-
tion: A Reexamination of the 'Pelz Effect.'" *Human Commu-
nication Research* 6 (3):210-20.
_____. 1981. "An Exploratory Study of Subordinates'
Perceptions of Supervisory Politics." *Communication Quarterly*
29 (4):269-75.
Jackson, D. D. 1965. "The Study of the Family." *Family
Process* 4 (1):1-20.
Jacobson, E. and S. Seashore. 1951. "Communication Practices
in Complex Organizations." *Journal of Social Issues* 7
(3):28-40.
Jaeger, Werner. 1939. *Paideia: The Ideals of Greek Culture.*
Trans. Gilbert Highet. New York: Oxford University Press.
Jakobson, Roman. 1962. *Selected Writings.* The Hague: Mouton.
_____. 1971. "The Metaphoric and Metonymic Poles."
Critical Theory Since Plato, ed. Hazard Adams, pp. 1113-16.
New York: Harcourt Brace Jovanovich.
James, L. R. and A. P. Jones. 1974. "Organizational Climate:
A Review of Theory and Research." *Psychological Bulletin* 81
(12):1096-1112.
Jameson, Fredric. 1972. *The Prison-House of Language: A
Critical Account of Structuralism and Russian Formalism.*
Princeton, N.J.: Princeton University Press.
_____. 1981. *The Political Unconscious: Narrative as a
Socially Symbolic Act.* Ithaca, N.Y.: Cornell University Press.
Janis, I. L. 1982. *Groupthink.* 2d ed. Boston: Houghton
Mifflin.
Janis, I. L. and L. Mann. 1977. *Decision Making: A
Psychological Analysis of Conflict, Choice, and Commitment.*
New York: The Free Press.
Johnson, B. M. 1975. "Images of the Enemy in Intergroup
Conflict." *Central States Speech Journal* 26:84-92.
_____. 1977. *Communication: The Process of Orga-
nizing.* Boston: Allyn & Bacon.

Johnstone, Christopher L. 1981. "Ethics, Wisdom, and the Mission of Contemporary Rhetoric: The Realization of Human Being." Central States Speech Journal 32 (3):177–89.

Johnstone, Henry W., Jr. 1978. Validity and Rhetoric in Philosophical Argument. University Park, Pa.: The Dialogue Press.

_____. 1982. "Communication: Thechology and Ethics." In Communication, Philosophy, and the Technological Age, ed. M. J. Hyde, pp. 38–53. University: University of Alabama Press.

Jones, E. E. and R. F. Baumeister. 1976. "The Self-Monitor Looks at the Ingratiator." Journal of Personality 44 (4):654–74.

Jourard, S. M. 1971. The Transparent Self. New York: D. Van Nostrand.

"Journalism History and Women's Experience: A Problem in Conceptual Change." 1964. Journalism History 8 (1).

Kanter, R. M. 1977. Men and Women of the Corporation. New York: Basic Books.

Katz, D. and R. L. Kahn. 1966. The Social Psychology of Organization. New York: John Wiley.

Katz, E., J. G. Blumler, and Michael Gurevitch. 1974. "Utilization of Mass Communication by the Individual." In The Uses of Mass Communication, Sage Annual Reviews of Communications Research, Vol. 3, ed. J. G. Blumler and E. Katz, pp. 19–32. Beverly Hills: Sage Publications.

Katzell, R. A., C. E. Miller, N. G. Rotter, and T. G. Venet. 1970. "Effects of Leadership and Other Inputs on Group Processes and Outputs." Journal of Social Psychology 80 (2):157–69.

Kelly, L. 1982. "A Critical Review of the Literature on Superior-Subordinate Communication." Paper presented at the annual convention of the International Communication Association, Boston.

Kelvin, P. 1973. "A Social-Psychological Examination of Privacy." British Journal of Social and Clinical Psychology 12 (3):248–61.

_____. 1977. "Predictability, Power and Vulnerability in Interpersonal Attraction." In Theory and Practice in Interpersonal Attraction, ed. S. Duck, pp. 339–54. London: Academic Press.

Kernan, Alvin B. 1982. The Imaginary Library: An Essay on Literature and Society. Princeton, N.J.: Princeton University Press.

Kline, F. Gerald. 1972. "Theory in Mass Communication Research." In Current Perspectives in Mass Communication Research, Sage Annual Reviews of Communication Research, Vol. 1, ed. F. Gerald Kline and P. J. Tichenor, pp. 17–40. Beverly

Hills: Sage Publications.

Knapp, M. L. and M. E. Comadena. 1979. "Telling It Like It Isn't: A Review of Theory and Research on Deceptive Communications." Human Communication Research 5 (3):270-84.

Knapp, M. L., C. Stohl, and K. K. Reardon. 1981. "'Memorable' Messages." Journal of Communication 31 (4):27-41.

Koch, Sigmund. 1971. "The Image of Man Implicit in Encounter Group Therapy." Journal of Humanistic Psychology 11 (2):109-28.

Koch, S. and S. Deetz. 1981. "Metaphor Analysis of Social Reality in Organizations." Journal of Applied Communication Research 9 (1):1-15.

Korzybski, Alfred. 1933. Science and Sanity. Lancaster: International Non-Aristotelian Library.

Kreps, G. 1983. "The Use of Interpretive Research to Develop a Socialization Program at RCA." In Organizing and Communicating: An Interpretive Approach, ed. L. L. Putnam and M. Pacanowsky. Beverly Hills: Sage Publications.

Kristeva, Julia. 1975. "The Subject in Signifying Practice." Semiotexte 1:19-26.

Kuhn, Thomas S. 1970. The Structure of Scientific Revolutions. 2d rev. ed. Chicago: University of Chicago Press.

Labov, William. 1972. Language in the Inner City. Philadelphia: University of Pennsylvania Press.

Lacan, Jacques. 1968. The Language of the Self. Trans. Anthony Wilden. Baltimore: Johns Hopkins University Press.

_____. 1977. Ecrits: A Selection. Trans. Alan Sheridan. New York: W. W. Norton.

Laclau, Ernesto. 1977. Politics and Ideology in Marxist Theory. London: New Left Books.

Laing, R. D. 1965. "Mystification, Confusion and Conflict." In Intensive Family Therapy, ed. I. Boszormenyi-Nagy and J. L. Framo, pp. 343-63. New York: Harper & Row.

_____. 1967. The Politics of Experience. New York: Pantheon.

_____. 1971. Self and Others. Middlesex: Penguin.

Lakatos, Imre. 1968. "Criticism and the Methodology of Scientific Research Programmes." Proceedings of the Aristotelian Society 69:149-86.

Landsberger, H. A. 1955. "Interaction Process Analysis of the Mediation of Labor-Management Disputes." Journal of Abnormal and Social Psychology 51 (4):552-58.

Lanzetta, J. T. and T. B. Roby. 1960. "The Relationship between Certain Group Process Variables and Problem-Solving Efficiency." Journal of Social Psychology 52 (2):135-48.

Larson, C. E. 1969. "Forms of Analysis and Small Group Problem-Solving." Speech Monographs 36 (4):452-55.

Lasch, C. 1979. The Culture of Narcissism. New York: W. W. Norton.

Laslett, B. 1973. "The Family as a Public and Private Institution: An Historical Perspective." Journal of Marriage and the Family 35 (3):480-90.

Lazarsfeld, P., B. Berelson, and H. Gaudet. 1948. The People's Choice. New York: Columbia University Press.

Leathers, D. G. 1972. "Quality of Group Communication as a Determinant of Group Product." Speech Monographs 39 (2):166-73.

Lee, Alfred McClung. 1937. The Daily Newspaper in America. New York: Macmillan.

Leff, Michael C. 1978. "In Search of Ariadne's Thread: A Review of Recent Literature on Rhetorical Theory." Central States Speech Journal 29 (2):73-91.

Leifer, A., W. A. Collins, B. M. Gross, P. H. Taylor, L. Andres, and E. R. Blackmer. 1971. "Developmental Aspects of Variables Related to Observational Learning." Child Development 42 (5):1509-16.

Leifer, A. and D. F. Roberts. 1972. "Children's Responses to Television Violence." In Television and Social Behavior, Vol. 2: Television and Social Learning, ed. J. P. Murray, E. A. Rubinstein, and G. A. Comstock. Washington, D.C.: U.S. Government Printing Office.

Leiter, K. 1980. A Primer on Ethnomethodology. New York: Oxford University Press.

Le Roy Ladurie, Emmanuel. 1979. The Territory of the Historian. Trans. Ben and Sian Reynolds. Paris: Gallimard.

Levi-Strauss, C. 1963. Structural Anthropology. Trans. C. Jacobson and B. G. Schoep. New York: Basic Books.

Levy, J. D. and F. O. Setzer. 1982. Measurement of Concentration in Home Video Markets. Staff Report, Office of Plans and Policy, Federal Communications Commission. Washington, D.C.: U.S. Government Printing Office.

Lewin, K. 1947. "Frontiers in Group Dynamics: Concept, Method and Reality in Social Science: Social Equilibria and Social Change." Human Relations 1 (1):5-41.

Lidz, V. 1981. "Transformational Theory and the Internal Environment of Action Systems." In Advances in Social Theory and Methodology: Toward an Integration of Micro- and Macro-Sociologies, ed. K. Knorr-Cetina and A. V. Cicourel, pp. 205-33. Boston: Routledge and Kegan Paul.

Lindlof, T. R. and G. A. Copeland. 1982. "Television Rules of Prepartum New Families." In Communication Yearbook 6, ed. M. Burgoon, pp. 555-82. Beverly Hills: International Communication Association, Sage Publications.

Litwin, G. and R. Stringer. 1968. Motivation and Organizational Climate. Cambridge, Mass.: Harvard University Press.

Lloyd-Kolkin, D. 1981. "The Far West Laboratory Project." In Education for the Television Age, ed. M. E. Ploghoft and J. A. Anderson, pp. 91-98. Springfield, Ill.: Charles C. Thomas.

Lofland, J. 1976. Doing Social Life. New York: John Wiley.

Louis, M. R. 1980. "Surprise and Sense Making: What Newcomers Experience in Entering Unfamiliar Organizational Settings." Administrative Science Quarterly 25 (2):226-51.

Lowe, Donald. 1982. The History of Bourgeois Perception. Chicago: University of Chicago Press.

Luckmann, T. 1973. "Philosophy, Science, and Everyday Life." In Phenomenology and the Social Sciences, Vol. 1, ed. M. Natanson, pp. 143-86. Evanston, Ill.: Northwestern University Press.

Lukacs, Georg. 1971. History and Class Consciousness: Studies in Marxist Dialectics. Trans. Rodney Livingstone. Cambridge, Mass.: MIT Press.

Lull, J. T. 1976. "Mass Media and Family Communication: An Ethnography of Audience Behavior." Doctoral diss., University of Wisconsin.

_____. 1978. "Ethnomethods of Television Viewers." Paper presented to the International Communication Association, Chicago.

_____. 1979. "Theoretical Approaches to Ethnographies of Mass Communication." Paper presented to the International Communication Association, Philadelphia.

_____. 1980a. "The Social Uses of Television." Human Communication Research 6 (3):197-209.

_____. 1980b. "Family Communication Patterns and the Social Uses of Television." Communication Research 7 (3):319-34.

_____. 1982. "Doing Ethnographic Research on Broadcast Media Audiences." In Broadcast Research Methods, ed. J. Dominick and J. Fletcher. Boston: Allyn and Bacon.

Lyle, J. and H. Hoffman. 1972. "Children's Use of Television and other Media." In Television and Social Behavior, Vol. 4: Television in Day-to-Day Life: Patterns of Use, ed. E. A. Rubenstein, G. A. Comstock and J. P. Murray, pp. 1-32. Washington, D.C.: U.S. Government Printing Office.

Lyotard, Jean-Francois. 1977a. "The Unconscious as Mise-en-Scene." In Performance in Post-Modern Culture, ed. Michel Benamou and Charles Caramello, pp. 87-98. Madison, Wis.: Coda Press.

_____. 1977b. "Energumen Capitalism." Semiotexte 6:11-26.

MacKay, Donald M. 1969. Information, Mechanism and Meaning. Cambridge, Mass.: MIT Press.

Maier, N. R. F. and R. A. Maier. 1957. "An Experimental Test of the Effects of 'Developmental' vs. 'Free' Discussions on the

Quality of Group Decisions." Journal of Applied Psychology 41:320-23.

Maines, D. R. 1977. "Social Organization and Social Structure in Symbolic Interactionist Thought." Annual Review of Sociology 3:235-59.

Malraux, Andre. 1978. The Voices of Silence. Trans. Stuart Gilbert. Princeton, N.J.: Princeton University Press.

March, J. G. and H. A. Simon. 1958. Organizations. New York: John Wiley.

Marzio, Peter C. 1973. The Men and Machines of American Journalism: A Pictorial Essay from the Henry R. Luce Hall of News Reporting. Washington, D.C.: National Museum of History and Technology, Smithsonian Institution.

Maslow, A. H. 1968. "Peak-Experiences as Acute Identity-Experiences." In The Self in Social Interaction Vol. I, ed. C. Gordon and K. J. Gergen, pp. 275-80. New York: John Wiley.

Mayer, J. E. 1957. "The Self-Restraint of Friends: A Mechanism in Family Transition." Social Forces 35 (3):230-38.

McCarthy, T. 1979a. The Critical Theory of Jürgen Habermas. Cambridge, Mass.: MIT Press.

_____. 1979b. "Translator's Introduction." In Communication and the Evolution of Society, ed. J. Habermas, trans. T. McCarthy. Boston: Beacon Press.

McDonagh, E. C. 1950. "Television and the Family." Sociology and Social Research 35 (2):113-22.

McGee, Michael C. 1975. "In Search of 'The People': A Rhetorical Alternative." Quarterly Journal of Speech 61 (3):235-49.

_____. 1980. "The 'Ideograph': A Link Between Rhetoric and Ideology." Quarterly Journal of Speech 66 (1):1-16.

McGrath, J. E. and I. Altman. 1966. Small Group Research: A Synthesis and Critique of the Field. New York: Holt, Rinehart and Winston.

McGregor, D. 1960. The Human Side of Enterprise. New York: McGraw-Hill.

McKeon, R. 1971. "The Uses of Rhetoric in a Technological Age: Architectonic Productive Arts." In The Prospects of Rhetoric, ed. Lloyd F. Bitzer and Edwin Black, pp. 44-63. Englewood Cliffs, N.J.: Prentice-Hall.

McKerns, Joseph P. 1977. "The Limits of Progressive Journalism History." Journalism History 4 (3):88-92.

McLeod, J. and B. Reeves. 1980. "The Nature of Mass Media Effects." In Television and Social Behavior: Beyond Violence and Children, ed. S. B. Withey and R. P. Abeles, pp. 17-54. Hillsdale, N.J.: Erlbaum Associates.

McLuhan, Marshall. 1962. Gutenberg Galaxy: The Making of Typographic Man. Toronto: University of Toronto Press.

McMullin, Ernin. 1974. "Two Faces of Science." Review of Metaphysics 27 (4):655-76.

McPhail, Thomas. 1981. Electronic Colonialism: The Future of International Broadcasting and Communication. Beverly Hills: Sage Publications.

McQuail, Denis. 1969. Towards a Sociology of Mass Communication. London: Collier-Macmillan.

McRobbie, Angela. 1980. "Settling Accounts with Subcultures: A Feminist Critique." Screen Education 34:37-49.

Mead, G. H. 1934. Mind, Self and Society. Chicago: University of Chicago Press.

Mead, M. 1949. Male and Female. New York: W. Morrow.

Mehan, H. and H. Wood. 1975. The Reality of Ethnomethodology. New York: John Wiley.

Merleau-Ponty, M. 1964. Signs. Trans. R. C. McCleary. Evanston, Ill.: Northwestern University Press.

Merrill, John C. 1969. The Elite Press: Great Newspapers of the World. New York: Pittman.

Merton, Robert K. 1968. Social Theory and Social Structure. New York: The Free Press.

Messaris, P. 1982. "The Influence of Family Background on Children's Interpretations of Television." Paper presented to the Popular Culture Association, Louisville.

Messaris, P. and C. Sarett. 1981. "On the Consequences of Television-Related Parent-Child Interaction." In Mass Communication Review Yearbook, Vol. 3, ed. D. C. Whitney, E. Wartella, and S. Windahl, pp. 365-83. Beverly Hills: Sage Publications.

Meyer, J. R., R. W. Wilson, M. A. Baughcum, E. Burton, and L. Caouette. 1980. The Economics of Competition in the Telecommunications Industry. Cambridge, Mass.: Oelgeschlager, Gunn & Hain, Publishers.

Meyer, T. P., P. J. Traudt, and J. A. Anderson. 1980. "Non-traditional Mass Communication Research Methods: Observational Case Studies of Media Use in Natural Settings." In Communication Yearbook 4, ed. D. Nimmo, pp. 261-76. New Brunswick, N.J.: International Communication Association, Transaction Books.

Meyer, T. P., J. McIntyre and S. J. Baran. In press. Mass Communication In Society: An Introduction to Media. Reading, Mass.: Addison-Wesley.

Miale, G. 1973. "Is Feeling More Real Than Thinking?" Journal of Humanistic Psychology 13 (2):53-59.

Millar, S. 1968. The Psychology of Play. London: Penguin.

Miller, James G. 1960. "Information Input, Overload, and Psychopathology." American Journal of Psychiatry 116 (7):695-704.

_____. 1976a. "The Nature of Living Systems." Behavioral Science 21 (5):295-319.

_____. 1976b. "Living Systems: The Supranatural System." Behavioral Science 21 (5):320-468.

Miller, G. R. 1981. "What Next? Three Knowledge Objectives for Communication Researchers." Central States Speech Journal 32 (4):212-18.

Mintzberg, H. 1973. The Nature of Managerial Work. New York: Harper & Row.

Mitroff, I. I. and R. H. Kilmann. 1976. "On Organizational Stories: An Approach to the Design and Analysis of Organizations Through Myths and Stories." In The Management of Organizational Design: Strategies and Implementation, ed. R. H. Kilmann, L. R. Pondy, and D. P. Slavin, pp. 189-207. New York: Elsevier.

Moles, Abraham. 1966. Information Theory and Esthetic Perception. Trans. Joel E. Cohen. Urbana: University of Illinois Press.

Monge, P. R., J. A. Edwards, and K. K. Kiriste. 1978. "The Determinants of Communication and Communication Structure in Large Organizations: A Review of Research." In Communication Yearbook 2, ed. B. D. Ruben, pp. 311-31. New Brunswick, N.J.: International Communication Association, Transaction Books.

Moreno, J. L. 1953. Who Shall Survive? Foundations of Sociometry, Group Psychotherapy and Sociodrama. New York: Beacon House.

Morgan, G. W. 1976. "Being Oneself with Others." Communication 2 (2):189-204.

Morley, David. 1980. The "Nationwide" Audience: Structure and Decoding. London: British Film Institute.

_____. 1981. "'The Nationwide Audience'—A Critical Postscript." Screen Education 39:3-14.

Morris, Charles. 1946. Signs, Language, and Behavior. Englewood Cliffs, N.J.: Prentice-Hall.

Morris, M. 1977. An Excursion into Creative Sociology. New York: Columbia University Press.

Mortensen, C. D. 1970. "The Status of Small Group Research." Quarterly Journal of Speech, 56 (3):304-09.

Mosco, V. 1979. Broadcasting in the United States: Innovative Challenge and Organizational Control. Norwood, N.J.: Ablex Publishing Corp.

_____. 1982. Pushbutton Fantasies: Critical Perspectives on Videotex and Information Technology. Norwood, N.J.: Ablex Publishing Corp.

Mosco, V. and J. Wasko. 1983a. Critical Communications Review: Volume I: Labor, the Working Class and Media. Norwood, N.J.: Ablex Publishing Corp.

_____. 1983b. Critical Communications Review: Volume II: Changing Patterns of Communications Control. Norwood, N.J.: Ablex Publishing Corp.

Moscovici, S. 1976. Social Influence and Social Change. London: Academic Press.

Mott, Frank Luther. 1962. American Journalism. New York: Macmillan.

Mowbray, C. and Z. Luria. 1973. "Effects of Labeling on Children's Visual Memory." Developmental Psychology 9 (1):1-8.

Munchinsky, P. M. 1977. "Organizational Communication: Relationships to Organizational Climate and Job Satisfaction." Academy of Management Journal 20 (4):592-607.

Murdock, G. 1978. "Blindspots about Western Marxism: A Reply to Dallas Smythe." Canadian Journal of Social and Political Theory 2 (2):109-18.

_____. 1981. "Television Programming, Audience Needs and the New Technologies." Conference paper, New Dimensions in Television. Venice, March 26-28.

_____. 1982. "Large Corporations and the Control of the Communications Industries." In Culture, Society and the Media, ed. M. Gurevitch, T. Bennett, J. Curran, and J. Woollacott, pp. 118-50. London: Methuen.

Murphy, J. P. 1973. "Attributional and Inferential Strategies in the Interpretations of Visual Communications: A Developmental Study." Doctoral diss., University of Pennsylvania.

Nelson, M. C. 1977. The Narcissistic Condition: A Fact of Our Lives and Times. New York: Human Sciences Press.

Nevins, Allan. 1959. "American Journalism and Its Historical Treatment." Journalism Quarterly 36 (3):411-22, 519.

Newcomb, Horace. 1978. "Assessing the Violence Profile Studies of Gerbner and Gross: A Humanistic Critique and Suggestion." Communication Research 5 (3):264-82.

Newmeyer, F. J. 1980. Linguistic Theory in America. New York: Academic Press.

Nichols, Bill. 1981. Ideology and Image. Bloomington: Indiana University Press.

Nilsen, T. R. 1966. Ethics of Speech Communication. New York: Bobbs-Merrill.

NIMH (National Institute of Mental Health), ed. 1982. Television and Behavior: Ten Years of Scientific Progress and Implications for the Eighties. Washington, D.C.: U.S. Government Printing Office.

Nisbet, Robert A. 1970. Social Change and History. New York: Oxford University Press.

_____. 1977. "Many Tocquevilles." American Scholar 46 (Winter):59-75.

Nisbett, R. and L. Ross. 1980. Human Inference: Strategies and Shortcomings of Social Judgment. Englewood Cliffs, N.J.: Prentice-Hall.

Oakeshott, M. 1962. Rationalism in Politics. New York: Basic Books.

O'Donnell-Trujillo, N. 1983. "'Performing' Mintzberg's Roles: The Nature of Managerial Communication." In Communication in Organizations: An Interpretive Approach, ed. L. L. Putnam and M. E. Pacanowsky, in press. Beverly Hills: Sage Publications.

"Official Minutes of the 1952 Convention." 1952. Journalism Quarterly 29 (3):502.

"Official Minutes of the 1956 Convention." 1956. Journalism Quarterly 34 (4):151.

Ogden, C. K. and I. A. Richards. 1930. The Meaning of Meaning. 3rd rev. ed. New York: Harcourt, Brace.

Olson, David R. 1977. "From Utterance to Text: The Bias of Language in Speech and Writing." Harvard Educational Review 47 (3):257-81.

O'Reilly, C. A. III. 1980. "Individuals and Information Overload in Organizations: Is More Necessarily Better?" Academy of Management Journal 23 (4):684-96.

Pacanowsky, M. E. 1981. "Writing: Science, Fiction, and the Interpretive Approach." In Proceedings of the Conference on Interpretive Approaches to Organizational Communication. West Lafayette, Ind.: Purdue University, Department of Communication.

Pacanowsky, M. E. and N. O'Donnell-Trujillo. 1982. "Communication and Organizational Culture." Western Journal of Speech Communication 46 (2):115-30.

Paine, R. 1969. "In Search of Friendship: An Exploratory Analysis in 'Middle-Class' Culture." Man 4 (4):505-24.

Palmer, R. C. 1969. Hermeneutics. Evanston, Ill.: Northwestern University Press.

Pap, L. 1979. "On the Scope of Semiotics: A Critique and Redefinition." In A Semiotic Landscape, ed. S. Chatman, U. Eco, and J. M. Klinkenberg. Paris: Mouton.

Park, Robert Ezra. 1923. "The Natural History of the Newspaper." American Journal of Sociology 29 (10):80-98.

Parke, R. D. and D. B. Sawin. 1979. "Children's Privacy in the Home: Developmental, Ecological and Child-Rearing Determinants." Environment and Behavior 11 (1):87-104.

Parks, M. 1981. "Ideology in Interpersonal Communication: Off the Couch and into the World." In Communication Yearbook 5, ed. M. Burgoon, pp. 79-107. Beverly Hills: International Communication Association, Sage Publications.

Parrington, Vernon. 1927. Main Currents in American Thought. New York: Harcourt, Brace and World.

Peirce, C. S. 1955a. Philosophical Writings of Peirce. Ed. J. Buchler. New York: Dover Publications.

_____. 1955b. Collected Papers. Vol. 2. Ed. J. Buchler. New York: Dover Publications.

Penley, L. E. 1982. "An Investigation of the Information Processing Framework of Organizational Communication." Human Communication Research 8 (4):348-65.

Perelman, Ch. and L. Olbrechts-Tyteca. 1969. The New Rhetoric: A Treatise on Argumentation. Trans. John Wilkinson and Purcell Weaver. Notre Dame, Ind.: University of Notre Dame Press.

Peters, John D. 1982a. "Seven Theses on Metaphor." Salt Lake City: University of Utah. Mimeographed.

_____. 1982b. "One Thesis on the Text." Salt Lake City: University of Utah. Mimeographed.

Peters, T. J. 1978. "Symbols, Patterns and Settings: An Optimistic Case for Getting Things Done." Organizational Dynamics 7 (2):3-23.

Pettigrew, A. M. 1979. "On Studying Organizational Cultures." Administrative Science Quarterly 24 (4):570-81.

Pfeffer, J. 1981. "Management as Symbolic Action: The Creation and Maintenance of Organizational Paradigms." In Research in Organizational Behavior, ed. L. L. Cummings and B. M. Staw, Vol. 3, pp. 1-52. Greenwich: J.A.I. Press.

Phillips, G. M. 1976. "Rhetoric and Its Alternatives as Bases for Examination of Intimate Communication." Communication Quarterly 24 (1):11-23.

Phillips, G. M. and N. J. Metzger. 1976. Intimate Communication. Boston: Allyn & Bacon.

Phillips, G. M., D. G. Pedersen, and J. T. Wood. 1979. Group Discussion: A Practical Guide to Participation and Leadership. Boston: Houghton Mifflin.

Phillipsen, Gerry. 1977. "Linearity of Research Design in Ethnographic Studies of Speaking." Communication Quarterly 25:42-50.

Phillpotts, Bertha. 1931. Edda and Saga. New York: H. Holt.

Plessner, Helmuth. 1970. Laughing and Crying. Trans. J. S. Churchill and M. Grene. Evanston, Ill.: Northwestern University Press.

Ploghoft, M. and J. Anderson, eds. 1981. Education for the Television Age. Springfield, Ill.: Charles C. Thomas.

Polanyi, Michael. 1958. Personal Knowledge. Chicago: University of Chicago Press.

Pondy, L. R. 1976. "Leadership is a Language Game." In Leadership: Where Else Can We Go?, ed. M. McCall and M. Lombardo, pp. 87-99. Durham, N.C.: Duke University Press.

Poole, Marshall Scott. 1978. "An Information-Task Approach to Organizational Communication." Academy of Management Review 3 (3):493-504.

_____. 1981. "Decision Development in Small Groups 1: A Comparison of Two Models." Communication Monographs 48:1-24.

Poole, M. S. and R. D. McPhee. 1983. "Bringing Intersubjectivity In: A Change of Climate." In Communication in Organizations: An Interpretive Approach, ed. L. L. Putnam and M. E. Pacanowsky, in press. Beverly Hills: Sage Publications.

Poole, M. S., R. D. McPhee, and D. R. Seibold. 1982. "A Comparison of Normative and Interactional Explanations of Group Decision-Making: Social Decision Schemes versus Valence Distributions." Communication Monographs 49 (1):1-19.

Poole, M. S., D. R. Seibold, and R. D. McPhee. 1982. "A Structurational Theory of Group Decision-Making: The Group as Permanent Process." Presented at Pennsylvania State University Conference on Group Communications Research, April, University Park.

Pratt, Mary Louise. 1977. Toward a Speech Act Theory of Literary Discourse. Bloomington: Indiana University Press.

Pulitzer, Joseph. 1904. "The College of Journalism." North American Review 578 (570):641-79.

Putnam, L. L. 1982a. "Paradigms for Organizational Communication Research." Western Journal of Speech 46 (2):192-206.

_____. 1982b. "Understanding the Unique Characteristics of Groups Within Organizations." Paper presented at the Conference on Research in Small Group Communication, Pennsylvania State University.

Putnam, L. L. and T. S. Jones. 1982. "Reciprocity in Negotiations: An Analysis of Bargaining Interaction." Communication Monographs 49 (3):171-91.

Putnam, L. L. and R. L. Sorenson. 1982. "Equivocal Messages in Organizations." Human Communication Research 8 (2): 114-32.

Putnam, L. L. and C. E. Wilson. 1983. "Communicative Strategies in Organizational Conflicts: Reliability and Validity of a Measurement Scale." In Communication Yearbook 6, ed. M. Burgoon, pp. 629-52. Beverly Hills: International Communication Association, Sage Publications.

Rabb, Theodore K. and Robert I. Rotberg, eds. 1982. The New History, NJ: The 1980s and Beyond. Princeton, N.J.: Princeton University Press.

Rabinow, Paul and William M. Sullivan, eds. 1979. Interpretive Social Science: A Reader. Berkeley: University of California Press.

Ramos, Reyes. 1974. "The Use of Improvisation and Modulation in Natural Talk: An Alternative Approach to Conversational Analysis." San Diego: University of California.

Mimeographed.

Ranson, S., B. Hinings, and R. Greenwood. 1980. "The Structuring of Organizational Structures." <u>Administrative Science Quarterly</u> 25 (1):1-17.

Rawlins, W. K. 1981. "Friendship as a Communicative Achievement: A Theory and an Interpretive Analysis of Verbal Reports." Doctoral diss., Department of Speech, Temple University.

_____. 1982. "Cross-Sex Friendship and the Communicative Management of Sex-Role Expectations." <u>Communication Quarterly</u> 30 (4):343-52.

_____. 1983. "Openness as Problematic in Ongoing Friendships: Two Conversational Dilemmas." <u>Communication Monographs</u> 50 (1):1-13.

Rayfield, Joan. 1972. "What's a Story?" <u>American Anthropologist</u> 74 (5):1085-106.

Read, W. H. 1962. "Upward Communication in Industrial Hierarchies." <u>Human Relations</u> 15 (1):3-15.

Redding, W. C. 1966. "The Empirical Study of Human Communication in Business and Industry." In <u>The Frontiers in Speech Communication Research</u>, P. E. Reid, pp. 47-81. Syracuse, N.Y.: Syracuse University Press.

_____. 1972. <u>Communication Within the Organization: An Interpretive Review of Theory and Research</u>. New York: Industrial Communication Council.

_____. 1979. "Organizational Communication Theory and Ideology: An Overview." In <u>Communication Yearbook 3</u>, ed. D. Nimmo, pp. 309-41. New Brunswick, N.J.: International Communication Association, Transaction Books.

Reeves, B. 1979. "Children's Understanding of Television People." In <u>Children Communicating: Media and Development of Thought, Speech Understanding</u>, ed. E. Wartella, pp. 115-55. Beverly Hills: Sage Publications.

Reeves, B. and B. S. Greenberg. 1977. "Children's Perceptions of Television Character." <u>Human Communication Research</u> 3 (2):113-27.

Reid, L. N. 1978. "The Impact of Family Group Interaction on Children's Understanding of Television Advertising: An Aspect of Consumer Socialization." Doctoral diss., University of Illinois.

_____. 1979a. "Viewing Rules as Mediating Factors of Children's Responses to Commercials." <u>Journal of Broadcasting</u> 23 (1):15-26.

_____. 1979b. "The Impact of Family Group Interaction on Children's Understanding of Television Advertising." <u>Journal of Advertising</u> 8 (3):13-19.

Reid, L. N. and C. F. Frazer. 1979. "Studying the Child/Television Advertising Relationship: A Symbolic Interactionist

Approach." Journal of Advertising 8 (4):13-19.

_____. 1980. "Television at Play." Journal of Communication 30 (4):66-73.

Report of the Federal Cultural Policy Review Committee. 1982. Ottawa: Department of Communications, Minister of Supply and Services, Government of Canada.

Rescher, Nicholas. 1977. Dialectics: A Controversy-Oriented Approach to the Theory of Knowledge. Albany: State University of New York Press.

Reusch, J. and G. Bateson. 1951. Communication: The Social Matrix of Psychiatry. New York: W. W. Norton.

Rice, M., A. Huston, and J. Wright. 1982. "Forms and Codes of Television: Effects on Attention, Comprehension and Social Behavior." In Television and Behavior: Ten Years of Scientific Progress and Implications for the Eighties, ed. National Institute of Mental Health. Washington, D.C.: U.S. Government Printing Office.

Richards, W. D. 1974. "Network Analysis in Large Complex Systems: Techniques and Methods — Tools." Paper presented at the Annual Meeting of the International Communication Association, New Orleans.

Richetto, G. M. 1977. "Organizational Communication Theory and Research: An Overview." In Communication Yearbook 1, ed. B. D. Ruben, pp. 331-46. New Brunswick, N.J.: International Communication Association, Transaction Books.

Ricoeur, Paul. 1964. History and Truth. Evanston, Ill.: Northwestern University Press.

_____. 1970. Freud and Philosophy: an Essay on Interpretation. Trans. Denis Savage. New Haven, Conn.: Yale University Press.

_____. 1976. Interpretation Theory: Discourse and the Surplus of Meaning. Fort Worth: Texas Christian University Press.

Roberts, D. F., C. Bachen, and P. Christenson. 1978. "Children's Information Processing: Perceptions and Cognitions about Television Commercials and Supplemental Consumer Information." Testimony to the Federal Trade Commission's Rulemaking Hearings on Television Advertising and Children, p. 123.

Roberts, K. H. and C. A. O'Reilly. 1974. "Measuring Organizational Communication." Journal of Applied Psychology 59 (3):321-26.

Robinson, J. P. 1977. How Americans Use Time: A Social-Psychological Analysis of Everyday Behavior. New York: Praeger.

Roeh, Itzhak. 1982. "Israel in Lebanon: Language and Images of Storytelling." In Television Coverage of the Middle East, ed. William Adams, pp. 76-88. Norwood, N.J.: Ablex Publishing

Corp.

Rogers, E. M.   1962.   Diffusion of Innovations.   New York: The Free Press.

_____. 1982. "The Empirical and the Critical Schools of Communication Research." In Communication Yearbook 5, ed. M. Burgoon, pp. 125-44.   New Brunswick, N.J.: International Communication Association, Transaction Books.

Rogers, E. M. and R. Agarwala-Rogers. 1976. Communication in Organizations. New York: The Free Press.

Rorty, Richard. 1982. "Method, Social Science, and Social Hope."   In Richard Rorty, Consequences of Pragmatism, pp. 191-210. Minneapolis: University of Minnesota Press.

Rosenblatt, P. C. and M. R. Cunningham. 1976. "Television Watching and Family Tensions." Journal of Marriage and the Family 38 (1):105-11.

Rossiter, J. R. and T. S. Robertson. 1975. "Children's Television Viewing: An   Examination   of   Parent-Child   Consensus." Sociometry 38 (2):308-26.

Rudner, R.   1953.   "The Scientist qua Scientist Makes Value Judgments." Philosophy of Science 20 (1):1-6.

Russell, Bertrand. 1927. An Outline of Philosophy.   London: Allen.

_____. 1935. Religion and Science. New York: Henry Holt.

Saal, C. D.   1982.   "A Historical and Present-Day View of the Position of the Child in Family and Society."   Journal of Comparative Family Studies 13 (2):119-32.

Salomon, G.   1979.   "Shape, Not Only Content: How Media Symbols Partake in the Development of Abilities."   In Children Communicating: Media and Development of Speech, Thought, Understanding, ed. E. Wartella, pp. 53-82.   Beverly Hills: Sage Publications.

Sanday, P. R.   1979.   "The Ethnographic Paradigm(s).   In Administrative Science Quarterly 24 (4):527-38.

Sapir, J. David.   1977.   "The Anatomy of Metaphor."   In The Social Use of Metaphor, ed. J. David Sapir and J. Christopher Cricker, pp. 3-32.   Philadelphia: University of Pennsylvania Press.

Sartre, J. P.   1966.   Being and Nothingness.   Trans. H. E. Barnes. New York: Citadel Publishers.

Saussure, F.   1959.   Course in General Linguistics.   Trans. W. Baskin. New York: Philosophical Library.

_____. 1974.   Course in General Linguistics.   London: Fontana.

Sayles, L. R.   1957.   Research in Industrial Human Relations. New York: Harper.

Scheidel, T. M. and L. Crowell. 1979. Discussing and Deciding: A Desk Book for Group Leaders and Members.   New York:

Macmillan.

Schiller, H. I. 1969. *Mass Communications and American Empire*. New York: Kelley.

_____. 1981. *Who Knows: Information in the Age of the Fortune 500*. Norwood, N.J.: Ablex Publishing Corp.

Schrag, C. O. 1980. *Radical Reflection*. West Lafayette, Ind.: Purdue University Press.

Schramm, W., J. Lyle, and E. Parker. 1964. *Television in the Lives of Our Children*. Stanford, Calif.: Stanford University Press.

Schudson, Michael. 1978. *A Social History of American Newspapers*. New York: Basic Books.

Schutz, Alfred. 1944. "The Stanger: An Essay in Social Psychology." *American Journal of Sociology* 49 (6):499-507.

_____. 1967. *The Phenomenology of the Social World*. Evanston, Ill.: Northwestern University Press.

Schwartz, B. 1968. "The Social Psychology of Privacy." *American Journal of Sociology* 73 (6): 741-52.

Scoresby, A. L. 1977. *The Marriage Dialogue*. Reading, Mass.: Addison-Wesley.

Scott, Robert L. 1967. "On Viewing Rhetoric as Epistemic." *Central States Speech Journal* 18 (1):9-17.

_____. 1976. "On Viewing Rhetoric as Epistemic: Ten Years Later." *Central States Speech Journal* 27 (4):258-66.

Scott, W. G. and D. K. Hart. 1979. *Organizational America*. Boston: Houghton Mifflin.

Scribner, Sylvia and Michael Cole. 1981. *The Psychology of Literacy*. Cambridge, Mass.: Harvard University Press.

Scult, A. 1981. "Dialogue and Dichotomy: Some Problems in Martin Buber's Philosophy of Interpersonal Communication." Paper presented at the SCA National Convention, Anaheim, California, November.

Searle, J. R. 1968. *Speech Acts*. Cambridge: Cambridge University Press.

_____. 1972. "Chomsky's Revolution in Linguistics." *The New York Review*, June 29, pp. 3-5.

"Seeking New Paths in Research." 1975. *Journalism History* 2 (2).

Seibold, D. R. 1979. "Criticism of Communication Theory and Research: A Critical Celebration." *Central States Speech Journal* 30 (1):25-39.

Seibold, D. R., R. D. McPhee, M. S. Poole, N. E. Tanita, and D. J. Canary. 1981. "Argument, Group Influence and Decision Outcomes." In *Dimensions in Argument: Proceedings of the Second Summer Conference on Argumentation*, ed. G. Ziegelmueller and J. Rhodes, pp. 663-92. Annandale, Va.: Speech Communication Association.

Seiden, M. 1974. Who Controls the Mass Media? Popular Myths and Economic Realities. New York: Basic Books.

Sennett, Richard. 1978. The Fall of Public Man. New York: Vintage.

Shannon, C. E. 1948. "A Mathematical Theory of Communication." Bell Systems Technical Journal 27:379-656.

Sharf, B. F. 1978. "A Rhetorical Analysis of Leadership Emergence in Small Groups." Communication Monographs 45 (2):156-72.

Shaw, M. E. 1981. Group Dynamics: The Psychology of Small Group Behavior, 3rd ed. New York: McGraw-Hill.

Siegmeister, E. 1965. Harmony and Melody. Belmont, Calif.: Wadsworth.

Sigman, S. 1980. "On Communication Rules from a Social Perspective." Human Communication Research 7 (1)-37-51.

Silverman, D. 1970. The Theory of Organizations: A Sociological Framework. London: Heinemann Press.

Simmel, G. 1949. "The Sociology of Sociability." American Journal of Sociology 55 (3):254-61.

Simon, H. A. 1976. Administrative Behavior: A Study of Decision-Making Process in Administrative Organization, 3rd ed. New York: The Free Press.

Simons, H. W. 1970. "Requirements, Problems and Strategies: A Theory of Persuasion for Social Movements." Quarterly Journal of Speech 56 (1):1-11.

_____. 1982. "Genres, Rules, and Collective Rhetorics: Applying the Requirements-Problems-Strategies Approach." Communication Quarterly 30 (3):181-88.

Singer, D., D. Zuckerman, and J. Singer. 1981. "Teaching Elementary School Children Critical Television Viewing Skills: An Evaluation." In Education for the Television Age, ed. M. Ploghoft and J. Anderson, pp. 71-81. Springfield, Ill.: Charles H. Thomas.

Singh, Jagjit. 1966. Great Ideas in Information Theory, Language and Cybernetics. New York: Dover.

Sisk, J. P. 1972. "Honesty as a Policy." The American Scholar 41 (Spring):251-64.

Skidmore, W. 1979. Theoretical Thinking in Sociology, 2d ed. Cambridge: Cambridge University Press.

Sklar, Robert. 1979. "The Sorrow and the Pity of Non-Fiction Film." The Nation 228 (9) (March 10):276-78.

Slack, J. D. and M. Allor. 1982. "The Political and Epistemological Constituents of Critical Communication Research." Conference paper, International Communications Association, Boston, May 1-5.

Smircich, L. and R. J. Chesser. 1981. "Superior's and Subordinates Perceptions of Performance: Beyond Disagreement." Academy of Management Journal 24 (1):198-205.

Smythe, D. 1977. "Communications: Blindspots of Western Marxism." Canadian Journal of Political and Social Theory 1 (Fall):1–27.

Snyder, M. 1974. "Self-Monitoring of Expressive Behavior." Journal of Personality and Social Psychology 30 (4):526–37.

Sorenson, J. R. 1971. "Task Demands, Group Interaction, and Group Performance." Sociometry 34 (4):483–95.

Speier, H. 1977. "The Communication of Hidden Meaning." Social Research 44 (Autumn):471–501.

Stanley, J. D. 1981. "Dissent in Organizations." Academy of Management Review 6 (1):13–19.

Stein, J. G. and R. Tanter. 1980. Rational Decision-Making: Israel's Security Choices, 1967. Columbus: Ohio State University Press.

Stein, W. 1975. "The Myth of the Transparent Self." Journal of Humanistic Psychology 15 (1):71–77.

Steiner, George. 1975. After Babel: Aspects of Language and Translation. Oxford: Oxford University Press.

Steiner, I. D. 1972. Group Process and Productivity. New York: Academic Press.

Stevens, John D. and Hazel Dicken Garcia. 1979. Communications History. Beverly Hills: Sage Publications.

Stewart, L. P. 1980. "'Whistle Blowing': Implications for Organizational Communication." Journal of Communication 30 (4):90–101.

Stock, Brian. 1938. The Implications of Literacy: Written Language and Models of Interpretation in the Eleventh and Twelfth Centuries. Princeton, N.J.: Princeton University Press.

Stohl, C. 1982. "The Impact of Social Networks on the Development of Communicative Competence." Doctoral diss., Purdue University.

Stone, Lawrence. 1980. The Past and the Present. Boston: Routledge and Kegan and Paul.

Stott, William. 1973. Documentary Expression and Thirties America. New York: Oxford University Press.

Strauss, Anselm. 1971. The Contexts of Social Mobility, Ideology and Theory. Chicago: Aldine.

_____. 1978. Negotiations: Varieties, Contexts, Processes, and Social Order. San Francisco: Jossey-Bass.

Sullivan, H. S. 1954. The Psychiatric Inverview. New York: W.W. Norton.

"Summary of Roundtables at Urbana Convention." 1951. Journalism Quarterly 28 (3):547.

Sussman, L. 1975. "Communication in Organizational Hierarchies: The Fallacy of Perceptual Congruence." Western Speech 39 (3):191–99.

Swensen, C. H. 1973. Introduction to Interpersonal Relations. Glenview, Ill.: Scott, Foresman.

"A Symposium: History in the Journalism Curriculum." 1981. Journalism History 8 (3-4).

Taylor, F. W. 1947. Scientific Management. New York: Harper & Row.

Thibaut, J. and H. H. Kelley. 1959. The Social Psychology of Groups. New York: John Wiley.

Thompson, K. 1980a. "Organizations as Constructors of Social Reality (I)." In Control and Ideology in Organizations, ed. G. Salaman and K. Thompson, pp. 216-36. Cambridge, Mass.: MIT Press.

_____. 1980b. "The Organizational Society." In Control and Ideology in Organizations, ed. G. Salaman and K. Thompson, pp. 3-23. Cambridge, Mass.: MIT Press.

Thonssen, Lester and A. Craig Baird. 1948. Speech Criticism. New York: Ronald Press.

Tichy, N. M. 1981. "Networks in Organizations." In Handbook of Organizational Design, vol. 2, ed. P. C. Nystrom and W. H. Starbuck, pp. 225-49. Oxford: Oxford University Press.

Tichy, N. M., M. L. Tushman, and C. Fombrun. 1979. "Social Network Analysis for Organizations." Academy of Management Review 4 (3):507-19.

Tompkins, P. K. 1962. "An Analysis of Communication Between Headquarters and Selected Units of a National Labor Union." Doctoral diss., Purdue University.

_____. 1977. "Management Qua Communication in Rocket Research and Development." Communication Monographs 44 (1):1-26.

_____. 1984. "Functions of Communication in Organizations." In Handbook of Rhetorical and Communication Theory, ed. C. Arnold and J. W. Bowers, in press. New York: Allyn & Bacon.

Tompkins, P. K. and G. Cheney. 1982. "Unobtrusive Control, Decision Making, and Communication in Contemporary Organizations." Paper presented at the annual meeting of the Speech Communication Association, Louisville.

_____. 1983. "Account Analysis of Organizational Decision Making and Identification." In Communication in Organizations: An Interpretive Approach, ed. L. L. Putnam and M. E. Pacanowsky, in press. Beverly Hills: Sage Publications.

Toulmin, Stephen E. 1958. The Uses of Argument. Cambridge: Cambridge University Press.

_____. 1969. "Concepts and the Explanation of Human Behavior." In Human Action, ed. T. Mischel, pp. 71-104. New York: Academic Press.

_____. 1972. Human Understanding. Vol. 1. Princeton, N.J.: Princeton University Press.

_____. 1974. "Rules and Their Relevance for Understanding Human Behavior." In Understanding Other Persons, ed. T. Mischel, pp. 184-215. Oxford: Oxford University Press.

Traudt, P. J. 1979. "Television and Family Viewing: An Ethnography." Master's thesis, University of Utah.

Tudor, Andrew. 1976. "Misunderstanding Everyday Life." Social Review 24 (3):479-503.

Turner, R. H., ed. 1974. Ethnomethodology. Middlesex: Penguin.

Turner, V. 1978. "Foreword." In B. Myerhoff, Number of Our Days, pp. ix-xiii. New York: Simon and Schuster.

Tushman, M. L. 1977. "Special Boundary Roles in the Innovation Process." Administrative Science Quarterly 22 (4):587-605.

Unger, Roberto M. 1975. Knowledge and Politics. New York: The Free Press.

U.S. House. 1980. Media Concentration, Parts 1 and 2. Hearings before the Subcommittee on General Oversight and Minority Enterprise, Committee on Small Business, 96th Cong., 2d sess. Washington, D.C.: U.S. Government Printing Office.

_____. 1981. Telecommunications in Transition: The Status of Competition in the Telecommunications Industry. Report by the Majority Staff of the Subcommittee on Telecommunications, Consumer Protection and Finance Committee on Energy and Commerce. 97th Cong., 1st sess. Washington, D.C.: U.S. Government Printing Office.

"U.S. Rests Its Defense in Fallout Trial." New York Times, November 17, 1982, p. A16.

Volosinov, V. N. 1973. Marxism and the Philosophy of Language. Trans. Ladislav Matejka and I. R. Titunik. New York: Seminar Press.

Von Wright, Georg H. 1971. Explanation and Understanding. Ithaca, N.Y.: Cornell University Press.

Vygotsky, Lev. S. 1978. Mind in Society. Ed. Michael Cole, Vera John-Steiner, Sylvia Scribner, and Ellen Souberman. Cambridge, Mass.: Harvard University Press.

Wallsten, T. S., ed. 1980. Cognitive Processes in Choice and Decision Behavior. Hillsdale, N.J.: Lawrence Erlbaum Associates.

Walsh, D. 1969. Literature and Knowledge. Middletown, Conn.: Wesleyan University Press.

Ward, S. and D. Wackman. 1973. "Children's Information Processing of Television Commercials." In New Models for Communication Research, ed. P. Clarke, pp. 119-46. Beverly Hills: Sage Publications.

Warren, C. and B. Laslett. 1977. "Privacy and Secrecy: A Conceptual Comparison." Journal of Social Issues 33 (3): 43-51.

Wartella, E. 1981. "The Child as Viewer." In Education for the Television Age, ed. M. Ploghoft and J. Anderson, pp. 28-34. Springfield, Ill.: Charles C. Thomas.

Wartella, E. and A. Alexander. 1978. "Children's Organization of Impressions of Television Characters." Paper presented to the International Communication Association, Chicago.

Wasko, J. 1982. Movies and Money: Financing the American Film Industry. Norwood, N.J.: Ablex Publishing Corp.

Watson, K. 1982. "An Analysis of Communication Patterns: A Method for Discriminating Leader and Subordinate Roles." Academy of Management Journal 25 (1):107-20.

Watt, J. and R. Krull. 1974. "An Information Theory Measure for Television Programming." Communication Research 1 (1):44-68.

Weaver, C. H. 1958. "The Quantification of the Frame of Reference in Labor-Management Communication." Journal of Applied Psychology 42 (1):1-9.

Weaver, Richard M. 1953. The Ethics of Rhetoric. Chicago: Henry Regnery.

_____. 1964. Visions of Order. Baton Rouge: Louisiana State University.

Webber, R. A. 1970. "Perceptions of Interactions Between Superiors and Subordinates." Human Relations 23 (3):235-48.

Weber, Max. 1968. Economy and Society: An Outline of Interpretive Sociology. Vol. 1, ed. Guenther Roth and Claus Wittrik. New York: Bedminster Press.

Weick, Karl E. 1979. The Social Psychology of Organizing, 2d ed. Reading, Mass.: Addison-Wesley.

Weider, L. 1974. "Telling the Code." In Ethnomethodology, ed. R. Turner, pp. 142-72. Middlesex: Penguin Books.

Weimer, Walter B. 1977. "Science as a Rhetoric Transaction: Toward a Nonjustificational Conception of Rhetoric." Philosophy and Rhetoric 10 (1):1-29.

_____. 1979. Notes on the Methodology of Scientific Research. Hillsdale, N.J.: Lawrence Erlbaum Associates.

Weinstein, E. A. 1969. "The Development of Interpersonal Competence." In Handbook of Socialization Theory and Research, ed. D. A. Goslin, pp. 753-75. Chicago: Rand McNally.

Whitehead, Alfred North. 1938. Aims of Society. New York: Macmillan.

Wilce, Gillian. 1979. "Hot Spots." New Statesman 98 (2522): 105-06.

Wilder, C. 1979. "The Palo Alto Group: Difficulties and Directions of the Interactional View for Human Communication Research." Human Communication Research 5 (2):171-86.

Williams, Raymond. 1965. The Long Revolution. London: Pelican Books.

_____. 1966. Culture and Society 1780/1950. New York: Harper and Row.

_____. 1973. "Base and Superstructure in Marxist Cultural Theory." New Left Review 82:3–16.

_____. 1974. Television: Technology and Cultural Form. London: Fontana.

_____. 1975. Television: Technology and Cultural Form. New York: Schocken.

_____. 1980. Problems in Materialism and Culture. London: Verso Editions.

Wilshire, B. 1982. Role Playing and Identity: The Limits of Theatre as Metaphor. Bloomington: Indiana University Press.

Wittgenstein, L. 1958. Philosophical Investigations. New York: Macmillan.

_____. 1969. The Blue and Brown Books. New York: Barnes and Noble.

Wolff, K. H. 1950. The Sociology of Georg Simmel. Glencoe, Ill.: The Free Press.

Wooldridge, Dean E. 1963. The Machinery of the Brain. New York: McGraw-Hill.

Working Papers in Cultural Studies, 1971–1977. Birmingham, England: Centre for Contemporary Cultural Studies.

Worth, S. and L. Gross. 1974. "Symbolic Strategies." Journal of Communication 24 (4):27–39.

Wyer, R. S. and D. E. Carlston. 1979. Social Cognition, Inference, and Attribution. Hillsdale, N.J.: Lawrence Erlbaum Associates.

Youngblood, G. 1977. "The Mass Media and the Future of Desire." Co-Evolution Quarterly 16 (Winter):6–17.

Zeller, Eduard. 1955. Outlines of the History of Greek Philosophy. London: Routledge and Kegan Paul.

Zey-Ferrell, M. and M. Aiken. 1981. "Introduction to Critiques of Dominant Perspectives." In Complex Organizations: Critical Perspectives, ed. M. Zey-Ferrell and M. Aiken, pp. 1–21. Glenview, Ill.: Scott, Foresman.

Zyskind, Harold. 1968. "A Case Study in Philosophic Rhetoric." Philosophy and Rhetoric 1 (4):228–54.

_____. 1970. "Some Philosophical Strands in Popular Rhetoric." In Perspectives in Education, Religion, and the Arts, ed. Howard E. Kiefer and Milton K. Nunitz, pp. 373–95. Albany: State University of New York Press.

INDEX

action, 110, 114–18; action
theory, 192, 194, 201
alphabet, 34
Althusser, Louis, 50–52, 53,
83
American cultural school of
communications, 29–30
American education, his-
tory/historiography of,
20–21
analysis, cultural, 65–70
antitrust, 73, 74
appropriating, 133, 136–38,
141
Aristotle, 108, 109
art, 12–13
art formula, 17
Association for Education in
Journalism, 29
audience 110–11
autonomy, 165–66

Babylonian empire, 33, 34
bad faith, 164, 167
Bailyn, Bernard, 20, 21
Barthes, Roland, 56–57
Bateson, Gregory, 9
Bavelas, J. B., 129
Beckett, Samuel, 7
bias of communication, 32,
33, 34, 35; Bias of Com-
munication, The, 30
Bleyer, Willard G., 26
books, 72
boundary spanning, 223
Bourdieu, Pierre, 59
Boyd-Barret, Oliver, 82
Braudel, Fernand, 30
broadcasting, 16
bureaucracy, 209

cable, 72, 73–74

Canada, 81
Canadians, 83
Carey, James W., 29
Chaney, David, 82
change, 208, 212, 218
children and television,
242–59; holistic research
on, 256–59; intervention
by parents and schools,
245–46
children compared to adults,
244–46
Cicero, 108
coalitions, 212, 220
code, 133
cognitive interest, 208, 210
communication: Act of 1934,
74; channels, 207, 213–15;
climate, 207, 213, 216–18;
and decisionmaking, limi-
tations of previous re-
search, 168–69; effectiveness, 215; in graduate
curriculum, 27, 28–29; and
group decisionmaking, ad-
vantages of model, 180;
and group decisionmaking,
directions for future re-
search, 181–82; and group
decisionmaking, problem
with previous research,
169; and group decision-
making, theoretical con-
ceptualization, 169–70;
history, captive, 20–21,
22, 25, 26–28, 36; history,
profession-driven concept
of, 21–22, 24–25, 26,
35–36; intellectual isolation of graduate training
in, 26–27; networks, 207,
213, 218–21; professional

321

ABOUT THE CONTRIBUTORS

RICHARD L. BARTON is Associate Professor of Telecommunications in the Department of Speech Communication at The Pennsylvania State University, University Park. His current research has been supported by a grant from the Canadian government, Department of External Affairs. His work has appeared in several journals, including Journal of Communication, Quarterly Journal of Speech, and Journalism Quarterly. Dr. Barton's research interests focus on media criticism and international mass communications. He holds a B.A. in English Literature from Ohio State University, an M.A. from Ohio University, and Ph.D. in Speech Communication from the University of Oregon.

JAMES W. CAREY presently is Dean of the College of Communications at the University of Illinois at Urbana-Champaign. Previously he occupied the George Gallup Chair at the University of Iowa and was Director of the Institute of Communications Research at Illinois. Dean Carey has published widely in the area of communications. His articles and reviews have appeared in American Journal of Sociology, Journal of Communication, Journalism Quarterly, Communication Research, Media, Culture and Society, American Historical Review, American Scholar, and Antioch Review. Dean Carey's research interests include popular culture and the history of communications. He holds a B.S. from the University of Rhode Island and an M.S. and a Ph.D. from the University of Illinois at Urbana-Champaign.

GEORGE CHENEY is a Doctoral Candidate and David Ross Fellow in the Department of Communication at Purdue University. His research interests center on the processes of intraorganizational influence and control, external organization communication — especially corporate advocacy — and organizational permanence and change in the Roman Catholic Church. His work has appeared in the Quarterly Journal of Speech and various collections, including Communication in Organizations: An Interpretive Approach. He holds a B.A. in Psychology from Youngstown State University and an M.A. in Communication from Purdue.

PETER G. CHRISTENSON is Assistant Professor of Telecommunications in the Department of Speech Communication, The Pennsylvania State University, University Park. His research on children and television has been published in the Journal of Communication and Communication Research. His most recent work appears in <u>Learning from Television,</u> edited by M. Howe. Besides children and media, Dr. Christenson is engaged in research on video aesthetics and the uses and social effects of new communications technologies. He holds a B.A. from Dartmouth, an M.A. from the University of Oregon, and a Ph.D. from Stanford University.

B. AUBREY FISHER is Professor of Communication in the Department of Communication, University of Utah. Recently he was elected Vice-President of the Western Speech Communication Association; he will be President of that organization in 1985-86. Dr. Fisher is widely published in the field. His articles have appeared in all the major journals of communication, including <u>Quarterly Journal of Speech</u>, <u>Human Communication Research</u>, <u>Journal of Communication</u>, and <u>Communication Quarterly</u>. His work also has been published in several collected additions. Dr. Fisher has authored <u>Perspectives on Human Communication</u> and <u>Small-Group Decision Making: Communication and the Group Process</u>. His research interests cover a wide range of topics, including group decisionmaking, the pragmatics of communication, communication theory, interpersonal communication, and group leadership. Dr. Fisher holds a B.S. from Northern State College (S.D.) and an M.S. and a Ph.D. from the University of Minnesota.

DENNIS S. GOURAN is Professor of Speech Communication at Indiana University. His previous publications include two books: <u>Discussion: The Process of Group Decision-Making</u>, and <u>Making Decisions in Groups: Choices and Consequences</u>. Dr. Gouran's research focuses on decisionmaking, leadership, and communication in small groups. He holds a B.S. and an M.S. in Speech from Illinois State University and a Ph.D. in Speech and Dramatic Arts from the University of Iowa.

LAWRENCE GROSSBERG is Associate Professor of Speech Communication, and Criticism and Interpretive Theory at the University of Illinois at Urbana-Champaign. His work has appeared in a number of journals, including <u>Semiotica</u>, <u>Man and World</u>, <u>Social Text</u>, and <u>Human Studies</u>. Dr. Grossberg is interested in the philosophy of communication, culture and interpretation (including semiotics, poststructuralism, Marxism, and psychoanalysis), and cultural studies and popular music. He has a B.A. from the University of Rochester and a Ph.D. in communications from the University of Illinois at Urbana-Champaign.

GERARD A. HAUSER is Associate Professor and Director of Graduate Studies in the Department of Speech Communication, The Pennsylvania State University, University Park. His most recent publications have appeared in <u>Pre/Text</u>, <u>Philosophy and</u>

Rhetoric, and Journal of Communication. Dr. Hauser is primarily interested in the historical development of rhetorical theory, with special emphasis on theories of invention and judgment. He also is investigating the philosophical foundation of rhetorical theories, the development of a rhetorical theory of the public, and political communication. He earned an A.B. in English from Canisius College and an M.A. and a Ph.D. in Speech Communication from the University of Wisconsin, Madison.

LEONARD C. HAWES is Professor of Communication at the University of Utah. Dr. Hawes is widely published in the field of communication. His reviews and articles have appeared in a variety of journals, including a recent piece, "Some Pragmatics of Talking on Talk Radio," which appeared in Urban Life. He also has authored Pragmatics of Analoguing: Theory and Model Construction in Communication. His research centers on discourse analysis and critical theory. Dr. Hawes holds a B.A. from Macalester College and an M.A. and a Ph.D. from the University of Minnesota.

RANDY Y. HIROKAWA is Assistant Professor in the Department of Speech Communication, The Pennsylvania State University, University Park. He has published a number of articles in such journals as Communication Monographs, Human Communication Research, and Communication Quarterly. He is interested in decisionmaking effectiveness in group and organizational settings, especially the relationship between communication processes and effectiveness of decisionmaking in the group and organization. Dr. Hirokawa received a B.A. from the University of Hawaii and an M.A. and a Ph.D. from the University of Washington.

THOMAS R. LINDLOF is Assistant Professor of Telecommunications in the Department of Speech Communication at The Pennsylvania State University, University Park. His work has appeared in Journalism Quarterly, Communications Research, and Communication Yearbook. Dr. Lindlof's research interests include cognitive processes of mediated communication, and the uses of media in family and institutional settings. He received his Ph.D. in Communications from the University of Texas at Austin.

MARY S. MANDER is Assistant Professor of Telecommunications in the Department of Speech Communication, The Pennsylvania State University, University Park. Her articles and reviews have appeared in Antioch Review, Journalism History, Journal of Popular Culture, Journal of Communication, Technology and Culture, Communications Research, American Journalism, and Philosophy and Rhetoric. Her research includes work on popular culture, the politics of interpretation, communications technologies

16802

and social change, and a cultural history of war correspondence. The last has been supported by grants from the Yank Foundation, the National Endowment for the Humanities, and the Institute for Arts and Humanistic Studies at Pennsylvania State University. Dr. Mander earned a B.A. in Latin from Fontbonne College in St. Louis and a Ph.D. in Communications from the Institute of Communications Research, University of Illinois at Urbana-Champaign.

CAROLYN MARVIN is Assistant Professor of Communications at the Annenberg School of Communication, University of Pennsylvania. Dr. Marvin's work has appeared in Journal of Communication, Journal of American Studies, Telecommunications Policy, and elsewhere. Her research concerns the social history of communications practices and technologies, the history of literacy, and the history of information. She earned a B.S. in Psychology from Texas Christian University, an M.A. in Communications from the University of Texas at Austin, an M.A. in History from the University of Sussex, England, and a Ph.D. in Communications from the University of Illinois at Urbana-Champaign.

NICK O'DONNELL-TRUJILLO is Assistant Professor in the Department of Communication at Purdue University. Dr. O'Donnell-Trujillo's research has appeared in a number of journals and books, including Communication Monographs and the Western Journal of Speech Communication. He is interested in organizational culture, managerial action, organizational politics, and relational development. He holds an M.A. from San Diego State University and a Ph.D. from the University of Utah.

MICHAEL E. PACANOWSKY is Assistant Professor of Communication at the University of Utah. His most recent work has appeared in Communication Monographs. Dr. Pacanowsky's research centers on interpretive studies of organizational cultures. He earned a B.A. in English from Harvard College, an M.A. from Michigan State University, and a Ph.D. in Communications from Stanford University.

MARSHALL SCOTT POOLE is Assistant Professor of Speech Communication at the University of Illinois at Urbana-Champaign. With J. P. Folger he has authored Working through Conflict. His work has been published in numerous journals and collections, including Human Communication Research, Communication Monographs, Small Group Behavior, and Communication Yearbook. His research interests encompass conflict management, group decisionmaking, theory of saturation, organizational climate, and methodology of interaction analysis. Dr. Poole holds a Ph.D. from the University of Wisconsin, Madison.

LINDA L. PUTNAM is Associate Professor of Communication at Purdue University. Her most recent publication is <u>Communication in Organizations: An Interpretive Approach</u>, edited with Michael Pacanowsky. Dr. Putnam's articles are published in several journals and collections, most recently in <u>Communication Monographs</u>, <u>Human Communication Research</u>, and <u>Communication Yearbook</u>. She is interested in conflict and bargaining in organizations, in paradoxes and contradictory messages as indexes of conflict and change, in interaction analysis and bargaining strategies, and in the role of groups in organizational communication. Dr. Putnam earned a B.A. from Hardin-Simmons University (Texas), an M.A. in Rhetoric and Public Address from the University of Wisconsin, Madison, and a Ph.D. in Communication from the University of Minnesota.

WILLIAM K. RAWLINS is Assistant Professor of Speech Communication at The Pennsylvania State University, University Park. His work has appeared in several journals and books, including <u>Human Communication Research</u>, <u>Communication Quarterly</u>, and <u>Communication Monographs</u>. Dr. Rawlins is interested in the functions of communication in ongoing relationships, particularly in friendship; he is also interested in human communication theory and development. He holds a B.A. from the University of Delaware and an M.A. and a Ph.D. from Temple University.

PAUL J. TRAUDT is Assistant Professor in the Communicative and Theatre Arts Department at the University of Iowa. Dr. Traudt's research interests are mass communication theory and audience behavior, with special interest in ethnographic methods and applications to the study of families and television. He earned a Ph.D. from the University of Texas at Austin.

JANET WASKO is Assistant Professor of Communication at Temple University. Recently she authored <u>Movies and Money: Financing the American Film Industry</u>. With Vincent Mosco, she is editor of <u>Critical Communications Review</u>, which is now in its third volume. Dr. Wasko's research interests center on critical studies and film. Her Ph.D. in Communication was earned at the University of Illinois at Urbana-Champaign.